ALCOHOLISM & SUBSTANCE

ABUSE

IN SPECIAL POPULATIONS

Contributors

Robert J. Aguilar, Sr., R.N., M.A.

David Archambault, M.A.

Daniel Ray Benson, M.A.

Freida Brown, Ph.D.

Stanley L. Eden, Psy.D.

Peter G. Fellios, M.A.

Benita Anne Glow, M.A.

Audrey Hill

Susann M. Jordan, M.A.

Yvonne Kress, M.A.

Ann W. Lawson, Ph.D., MFCC

Gary W. Lawson, Ph.D.

Gary R. Lewis, Ph.D., R.N.

Herbert Martin, M.A.

Nancy P. Moore, M.A.

Christine M. O'Sullivan, M.A.

P. Clayton Rivers, Ph.D.

Delia Thrasher, M.A.

Joan Tooley, M.A.

Thomas J. Young, Ph.D.

ALCOHOLISM & SUBSTANCE

ABUSE

IN SPECIAL POPULATIONS

Edited by

Gary W. Lawson, Ph.D.
Professor of Psychology
Director of Graduate Studies
in Chemical Dependency

Ann W. Lawson, Ph.D., MFCC
Director
Addiction Counselor Training Program

United States International University
San Diego, California

AN ASPEN PUBLICATION®
Aspen Publishers, Inc.   1989   Gaithersburg, Maryland

Library of Congress Cataloging-in-Publication Data

Alcoholism and substance abuse in special populations / edited by
Gary W. Lawson, Ann W. Lawson.
p. cm.
"An Aspen publication."
Bibliography: p.
Includes index.
ISBN: 0-8342-0007-4
1. Alcoholism—United States—Prevention.
2. Drug abuse—United States—Prevention.
3. Alcoholism—Treatment—United States.
4. Drug abuse—Treatment—United States.
I. Lawson, Gary. II. Lawson, Ann W.
HV5292.A389   1989
362.2'9—dc19   88-7600
CIP

Aspen Publishers, Inc., grants permission for photocopying for limited personal or
internal use. This consent does not extend to other kinds of copying, such as
copying for general distribution, for advertising or promotional purposes, for
creating new collective works, or for resale. For information, address
Aspen Publishers, Inc., Permissions Department, Suite 200,
200 Orchard Ridge Drive, Gaithersburg, Maryland 20878.

Editorial Services: Jane Coyle Garwood

Library of Congress Catalog Card Number: 88-7600
ISBN: 0-8342-0007-4

Printed in the United States of America

3 4 5 6

Table of Contents

Preface

This book examines the special issues involved in the etiology, treatment, and prevention of alcoholism and other types of substance abuse among specific populations. These populations have been chosen either because of their high risk for substance abuse problems in relation to the general population, as with Native Americans and adolescents, or because of a lack of resources available to provide up-to-date, appropriate information, as in the case of blacks.

Each contributor has carefully reviewed the existing literature on a specific population in order to include the most current substance abuse information on that population. In most cases, the contributors have had personal experience working with their specific populations in clinical settings. In several cases, the contributors are members of the specific population they are writing on, giving them special insights into the problems of that population.

For some of the populations there was a great deal of information available and for others there was very little. Because of the similarities in the nature of substance abuse among some of these populations, the information in one chapter sometimes will overlap with the information in other chapters. This is not an oversight; it is a deliberate attempt to provide the reader with a reference that can be used at any time for information on one specific population that the reader may wish to learn about. Thus it is not necessary to read the entire book to understand the issues of one population. However, we feel that the book will be most beneficial to those working in the field of substance abuse if it is read in its entirety.

Although the contributors were given latitude to write their chapters as they saw fit, they were each provided with a brief outline to follow. Therefore most chapters will resemble one another in structure. For example, most chapters begin with a review of demographic information, substance abuse rates, and kinds of substances abused by the specific population.

The majority of the contributors have had close professional contact with the editors and share similar beliefs regarding the etiology and approaches to treatment and prevention of substance abuse. More specifically, they are likely to believe that alcoholism and other types of substance abuse are multifaceted problems that should be examined from physical, social, and psychological perspectives. They are further likely to believe that the family, both the family of origin and the nuclear family, plays a major role in the cause or etiology of substance abuse and that treatment and prevention efforts are best undertaken with the family fully involved. As the editors of this volume, we feel that the message regarding the role of the family is an important one and cannot be overstated.

Although there have been enormous strides in knowledge and attitudes regarding substance abuse, we are just beginning to comprehend the significance of substance abuse problems with regard to our society and our world. Substance abuse problems are emerging as major political and economic issues, offering many challenges for those working in the field of substance abuse. It becomes ever more important that we learn from, yet not be bound by, our past. We must understand and use the information provided by research and clinical experience to guide us in planning programs to prevent and treat substance abuse. The significant progress made over the past 50 years in identifying and understanding substance abuse has not been equaled in the areas of treatment and prevention of substance abuse. It is time to develop programs, designed for specific populations, that can be proven over time to be effective in the elimination of these most pressing of problems. We hope this book will be a step in that direction.

Gary Lawson
Ann Lawson

Acknowledgments

We thank our children, Lindsey and London, for the understanding they showed while Mom and Dad spent too many hours upstairs on the computer. We promise they can use it for a while. We also thank the contributors to this volume and their families for the sacrifices they made for this book. Finally, we thank Laurie Brown for her typing expertise and editorial assistance.

Chapter 1

A Rationale for Planning Treatment and Prevention of Alcoholism and Substance Abuse for Specific Populations

Gary W. Lawson

INTRODUCTION

The primary purpose of this chapter is to encourage the reader to consider the treatment and prevention of substance abuse, including alcoholism, from a viewpoint that takes into consideration the attributes that the abuser brings from the specific population he or she primarily identifies with. This may involve a new way of thinking about alcoholism or substance abuse. This chapter presents a model of treatment and prevention that allows for special consideration of the issues of specific populations.

In order to develop a model for the treatment or prevention of any disorder, it is useful to understand the etiology of the disorder. There are three important factors to consider in the etiology of alcoholism or substance abuse: physiological, sociological, and psychological factors. It is yet unclear how much of a role each factor plays in the development of alcoholism or substance abuse. From a physiological perspective, it has been clearly shown that alcoholism, at least, has a genetic factor (Cotton, 1979). Less physiological research is available for other types of substance abuse. Sociological factors, whether they are related to the family, a peer group, fellow workers, or several of these in combination, have a great deal to do with the likelihood that a person will abuse drugs or alcohol (Cahalan, 1970). The psychological makeup of an individual, which can be defined as the personality and emotional stability of the person, also plays a major part in the likelihood that the individual will use or abuse drugs or alcohol (Lawson, Peterson, & Lawson, 1983). All three aspects, physical, social, and psychological, must be considered in combination in developing plans for the prevention and treatment of alcoholism or substance abuse. But before examining these three factors and their specific roles in treatment and prevention, a clear definition of what it is to be treated or prevented would be useful.

Alcoholism, substance abuse, problem drinking, drug abuse, drug dependence, addiction, and many other terms are used to describe the behavior involved in a person's destructive relationship with a chemical or a behavior. Although these may include subtle or even major differences, they all include a common denominator: These conditions exist when an individual is in a relationship with a chemical substance (e.g., alcohol) or a particular behavior (e.g., gambling) and there are continuing difficulties, of any kind, in that person's life as a result of using the chemical substance or exhibiting the offending behavior. These life difficulties can be physical problems, relationship problems, social problems, work-related problems, or any other type of problem.

Using a drug, drinking alcohol, and gambling excessively are all behaviors. It is often a secondary or related behavior, rather than the drug using behavior, that causes most of the problems for the individual or those around him or her (e.g., driving drunk, fighting). Therefore, the problems ultimately addressed in treatment or prevention are behaviors. In most cases, these behaviors cause problems not only for individuals using drugs or alcohol but also for those around them. At times, the alcoholic or drug user may be unaware of the degree of difficulties they are causing the significant people in their life. Sometimes even the family or others close to the user are unaware of the negative effect the behavior has on the social or family system they live in. In those cases, part of the role of the therapist or treatment staff is to create an awareness in the family of the current and potential negative consequences of the drinking or drug taking behavior. However, it is equally important for the therapist to examine what may appear to the user to be the positive consequences of the drug taking or other disruptive behavior. This systems view of behavior is important when planning strategies to help the patient change the drug using behavior. The concept of considering both positive and negative consequences of substance abuse is discussed later in this chapter and throughout this book. But first, it would be useful to examine why there are those who might be reluctant to admit that alcoholism and other substance abuse are behaviors with social and psychological causes rather than a disease that people "get" or have, like cancer. The best example of this reluctance can perhaps be found in the field of alcoholism.

Not all of those working in the field of alcoholism want to admit that alcoholism is primarily a behavior. Many prefer to see alcoholism as a "disease," yet it is not often that one hears addiction to heroin or addiction to cigarettes referred to as a disease. There are many reasons treatment professionals, as well as alcoholics themselves, would be reluctant to admit that alcoholism and other substance abuse are behaviors. Dr. Alfred Smith, a psychiatrist who spent 15 years seeking a biological cause for alcoholism, stated before the National Safety Congress in Chicago: "it's a terrible disappointment to me to finally face up to the fact that alcoholism is a behavioral disorder" (Vogler & Bartz, 1982, p. 8). It is understandable why someone who spent so much time and effort looking for a biological cause for alcoholism would be disappointed to find little if any evidence of its existence. It is also understandable that it would be a disappointment for that person to realize that social factors, environment, and the psychological makeup of the individual, not biological causes, are primary factors in alcoholism and substance abuse.

To admit that alcoholism is a behavioral disorder is to imply that the individual has control over the behavior. This implication is threatening to those who have resolved personal guilt issues by convincing themselves that they were not responsible for their past behavior because they had a "disease" with a biological basis. There may never be agreement among professionals with regard to the cause and effect of alcoholism. There are too many economic, social, and personal considerations involved. An excellent example of the conflict is the recent Supreme Court decision relating to alcoholism as a disease. This is an issue that volumes have been written on; yet it is not close to resolution.

Davis (1987) stated "Therapists are ill-advised to take sides on the issues of cause versus effect when it comes to alcoholism " (p. 5). Whether one takes sides or not, it is important with regard to the plan developed for treatment or prevention to understand the dynamics of the disorder to be treated or prevented. If the disorder is misunderstood, there can be problems when planning treatment or prevention. For example, if excessive drinking or drug use is seen as only maladaptive (as opposed to adaptive) with one ultimate cause, either biological or psychological, this may lead to moral exhortations and scare tactics by treatment persons, a punitive legal approach, and generally aversive therapeutic approaches, such as the use of disulfiram (Antabuse), apomorphine injections, or videotaped self-confrontation. Therapeutic approaches based on an "ultimate cause" hypothesis rather than on a multicausal hypothesis have led therapists to apply uniform therapies to all "alcoholics." These therapeutic approaches may lead to short-term improvements. However, they usually lead to relapse and increased frustration for both the therapist and the patient. Working with this model can have the added negative effect of separating the control of behavior from the behavioral contingencies (Davis, 1987; Lawson, Ellis, & Rivers, 1984). In other words, patients feel there are no logical reasons for their behavior and that they have no control over their actions. The attitude that some external unknown factor "made me do it" is likely to lead only to a continuation of the behavior and a feeling of helplessness on the part of the patient.

As an alternative to this approach, a behavioral-adaptive model in which the emphasis is placed on finding what seems to be adaptive and reinforcing for the drinking or drug taking behavior is recommended. Rather than viewing the use of alcohol or other drugs as maladaptive with one ultimate cause, Davis (1987) presented the following three hypotheses:

(1) The abuse of alcohol has adaptive consequences. [No implication is made that adaptive means "good" or "moral" or necessarily desirable.]

(2) These adaptive consequences are sufficiently reinforcing to serve as the primary factors maintaining a habit of drinking, regardless of what underlying causation there may be.

(3) The primary factors for each individual differ and may be operating at an intra-psychic level, intra-couple level, or at the level of maintenance of homeostasis in a family or wider social system (p. 17).

the case for Behavioral

Given that these hypotheses are reasonable, it becomes clear that a therapist who knew which factors motivate specific populations to abuse drugs or alcohol would be at an advantage when planning treatment or prevention for specific groups. It would further seem likely that a therapist who based plans for treatment on factors pertaining to one group could not be successful using the same factors to plan treatment for a different group. For example, the adaptive consequences for a male drinker may not be the same as for a female drinker, and the adaptive consequences for an individual with handicaps are unlikely to be the same as for a high-performance athlete. It is also likely that individuals in specific groups (e.g., blacks, women, Native Americans) would share some adaptive consequences.

The remaining chapters in this book provide information on many specific groups with regard to their physiological, sociological, and psychological risk for drug or alcohol abusing behavior and with regard to the adaptive consequences of this type of behavior. With this information, the therapist or prevention specialist can design treatment and prevention strategies based on the needs most often seen in that specific group.

It would be ideal to plan treatment for each individual after considering his or her specific needs. However, from a practical standpoint this is difficult. There are only a limited number of treatment professionals, and there are many, many people who need treatment. Planning for specific groups is the next best approach. With the limited amount of funds available for prevention programs, it makes sense to target spending for programs for populations that are at high risk.

CHARACTERIZING INDIVIDUALS AND ASSESSING THEIR NEEDS

There is no "typical" chemically dependent person, and there is no specific personality type, family history, socioeconomic situation, or stressful experience that has been found to predict categorically the development of chemical dependency (Lawson et al., 1984). However, in assessing or diagnosing the chemically dependent person, many of these factors as well as others may play important roles in the individual's adaptive behavior of using, and they should be evaluated. In order to ensure that all the necessary information is obtained, it is best to cover systematically all important aspects of the three areas mentioned earlier: physiological, sociological, and psychological. Some of the major factors in each area are listed in Table 1-1.

Physiological Factors

In assessing the physiological nature of the problem, it is important to determine if physical addiction is present. Obtaining a detailed history of drug and/or alcohol use is often appropriate at this beginning point in treatment. If physical addiction is present, the first order of treatment will be to detoxify the individual. This is usually done under the supervision

---

Table 1-1 Factors To Consider in the Etiology, Treatment, and Prevention of Alcoholism and Substance Abuse

Physiological Factors	Sociological Factors	Psychological Factors
Physical addiction	Ethnic and cultural differences	Social skills
Disease or physical disorders	ences	Emotional level
Related medical problems	Family background	Self-image
Inherited risk	Education	Attitude toward life
Mental disorders (with physiological causes)	Employment	Defense mechanisms
	Peer relationships	Mental obsessions
		Judgment
		Decision making skills

of a medical practitioner; therefore, a referral will be called for if the therapist is not a physician. This is also a good time to rule out other addiction-related or physical diseases or disorders. Other aspects of a physical nature that need to be ruled out are underlying psychopathological problems, such as chronic depression, schizophrenia, or other mental disorders, that are likely to respond to psychotropic medications. (For more detailed information on this topic, see chapter 3.)

Finally, it is useful to assess the family's background to determine if a family history of substance abuse exists. If there is a history of alcoholism or substance abuse in the parents or grandparents of the individual being evaluated, then a physical predisposition to the condition can be assumed. There is little or nothing of a physical nature that can be done to reduce this predisposition, but it is useful to pass this information on to clients or patients so they will know that they must take precautions to see that the sociological and psychological areas of their lives do not cause undue risk or pressure for them to abuse drugs or alcohol.

Sociological Factors

Sociological factors are all factors related to the interactions between the individual in question and those around him or her. These include family processes with both the family of origin and the nuclear family as well as extended family members. Education, or the lack of it, is often important with regard to a person's self-image. Employment history, peer group, and cultural or ethnic background are all very important factors to learn about before developing a treatment plan. These are all related to the motivation the person is likely to have to change the offending behavior.

Social factors determine not only whether people will drink but also how people will view themselves after drinking. In a review of a 33-year prospective study of alcoholism, Vaillant and Milofsky (1982) found data suggesting that ethnicity (in this instance, South European) and the number of alcoholic relatives accounted for most of the variance in adult alcoholism.

Tarter and Schneider (1976) identified 14 variables that have an impact on an individual's decision to start, continue, or stop drinking. These are (a) childhood exposure to alcohol and drinking models, (b) the quantity of alcohol that is considered to be appropriate or excessive, (c) drinking customs, (d) the type of alcoholic beverage used, (e) the levels of inhibition considered safe, (f) the symbolic meaning of alcohol, (g) the attitude toward public intoxication, (h) the social group associated with drinking, (i) the activities associated with drinking, (j) the amount of pressure exerted on the individual to drink and continue drinking, (k) the use of alcohol in the social or private context, (l) the individual's mobility in changing drinking reference groups, and (m) the permanence of and the social rewards or punishments for drinking.

Four "parent types" have also been identified as producing high-risk offspring. These are the alcoholic parent, the teetotaling parent, the over-demanding parent, and the overprotective parent (Lawson et al., 1983). A complete social history would include asking about these parent types, and a good treatment plan would involve dealing with the effects these parent types had on the patient.

Psychological Factors

Among the major psychological factors involved are the emotions or feelings and the personality of the individual. A person's personality is loosely measured by how that person interacts with his or her environment, what his or her defense mechanisms are, and what rules he or she abides by. These psychological factors are often directly related to sociological factors. For example, an individual may develop certain methods of coping with stress or may learn to withdraw from stress altogether after growing up in a family where there was a great deal of stress. On the other hand, an individual who grew up where there was very little stress might not handle stress well at all in his or her later life.

Among the psychological aspects to look for are mental obsessions, emotional compulsions, a poor self-image, negative attitudes, rigid defense systems, and delusions. Problem areas include low identification with viable role models; low identification with family; and inadequate interpersonal skills, including communication, cooperation, negotiation, empathy, listening, and sharing. Another psychosocial problem is inadequate systemic skills, or the inability to respond to the limits inherent in a situation (responsibility) and the inability to adapt behavior constructively to a situation in order to get needs met (adaptability). Irresponsibility, refusal to accept the consequences of behavior, and scapegoating are all expressed when there is a weakness in this area. There are also inadequate judgmental skills, which include the inability to recognize, understand, and apply appropriate meanings to relationships. Weaknesses in judgment are manifested as crises in sexual, natural, consumer, and drug and alcohol environments and as repetitive self-destructive behavior (Glenn, 1981).

TREATMENT AND PREVENTION

When clients come in or are sent in for treatment, they need to change their behavior. What is prevented in prevention work is a specific behavior or a series of behaviors. It may be using drugs, drinking alcohol, or specific behaviors like gambling or fighting that need to be treated or prevented. The behavioral situation needs to be changed.

Three things can change in an individual: behavior, thinking, and feeling. That is, one can change one's behavior, one's thinking or way of looking at certain things, or the way one feels about something. These are inter-related. How one thinks is related to how one feels and vice versa. How one behaves is related to how one feels and thinks. The job of treatment is to facilitate change. The job of prevention is to guide change.

What makes a person change his or her behavior, thinking, or feeling? What can a therapist do to help the client or patient to change? One way to help someone change is to help him or her and his or her family be aware of all of the consequences of the drinking, drug using, or specific behavior in question. This does not always work, but sometimes it does. This may be the simplest way to facilitate change. If the person providing the new information is held in high esteem by the receiver of the infor-mation, this could increase the chance of a change. For example, a physician telling a patient about a major health risk from a behavior could have enough effect on the patient to help him or her to change that behavior. A wife making it clear during therapy that she will leave her husband if he drinks again could change his behavior. Her plan might also be the reason he drinks again, to rid himself of her. To avoid making major mistakes in therapy, the therapist should find out all he or she can about what is motivating a behavior. For example, if an alcoholic is drinking to kill himself (suicide on the installment plan), the therapist who knows this can avoid statements to the patient such as "if you keep drinking you are going to die." That is exactly what the patient wants to hear.

As a therapist and educator in the field of addiction treatment, this author has asked many hundreds of recovering alcoholics and drug addicts why they decided to quit using and change. All of them had an answer, and all of them knew something that caused them to change. One man with a 15-year history of drug and alcohol abuse who had been sober for 3 years was asked why he stopped using. He said, "because my 10-year-old son asked me to." When asked why he had not stopped much earlier when his parents and wife had asked him to, he said, "because they were the reason I was using." For this man, it took his son's request to cause him to change his behavior.

For each person, there is a reason and perhaps many reasons he or she is using, and there are also reasons or perhaps just one reason he or she would be willing to stop using and change. For the therapist, the task is to identify these reasons. The clues to what will cause change in the present are found in the past of the individual. What was it that caused the person to think, feel, and behave the way he or she did to begin with? By knowing that, a therapist can plan events to change what is necessary. For change to be lasting, the precipitating event or motivation to change needs to be as powerful or meaningful as the event or events that caused the person to behave, think, or feel the way he or she did to begin with. For example, individuals who have low self-esteem because they were adopted and who feel that they were unwanted and unloved by their natural parents could change those feelings by meeting the natural parents and finding out what happened to make the natural parents give them up. It might not be enough for a therapist to say "I'm sure your parents loved you." But the event of actually meeting the natural parents could change individuals' self-esteem by changing the way they think and feel about why their natural parents gave them up. They could say to themselves: "I was lovable and my parents loved me but given the circumstances they were unable to keep me, so I'm not unlovable after all."

The remainder of this book attempts to examine different populations that can be differentiated by the types of things or events that might play a role in their potential for alcoholism or substance abuse. This information will be useful in the planning of treatment or prevention programs. In some chapters, the author presents current approaches to treatment and prevention. With other chapters, readers can use the information to develop their own plans for the specific population they work with.

For this author, treatment planning always includes the family. The events that mold individuals almost always evolve from the family. If the family is included in the treatment and prevention process, the chances of success will be greatly increased. There are increasing numbers of family treatment books (Barnard, 1981; Davis, 1987; Lawson et al., 1983; Stanton & Todd, 1982), and the addiction counselor should read all of them.

The remaining chapters in this book are diverse in their viewpoints and presentations of issues for specific populations. Readers are advised to keep an open mind, to take the information that is useful and use it, and to reflect on the viewpoints that do not support their own.

REFERENCES

Barnard, C. (1981). *Families, alcoholism, and therapy*. Springfield, IL: Charles C Thomas.

Cahalan, D. (1970). *Problem drinkers: A national survey*. San Francisco: Jossey-Bass.

Cotton, N.S. (1979). The familial incidence of alcoholism: A review. *Journal of Studies on Alcohol, 46*, 98–116.

Davis, D. (1987). *Alcoholism treatment: An integrated family and individual approach*. New York: Gardner.

Glenn, S. (1981, February). *Directions for the eighties*. Paper presented at the Nebraska Prevention Center, Omaha.

Lawson, G., Ellis, D., & Rivers, C. (1984). *The essentials of chemical dependency counseling.* Rockville, MD: Aspen.

Lawson, G., Peterson, J., & Lawson, A. (1983). *Alcoholism and the family: A guide to treatment and prevention.* Rockville, MD: Aspen.

Stanton, M.D., & Todd, T. (1982). *The family therapy of drug abuse and addiction.* New York: Guilford.

Tarter, R.E., & Schneider, D.V., (1976). Models and theories of alcoholism. In R.E. Tarter & A.A. Sungleman (Eds.), *Alcoholism: Interdisciplinary approaches to an enduring problem* (pp. 202–210). Reading, MA: Addison-Wesley.

Vaillant, G.E., & Milofsky, E.S. (1982). The etiology of alcoholism: A prospective viewpoint. *American Psychologist, 37,* 494–503.

Vogler, R., & Bartz, W. (1982). *The better way to drink.* Oakland, CA: New Harbinger.

Chapter 2

Alcoholism in Women: Causes, Treatment, and Prevention

Peter G. Fellios

INTRODUCTION

Most of the literature dealing with alcoholism in women as a subgroup makes one point: until recently, women had received little attention from researchers in the field of alcoholism. As an example, Doshan and Bursch (1982) stated that research on the special problems of women who abuse drugs and, in particular, on effective treatment modalities is in an embryonic stage. According to Sandmaier (1980), only 28 English language studies of alcoholic women had been done. Men, on the other hand, had received considerably more attention.

Though public concern about women's problems with alcohol was increasing in the 1970s, research in the field lagged behind. In 1975, a group of researchers defined the area of alcohol and drug abuse in women as a "non-field" with few acknowledged experts and practically no specialized literature (Kalant, 1980). Common beliefs about alcoholic women included the notions that they were primarily white middle-class housewives who successfully hid their drinking from everyone; that most of them were sexually promiscuous, especially when under the influence; that they were sicker than male alcoholics; and that they had poorer treatment outcomes than men. In fact, even when information became available to contradict certain assumptions, the assumptions persisted for years (Wilsnack & Beckman, 1984). However, the public has become much more aware of the problems of the chemically dependent woman. Much has happened during the past 15 years to heighten the awareness. The women's movement, as an example, focusing on various feminine issues, has brought to light some of the difficulties women face. Also, the medical profession through its increased attention to fetal alcohol syndrome (FAS) has pinpointed some special feminine problems.

11

Today, more women drink than ever before, and alcohol dependence among women has grown steadily. There are approximately 5 million women experiencing problems with alcohol (Kirkpatrick, 1977/1978). Women of all ages and socioeconomic backgrounds fall victim to alcoholism, which, among women, as among men, knows no boundaries. Adolescents and those advanced in years, housewives and executives, the rich and the poor, the single and the married are all susceptible to alcoholism. The alarming statistic is that the number of alcoholic women has been growing much faster than the number of alcoholic men. (The term "women," understandably, is a general term covering many subgroups with which this chapter will not deal. For more specific information on some of these subgroups, see other chapters in this book.)

As the literature shows, the amount of research has increased since the 1970s. Many researchers from various fields have become interested in all aspects of alcoholism in women. Female researchers have been actively seeking answers to various questions. In 1982, *The Journal of Studies on Alcohol* abstracted 49 studies of drinking, problem drinking, and alcoholism in women. This number constituted more than the total number of studies published in English between 1929 and 1970 (Wilsnack & Beckman, 1984). The National Institute on Alcohol Abuse and Alcoholism (NIAAA) has not only sponsored working conferences for specialists in the field, but it has also sponsored special research projects in the area of alcoholic women.

Empirical data have been accumulating in this new area of alcohol studies. These new data are opening avenues of research and concentration and indicate that much more needs to be done. The research is uncovering the special causes, needs, and methods of treating women who are chemically dependent. This chapter attempts to summarize some of the literature and provide an overview of the problem.

CAUSES

No simple profile can accurately describe the heterogeneous population of women who can be described as alcoholics. Though many generalizations describing alcoholic women have been proposed, one must be cautious in his or her acceptance of them. Some studies have been criticized for their biases, inconsistencies of definition criteria, and imprecise measurements (Braiker, 1984). The stereotype of a female alcoholic, as an example, is that of a homemaker who hides her bottles throughout her house and who is protected by other members of her family. This stereotype is not totally correct, however. First, less than half of adult women are non-wage-earning homemakers: working women, single parents, and single women who are divorced or separated, widowed, or never married comprise the majority. Second, in recent national surveys, the greatest number of alcohol-related problems were reported by women aged 18 to 20 years and unemployed women looking for work (Wilsnack & Beckman, 1984).

Modern literature relating to the causes or antecedents of alcoholism in women tends to divide risk factors into physiological, psychological, or sociological categories (Gomberg, 1980). On the basis of this information, the stereotype of the alcoholic woman is seen to be incomplete and inappropriate, and a more specific examination of the causes of female alcoholism is warranted.

Physiological Causes and Effects

Research has shown that women appear to be more prone to some of the complicating medical consequences of heavy drinking than are men, but one cannot designate these effects of alcohol as antecedents of alcoholism (Gomberg & Lisansky, 1984). Even though many specialists in the field consider alcoholism to be a disease, the cause of the disease continues to be researched. Consistent with the disease model, the role that heredity plays in the development of the disease has been investigated intensely. In 1973, Goodwin studied a group of 55 men who had been adopted as infants and raised by nonrelatives. These men, each of whom had at least one alcoholic biological parent, were compared with a control group of 78 adopted men whose parents were not known to be alcoholic. Drinking problems and alcoholism were noted in the first group of men almost 4 times more frequently than in the control group (Langone & Langone, 1980).

The data for adopted women, however, were not known until recently. Brohman (1981) showed that adopted daughters with biological parents who were alcoholic were 3 times more at risk of abusing alcohol than adopted women whose parents were not alcoholic. The maternal relationship was most important in the prediction of alcohol abuse. Brohman concluded that alcoholic mothers had more alcoholic children than did alcoholic fathers.

Alcoholism in one's family background, however, does not predestine an individual to abuse alcohol. Heredity provides an indication of risk for the development of the disease, but it is only one of many factors that may combine to cause alcoholism.

Studies of women with alcohol problems have suggested that heavy drinking often began as a response to obstetrical stress and disappointment.

This might include difficulty in conceiving, difficulty in carrying to term, miscarriage, abortion, childbirth, and hysterectomy (Gombert & Lisansky, 1984). Wilsnack (1973) found that 26% of her female subjects were unable either to become pregnant or to carry to term. Though some of these women engaged in heavy drinking before the onset of infertility, the study suggested that in some cases, infertility may have caused the drinking. Rathbone-McCuan and Roberds (1980) found that the events most mentioned as precipitating problem drinking were biological: childbirth, breast removal, and hysterectomy.

Jones and Jones (1976) reported that blood alcohol level (BAL) varies with the phases of the menstrual cycle. This suggests a link between hormonal status and the effects of alcohol. However, premenstrual and menstrual difficulties and stresses may be antecedents to alcoholic drinking in that such stresses may precipitate a drinking bout (Gombert & Lisansky, 1984). However, the case for menstrual discomfort as well as other stressful conditions bringing on alcoholism in adults remains weak, and more research is needed in this area. (See, examples, Allan and Cooke, 1985, and Cook and Allan, 1984). Braiker (1984) suggested that the clinician must be alert for correlations between drinking level and menstrual midcycle, and premenstrual periodicity patterns. The clinician should also be alert to the patient's mood swings accompanying hormonal changes.

Various sexual problems for female substance abusers have been identified. Sclare (1975) reported that female patients more often reported sexual problems than did men. The main difficulty was a lack of sexual interest and drive. Beckman (1979) also found a general sexual dissatisfaction among female alcoholics. Cuskey, Berger, and Densen-Gerber (1977) called attention to the fact that at least 25% of female addicts have experienced sexual relationships with family members or other relatives, and that two thirds of the female addicts reported frigidity with men. Evans and Schaefer (1980) supported this theory of sexual dysfunction as a cause for alcoholism when they found that female alcoholics identified marital problems, often including sexual difficulties, as initial reasons for drinking. Wilsnack (1973) found that 76% of married female alcoholics but only 34% of the controls reported an obstetrical or gynecological disorder such as infertility or miscarriage. Covington and Kohen (1984) also concluded that sexual abuse early in a woman's life may add to both the probability of her sexual dysfunction and her propensity for alcohol abuse. All researchers suggested that research in this area of sexual dysfunction continue.

Women become intoxicated more easily than men on the same amount of alcohol even if they weigh the same because women generally have less muscle tissue, which contains the water to break down the alcohol. Humphrey and Friedman (1986) summarized their findings by stating that an individual's body weight, metabolic rate, emotional state, and experience with alcohol tend to affect alcohol consumption. Jones and Jones (1976) suggested that hormonal differences between men and women may be responsible for women reaching higher BALs at a faster rate than men when given the same dose; Goist and Sutker (1985) found that these findings may have resulted from the practice of dosing subjects based on total body weight rather than based on body *water* weight. When doses were based on total body water weight, no significant differences in BAL between men and women were found. Brick, Nathan, Westrick, Frankenstein, and Shapiro (1986) found that neither the pharmacokinetics of alcohol nor certain behaviors affected by alcohol were affected by menstrual cycle phase. This study concluded that naturally occurring hormonal variations in women do not mediate the effects of alcohol in certain behaviors.

Alcohol's physical effects on women are numerous. Women may develop cirrhosis of the liver at lower levels of alcohol consumption and after a shorter history of excessive drinking than do men. It is difficult to establish whether women in general are at greater risk for developing alcoholic liver disease since more than half the number of heavy drinkers never seek treatment, and the extent of their liver disease may not be known (Edwards, Hawker, Hensman, Peto, & Williamson, 1973).

Krasner, Davis, Portmann, and Williams (1977) found that 11.5% of alcoholic women had alcoholic hepatitis and central sclerosing hyaline necrosis compared with 3.3% of alcoholic men. Wilkinson, Santamaria, and Rankin (cited in Saunders, Davis, & Williams, 1981) found that women with alcoholic cirrhosis had drunk excessively for a mean period of 13.5 years compared with 20.0 years for men with cirrhosis. All grades of liver damage seemed to develop more rapidly in women. Saunders et al. (1981) supported these findings by stating that as alcoholic liver disease develops more rapidly and at a lower daily intake in women, different pathogenic mechanisms may be responsible. Evidence is mounting that in addition to the direct hepatotoxic effects of alcohol, immunological reactions directed against the liver play a part in the development of alcoholic liver disease. Humoral and cell-mediated immune reactions, particularly alcoholic hepatitis, have been observed in patients with alcoholic liver problems and may form the basis for a sex related difference in pathogenesis.

Women who are heavy drinkers have more gynecological problems than do light or moderate drinkers. Habitual drinking in women is associated with infertility, miscarriage, and stillbirth as well as FAS and fetal alcohol defects. According to Wilsnack, Klassen, and Wilsnack (1984), infertility, miscarriage or stillbirth, prematurity, and birth defects were elevated only at extreme drinking levels. Thresholds were six or more drinks per day at least three times per week for miscarriages or stillbirths and prematurity and six or more drinks per day at least five times per week for infertility and birth defects. FAS, fetal alcohol defects, dysmenorrhea, abruptio placentae, spontaneous abortion, and preterm delivery have all been well documented in the literature and are not dealt with in this chapter. The research, however, does point to the fact that though these complications may be the result of abnormal drinking, some may also be the cause.

In a study of 26 female alcoholics and 41 controls, Jacobson (1986) researched the clinical associations between computerized tomographic (CT) scan changes and drinking. She found that the female alcoholics had larger ventricles and a greater degree of widening of sulci and sylvian and interhemispheric fissures than did controls. The CT scans of all the alcoholic women showed significant differences when compared with those of healthy female controls. Almost all had the features of "alcohol dependence syndrome" even after a considerably shorter drinking history than reported by male alcoholics.

Schatzkin et al. (1987) in a follow-up cohort study of 7,188 women between the ages of 25 and 74 examined the relationship between drinking and breast cancer. They found that consumption of any amount of alcohol conferred an increase in the risk for breast cancer of 40% to 50% among women who drank less than 5 g of alcohol per day (equivalent to about three drinks per week). The greatest risk was seen among women who drank 5 g of alcohol or more per day. The association between drinking and breast cancer was stronger among younger women rather than older, leaner rather than heavier, and premenopausal rather than postmenopausal. This increased risk for younger women may simply reflect the fact that drinking at earlier ages is more hazardous.

Even though women in the general population have lower death rates than men, alcoholism reduces this advantage so that mortality is the same or greater for women (Schmidt & Popham, 1980). Follow-up studies, ranging from 3 to 14 years, have found that observed rates of death for alcoholic women range from more than 3 (Schmidt & DeLint, 1972) to 9 times (Gorwitz, Bahn, Warthen, & Cooper, 1970) the expected rate for women in the general population. Elevated mortality rates from breast cancer have been observed in women with a history of heavy drinking (Adelstein & White, cited in Schatzkin et al., 1987). Alcoholic women are significantly younger at death than are women in the general population (Smith, 1983). The approximate mean age of the study subjects was 66.5 for nonalcoholic women, while the mean age for the alcoholic subjects was 51. The life span of the alcoholic women was shortened by 15 years.

The study by Smith, Cloninger, and Bradford (1983) indicated that the leading causes of death were digestive system disorders, cirrhosis of the liver and other liver diseases, and pancreatitis, which accounted for 29% of all deaths. The study concluded that the earlier the onset, the higher the correlation with various symptoms, and that women who are older when they seek treatment, who have developed alcoholism before the age of 30, and who have a history of frequent binges are at the highest risk for death.

Sociological Factors

As a group, women suffer a great deal of stress that may be different from that faced by men. Traditional roles society has defined for women and men produce quite different behavior and goals. Women have been raised traditionally as the "second sex," and they have been expected to derive their fulfillment primarily through their relationships with men rather than through achievements of their own. Recently, however, women have been encouraged to develop as independent persons with strong identities; social pressures affect women severely.

The Work Role

In our changing society, work roles and ethics change constantly. In 60% of families with children, both spouses work (U.S. Department of Labor, 1981). The proportion of the families in which only the husband works is decreasing, while the number of households in which both spouses work or are composed of single parents with children and single, divorced, separated, widowed, or never married individuals is increasing drastically (Masnick & Bane, 1980). Divorced mothers are more likely to be working or looking for work than mothers of any other marital status (U.S. Department of Labor, 1981).

Several studies have suggested implications of these demographic trends. Johnson, Armor, Polich, and Stambul (1977) found that the highest rates of problem drinking occurred among women seeking work, followed closely by employed women. Married working women reported drinking problems twice as often as did single working women. The largest population of female drinkers was found in professional, semiprofessional, technical, and business jobs, and the lowest proportions were among farm women, laborers, and service workers (*Alcohol and Health,* 1971). The highest percentages of heavy drinkers, however, were found among service workers, semiskilled workers, laborers, and business women.

Work is a stressful environment. The working woman is faced with many problems. The world still holds the double standard (Bete Co., 1983) and often labels the woman inferior, forcing her to work harder, at times, than her male counterpart just to prove that she is competent. As a result, the social and psychological pressures may be overwhelming. A woman is expected to work like a man in a fast-paced environment that does not treat her equally. Soon, the opportunities to drink like a man arise, and a woman finds herself drinking during lunch and dinner and during business routines (Sandmaier, 1977).

Johnson (1982) and Kleeman and Googins (1983) found that conformity to new drinking norms or increased exposure to drinking situations is seen as a possible cause of problem drinking among women. Occupational stress induced by the competitive work role, a relative lack of familiarity with the rules of the game, or discrimination against women is also seen as a potential precipitant of heavy or problem drinking. Shore (1985) concluded that there is a possibility that women who drink tend to move toward managerial and professional jobs or that women in such jobs quickly become a part of the drinking world.

The Home Role

Though many women derive great satisfaction from a full-time career as a mother and a homemaker, others find it difficult to deal with the pressures and escape through drinking. Not every wife is interested in being a housewife, but many women abandon outside interests because society "dictates" that they must fulfill their "role." This "pressure" puts many women's life styles at odds with their goals, and they become increasingly frustrated, angry, and overwhelmed. An Alcoholics Anonymous (AA) member expressed her feelings succinctly: "I drank because I was lonely and because of sheer, unadulterated boredom. I was a housewife" (Sandmaier, 1977, p. 10).

A woman who enjoys being a housewife may find that her family is changing. Female alcoholics experience greater marital instability (Rathod & Thompson, 1971) and instability in the family of origin (Curlee, 1970) and are more likely to have alcoholic spouses (Lisansky, 1958). They have lower self-esteem than male alcoholics (Beckman, 1978a) and more frequently report that they began to drink heavily in response to a major life crisis (Wilsnack, 1973). This family crisis may be a serious illness in the family, divorce, or children leaving home. As a result, the center of their life—their home—is suddenly empty. As they search for outside help they find few resources: no job, few close friends, and no interests outside the family. The result is anxiety, panic, profound loneliness, and nothing to cling to but drinking.

There is no clear answer concerning whether or not the strain of parenting acts as an antecedent of problems with alcohol. Bearing and raising children, particularly for women who work regularly, may provide dual-role stress. As children leave home, many women are faced with a period in which they are still relatively young and vigorous but in which their major caretaking role is no longer needed. The resulting "empty nest" can contribute to the drinking problems of some women (Sclare, 1970). Cahalan, Cisin, and Crossley (1969) found that the highest proportion of heavy drinkers among drinking women was in the 45 to 49 age group, which suggests that most women by then have raised their children and have completed the major role of their life. The proportion of heavy drinking dropped to 3% for the 50 to 54 age group and remained there for older women.

Divorced women or single parents face more difficulties than do married women. Some studies have found that female alcoholics are more likely to be divorced and the single head of a household than are male alcoholics (Rathod & Thompson, 1971). Some 9 million families in the United States are headed by women (Sanmaier, 1977) who work full time and have no one at home to care for their children, cook their meals, and clean their home. Many of these women may drink because they have few skills, they are underpaid in the jobs they have, and one of every three supports her family on an income below the poverty level. The pressures that such a woman faces are immense. Financial difficulties, home responsibilities, and child care pressure her to the point that she feels inadequate or overburdened. Such pressures can cause a woman to drink.

Psychological Factors

Recent data reported in the National Institute of Mental Health Epidemiological Catchment Area Survey revealed that alcohol abuse/dependence was the first ranked psychiatric disorder for noninstitutionalized men and the third-ranked psychiatric disorder for noninstitutionalized women in the United States (Eaton et al., 1984). Filmore's (1975) longitudinal study of college drinkers followed into midlife suggested that when young women manifest psychological dependence on alcohol for relief from unpleasant feelings, they are more likely to develop problems in adult life. Kielholz (1970) found that what both sexes wanted was relief or escape from the pressures, tension, and unhappiness generated from difficult life areas. Alcoholic women, however, reported more feelings of powerlessness and inadequacy before drinking than did the other groups (Beckman, 1980). Alcoholic women are more likely to have a poor self-concept and low self-esteem than male alcoholics, as well as high denial of their drinking problems, possibly due to social stigmatization (Beckman, 1978a).

It has also been suggested (Blane, 1968) that the central feature of alcoholism in women is a preoccupation with being inadequate and inept and a sense of futility about being able to fulfill the female role. Beckman (1978a) found that in female alcoholics, in addition to social factors, neurosis, anxiety, and depression had relatively high negative correlations with self-esteem. She suggested that there may exist bidirectional causality: women with low self-esteem are more likely to abuse alcohol, and the misuse of alcohol further decreases self-esteem. MacAndrew (1986) supported this theory of neuroticism with his findings that the model female alcoholic is a neurotic who drinks too much.

Problem-drinking women experience depression, severe anxiety, and delusions and make suicidal threats more frequently than do men (Langone & Langone, 1980). The area of depression and alcoholism has been receiving much attention lately. Clancey (1986) stated that there is little doubt that secondary depression is common among alcoholics. Harlow, Newcomb, and Bentler (1986) found that depression and self-derogation may lead to a lack of purpose in life, which, in turn, may lead to substance abuse. Sclare (1970) reported that there was a striking incidence (20%) of primary depression, i.e., antedating the onset of alcoholism, in women. Recognition of such depressive symptoms is of value in that appropriate therapy may follow. Women with a history of major depression more frequently reported drinking to forget their worries than did women without a history of major depression (Hesselbrock, Hellelbrock, & Workman-Daniels, 1986). Sugerman (1975) found that female alcoholics turn their anger toward themselves, which predisposes them to anxiety and depressive disorders.

Haver's (1986) findings suggested a predisposition to severe personality disturbances and difficulties in establishing rewarding relationships for some women, which may influence alcohol abuse. For both men and women, the development of alcoholism was accelerated in those patients with antisocial personality (ASP) compared with alcoholic patients with a history of major depression and with alcoholics with no other psychiatric disorder. The Hesselbrock et al. (1986) study suggested that alcoholic women without ASP or major depression more frequently reported that they drank because it was the polite thing to do, whereas alcoholic women with a history of major depression more frequently reported that they drank to forget their worries.

Another area that has been studied as a contributing factor to female alcoholism is the relationship between eating disorders and alcohol abuse. Beary (1986) compared 20 alcoholic women aged 40 or under with 20 age-matched bulimia nervosa patients and 17 age-matched controls. The results of the study indicated that eating disorders commonly start significantly earlier than does alcohol abuse. Patients appeared to substitute alcohol abuse for eating. The patients with bulimic disorders were at high risk for developing alcoholism.

The association between suicide and alcoholism has also received much attention. The reported rates of completed suicide among alcoholics is 6 to 20 times that of the general population (Goodwin, 1973). Among alcoholic women, the incidence of suicide attempts exceeds that for the general female population and that of alcoholic men (Rimmer, Pitts, Reich, & Winokur, 1971). Suicide rates are 44% for female alcoholics and 26% for male alcoholics (Rimmer et al., 1971). Curlee (1970) found attempted suicide rates of 1% for men and 11% for women in a sample of alcoholic patient case histories.

Women who drink heavily often feel shame, guilt, and loneliness, and they try to hide their drinking. They may drink gin or vodka, which is more difficult to detect on the breath, and they secretly dispose of empty bottles (Bete Co., 1983). This problem in many cases remains hidden for years before family and friends become aware of it. This idea of denial has been supported by Shore (1985) who found that women were unwilling to acknowledge high alcohol consumption; yet, most of the women said that they preferred the company of other heavy drinkers, and that they drank as much as the other heavy drinkers.

Unfortunately, too, there appears to be a number of accomplices that contribute to the female alcoholic's denial. These accomplices include friends, employers, physicians, and worse, family members. Female alcoholism, therefore, is a multifacted problem that is caused by many contributors, including stress. The clinician must be alert to the personal, familial, social, and psychological causes in order to develop a meaningful therapy program.

THE TREATMENT PROCESS

Whether genetic, physical, social, or psychological in nature, the etiology of alcoholism in women differs from that in men. The differences in the development of alcoholism in women necessitate a different approach to the treatment of women. The aim of the treatment should be to make the female patient a stronger, happier, more self-aware person who does not need alcohol to function in her day-to-day routine.

Because women have a high degree of denial, and because husbands, family, and friends may be unaware of how seriously ill a woman is or may refuse to recognize her problem, treatment is very difficult (Bete Co., 1983). Once a woman gets into treatment, her job and/or family responsibilities may draw her away. Nonetheless, strong beliefs notwithstanding, there are still relatively few solidly established facts about the outcomes of treated female alcoholics (Litman, 1986). There are few data to substantiate or refute the notions that women have a poorer prognosis than men or that women need to be treated in separate facilities.

No recovery program can begin until a woman recognizes that she may be an alcoholic and accepts the fact that she needs help. For successful treatment, she must be willing to recover, and she must be ready and willing to seek solutions. Once she decides to seek help, the therapy process can begin.

Therapy begins with an initial interview, which, in the case of female patients, should be handled with great delicacy (Braiker, 1984). The professional therapist must be careful with fact gathering and the analysis of the patient so that the right treatment plan may be developed. A woman who has a primary affective disorder, e.g., who drinks to medicate depressive symptoms, will require a different therapeutic process from a female executive who drinks to alleviate work related stress. The therapist must gather information about the patient's environmental factors, consumption patterns and amounts, family background (including family of origin and nuclear family), and social behavior. The therapist should ask the patient about the type of alcohol consumed (including proof), the number of drinks in a typical day, the number of drinking days per week, and the time of day or week of drinking. He or she should ask the patient if she is still drinking when she enters treatment. He or she should be alert for correlations between drinking levels and menstrual, midcycle, and premenstrual periodicity patterns (Braiker, 1984). This information can be crucial in the development of a good treatment plan.

The therapist must keep in mind, too, that the woman may have been protected by family and friends, that she may deny her alcohol problems, and that she may be confused about her social roles. The types of questions asked, the therapist's empathy, the rapport established, and the candor and accuracy with which the patient reports her behavior, thoughts, and feelings are indeed important (Braiker, 1984). Human, positive attitudes are important in a situation involving such a patient. Haver (1986) reported that if the treatment was of any help, its success was attributed to the contact with a therapist who was tolerant, stable, likable, and available for future crises. Some of the young women in the study experienced the detoxification center as the only place they had encountered positive human attitudes.

The patient may exhibit signs of depression such as tearfulness and retarded speech and thought (Braiker, 1984). She may exhibit signs of or discuss issues that indicate low self-esteem. She may be sensitive and embarrassed. The therapist must respect the patient's psychological state and attempt to eliminate any inhibitions the patient may have that may interfere with the process of therapy. He or she should provide ample opportunities for the patient to relate positive experiences in life along with obvious problems. This would help the patient begin to recover her self-esteem.

The therapist must realize, obviously, that the causes of alcoholism are numerous. He or she must attempt, then, to minimize those causes—and ideally to eliminate them. Social and psychological situations must be carefully scrutinized and changed to provide the best possible therapeutic environment. Dealing with the causes of alcoholism will help the patient deal with the disease. The therapy must focus on changing self-destructive behavior.

Henderson, Hall, and Lipton (1979) identified three general psychological models that best relate to changing self-destructive behavior: the rational (or cognitive), the behavioral, and the psychodynamic. In explaining the cognitive model, Beck (1976) stated that emotional disorders arise from faulty, illogical, or inaccurate assumptions. It is these faulty assumptions that the therapist must analyze and correct. Because women have hidden their drinking habits and because they have been protected, they possibly do not have direct and accurate information about alcohol and its effects on health. The therapist must provide accurate, frank, and recent information. Women's beliefs that alcohol may help them feel sexier, may help them relax and reduce their tensions, or may make them feel more social are examples of thinking based on illogical assumptions. The cognitive approach to therapy would deal with these issues.

The behavioral model was developed in response to the theory that people learn to drink excessively because their behavior has primary and secondary reward value (Heather & Robertson, 1981). The behavioral approach attempts to change excessive drinking by changing the conditions or cues by which drinking has been conditioned and by changing the reinforcement values of drinking itself. The behavioral approaches are especially useful when the specific treatment goal is controlled drinking or moderation rather than total abstinence. Under this treatment plan, the patient should be asked to monitor her drinking and to identify the kinds of situations that act as stimuli to her drinking. The patient should be taught to identify these stimuli and helped to change her environment to reduce her exposure to such stimuli.

The psychological model was developed as a response to the belief that alcoholism is a behavior rooted in unresolved conflicts that develop early in life. Because they have developed so early, many of these conflicts are subconscious. In order to be effective, then, therapy, according to this model, must uncover these hidden subconscious conflicts and resolve them (Braiker, 1984). Any other therapy will be largely ineffective. McClellan,

Davis, Kalin, and Wanner (1972) in their "power theory" stated that executives drink excessively because they have an unsatisfied need for personal power. Though no empirical data have been reported to support this theory with women, it could explain the excessive drinking of the modern female executive who is compelled to succeed in a business world dominated by men.

Kinsey (1966) and Blane (1968), in two different studies, supported each other with their findings that unsatisfied dependency needs could be one of the causes of female abusive drinking. Wilsnack (1976) found that her subjects consciously valued their femininity and wanted to feel more like traditional women. Wood and Duffy (1966), however, suggested that women abuse alcohol because—among other reasons—they have a masculine identification, a poor feminine identification, and difficulty in adjusting to a female role. The discrepancy between the findings of these two studies points out the need for more research. Nonetheless, the point that underlying causes concerning unresolved psychological issues may contribute to alcohol abuse is well made. The therapist must be alert in detecting such factors.

Kinds of Treatment

The severely alcoholic patient must recover from acute intoxication and withdrawal before she can begin to change her life in more active ways. The detoxification may be on either an inpatient or outpatient basis. A physician may prescribe medication to reduce discomfort and may require that the patient follow a regular diet supplemented by vitamins (Bete Co., 1984). In addition, the physician should follow any signs of physical illnesses carefully. Liver cirrhosis, gastritis, malnutrition, and dehydration should be closely monitored. However, detoxification is a short-term treatment that is designed to cleanse the patient and to force her to break the habit of drinking. Once the detoxification process is over, therapy must continue. Therapy can be accomplished by various means.

Individual Counseling

During such therapy, the female patient should be guided by the therapist to deal honestly with her feelings, her fears, her emotions, her strengths, and her weaknesses. She must be helped to see that alcoholism is not a moral problem but an illness that needs to be treated: that it is a complicated disease all too often misunderstood. She must be helped to deal with the causes of her drinking be they physical, social, or psychological. She must be guided to grow emotionally and spiritually so that she may understand that she is a competent woman with much to give to others. Though this may take a long time, it is indeed important because it is the key to self-esteem.

During individual counseling, the female patient must be helped to overcome her negativism, which usually precedes drinking bouts. One of the most often used excuses (Kirkpatrick, 1978) "who cares" or "what's the use," has offered women an escape from reality and has helped them develop negativism. The patient must be directed toward the happiness that a sober life offers. The patient must learn to make life great because she can be in control. She must be guided to put her past into perspective and to realize that the past is gone forever. Alcoholic women are prone to carry into the present the burden of the past, which can cause guilt and remorse, which, in turn, can destroy the present.

Group Therapy

Group therapy has proven to be an effective model of treatment, and women-only groups have been suggested to be the most effective (Doshan & Blursch, 1982). Groups, especially homogenous ones, provide acceptance and nurturance; they provide kinship and identification, making the female patient feel more comfortable, more at ease. Groups provide love, help, and care which may be bidirectional, and the female patient understands, feels, and experiences the care of others and for others. By searching within herself, she may find all those feelings and emotions that she had forgotten. She learns to commit to a relationship based on her true abilities and her own unique female characteristics.

Groups should be nonjudgmental; they should foster and reinforce basic human values by allowing each participant to express her feelings honestly. Groups should be an opportunity for the female patient not only to express her anxieties and worries but also to listen to others' difficulties in life. Providing a place for the female patient where she can go and talk and relate with others with the same problems could be therapeutic. The female alcohol abuser, with the expert guidance of the counselor, can begin to change the past, full of alcohol and hardships, and begin a future based on love, understanding, courage, and determination. Group members should be patient with one another because recovery can take a long time.

Women-only groups may be more effective than mixed groups. Beckman (1978b) found that women may be more honest and reveal more to a female group than they would to a mixed group. According to McLachlan, Walderman, and Birchmore (1979), in most treatment groups, men outnumber women three to one, and women frequently allow the men to do most of the talking and relating. Mandel, Schulman, and Monteiro (1979) commented that a group for feminist awareness in a coed therapeutic community met with resistance and interruption by the male residents.

Counseling groups in which a woman is exposed to other women as models functioning at higher levels of ego development can provide a necessary condition for developmental advancement to take place (Hoar, 1983). The counselor should develop a group composed of members at different developmental levels and thereby provide conditions in which group members can experience different challenges for thinking and for discovering their own potential. Even though male/female groups would seem to have the potential for the greatest challenge, they could very well be destructive to the devaluing woman who is not confident enough to participate in a mixed group. In this situation, it would be prudent for the counselor to place the patient in a women-only group and eventually, as she progresses, place her in a mixed group.

However, in view of the fact that the world is a male/female group, the therapist should strive for the best reality therapy—a mixed group (Hoar, 1983). Specific workshops related to issues of common concern to persons in early recovery, such as sexuality, family status, rebuilding relationships, and coping with stress, could be planned to include both men and women as a means of broadening awareness and social skills.

Family Therapy

If, as Fewell and Bissell (1978) reported, other family members play an important protective role in helping the woman conceal her alcohol problems, the family, then, is one of the causes of the continuation of the disease. They, in effect, increase the chances that the woman will deny her problems and that she will continue to drink. The family, then, has the responsibility of dealing with the problem. If the environment (family) has caused the patient to begin or to continue to drink, that environment needs to be altered through therapy so that the patient may be helped. Men are more likely to leave or divorce their alcoholic spouse than are women. (Lemay, 1980). By leaving, husbands could be denying the reality of the situation, and divorce can precipitate a drinking bout or help the patient continue to drink.

Female patients must identify the environmental cues for their drinking, and the family—the most consistent environment—must be taught to help. Counselors agree (Lemay, 1980) that female patients must understand the differences in male/female relationships and look at their own conflicts concerning expected roles of behavior. A woman who is expected to fulfill both male and female roles, for example, may find it difficult to do so and resort to drinking. Without realizing it, the family may have exerted too much pressure on the female patient. That pressure must be lifted before she can begin therapy in earnest.

During family therapy, the family, together, should learn to face and accept the truth—that alcoholism is a multifaceted disease and that they should work together to help the alcoholic. They should learn that honesty with the children is important. Mulford (1977) indicated that more than 25% of problem-drinker female patients in treatment felt that their children were the most critical of their drinking and exerted pressure on them to stop. If this is the case, children must learn, through family therapy, that they may have contributed to the drinking and that they must accept some of the responsibility, not for the disease, but for its treatment. They must learn that forcing the patient to seek therapy does not end their responsibility.

Children and adult members of the family must learn to give love and understanding. Overcoming alcoholism takes a long time, a great deal of courage, and determination. There may even be relapses. The family unit can be the most important source of strength and support. The therapist sees the patient for only a short period of time during the day or week. The family, on the other hand, spends much more time with the patient. They have the power to support and augment the therapist and his or her plan for the patient, or they can destroy such a plan. Family therapy can be used to help the members of the family contribute positively to the outcome of therapy.

Family members can lend encouragement. They can learn to motivate the patient to continue on with the treatment program, attend therapy meetings, and discuss her feelings and emotions. They can learn to be patient because recovery takes a long time (Bete Co., 1983). They must come to accept the fact that the patient may need inpatient treatment. They must realize that family life may change in order to effect a positive direction for the entire family. They must learn to help the patient make a responsible decision that will affect her environment. Quitting her job or finding one and becoming involved in a project or in socially rewarding activities may be examples of these. Enrolling in college or in an evening class may break up the boredom and change the environment that may have contributed to the development of the disease.

Family therapy may help the members of the family deal with their own problems. Watching a loved one destroy her life affects one's thinking. Feelings about alcohol, alcoholic behavior, treatment, and acceptance must be dealt with. If the family members are not healthy, they cannot effect a healthy change in the patient. Family members must also understand the reactions of society once society discovers that a member of the family is an alcoholic. They must learn the facts about alcoholism: that the family must insist on treatment and that the behavior of an alcoholic family member does not reflect negatively on the other members. They do not have to make excuses; they do not have to provide coverups.

Family members must learn that covering up the disease will not help; if anything, it will only weaken a woman's desire to get help, and it will perpetuate the problem. They should learn that they must not accept broken promises because they will lead to failure, more lies, and distrust. Threats, bribes, and punishment lead to increased guilt and self-hatred, which may give the alcoholic another excuse to drink (Bete Co., 1983).

Assertiveness Training

Since many alcoholic women report a lack of skills to deal effectively and assertively in the social world as a cause of alcoholism, they show abnormally high levels of fear revolving around interpersonal situations. Assertiveness training may be instrumental in reducing the emotional factors that trigger the drinking behavior. Assertiveness training can help the patient express, in an appropriate fashion, personal rights and feelings in the presence of others and to improve communication and interpersonal problem solving (O'Neil and Roitzch, 1977).

In addition, assertiveness training can provide the patient with an opportunity to learn or relearn social skills in a drug-free environment. Assertiveness training can help the female alcoholic by giving her the opportunity to develop socialization skills and avoid the loneliness, the lack of self-esteem, and the low self-concept that characterize most alcoholic women.

Child Care Facilities

The availability of child care service has been identified as a factor for consideration in a woman's decision to enter and remain in a residential treatment program for substance abuse (National Clearing House, 1979). Though there are no data indicating how many women are prevented from entering a treatment program because of this, the lack of child care is a potential barrier to treatment. A common factor in the need for child care services is that the alcoholic woman often feels alienated from family and other support systems. Whether the alienation is real or imagined, she may postpone or avoid seeking treatment for herself rather than request child care assistance (Reckman-Williams, Babcock, & O'Bryan, 1984). An alcoholic woman's seeking of treatment may constitute a role shift in the family that may be dramatic. To avoid such a shift, she may not seek treatment.

In order to encourage women to seek treatment, care professionals must deal with a mother's concern for her children, especially if she is single and working. Of the female addicts in a study by Suffet and Brotman (1976), 78% were unmarried and 50% had children. The female patient has problems of guilt, and such feelings should not be magnified by child care responsibilities. Anyone planning a program for female alcoholic therapy must consider providing child care or at least aiding in the location of reliable child care services. Such a center is the Eaton Treatment Center at Beech Acres, Cincinnati, Ohio. The center provides a range of services to the women who are dependent on alcohol and a combination of alcohol and other mood-altering drugs. This center established a child care unit because they believed that recovery from the acute phase of chronic illness required both rest and the focusing of a person's energy and attention on treatment and that this process is facilitated for a mother if her children are not present (Reckman, et al. 1984).

PREVENTION AND INTERVENTION

Women have stated (Haver, 1986) that treatment was only one life event among many that influenced the outcome of therapy. They attributed meeting a new partner and forming a good relationship, having a child, obtaining a place to live, having a better job, the death of a drinking companion, a serious somatic illness, a religious conversion, or a combination of these factors to a positive change in their drinking career. Though a woman (and her therapist) has no control over some of these factors, she does have control over others. New friendships, a new religion, a new job—a change in her social environment—could be very helpful in establishing a better feeling and consequently a change in drinking behavior.

Prevention can be a positive influence in the fight against alcoholism. There are structural points of view that apply equally to men and women (Litman, 1986). According to the structural view, increased taxation on alcohol, prevention of alcohol sales in certain locations, and increased restrictions on advertising could help. According to Sandmaier (1980), the liquor industry has recognized the changing drinking norms for women. In contrast to the 1958 code that forbade the depiction of women in the liquor industry's advertisements, by 1976, a popular women's periodical, *Cosmopolitan,* ranked as one of the top 15 magazines in liquor advertising revenue. A cursory search through the 1987 issues of *Working Woman,* a magazine directed toward the female executive or aspiring female entrepreneur, revealed many alcohol advertisements. These advertisements portrayed alcohol as the reward of a hard day's work, the complement to a beautiful relationship, the culmination of a long search, and the symbol of prestige and independence.

Alcohol advertisers have been using television to their advantage by promoting alcohol as the socially accepted refreshment, making it the symbol of prestige, independence, and reward. Weekends are advertised as having been made for good times, and good times are always accompanied, according to the advertisements, by alcohol. Young women, then, may accept these idealistic, distorted advertisements as truth and succumb to their pressure as they attempt to establish identities for themselves. Keil (1978) studied a group of women in Pennsylvania and found that the breakdown of barriers based on sex roles exposed women to new social opportunities in which drinking was not only acceptable but expected of women. Such expectations were sufficiently strong to counter ethnic or religious prescriptions for more conservative norms for female drinking.

Although there is little evidence to indicate that the mass media play a role in changing drinking behavior, the glamorous portrayal of the drinking woman (reminiscent of the glamorous smoker of the 1940s and 1950s) as a role model could be discouraged (Litman, 1986). In terms of changing individual beliefs, attitudes, and behavior, prevention strategies must be geared and evaluated in relation to the specific characteristics of women.

As a preventative measure, education about the physiological, social and psychological illnesses that accompany alcoholism should be stressed. An emphasis on earlier diagnosis must be accompanied by educational programs to increase public awareness of hazardous drinking levels. Women should be advised not to exceed 40 g of alcohol per day on a regular basis (Saunders et al., 1981). Masi (1981) pointed out that in 1975, of $75 million allocated for alcoholism, only $2.5 million was targeted for women's problems. By 1978, women's needs were not being met; among 14 treatment centers for women, only one had child care components.

But in order to be successful, a program must disaggregate alcoholism and talk about the prevention of the specific kinds of problems which are included under that label (Room, 1974). To some extent, current programs for women have focused on specific alcohol-related problems such as FAS, and such programs are most likely to succeed (Wilsnack & Beckman, 1984). Programs must also be directed to a specific group at risk because the message can be more specific and can include role models that more closely resemble members of the group. Such groups may be composed of young single women, adolescents, or women who have been identified as being depressed.

The best prevention program, then, is one that focuses on the social and psychological factors of female alcoholism. Research has not shown how hereditary causes can be cured. But something can be done about the social and psychological factors. More money should be spent on alcoholism research, prevention, and treatment.

REFERENCES

Alcohol and health: First special report to the U.S. Congress from the Secretary of Health, Education, and Welfare (DHE Pub. No. HSM 72-9099). 1971, December. Washington, DC: Government Printing Office.

Allan, C., & Cook, D.J. (1985). Stressful life events and alcohol misuse in women: A critical review. *Journal of Studies on Alcohol, 2,* 147–152.

Beary, M.D., Lacey, J.H., & Merry, J. (1986). Alcoholism and eating disorders in women of fertile age. *British Journal of Addiction, 81,* 685–689.

Beck, A.T. (1976). *Cognitive therapy and the emotional disorders.* New York: International University Press.

Beckman, L.J. (1978a). Self-esteem of women alcoholics. *Journal of Studies on Alcohol, 39,* 491–498.

Beckman, L.J. (1978b). Sexual conflict in alcoholic women: Myth or reality. *Journal of Abnormal Psychology, 87,* 4, 408–417.

Beckman, L.J. (1979). Reported effects of alcohol on the sexual feelings and behavior of women alcoholics and nonalcoholics. *Journal of Studies on Alcohol, 40,* 272–282.

Beckman, L.J. (1980). Perceived antecedents and effects of alcohol consumption in women. *Journal of Studies on Alcohol, 41,* 518–530.

Bete Co., Channing L. (1983). *About women and alcohol.* [A scriptographic booklet]. (Pub. No. 1214C-5-83). South Deerfield, MA: Author.

Blane, H.T. (1968). *The personality of the alcoholic: Guises of dependency.* New York: Harper & Row.

Braiker, H. (1984). Therapeutic issues in the treatment of alcoholic women. In S.C. Wilsnack & L.J. Beckman (Eds.), *Alcohol problems in women* (p. 349). New York: Guilford.

Brick, J., Nathan, P.E., Westrick, E., Frankenstein, W., & Shapiro, A. (1986). The effects of menstrual cycle on blood alcohol levels and behavior. *Journal of Studies on Alcohol 47,* 6, 472–477.

Brohman, M. (1981). Maternal inheritance of alcohol abuse: Cross fostering analysis of adopted women. *Archives of General Psychiatry, 38,* 965–969.

Cahalan, D., Cisin, I.H., & Crossley, H.M. (1969). *American drinking practices: A national study of drinking behavior and attitudes.* (Monograph No. 6). New Brunswick NJ: Rutgers Center of Alcohol Studies.

Clancey, J. (1986). Alcoholism and depression. *Iowa Medicine,* March, 118–119.

Cooke, D.J., & Allan, C. (1984). Stressful life events and alcohol abuse in women: A general population study. *British Journal of Addiction, 79,* 425–430.

Covington, S., & Kohen, J. (1984). *Women, alcohol, and sexuality: Social and sociological aspects of alcoholism and substance abuse.* New York: Hawthorne Press.

Curlee, J. (1970). A comparison of male and female patients at an alcoholism treatment center. *Journal of Psychiatry, 74,* 239–247.

Cuskey, W., Berger, L., & Densen-Gerber, J. (1977). Issues in the treatment of female addiction: A review and critique of the literature. *Contemporary Drug Problems, 6,* 307–371.

Doshan, T., & Bursch, C. (1982). Women and substance abuse: Critical issues in treatment design. *Journal of Drug Education, 12,* 229–239.

Eaton, W.W., Holzer, C.E. III, Von Korff, M., Anthony, J.C., Helzer, J.C., George, L., Burnam, M.A., Boyd, J.M., Kessler, L.G., & Lock, B.Z. (1984). The design of the epidemiological catchment area surveys. *Archives of General Psychology, 41,* 942–948.

Edwards, G., Hawker, A., Hensman, C., Peto, J., & Williamson, V. (1973). Alcoholics known or unknown to agencies: Epidemiological studies in a London suburb. *British Journal of Psychiatry, 123,* 179–183.

Evans, S., & Schaefer, S. (1980). Why women's sexuality is important to address in chemical dependency treatment programs. *Grassroots, 37,* 37–40.

Fewell, C.H., & Bissell, L. (1978). Alcoholic denial syndrome: An alcoholic focused approach. *Social Casework, 59,* 6–13.

Filmore, K.M. (1975). Relationships between specific drinking problems in early adulthood and middle age. *Journal of Studies on Alcohol, 36,* 882–907.

Goist, K.C., Jr., & Sutker, P.B. (1985). Acute alcohol intoxication and body composition in women and men. *Pharmacology, Biochemistry and Behavior 22,* 811–814.

Gomberg, E.S.L. (1980). Issues in prevention of alcohol problems: A review. In S.C. Wilsnack & L.J. Beckman (Eds.) *Alcohol problems in women.* New York: Guilford.

Gomberg, E.S.L., & Lisansky, J. (1984). Antecedents of alcohol problems in women. In S.C. Wilsnack & L.J. Beckman (Eds.), *Alcohol problems in women* (p. 249). New York: Guilford.

Goodwin, D.W. (1973). Alcohol in suicide and homicide. *Quarterly Journal of Studies on Alcohol, 34,* 144–156.

Gorwitz, K., Bahn, Warthen, & Cooper (1970). Some epidemiological data on alcoholism in Maryland. *Quarterly Journal of Studies on Alcohol, 31,* 423–443.

Halrow, L.L., Newcomb, M., & Bentler, P.M. (1986). Depression, self-derogation, substance abuse, and suicide ideation: Lack of purpose in life as a mediational factor. *Journal of Clinical Psychology, 42,* 5–19.

Haver, B. (1986). Female alcoholics: 1. Psycho-social outcome six years after treatment. *Acta Psychiatrica Scandinavica, 74,* 102–111.

Heather, N., & Robertson, I. (1981). *Controlled drinking.* London: Methuen.

Henderson, J.B., Hall, & Lipton (1979). Changing self-destructive behaviors. In G.C. Stone, et al. (Eds.) *Health psychology: A handbook.* San Francisco: Jossey-Bass.

Hesselbrock, V., Hellelbrock, M., & Workman-Daniels, K. (1986). Effects of major depression and antisocial personality on alcoholism: Course and motivational patterns. *Journal of Studies on Alcohol, 47,* 207–211.

Hoar, C. (1983). Women alcoholics—are they different from other women? *International Journal of Addictions, 18,* 251–270.

Humphrey, J., & Friedman, J. (1986). The onset of drinking and intoxication among university students. *Journals of Studies on Alcohol, 47,* 455–458.

Jacobson, R. (1986). Female alcoholics: A controlled CT brain scan and clinical study. *British Journal of Addiction, 81,* 661–669.

Johnson, P.B. (1983). Sex differences, women's roles and alcohol use: Preliminary national data. *Journal of Social Issues, 38,* 93–116.

Johnson, P. (1984). U.S. adult drinking practices: Time trends, social correlates and sex roles. In S.C. Wilsnack & L.J. Beckman, (Eds.) *Alcohol problems in women* (p. 282). New York: Guilford.

Jones, B.M., & Jones, M.K. (1976). States of consciousness and alcohol: Relationship to the blood alcohol curve, time of day, and the menstrual cycle. *Alcohol Health and Research World, 1*(1), 10–15.

Kalant, O.J. (Ed.). (1980). *Research advances in alcohol and drug problems* (Vol. 5). New York: Plenum.

Keil, T.J. (1978). Sex role variation and women's drinking. *Journal of Studies on Alcohol, 29,* 859–868.

Kielholz, P. (1970). Alcohol and depression. *British Journal of Addiction, 65,* 187–193.

Kinsey, B.A. (1966). *The female alcoholic: A social psychological study.* Springfield, IL: Charles C Thomas.

Kirkpatrick, J. (1978). *Turnabout: Help for a new life.* New York: Doubleday.

Kleeman, B., & Googins, B. (1983). Women alcoholics in management: Issues in identification. *Alcohol Health and Research World, 7*(3), 23–28.

Krasner, N., Davis, M., Portmann, B., & Williams, R. (1977). Changing pattern of alcoholic liver disease in Great Britain: Relation to sex and signs of autoimmunity. *British Medical Journal, 1,* 1487–1550.

Langone, J. & Langone, D. (1980). *Women who drink.* New York: Addison-Wesley.

Lemay, D. (1980). The need of an awareness of specialized issues in counseling alcoholic women. *Personnel and Guidance Journal,* October, 103–105.

Lisansky, E.S. (1958). The woman alcoholic. *Annals of the American Academy of Political and Social Science, 315,* 73–81.

Litman, G.K. (1986). Women and alcohol problems: Finding the next question. *British Journal of Addiction, 81,* 601–603.

MacAndrew, C. (1986). Similarities in self-depictions of female alcoholics and psychiatric outpatients: Examination of Eysenck's demention of emotionality in women. *Journal of Studies on Alcohol, 47,* 478–484.

Mandel, L., Schulman, J., & Monteiro, R. (1979). A feminist approach for the treatment of drug abusing women in a coed therapeutic community. *International Journal of Addictions, 14,* 589–597.

Masi, D.A. (1981). *Organizing for women.* Lexington, MA: Lexington Books.

Masnick, G., & Bane, M.J. (1984). The nation's families: 1960–1990. In S.C. Wilsnack & L.J. Beckman (Eds.), *Alcohol problems in women* (p. 282) New York: Guilford.

McClellan, D.C., Davis, W.N., Kalin, R., & Wanner, E. (1972). *The drinking man: Alcohol and human motivation.* New York: Free.

McLachlan, J.F.C., Walderman, R.L., & Birchmore, D.F. (1979). Self-evaluation, role satisfaction, and anxiety in the woman alcoholic. *International Journal of Addictions, 14,* 809–832.

Mulford, H.A. (1977). Women and men problem drinkers: Sex differences in patients served by Iowa's community alcoholism centers. *Journal of Studies on Alcohol, 38,* 1624–1639.

National Clearing House for Drug Abuse Information. (1979, April). *Child care provision in drug abuse treatment programs.* (DHEW Pub. No. ADM 79-830). Rockville, MD: National Institute on Drug Abuse.

O'Neal, P.M., & Roitzsch, J.C. (1977). Assertiveness training for alcohol abusers: Rationale and application. *British Journal of Alcohol and Alcoholism, 12,* 107–113.

Rathbone-McCuan, E., & Roberds, L. (1980). Treatment of the older alcoholic. *Focus on Women, 1,* 104–139.

Rathod, J.H., & Thompson, I.G. (1971). Women alcoholics: A clinical study. *Quarterly Journal of Studies on Alcohol, 32*, 45–52.

Reckman-Williams, L., Babcock, P., & O'Bryan, T. (1984). Meeting the child care needs of the female alcoholic. *Child Welfare, 63*, 541–546.

Rimmer, J., Pitts, F.N. Jr., Reich, T., & Winokur, G. (1971). Alcoholism: 2. Sex, socio-economic status, and race in two hospitalized samples. *Quarterly Journal of Studies on Alcohol, 32*, 942–952.

Room, R. (1974). Minimizing alcohol problems. *Alcohol Health and Research World*, 12–17.

Sandmaier, M. (1977). Alcohol abuse and women: A guide to getting help. Washington, DC: Government Printing Office.

Sandmaier, M. (1980). *The invisible alcoholics: Women and alcohol abuse in America.* New York: McGraw-Hill.

Saunders, J.B., Davis, M., & Williams, R. (1981). Do women develop alcoholic liver disease more readily than men? *British Medical Journal, 282*, 1141–1143.

Schatzkin, A., Jones, Y., Hoover, R.N., Taylor, P.R., Brinton, L.A., Ziegler, R.G., Harvey, E.B., Carter, C.L., Licitra, L.M., Dufour, M.C., & Larson, D.B. (1987). Alcohol consumption and breast cancer in the epidemiologic follow-up study of the first national health and nutrition examination survey. *New England Journal of Medicine, 316*, 1169–1173.

Schmidt, W., & DeLint, J. (1972). Cause of death of alcoholics. *Quarterly Journal of Studies on Alcohol, 33*, 171–185.

Schmidt, W., & Popham, R.E. (1980). Sex differences in mortality: A comparison of male and female alcoholics. In O.J. Kalant (Ed.), *Research advances in alcohol and drug problems* (Vol. 5). New York: Plenum.

Sclare, A.B. (1970). The female alcoholic. *British Journal of Addiction, 65*, 99–107.

Sclare, A.B. (1975). The woman alcoholic. *British Journal of Alcohol and Alcoholism, 10*, 134–137.

Shore, E.R. (1985). Alcohol consumption rates among managers and professionals. *Journal of Studies on Alcohol, 46*, 153–156.

Smith, E., Cloninger, & Bradford (1983). Predictors of mortality in alcoholic women: A perspective follow-up study. *Alcoholism: Clinical and Experimental Research, 7*, 232–243.

Suffet, F., & Brotman, R. (1976). Female drug use: Some observations. *International Journal of Addictions, 11*, 19–33.

Sugerman, A.A., Sheldon, J.B., & Roth, C. (1975). Defense mechanisms in men and women alcoholics. *Journal of Studies on Alcohol, 36*, 422–424.

U.S. Department of Labor. Bureau of Labor Statistics. (1981, November 15). *News.*

Wilsnack, S.C. (1973). Sex role identity in female alcoholism. *Journal of Abnormal Psychology, 82*, 253–261.

Wilsnack, S.C. (1976). The impact of sex roles in women's alcohol use and abuse. In M. Greenblat & M.A. Schuckit (Eds.), *Alcoholism problems in women and children* (p. 178). New York: Grune & Stratton.

Wilsnack, S.C., & Beckman, L.J. (Eds.) (1984). *Alcohol problems in women.* New York: Guilford.

Wilsnack, S.C., Klassen, A., & Wilsnack, R. (1984). Drinking and reproductive dysfunction among women in a 1981 national survey. *Alcoholism: Clinical and Experimental Research, 8*, 451–458.

Wood, H.P., & Duffy, E.L. (1966). Psychological factors in alcoholic women. *American Journal of Psychiatry, 123*, 341–345.

Appendix 2-A

Sources of Help

The following is a partial list of sources to which the alcoholic woman may turn for help:

- *Physicians:* They can provide needed medical care and can also help locate other needed services.
- *Mental health centers:* Most of them are beginning to offer a full range of alcoholism services. Since alcoholism has psychological causes, these centers can be very helpful.
- *Hospitals and health clinics:* They provide information and services for alcoholism and related health problems. Many of them provide inpatient and outpatient services.
- *On the job health services:* Many companies realize that alcoholism is a disease that can be treated. As a result, they offer occupational services.
- *Counselors and therapists:* These people are specialists in their fields, and they can provide support, understanding, and guidance to people in need. Though most of the therapists are men, many women should be encouraged to enter the field as specialists.
- *Alcoholics Anonymous (AA):* This well-known program is made up of people who help each other stop drinking and rebuild their lives. Based on 12 steps (see Appendix A), the philosophy of AA is to reestablish the patient's self-esteem by providing support and understanding. Its affiliates, Al-Anon and Al-Ateen, provide fellowship and advice to families, friends, and children of alcoholics. However, because the group is directed to all alcoholics, women may feel uncomfortable as members.

Source: From *About Women and Alcohol,* 1983, South Deerfield, MA: Channing L. Bete Company, Inc. Copyright 1983 by Channing L. Bete, Company, Inc.

- *Women for Sobriety (WFS):* This group was founded by a critic of AA, Jean Kirkpatrick (1978), who joined AA twice and did not stop drinking. WFS is a program designed to help female alcoholics develop a sense of self-esteem and positive attitudes in everyday life. WFS has 13 statements that are acknowledgments of the problems alcohol causes for the individual. In contrast to the AA approach which admits a powerlessness over alcohol and professes a belief that recovery requires a help from a "power greater than ourselves," the 13 statements of WFS appear to recognize that the power of change lies within the alcoholic. This is a key point in WFS because most female alcoholics have been characterized as helpless and lacking self-esteem.

Chapter 3

Substance Abuse and Psychopathology: The Special Population of the Dual-Diagnosis Patient

P. Clayton Rivers

INTRODUCTION

Dual-diagnosed clients, i.e., those with both substance abuse and mental health problems, create difficulties for both substance abuse and mental health treatment systems. These clients are frequently misfits in both care giving systems and/or receive treatment for only one aspect of their problem. One of the difficulties is, of course, that most treatment personnel in this country are trained in only one care modality, i.e., either mental health or substance abuse. In addition, the treatment philosophies, program structures, and even the length of care vary greatly between these treatment orientations.

Because of these differences in treatment programs across the mental health and substance abuse fields, these clients can often get in a "revolving door" pattern from one type of treatment program to another. For example, a client may have delusions and hallucinations, use alcohol to medicate these problems, abuse alcohol, and be sent to an alcohol treatment center. After alcohol treatment begins, the hallucinations and delusions recur, and the person is referred back to a mental health facility and receives major tranquilizers. Then he or she is released, then quits taking medications and begins to use alcohol again, abuses, and may be readmitted to an alcohol center. This pattern, which is only one of many that may be followed, can be repeated several times by individuals who hve conjoint occurrence of mental health and substance abuse problems.

This chapter focuses on this special population. It is a special population not only in name but in the way that professionals must respond to their problems. Specifically, this chapter focuses on the conjoint occurrence of the following problems: (a) substance abuse and depression, (b) substance abuse and sociopathy, and (c) substance abuse and schizophrenia. Obviously, the list could be extended to all types of mental health problems and various combinations of substance abuse. However, the specific mental health–substance abuse pairings chosen as the main focus of this chapter are based on those disorders for which sufficient clinical and research data are available on which to base at least an initial description of the problem pairing.

DEPRESSION AND SUBSTANCE ABUSE

The relationship between affective disorder and alcoholism has been studied extensively (O'Sullivan, 1984). The positive relationship between affective disorder and alcoholism can be inferred from the finding of a high incidence of affective disorder in the families of alcoholics (Winokur, Clayton, & Reich, cited in Mayfield, 1985; Winokur, Reich, Rimmer, & Pitts, cited in Mayfield, 1985). There is also a high rate of suicidal attempts and contemplation with both affective disorder and alcoholism. As O'Sullivan (1984, p. 379) noted: "Studies reporting on the prevalence of affective disorder in alcoholic populations give ratio rates of 5-9% while conversely 8-36% of manic-depressives are said to exhibit coexisting alcoholism." Other researchers (e.g., Zimberg, 1985) have provided somewhat varying figures. Addiction to substances other than alcohol and the relationship of these addictions to depression have been less well researched.

Alcohol and Depression

There has been an association established between depression and alcoholism for a relatively long period of time, particularly in terms of suicide (East, cited in Mayfield, 1985; Sullivan, cited in Mayfield, 1985). More recently, there has been a more direct relationship established between alcoholism and affective disorder. Before launching into those studies, some differences in how alcohol abuse can be associated with depression should be outlined. First, there are relatively consistent test data that suggest that alcohol abuse leads to elevated scores on the depression scale of the Minnesota Multiphasic Personality Inventory (MMPI). However, in the majority of cases, the score on the depression scale declines as the individual begins to recover from the toxic state of alcohol abuse. This indicates that there is probably some depression brought on by alcohol abuse itself. This depression clears up as individuals begin to cope with the toxic state of alcohol abuse and resolve their guilt over the harm they may have done to significant people in their life. These individuals typically show no history of depression. The type of depression that usually occurs in reaction to the physical and psychological consequences of drinking is reactive, or exogenous, depression.

Endogenous depression can be defined as depression that is not related to a precipitating event, does not seem to be improved by a change in the person's situation, and reoccurs over the person's life cycle. There is sometimes, but not always, a family history of depression that can be readily documented. There are two types of endogenous depression identified in the psychiatric literature. The first type, unipolar depression, refers to a disorder that is expressed by deep depression and melancholia. Persons may, over their life span, move from a mood that would be classified as "normal" to severe depression several times.

The second type of endogenous depression is called "bipolar depression" and has been referred to in earlier classification schemes as manic-depressive disorder. Individuals show a typical cycle of moving from normal affect to maniclike behavior where they sleep very little, are very active, talk and move constantly, and show a rapid shift in ideas and verbal material. They are so active that they may exhaust the onlooker. They also may have grandiose schemes and be temporarily amusing to the people with whom they interact, although eventually they push the limits too far and are perceived as rude and insensitive. This part of the cycle is then followed by depression. The depression cycle shows the same or similar type of depression as the unipolar depression. Sometimes it may show a typical pattern of going from normal behavior to manic and then depression. Finally, then, the person will return again to a normal mood state.

Depression has shown an unusual association with alcoholism. Studies at the beginning of the century showed a high rate of alcoholism among those who committed suicide (East, cited in Mayfield, 1985; Sullivan, cited in Mayfield, 1985). More recent research has tended to confirm those findings (e.g., Robins, Murphy, Wilkinson, Gassner, & Kayes, 1959, cited in Mayfield, 1985).

Mayfield (1985) noted that the co-occurrence of alcoholism and affective disorder is a more recent finding. For example, Mayfield and Coleman (1968) found alcoholism in 20% of their bipolar patients. For individuals whose primary diagnosis is alcoholism, Mayfield (1985) reported less striking but reliable co-incidences of about 7% to 9% who were also diagnosed as having an affective disorder.

Perhaps one of the major hypotheses regarding affective disorders in general and alcoholism is that they may reflect the same underlying problem in different ways, i.e., expressed as alcoholism in men and as depression in women. This hypothesis has been generated from the research on family co-incidences of alcoholism and depression noted above. As Mayfield

(1985) indicated, Winokur and his colleagues used the research on concurrence of depression and alcoholism "to devise a hypothetical subdivision of unipolar affective disorder" (Mayfield, 1985, p. 71). These included:

- depressive spectrum disease, a serious unipolar depression occurring in a person with a first degree relative suffering from either alcoholism or antisocial personality with or without a first degree relation with unipolar depression
- familial pure depressive disease, occurring in an individual with a first degree relative suffering only from unipolar depression
- sporadic depressive disease, occurring in the absence of any psychiatric illness among first degree relatives.

It is the first, depressive spectrum disease, that suggests a common underlying familial attribute that may be expressed as either unipolar affective disease or alcoholism.

There has also been research on the role of alcohol abuse in relationship to bipolar affective disorder. One of the important studies in this area was done by Mayfield and Coleman (1968). In a group of 59 patients with cyclic affective disorders, they found that 20% of that group drank excessively. They also found that a change in drinking with mood swing was quite common. Contrary to what might be expected, they found that increased drinking was associated with elation and not depression. When depression occurred, drinking in general decreased. An increase in drinking was predominant in the elation cycle. This type of association between affect and alcohol has also been found by other researchers. These findings suggest that the notion that abusive alcohol use by people suffering from bipolar disorder is an attempt to cope with a severely depressed mood is erroneous.

One issue that must be addressed is the fact that alcohol is used by many people to alter their mood state. If the self-reports of drinkers can be accepted, alcohol does modify mood. Moderate social drinkers when experimentally intoxicated in a laboratory setting show improved mood at low levels of alcohol intoxication. However, this change in mood does not appear to be euphoric and seems to be below the positive affect changes reported for cocaine or amphetamines. At high levels of intoxification, there is a deterioration of mood.

These findings do not support the notion that the alcoholic drinker abuses alcohol to reach a euphoric state. Indeed, research on alcoholics suggests that alcoholics in laboratory settings have deterioration in mood (i.e., become more depressed and anxious) under chronic heavy alcohol intake (Mendelson, 1964). These results have been replicated by several other researchers. Mood changes have been observed to proceed to the point of a severe depressive syndrome with suicidal ideation. A question arises: why do alcoholics who suffer this depressive affect continue to drink? One possibility is that although they are not finding euphoria from their drinking, they may be relieved from dysphoria (a sense of melancholia or sadness, depression), i.e., returning to a more moderate and midrange mood state. That this may occur has been supported to some degree by laboratory research on acute severe depression (Mayfield & Allen, 1967). The subjects in these studies showed profound improvement in most mood factors after mild acute intoxication. While these findings suggest that alcohol can have positive effects on severely depressed people, it was also found that those subjects who had a history of excessive drinking showed much less improvement than did subjects who had never been excessive drinkers.

Pharmacotherapy for Depressed Alcoholics

Having a dual diagnosis usually means a longer period of treatment than would be true for a person with one of the problems. This is especially true when compared with the treatment time of the typical alcohol program. Within general alcohol treatment programs, there is also a concern with the use of psychotropic drugs as a part of treatment, i.e., that they should not be used at all if their use can be avoided. Despite these concerns, there have been several ways that pharmacotherapy has been used with depressed alcoholics. It is important to note that the alcoholic should be sober and abstinent before any psychotropic drugs are prescribed.

In terms of the neurotic, or reactive (exogenous), depression so often seen in alcoholics, overall, Brown, Williams, and Neil (1973) found that phenothiazine and tricyclic antidepressants in low dosages may be of assistance. These two types of medication were more effective than diazepam in producing symptom relief in separate groups of detoxified alcoholics with the anxiety depression syndrome. This is an important finding since many people feel that the prescribing of minor tranquilizers is not a realistic treatment option in view of the addiction potential of these drugs. In general, it can be said that research has not supported the initial enthusiasm for treating depressed alcoholics with antidepressants (O'Sullivan, 1984).

A similar finding seems to have been established for the use of lithium carbonate in the treatment of depression in alcoholics. While this treatment does seem to be effective with patients who have a primary affective disorder, it is not useful with reactive depression. Severe depressive disorders occur only occasionally in alcoholics. When these disorders do occur, the pattern of using lithium treatment is similar to that followed in treating nonalcoholics with an affective disorder (O'Sullivan, 1984).

When treating the alcoholic with depression, it is frequently helpful to have as specific a description of the client as possible. Mayfield (1985) outlined four subtypes of depression in alcoholics that need to be considered:

1. depression developed in reaction to chronic intoxication (disappears promptly upon cessation of drinking)
2. suicidal/reactive depression
3. depression that might be called characterological depression, which is long standing and independent of life events ("normally" a depressed individual)
4. severe affective disorder or endogenous depression.

The first of these is not helped by medication. It is only the last type, i.e., severe affective disorder, for which medication may be helpful (Mayfield, 1985).

Comprehensive Treatment of Mood Disorders with Alcoholics

The preferred ordering of treatment with the dual diagnosis of alcoholism and depression was commented on by O'Sullivan (1984). He suggested that control over problem drinking takes priority in the early phase of treatment. Only after the alcoholic is abstinent can a true picture of the underlying pathology emerge and be dealt with over time. Once abstinence has been accomplished, the type of treatment offered will depend on many factors, including the patient's capacity for insight, the intactness of the personality, and the presence or absence of intellectual impairment. O'Sullivan suggested obtaining a collateral history from a significant other to help deal with the issue of denial or memory lapses by the patient. The use of family members and other possible sources of support were also encouraged. Support from others is particularly helpful in dealing with the reactive depression found in alcoholics suffering with guilt related to drinking associated actions. This is especially an issue when the alcoholic is forced to deal with these guilt feelings without the support of alcohol.

Blume (1985) discussed dealing with depression in the group psychotherapy session. She suggested that the therapist make an effort to draw persons out slowly so that they may express their feelings, including crying or mourning, if appropriate. She noted that depressed persons are usually very quiet in the group. Once the depression and its possible causes are expressed, the group can sympathize with depressed persons and comfort them. The group can then help such patients win a series of small victories to help them gain a sense of mastery over their life and their environment. A helpful question, once the depression begins to lift, is: "Do you deserve to be happy?" Once the patients admit they have that right, the leader can ask each of them to go to each member, make eye contact, and repeat: "I deserve to be happy." According to Blume, "not guilty" is an excellent motto for some depressed people in such group sessions.

While reactive depression is a frequent occurrence in both sexes, the presence of a major affective disorder is much more common in female alcoholics. For example, Zimberg (1985) indicated that only 5% or fewer of male alcoholics have major affective disorders, while 25% to 50% of female alcoholics may suffer from this type of problem. He suggested treatment with lithium carbonate for these patients. A similar finding regarding the rates for severe affective disorders in women was made by Tamerin (1985).

One result of depression in female alcoholics is a syndrome called "inhibited sexual desire." Powell (1985) outlined ways of treating this disorder. His techniques are included here because some of them are quite effective in dealing with depression in general in both men and women. Powell suggested that the therapist intervene to disrupt depression in a number of ways:

- *Behavioral interventions:* These include increasing positive reinforcers, dealing with learned helplessness, reducing stress, and teaching problem-solving skills.
- *Affective interventions:* These include dealing with anger, resentment, and guilt; reducing passivity and distrust; and dealing with negative self-fulfilling prophecies.
- *Cognitive Interventions:* These include eliminating negative thoughts, teaching thought-stopping techniques, reframing myths and cognitions, and dealing with boredom.
- *Systematic relational interventions:* These include modifying relationships and roles/expectations, changing destructive interactions, and reducing tendencies toward being a workaholic.

Other Drugs and Depression

Several studies have shown a strong association between alcohol and depression. As Mayfield (1985) noted, there is little evidence of an association between the user of other "recreational" drugs and depression. While this is contrary to what one would predict from substance abuse theories, it is what the data suggest at this point in time. Both psychodynamic and behavioral theories hold that most drugs are used in a manner similar to alcohol, i.e., to meet similar psychodynamic needs or as reinforcers of behavior.

Since alcohol use and abuse are so pervasive, they have been closely examined by researchers. It may be that too little research on drugs other than alcohol and depression is available to allow the establishment of a relationship between the two. Despite the failure of association, the research and clinical/theoretical thinking concerning opiate and nonopiate drug abuse and depression are briefly examined.

Opiates

With the exception of alcohol, opiate abusers have been more widely studied than any other drug users. The most probable reason is that most of them, like most alcoholics, employ only one drug of addiction. They are also more often what Mayfield (1985) called a "captive audience." For example, over the past 50 years, there has been extensive research on opiate abusers at the Lexington Federal Narcotics Hospital.

When the same research strategies used for alcoholics are followed with opiate abusers, i.e., looking at depression rates in opiate abusers or looking at opiate abuse in depressed psychiatric patients, the findings are not persuasive. For example, Mayfield and Coleman (1968) conclude that few opiate abusers are found in diagnosed depressives. Valliant (1966) followed 100 New York addicts over 12 years who were treated at the Lexington Narcotic Hospital and found few subjects with a clearly definable affective disorder.

Blatt, Rounsville, Eyre, and Wilbur (1984) at Yale illustrated a more positive relationship between opiate abuse and depression. Working from a psychodynamic framework, they used the Depressive Experience Questionnaire to assess depression in 86 drug abusers. Of that group, 36 men and 11 women were primarily addicted to opiates. Data from these subjects suggested that depression is a central issue for opiate addicts.

Blatt et al. (1984) found that the opiate addicts were significantly more depressed than a group of polydrug users who were not yet opiate addicted. Their data also indicated that the elevation in depression by opiate addicts focused primarily on issues of self-criticism, guilt, and shame. Issues of dependency and feelings of rejection, abandonment, and neglect do not appear to be common in depressed opium addicts.

The contrasting conclusions one can find in the literature regarding the association of depression and opiate abuse are illustrated by the research outlined. These studies are reflective of the general findings in this research today. A common thread in this research is that the depression found in opiate addicts seems to be reactive or exogenous rather than the result of a major affective disorder. Apparently, severe depression does not occur more frequently in opiate addicts than in the population at large.

Nonopiates

Well-designed studies on nonopiate drug abusers who have affective disorders are even less frequent than those for opiate addicts and even more inconclusive (Mayfield, 1985). The studies that have been directed at establishing correlations between type of drug use and type of psychopathology have not indicated a high coincidence of affective disorder and substance abuse. McLellan and Druley (1977) found an interesting differential association of diagnosis and type of drug abused. They systematically interviewed patients admitted to psychiatric wards with a questionnaire designed to detect substance abuse. They found that 50% of the patients should have had a substance abuse diagnosis who had initially been missed in the diagnostic process. A comparison was made between patients' psychiatric diagnoses and their type of drug abuse. The following relationships were found:

1. Barbiturate use had a high association with depressive diagnosis and a low association with schizophrenia.
2. Alcohol and heroin abuse had about the same association with depression as did the general population.
3. Amphetamine and hallucinogen abuse was highly correlated with paranoid schizophrenia.

While these findings are provocative, there are few examples of how to proceed in treatment with depressed people who are addicted to drugs other than alcohol.

One positive factor is that inpatient drug treatment is often of a longer duration and typically has a more comprehensive focus than that found in the typical alcohol treatment programs of 28 to 30 days. When this is true, the programs allow more time to be spent with the patient and allow a longitudinal monitoring of mood. In addition, there is usually an emphasis in these programs on "habilitating," which implies a more client centered, personalized approach and comprehensive attention to issues the patient must modify. This includes ways of handling mood (both positive and negative extreme mood swings are seen by some as relapse inducing, see Baker, 1987) and the redeveloping of a value structure that is more consistent with society in general. The person must also learn to deal with life without drugs, and that alone can be a major loss for the long-time user. These types of changes are difficult when there is not a major concern with depression. When depression is present, more time in a supportive atmosphere is needed. In addition, the wise and judicious management of psychotropic medication may be necessary.

SOCIOPATHY AND SUBSTANCE ABUSE

A discussion of this dual problem is difficult without first describing and defining sociopathy. This diagnostic category is frequently vaguely defined and is complicated by the way sociopathy is viewed in relation to substance abuse by different researchers.

Definitions and Descriptions of Sociopathy

The term *psychopath/sociopath* (often used interchangeably) has evolved over the history of abnormal psychology. While a review of that history is beyond the scope of this chapter, a review of the clinical profile presented by Cleckly (1941) is useful in understanding the general characteristics of abnormal behavior. These characteristics include:

- superficial charm and good intelligence
- absence of delusions and other signs of irrational thinking
- absence of nervousness or psychoneurotic tendencies
- unreliability
- untruthfulness and insincerity
- lack of remorse or shame
- inadequately motivated antisocial behavior
- poor judgment and failure to learn from experience
- pathological egocentricity and incapacity for love
- general poverty in major affective relations
- specific loss of insight
- unresponsiveness in general interpersonal relationships
- fantastic and uninviting behavior with drink and sometimes without
- threats of suicide, rarely carried out
- sex life impersonal, trivial, and poorly integrated
- failure to follow any life plan

More recently, Robins et al. (cited in Mayfield, 1985) defined the sociopathic personality. Their criteria included (a) chronic failure to conform with social norms, (b) a failure to maintain close interpersonal relationships, (c) a poor work record, (d) engaging in illegal activities, (e) problems of maintaining support, (f) sudden changes in plans, and (g) a low frustration tolerance.

The current *Diagnostic and Statistical Manual of Mental Disorders* (DSM III) of the American Psychiatric Association (the prevailing psychiatric diagnostic system in the United States) does not contain a sociopathic category. However, the antisocial personality disorder, which replaced the sociopathic label, is characterized by

> a current age over 17; onset before age 15 of three of the following: truancy, school misbehavior, delinquency, running away from home, persistent lying, repeated substance abuse, thefts, vandalism, school underachievement, chronic rule violations, initiation of fights; evidence after 18 of four or more of the following: inability to sustain consistent work behavior, lack of ability to parent responsibly, repeated illegal behavior, marital failure, physically aggressive behavior, financial failure, impulsivity, repeated lying or recklessness; no spontaneous break in anti-social behavior over 5 years after the age of 15 and absence of mental retardation, schizophrenia or mania (pp. 179–182).

The general movement in defining sociopathy/psychopathy has been an increased emphasis on socialization issues in positing the cause of the disorder. There has also been a more social/behavioral (as opposed to intrapsychic) use of diagnostic signs for diagnosing the problem.

The Relationship of Substance Abuse and Sociopathy

Across time, there has been a consistent relationship between sociopathic behavior (or antisocial behavior) and substance abuse throughout the substance abuse literature. Kay (1985) included all violations of socially approved behaviors, even if these behaviors did not involve breaking rules and laws, in his discussion of substance abuse and sociopathy. He pointed out in his review of the literature that there has been an association established between thrill seekers and habitual criminals and substance abuse. Another common finding is that the psychopathic deviate (Pd) scale on the MMPI has been frequently elevated in substance abusers. When this subscale was factor analyzed, several independent factors were established. For example, Monroe, Miller, and Lyle (cited in Kay, 1985) derived six major independent factors from Pd scale items on the MMPIs of alcoholics. These were intrapunitiveness, denial of shyness, hypersensitivity, impulse control, emotional deprivation, and social maladaptation. In another study (Hill, Haertzen, & Davis, 1962), criminals, opiate addicts, and alcoholics had remarkably similar profiles on the MMPI, with only an elevation of the depression scale score discriminating the two addict groups from the criminal group. In general, the findings suggested that most substance abuse groups have an elevated Pd scale score on the MMPI.

Alcohol and Sociopathy

Barry (1974) indicated that sociopathy has been associated with alcohol abuse in research spanning several decades. He pointed out that sociopathy is a rather vague and poorly established psychodiagnostic category. It is, he suggested, manifested by a variety of irresponsible, impulsive, and destructive actions. He also noted that the chronic, excessive drinking by the alcoholic is one of the antisocial behaviors and is associated with many others. For example, alcoholism is found in a high proportion of felons (43%) (Goodwin, Crane, and Guze, 1971). Sociopathy characterizes a much higher proportion of alcoholic than nonalcoholic felons (Barry, 1974). Abusive drinking has also been associated with antisocial behavior in young black men (Robins et al., cited in Mayfield, 1985).

Kissin (1977) suggested that the character disorders, of which antisocial behavior is one category in his scheme, account for 70% to 80% of the psychopathology seen in alcoholics. He also noted that alcoholics have a tendency to score high on the Pd and mania scales of the MMPI (see Hill et al., 1962). However, Kissin also suggested that if the items on the Pd scale that pertain to acute alcoholics are omitted, the level of sociopathy for alcoholics is not significantly different from that of normal subjects. He doubted that alcoholics are as psychopathic as has been generally concluded, especially since most of the antisocial behavior occurred under the influence of alcohol, a psychotoxic drug.

Kissen's (1977) suggestion concerning the MMPI Pd scale would indicate that the endorsement of the items by chronic alcohol abusers does not mean that they are sociopathic in the traditional sense of the term. However, at the same time, Kissen reported that the consistency in finding certain personality characteristics in alcoholics suggests there may be some reliability to the diagnosis of character disorder for alcoholics.

The antisocial personality he described showed a mild to moderate level of socially oppositional behavior, depending on the degree of psychopathology. In most respects, these patients exhibited the major aspects of character disorders, e.g., they were immature, impulsive, and showed a low frustration tolerance, a high degree of hostility, and a tendency to act out. Often these individuals came from families with a high incidence of antisocial behavior, broken homes, alcoholism, and low socioeconomic status.

A similar description (with the possible exception of low socioeconomic status) has been given by several researchers (e.g., Zucker, 1987) for antisocial personality. Zucker (1987) found, in preliminary results, that married couples (in which one spouse was arrested for driving while intoxicated [DWI]) differed in significant ways from community control families. For example, "alcoholic" fathers (those arrested for DWI) and their wives reported more delinquent activity (e.g., truancy, joyriding, and shoplifting); more overaggression (e.g., fighting in school, beating up people, killing animals); and more school-related antisocial behavior (e.g., suspension from school, cursing at teachers during adolescence). In adulthood, these same alcoholic fathers and their wives reported more job-related antisocial behavior (e.g., fired for absenteeism, three or more jobs per year). They also reported more trouble with the law (e.g., taking part in robberies and resisting arrest) than did community control couples.

Zucker (1987) reviewed data from the Epidemiologic Catchment Area (ECA) study to establish the relation of alcohol related diagnoses to other psychiatric diagnoses. The data showed that alcohol related diagnoses were most likely to be associated with antisocial personality, followed by manic episodes, drug abuse or dependence, and to a lesser but still significant degree, by major depressive episodes. These data are important because the sample was not a treatment-based one, and hence the selectivity that surrounds treatment-based samples was avoided.

Both of the findings by Zucker (1987) suggest that alcohol abuse and antisocial behavior are closely associated. A study by Hoffman, Loper, and Kammier (1974) compared the MMPI profiles of freshmen at the University of Minnesota with their later profiles while in treatment for alcoholism. As freshmen, these prealcoholics showed elevation on the Pd scale and the hypomania scale, suggesting that these individuals were more gregarious, impulsive, and nonconforming than their peers who were not prealcoholics. The onset of alcoholism later in life led to a somewhat different picture with clear evidence of subjective distress, in addition to the psychopathy noted while they were students.

This study suggests that there may be behaviors and personality factors that can precede alcohol abuse in at least some alcoholics. Hill, Steinhauer, and Zubin (1987) noted that research by Jones (1968, 1971), Jessor (1977, 1978), and Kandel (1978, 1980) suggested that addicts' behavior while in adolescence (specifically, greater independence, rebelliousness, and failure to value conventional institutions) is related to alcohol and drug abuse as adults.

Treatment of Alcohol Abuse and Sociopathy

The relationship of alcohol abuse and sociopathy can be seen in a number of ways. The descriptions are often confusing. It is difficult to decide exactly what the relationship is between substance abuse and sociopathy. Are there some patients who are sociopathic and alcoholic? Are there other patients who develop sociopathic behaviors in reaction to substance abuse? Perhaps the safest answers would be that at least these two basic co-occurrences are present in populations needing alcohol and/or psychiatric treatment. When the sociopathic behavior is in reaction to alcohol abuse, much of the sociopathic problem is dealt with as a normal function of the alcohol treatment programs followed in this country. As Kissen (1977) noted, many of the items endorsed on the MMPI that produced elevated Pd scores can be seen as being related to alcohol abuse itself.

It is possible to see some of the philosophy and steps of Alcohol Anonymous (AA) as directed toward dealing with sociopathic behavior in the alcoholic (see Appendix A). For example, the emphasis on total honesty is directed at changing the deceit and dishonesty many alcoholics have engaged in while drinking. Steps 2 and 3 deal with the alienation of alcoholics and encourage them to seek support from outside themselves, offering the emotional support of the group as well as God in dealing with this tendency to go it alone. Step 4 recognizes the rationalization of alcoholics and encourages them to see and accept themselves as they are. Jellinek (1983), in discussing the chronic phase of drinking and the prolonged intoxication of the alcoholic, noted: "This latter drinking behavior meets with such unanimous rejection that it involves a grave social risk. Only an originally psychopathic personality or a person who had later in life undergone a psychopathological process would expose himself to such risk" (p. 22). One way to see sociopathy is as a method to defend oneself against guilt and social pressure from other people. Step 8 of AA has the alcoholic make restitution to those he or she has harmed.

Some researchers (e.g., Tournier, 1983) believe that the AA philosophy and methods have come to dominate the alcohol treatment approaches in the United States. Whether Tournier's assertions are correct or not, it is true that issues of total honesty (not lying or deceiving either yourself or others) are an important part of most alcohol treatment programs in the United States. The point to be made here is that inherent in all alcohol treatment programs are procedures to deal with "sociopathic" behavior, particularly as it is associated with alcohol abuse. One could also note confrontation, the use of the group to keep the alcoholic in treatment honest, etc. as procedures that help to deal with sociopathic behaviors. However, these may be seen as attempts to break dysfunctional behavior patterns that have developed as a function of alcohol abuse. They do not seem to be directed at deep characterological changes that require more intense and longer treatment.

While confrontation does exist in most alcohol treatment programs, some researchers caution against severe confrontation with alcoholism. For example, Wallace (1985) suggested using only the minimal amount of confrontation needed for change in the alcoholic. He stated that heavy confrontation may lead to less internal change in the person being treated. Individuals with alcohol problems placed under heavy confrontation may rebel or decide to conform just to avoid the heavy confrontation, i.e., simply tell the person what he or she wants to hear to get him or her off your back. Neither of these postures leads to internal value change, which some researchers feel is crucial in the recovery of the alcoholic (e.g., Wallace, 1985). Other researchers (Landfield & Rivers, 1975, Rivers & Landfield, 1985) have noted that heavy confrontation leads to an arousal of general defensive behavior in the client.

Many, if not most, of the alcohol abusers in treatment may not need a level of confrontation that would be seen as necessary with individuals who have shown the development of sociopathic behavior over the life span. The author, in discussion with a director of a major alcohol treatment center in the Midwest, was told that perhaps 20% of the alcoholics who arrived at their free standing, nonprofit, third party payment treatment centers need a heavy, confrontive approach (William Leipold, Ph.D., personal communication, 1978). The focus of treatment seems to be on helping put self-esteem back together and getting people to accept more responsibility for their behavior. The first part of this treatment approach is not served well by heavy confrontation and personal attacks on the individual.

Clearly, there are some alcoholics that may need the more confrontive treatment. These individuals may be more frequent patients in some alcohol treatment programs, particularly those where referrals have come through the criminal justice system and/or the person is in prison. It is also possible that many alcoholics who show high rates of recidivism in traditional alcohol treatment programs may need a program with heavier confrontation and one that restricts and structures programs to a greater degree. The question is: What should be done in these programs where the sociopathic behavior is more resistant to change?

Kay (1985) reviewed the procedures at the Houston Veterans Administration (VA) Program. He noted that ordinary psychotherapeutic contracts could not be made with sociopathic patients there because of their mistrust and manipulation of words. He saw it as appropriate to demand specific (not specified) behaviors before members could qualify for individual or group therapy. At the Houston VA substance abuse program, only ward officers qualify for individual therapy. This decision is made on the basis that they are maximizing the inhibition of sociopathic behavior and as a result are experiencing the maximum of stress. Kay also suggested that since substance abusers learn more by doing than by saying, variants of psychodrama and other action therapies deserve testing. Because psychoactive drugs are associated with active avoidance of "suffering," learning an increased tolerance for suffering would seem to be an important focus on therapy.

Sociopathy and Other Drugs

Many of the same factors hold for this group of abusers as for the alcoholic. One aspect of this group that tends to increase the probability of sociopathic behavior is the criminal behavior associated with drug use. Since most drugs are illegal to purchase without a physician's prescription, drug abusers are typically forced into illegal behaviors to obtain various mood-altering chemicals. In addition, the maintenance of an addictive drug habit (e.g., heroin, cocaine) can lead to stealing and fraud to obtain the money for the drug habit. Under these conditions, it is easy to acquire rapidly a life style that is antisocial and that operates against traditional life patterns. It is also difficult to change because it involves people with core values that are antithetical to those held by mainstream society.

Kay (1985), in his description of the Houston VA program, stated that adequate therapy for sociopathic substance abusers must begin with behavioral and/or chemical inhibition of their antisocial behavior. This belief led the Houston program to have:

- daily collection of urine with random testing of common drugs of abuse
- have confrontation by members of the therapeutic community to reduce the ignoring of rules and violations
- have confrontation in therapy groups to inhibit common nonproductive transactional analysis games.

This program also used lithium and neuroleptics to inhibit behavior. These medications are not popular in the program, according to Kay. Unfortunately, he did not relate whether it was the staff or the patients who disliked the drugs' use.

Kay defined a term, *hypophoria*, that can be considered the absence of a positive mood (euphoria) rather than the presence of a negative mood (dysphoria). He suggested that some people may drink or use drugs because they wish to obtain a positive mood state. *Psychopathic state*, his second concept, incorporates the idea of a variable mood or feeling state (including euphoria and dysphoria) that may be acute or chronic (if chronic, it is equivalent to a psychopathic personality). A psychopathic state is often related to the chronic use of psychoactive drugs (or drug induced psychopathic state), which has a better prognosis than does a chronic psychopathic state associated with either a major mood disorder or persistent antisocial behavior. As Kay noted, the treatment of sociopathy associated with substance abuse is tied to the degree to which external control is needed to help the abusers inhibit some of their behaviors. Those who have severe sociopathic and drug problems will have to be treated while imprisoned, or at least under strict limitations. He also suggested that physiological-medical drug interventions may need to be developed in the future.

SCHIZOPHRENIA AND SUBSTANCE ABUSE

While the exact etiology of both schizophrenia and substance abuse is still being debated, research has confirmed that alcohol and drug abuse is frequently a complicating factor in schizophrenia. Several researchers (e.g., Alterman, 1985) have seen the typical psychiatric staff member as ill equipped to deal with psychiatric patients who are substance abusers. Unfortunately, there are almost no programs designed to deal with patients with the conjoint occurrence of severe psychiatric difficulties and substance abuse problems. In brief, although conjoint occurrence is well established, there has been relatively little attention paid to this population by clinicians or researchers.

As a result of this lack of attention, diagnostic procedures to detect this disorder have not been fully developed and/or clinicians in both substance abuse and psychiatric facilities fail to question the patient about possible secondary diagnoses. Thus many psychiatric patients who have substance abuse problems are being missed; the same failure in diagnosis is true for psychiatric difficulties of patients in some substance abuse agencies. Because of this failure in diagnosis, the exact prevalence of this conjoint disorder is not known.

Schizophrenia may be described as a group of disorders that are characterized by severe impairment of cognitive processes, personality disintegration, and social withdrawal. The schizophrenic disorders are severe disturbances (psychoses) that always involve some disruption of thought processes. Affected individuals may lose contact with reality, may see or hear things that are not actually occurring, or may develop false beliefs about themselves or others (Sue, Sue, & Sue, 1986, p. 426).

In addition, DSM III contains specific criteria for a diagnosis of schizophrenia. According to the DSM III, this diagnosis should be given only if delusions, auditory hallucinations, or marked disturbances of thought or speech are present. The person must have also displayed a deterioration from a previous level of functioning with regard to work, relationships with others, personal care and hygiene, etc. The disorder should have had a duration of at least 6 months during some period of the person's life and be currently present for at least 2 weeks. Organic mental disorders and affective disorders (i.e., mania and depression) must be able to be ruled out. The major symptoms of this disorder must appear before the person is 45 years of age.

Schizophrenia and Alcoholism

Alterman (1985) reviewed several studies regarding the incidence of schizophrenia and alcoholism. He noted that about one-fourth of admissions to psychiatric hospitals bear a diagnosis of alcoholism. Few of these early studies provided a second diagnosis, if appropriate, for the incarcerated alcoholic. Other studies by Parker, Meiller, and Andrews (1960) indicated that 22% of the schizophrenic and 33% of the manic-depressive patients in a VA hospital were also diagnosed as alcoholic. Panepento, Higgins, Keane-Dawes, & Smith (1970) reported doing group therapy with schizophrenic alcoholics who constituted 18% of the total alcoholic population. Alterman, Erdlen, McLellen and Mann (1980) provided evidence of the existence of the conjoint occurrence of schizophrenia and alcoholism in about 10% to 15% of the psychiatric population. Alterman, Erdlen, and Murphy (1981) found 13.4% of psychiatric patients who did not have a primary diagnosis of substance abuse carried a secondary or tertiary diagnosis of alcoholism. About one-third of these patients were diagnosed as paranoid schizophrenics. They also found that a higher proportion of conjoint diagnosed patients were black when compared with those who did not have alcoholism problems (31% to 20%).

It is apparent that there is a significant conjoint occurrence of alcohol abuse and serious psychiatric disorders. As Alterman (1985) noted, schizophrenia with complicating alcoholism represents a significant proportion of the patients in psychiatric treatment facilities. Although these conjoint-diagnosis patients are nowhere near a majority of the schizophrenic patients, they are in sufficient numbers to cause significant problems for the society at large and the treatment facilities in particular. Alterman also cautioned that these samples were all hospitalized patients. The rate of co-occurrence of alcoholism and schizophrenia in the general population is unknown.

Treatment issues for the schizophrenic patient who also has alcoholism as a primary and secondary diagnosis must be considered. Alterman and his colleagues appear to be the authority on this topic. It is important to remember the characteristics of the patients with whom they worked:

- About 15% of these VA schizophrenics were also diagnosed as alcoholic.

- About one half of these patients continued to abuse alcohol while in treatment.
- These problem-drinker schizophrenic patients were significantly younger and more likely to be black. They also had many more previous admissions than the schizophrenic patients without an alcohol diagnosis.
- Those with an alcohol diagnosis were more likely to bear a diagnosis of paranoid schizophrenia (77%) than were those without an alcohol diagnosis (55%).

Staff reported a number of treatment and management problems that were associated with alcohol abuse in these patients. These included mood and behavior change, hallucinations, blackouts, and "the shakes." They also frequently had a greater need for supervision, were unruly, displayed poor money management, missed roll calls, did not complete assignments, and had problems with their families. In addition, almost half the alcohol abusing patients had serious medical conditions that contraindicated alcohol use and especially abuse. These included seizures, diabetes, hypertension, peripheral neuropathy, and ulcers.

These patients were, in almost every case, being given major tranquilizers. This is an important issue, since all of them had potential adverse cross reactivities with alcohol. Reports from nursing staff suggested that several patients became combative after using alcohol on the hospital grounds. Alcohol use also seemed to precipitate hallucinations.

All of these factors present difficulties for treatment. However, as Alterman (1985) indicated, there is almost no research on what works with these patients. This makes it difficult for agencies to plan treatment programs. The little that is known suggests the following:

- Panepento et al. (1970) reported that alcoholics who were schizophrenic were able to remain in therapy longer and maintain a better relationship with their therapist in a nonintensive supportive drug program than alcoholics with a diagnosis of sociopathy.
- A study by Hall, Popkin, DeVaul, and Stickney (1977) examined the effects of illicit drug use by psychiatric outpatients on their diagnosis and treatment course. They found that drug users were more likely to be incorrectly diagnosed as schizophrenic and were more likely to miss therapy sessions and discontinue therapy. They also made their therapists more uncomfortable and were much less likely to benefit from treatment than were non-drug-using psychiatric outpatients. One has to remember that these results may be compounded by the chaotic life style that frequently accompanies drug use.

- Dual-diagnosed patients with alcohol problems do more poorly, in general, than do patients without substance abuse problems.
- How these patients will respond to the use of psychotropic medication and ways of managing that part of treatment with individuals who are using a mood-altering substance like alcohol are still unclear.

This information is very limited. It tells working clinicians much less than most would like to know about how to deal with these patients. The following general comments about a treatment program may be useful to the working clinician.

Drug Abuse in Psychiatric Patients

There has been documented evidence of amphetamine use triggering or exacerbating symptoms of schizophrenia (Robinson & Wolkin, 1980). These researchers confirmed their findings with laboratory assays. However, Alterman, Erdlen, LaPorte, and Erdlen (1982) indicated that without the backup of laboratory assay, the staff seems to be less aware of patients' drug abuse than they are of patients' alcohol abuse. Sharp changes in mood were the only psychological change the staff associated with drug abuse. Drug abusing psychiatric patients were more likely to have a larger number of previous admissions to the same facility, with shorter duration, than a comparison group of non-substance-abusing psychiatric patients.

Less is known about drug abusing psychiatric patients than is known about alcohol abusing psychiatric patients. However, there are a few things that may be helpful in treating this population. For example, a study by Hall et al. (1977) found that drug using psychiatric patients were more likely to be diagnosed as schizophrenic. They were also more likely to miss sessions and to discontinue therapy. These findings suggest that more effort is required on the part of the caregiver in terms of helping to maintain motivation and support than in psychiatric patients in general.

Perhaps a more severe impediment to therapy is the finding by Hall et al. (1977) that these patients induced more discomfort in their therapists (which would seem to work against the therapist becoming more involved with the patient). In addition, drug using patients were less likely to benefit from therapy than were non-drug-using psychiatric outpatients. These findings suggest that these patients are difficult to treat, difficult for therapists to establish relationships with, and overall do more poorly in therapy than the nonabusing psychiatric clients.

Unfortunately, the literature does not give many guidelines about how to improve success with these patients. The one point that does seem relevant is that therapy may have to be extended over a longer period of time. In addition, careful monitoring of the patient's drug use must be sustained throughout the treatment.

SPECIALIZED TREATMENT OF THE DUAL-DIAGNOSED PATIENT: AN EXAMPLE

The following summary of the treatment program at St. Paul–Ramsey Medical Center (Harrison, Martin, Tuason, & Hoffman, 1985) should give the reader an overview of some of the issues with which a specialized treatment program for the dual-diagnosed patient must deal. Since space considerations allow only highlights of the program, the reader is referred to the original report. Only a complete reading of the report will allow a full understanding of the program and how it was operationalized.

Originally, the program had only an outpatient program. However, the greater dysfunction of the patients with dual diagnoses led to the establishment of an inpatient treatment unit. These treatment services had a relatively brief duration before funding caused them to curtail their efforts. However, this is one of the few descriptions in the literature of a working treatment program for dual-diagnosed patients. Some of the procedures and ideas from that unit that are potentially useful in establishing a dual diagnosis treatment unit are:

1. The program found over time that treatment issues are complex with dual-disorder patients and that there is a need for flexibility in the program.
2. The skills of one subspeciality are not sufficient to meet the needs of patients. Patients' needs often cross professional boundaries that are more relevant to practitioners than they are to patients. Therefore, staff cannot adhere to strict professional turf rates with this population.
3. There is a need for individualized assessment and programming for each patient rather than rigid programmatic treatment approaches.
4. To illustrate the possible diversities of patients and the complexity of their problems, the authors gave their characteristics (see Tables 3-1 and 3-2).
5. There was a great deal of variability in the patients. Other demographic characteristics important in understanding the type of patients treated in this unit include (a) sex: two thirds were male; (b) age: more than half the patients were under 30; one third were in their 30s; (c) two thirds were unemployed at intake; (d) 62% had at least

Table 3-1 DSM III Psychiatric Diagnoses of Dual-Disorder Patients (N = 207)

Axis I	
Major affective disorder	29%
Schizophrenia and other psychotic disorder	24%
Adjustment disorder	19%
Dysthymia	9%
Anxiety disorder	7%
Impulsive control disorder	6%
Other	5%
Axis II: Personality Disorders	
Dependent	30%
Antisocial	17%
Avoidant	14%
Borderline	11%
Passive/aggressive	9%
Compulsive	7%
Narcissistic	7%
Schizoid	3%
Schizotypal	1%
Atypical, mixed, or other	10%

Source: From *Substance Abuse and Psychopathology* (p. 370) by A.I. Alterman (Ed.), 1985, New York: Plenum Publishing Corporation. Copyright 1985 by Plenum Publishing Corporation. Reprinted by permission.

---

one previous psychiatric admission; (e) 51% had at least one admission to a chemical dependency treatment program; (f) 50% reported a suicide attempt; (g) during treatment in the dual diagnosis unit, psychotropic medication, was being used by almost half the population.

6. The majority of female patients report being victims of physical and sexual abuse; a smaller but significant proportion of male patients reported abuse.

7. "Recovery" for many of these patients is probably unrealistic. Rather it may have to be measured in terms of less frequent and severe use of chemicals, increased length of abstinence, compliance with medication maintenance, and a reduction in the number of hospitalizations.

Perhaps of more central interest is the philosophy of the program. Because of the hopelessness felt by those suffering from chemical dependency and psychopathology, treatment personnel see the instilling of optimism as one of their main roles. They reinforce even small and often uneven progress. They see the reduction of guilt because of the need for the extended hospitalization as a factor that must be dealt with therapeutically.

Table 3-2 DSM III Substance Use Diagnoses of Dual-Disorder Patients (N = 207)

Alcohol only	49%
Alcohol/polydrug	22%
Alcohol/cannabis	17%
Alcohol/single other drug	3%
Cannabis only	3%
Single substance other than alcohol or cannabis	3%
Polydrug (no alcohol)	3%

Source: From *Substance Abuse and Psychopathology* (p. 371) by A.I. Alterman (Ed.), 1985, New York: Plenum Publishing Corporation. Copyright 1985 by Plenum Publishing Corporation. Reprinted by permission.

Patients are asked to set short-term goals so that they can assess their progress.

Treatment is created to respect the individual patient's pace and boundaries. Staff do not attack the patient's defenses (something that frequently is done in many chemical dependency agencies). Instead they model other responses that may allow patients to lower their defenses when they feel safer, or they may help the patient identify defenses and learn more satisfying ways to cope. Self-disclosure about personal issues is not demanded during group sessions. Individual counseling is available as needed for patients who choose not to reveal or who are unable to reveal certain information about themselves in a group situation. Such information is frequently of a sexual nature (this is another divergent approach since many group therapists feel removing material from the group disrupts therapy).

The program employs a patient contract to specify the expectations for the patients. For example, attendance, compliance with medication regimens and physician's orders, appropriate ingroup behavior, abstinence from alcohol and drugs, the reporting of use of chemicals by self or others, a prohibition of verbal and physical abuse, and the explicit requirements of confidentiality are all included in the contract.

Staff interpret the diagnoses the patient receives in a straightforward manner with the patient. After explaining the limitations of the evaluation procedures, patients are encouraged to not equate an evolving diagnosis with self. Instead, they are asked to explore their own experience of their disorder and to avoid a focus on diagnostic language.

Perhaps one of the most radical departures of this program, from the substance abuse perspective, is that it does not adhere to the AA model of substance abuse. The authors noted that the AA model may be limited in its flexibility to adapt to the complex clinical picture presented by dual-diagnosis patients. For example, in many cases substance abuse must be explored as an attempt to reduce psychiatric distress by the patient and/ or as a behavioral maladaptation. The program designers suggested that the use of a multifactoral etiology of chemical dependency may be more appropriate with these patients than the traditional AA model. It is important to point out that the AA philosophy is offered as one way to recovery, but it is only one of many strategies that are employed.

Although individual treatment is available to meet a given patient's needs, most of the treatment is done through counseling groups. These include *discovery groups, horizon groups,* and *transition groups.*

Discovery groups meet three times a week for 90 minutes each session. Most of the people in these groups have major psychiatric problems that typically require maintenance medication. Typical diagnoses in this group include (a) organic mental disorder, i.e., drug induced psychosis or substance delusional disorders; (b) schizophrenia; (c) paranoid disorders; (d) atypical psychosis; (e) major affective disorder, usually mania or major depressive disorder with psychotic feature; and (f) borderline personality disorder, usually schizotypical personality disorder or other personality disorder where brief psychotic states may occur.

Horizon groups meet for 90 minutes twice per week. The majority of patients have nonpsychotic psychiatric conditions. Typical diagnoses include (a) affective disorders largely without psychotic features, (b) anxiety disorders, (c) impulse control disorders, (d) personality disorders not involving psychotic states, (e) psychosexual disorders, and (f) severe adjustment disorders with limited responsiveness to traditional chemical dependency programs.

Transition groups meet once a week in the evenings. Most of the patients in this group have been involved in either the horizon or the discovery group, although program dropouts and others may also be included.

The authors also named a series of educational workshops that are directed at more general topics for patients with this alternative so that these issues do not have to be dealt with in the counseling groups. The workshops are designed for members of the first two groups. One sequence of workshops is designed primarily for discovery group members and discusses:

- cognitive therapy: an examination of attitudes, beliefs, and feelings and learning to differentiate feelings from thoughts
- symptom patterns (in behavioral terms) of major mental illnesses
- common reactions to stress and grief
- coping skills in dealing with life events
- functional areas of the brain affected by mental illness
- the role of medications in the treatment of mental illness.

A second series of workshops is designed for both discovery and horizon group members. These workshops include (a) group process, rules, and interpersonal skills; (b) communication skills, especially assertiveness; (c) sexuality as an expression of self; and (d) family roles and communication patterns.

Depending upon the stage of involvement, a patient could be attending from one to five sessions per week. In addition, chemical dependency patients attend a traditional program during the remaining days or evenings. Psychiatric patients attend scheduled groups on their residential units.

The multidisciplinary staff includes a psychiatrist, a psychologist, certified chemical dependency counselors, and nurses. They plan to add a social worker. While staff members contribute from their own speciality expertise, e.g., psychological assessment, psychiatric diagnosis, and medication monitoring and nursing plan, the professional's role is very flexible. Staff members are expected to develop their own unique styles and contributions. Those who provide direct counseling services are supervised by a psychologist who has experience in substance abuse.

The St. Paul–Ramsey Medical Center Program gives an overview of the issues faced by one dual-diagnosis treatment unit. The description demonstrates the complexity of diagnosing and treating patients with conjoint substance abuse and mental health problems. In the next few years it is anticipated that there will be many more specialized units to treat the dual-diagnosis patient. These units and increasing research interest in this type of patient may help clarify how treatment teams should proceed with this complex problem. The complexity of the issues surrounding these patients will probably make the development of a simple unimodal treatment approach an impossible goal for the foreseeable future. The problem does offer an opportunity for a dialogue between substance abuse and mental health workers. Whether the professional gulf between these two groups can be bridged to help patients with whom both have legitimate concerns is unknown.

SUMMARY

This chapter examined the relationships between alcohol and drug abuse and the psychiatric diagnosis of affective disorders, sociopathy, and schizophrenia. Relevant issues of etiology, asessment, treatment, and research were reviewed for each diagnosis.

Dual-diagnosis patients are unique in the field of chemical dependency. As a specific population they are emerging as a complex and difficult group to treat. The etiology of these dual diagnoses is not thoroughly understood. In some cases it appears that the psychiatric problem preceded the chemical abuse and in others this is reversed. Some patients may be medicating symptoms with the chemical abuse, while others may be covering substance abuse with psychiatric symptoms.

These patients are often misdiagnosed, undertreated, or shifted between mental health and chemical dependency treatment units. To reduce treatment failures with this population, mental health professionals and substance abuse counselors must be cross trained in both disciplines, treatment programs should be designed to meet their multiple needs, and professionals in these two fields must be willing to put aside their differences for the benefit of the patients.

Assessments, treatment plans, and staffing problems must be examined in light of the dually diagnosed. This is especially crucial when medications are being used with chemically dependent patients. Rigid approaches must be avoided, and flexibility of policies, programs, and treatment professionals is essential to improve the prognosis for this population.

REFERENCES

Alterman, A. (1985). Substance abuse in psychiatric patients: Etiological, developmental, and treatment considerations. In A. Alterman (Ed.), *Psychopathology and substance abuse* (pp. 121–136). New York: Plenum.

Alterman, A., Erdlen, F., McLellan, A., & Mann, S.C. (1980). Problem drinking in a psychiatric hospital: Alcoholic schizophrenics. In E. Gottheil, A. McLellan, & K. Druley (Eds.), *Substance abuse and psychiatric illness* (pp. 27–37) New York: Pergamon Press.

Alterman, A., Erdlen, F., & Murphy, E. (1981). Alcohol abuse in the psychiatric hospital population. *Addictive Behaviors, 6,* 69–73.

American Psychiatric Association (1980). *Diagnostic and statistical manual: Mental disorders* (DSM III). Washington, D.C.: APA.

Baker, T.B. (1987). The motivation to use drugs: A psychobiological analysis of urges. In P.C. Rivers (Ed.), *Alcohol and addictive behavior: Vol. 34. Nebraska symposium on motivation* (pp. 257–323). Lincoln: University of Nebraska Press.

Barry, H. (1974). Psychological factors in alcoholism. In B. Kissen & H. Begleiter (Eds.), *The biology of alcoholism* (Vol 3). (pp. 83–107). New York: Plenum.

Blatt, S.J., Rounsville, B., Eyre, S.L., & Wilber, E. (1984). The psychodynamics of opiate addiction. *Journal of Nervous and Mental Disease, 172,* 342–352.

Blume, S.B. (1985). Group psychotherapy in the treatment of alcoholism. In S. Zimberg, J. Wallace, & S.B. Blume (Eds.), *Practical approaches to alcoholism psychotherapy* (2nd ed.) (pp. 73–107). New York: Plenum.

Cleckly, H. (1941). *The mask of sanity.* St. Louis: C.V. Mosby.

Goodwin, D.W., Crane, J.B., & Guze, S.B. (1981). Felons who drink. *Quarterly Journal of Studies on Alcohol, 32,* 136–147.

Hall, R.C.W., Popkin, M.K., DeVaul, R., & Stickney, S.K. (1977). The effect of unrecognized drug abuse on diagnosis and therapeutic outcome. *American Journal of Drug and Alcohol Abuse, 4,* 455–465.

Harrison, P., Martin, J., Tuason, V., & Hoffman, N. (1985). Conjoint treatment of dual disorders. In A. Alterman (Ed.), *Psychopathology and substance abuse* (pp. 367–390). New York: Plenum.

Hill, H.E., Haertzen, C.A., & Davis, H. (1962). An MMPI factor analytic study of alcoholics, narcotic addicts and criminals. *Quarterly Journal of Studies on Alcoholism, 23,* 411–431.

Hill, S.Y., Steinhauer, S.R., & Zubin, J. (1987). Biological markers for alcoholism: A vulnerability model. In P.C. Rivers (Ed.), *Alcohol and addictive behavior: Vol. 34. Nebraska symposium on motivation* (pp. 208–256). Lincoln: University of Nebraska Press.

Hoffman, H., Loper, R.G., & Kammier, M.L. (1974). Identifying future alcoholics with MMPI alcoholism scales. *Quarterly Journal of Studies on Alcohol, 35,* 490–498.

Jellinek, E.M. (1983). Phases of alcohol addiction. In D.A. Ward (Ed.), *Alcoholism: Introduction to theory and treatment* (2nd ed.) (pp. 14–24). Dubuque, IA: Kendall/Hunt.

Jessor, R., & Jessor, S. (1977). *Problem behavior and psychosocial development: A longitudinal study of youth.* New York: Academic.

Jessor, R., & Jessor, S. (1978). Theory testing on longitudinal research on marijuana use. In D. Kandel (Ed.), *Longitudinal research on drug use* (pp. 41–71). Washington, DC: Hemisphere.

Jones, M.C. (1968). Personality correlates and antecedents of drinking patterns in adult males. *Journal of Consulting & Clinical Psychology, 32,* 2–12.

Jones, M.C. (1971). Personality antecedents and correlates of drinking patterns in women. *Journal of Consulting & Clinical Psychology, 36,* 61–69.

Kandel, D.B. (1978). *Longitudinal research on drug use: Empirical findings and methodological issues.* Washington, DC: Hemisphere.

Kandel, D.B. (1980). Drug and drinking behavior among youth. In A. Inkeles, N.J. Smelser, & R.H. Turner (Eds.), *Annual review of Sociology* (Vol. 6). Palo Alto, CA: Annual Reviews.

Kay, D.C. (1985). Substance abuse in psychopathic states and sociopathic individuals. In A. Alterman (Ed.), *Psychopathology and substance abuse* (pp. 91–119). New York: Plenum.

Kissen, B. (1977). Medical management of the alcoholic patient. In B. Kissen & H. Begleiter (Eds.), *The biology of alcoholism* (Vol. 3) (pp. 53–103). New York: Plenum.

Landfield, A.W., & Rivers, P.C. (1975). An introduction to interpersonal transaction and rotating dyads. *Psychotherapy: Theory, Research and Practice, 12,* 366–374.

Mayfield, D. (1985). Substance abuse in the affective disorders. In A. Alterman (Ed.), *Psychopathology and substance abuse* (pp. 69–90). New York: Plenum.

Mayfield, D., & Allen, D. (1967). Alcohol and affect: A psychopharmacological study. *American Journal of Psychiatry, 123,* 1346–1351.

Mayfield, D., & Coleman, L.L. (1968). Alcohol use and affective disorder. *Diseases of the Nervous System, 29,* 467–474.

McLellan, A.T., & Druley, K.A. (1977). Non-random relation between drugs of abuse and abusers. *Journal of Psychiatric Research, 13,* 179–184.

Mendelson, J.H. (Ed.). (1964). Experimentally induced chronic intoxication and withdrawal in alcoholics. *Quarterly Journal of Studies on Alcohol,* (Suppl. 2).

O'Sullivan, K. (1984). Depression and its treatment in alcoholics: A review. *Canadian Journal of Psychiatry, 29,* 289–384.

Overall, J.E., Brown, D., Williams, J.D., & Neil, L.T. (1973). Drug treatment of anxiety and depression in detoxified alcoholic patients. *Archives of General Psychiatry, 29,* 218–221.

Panepento, W.C., Higgins, M.J., Keane-Dawes, W.Y., & Smith, D. (1970). Underlying psychiatric diagnosis as an indicator of participation in alcoholism therapy. *Quarterly Journal of Studies on Alcohol, 31,* 950–956.

Parker, J.B., Meiller, R.M., & Andrews, G.W. (1960). Major psychiatric disorders masquerading as alcoholism. *Southern Medical Journal, 53,* 560–564.

Powell, D.J. (1985). Management of sexual dysfunctions in alcoholics. In S. Zimberg, J. Wallace, & S.B. Blume (Eds.), *Practical approaches in alcoholism psychotherapy* (2nd ed.) (pp. 213–237). New York: Plenum.

Rivers, P.C., & Landfield, A.W. (1985). Personal construct theory and alcohol dependence. In E. Button (Ed.), *Personal construct theory and mental health,* (pp. 169–181). Beckenham, Kent, England: Croom Helm.

Robins, L.N. (1966). *Deviant children grown up: A study of psychopathic personality.* Baltimore: Williams & Wilkins.

Robinson, A.E. & Wolkind, S.N. (1980). Amphetamine abuse among psychiatric inpatients: the use of gas chromatography. *British Journal of Psychiatry, 116,* 643–644.

Sue, D., Sue, D., & Sue, S. (1986). *Understanding abnormal behavior* (2nd ed.). Boston: Houghton Mifflin.

Tamerin, J.S. (1985). The psychotherapy of alcoholic women. In S. Zimberg, J. Wallace, & S.B. Blume (Eds.), *Practical approaches to alcoholism psychotherapy* (2nd ed.) (pp. 259–279). New York: Plenum.

Tournier, R.E. (1983). Alcoholics Anonymous as treatment and ideology. In D.A. Ward (Ed.), *Alcoholism: Introduction to theory and treatment* (pp. 343–369). Dubuque, IA: Kendall/Hunt.

Valliant, G.E. (1966). A 12 year followup of New York narcotic addicts. *Archives of General Psychiatry, 15,* 599–609.

Wallace, J. (1985). Critical issues in alcoholism therapy. In S. Zimberg, J. Wallace, & S.B. Blume (Eds.), *Practical approaches to alcoholism psychotherapy* (2nd ed.) (pp. 37–49). New York: Plenum.

Zimberg, S. (1985). Principles of alcoholism psychotherapy. In S. Zimberg, J. Wallace, & S.B. Blume (Eds.), *Practical approaches to alcoholism psychotherapy* (2nd ed.) (pp. 27–83). New York: Plenum.

Zucker, R.A. (1987). The four alcoholisms: A developmental account of the etiologic process. In P.C. Rivers (Ed.), *Alcohol and addictive behavior: Vol. 34. Nebraska symposium on motivation* (pp. 27–83). Lincoln: University of Nebraska Press.

Chapter 4

Alcoholism, Drugs, and the Disabled

Benita Anne Glow

INTRODUCTION

Drug and alcohol treatment programs for people with handicaps must include an awareness of the particular aspects of each condition being treated and must be integrated with the general population. Therefore, this chapter focuses on an overview of certain aspects of the conditions of blindness, deafness, spinal cord injury, epilepsy, and developmental disabilities. Caregivers should continue in an in-depth study of particular conditions.

Two problems surfaced in the writing of this chapter: (a) there is a lack of available information on the treatment of people with handicaps; and (b) there is a lack of information on treatment programs that are integrated with the general population.

EARLY DEVELOPMENTS THAT LED TO THE EMANCIPATION OF PEOPLE WITH HANDICAPS

In the 1960s there was a movement to integrate minorities into the mainstream of American life. This movement was not only beneficial to racial minorities and women but thrust the isolation of the "disabled" into focus so that they too could move into the mainstream of American life. With the passage of the Landmark Bill 94-142, which was the equal rights bill for the disabled, public schools had to open their facilities and programs to people with handicaps and disabilities.

Special programs were initiated for people with handicaps, and they were allowed to participate in the same activities as did the other students. Public schools built ramps to make classrooms available to blind, wheelchair-bound, and walker-bound students. Interpreters for the deaf were provided so that deaf students could attend mainstream classes. Teachers were schooled in teaching "the handicapped."

With the advent of the movement of those with handicaps into the mainstream of American life came the urge to enjoy that capability in all areas: jobs, transportation, and even in alcohol treatment facilities. Thus there began a growing awareness among treatment facilitators of the need to provide special treatment within the framework of the general population's treatment of drug and alcohol abuse.

In an article for the *Los Angeles Times* (October 1987), Jim Murray, a sportswriter, quoted Bard Parks, a former skiing-surfing star who is now a paraplegic tennis player. Parks said: "It's [being a paraplegic] not the worst thing in the world. People think being in a wheelchair is the worst thing in the world, but I find myself very happy. I think anybody who is able to go out and play three sets of tennis is very lucky" (Murray, 1987, p. 1). "It's the stand-up tennis that makes you feel sorry for yourself" (Murray, 1987, p. 1). Murray was writing about the upcoming Everest & Jennings U.S. Wheelchair Tennis Championships to be played the following week. The tournament had grown out of Parks's need to participate in a competitive sport despite the "handicap" of being paraplegic.

As may be seen from Bard's statement, being "handicapped" depends on one's point of view. Very often, caregivers of alcoholics with handicaps see only the handicap and not the person who has the handicap. The disabled can be viewed from the perspective of "What can they do?" rather than "What can't they do?" One agency, when writing about the disabled, writes the word *dis-abled* with a slash through the *d* to accentuate the *is-abled*.

Sometimes, some people with disabilities ease their physical and mental pain, lack of "do-ableness," isolation, and feelings of low self-worth through the use of drugs and alcohol: often drugs that have been prescribed by a physician. Some of the questions this chapter addresses are: "Do the disabled use alcohol and drugs to the same extent, or more, as do people in the general population?" "Why do the disabled abuse alcohol and drugs?" "What kinds of treatment programs and preventative measures can best serve the disabled?"

DO THE DISABLED USE AND ABUSE ALCOHOL AND DRUGS?

A survey of several studies indicates that the disabled use and abuse alcohol and drugs.

It's common knowledge that about 10 percent of the U.S. population actively abuses alcohol. Given the number of people with disabilities in the United States, estimates from the U.S. Census Bureau hover around 36 million, it is reasonable to assume that there is a large group of physically disabled substance abusers. Based on the incidence of substance abuse problems among clients of the Center for Independent Living (CIL) in Berkeley, we estimate that the actual proportion of persons with disabilities who abuse substances is much higher than 10 percent (Hepner, Kirshbaum, & Landes, 1980, p. 11).

Alcoholism is the biggest single diagnosis in the VA health care system. We treat over 100,000 patients each year—somewhere between 25 and 30 percent of the Vietnam-era veterans. We treat twice as many Vietnam-era veterans for alcoholism as we do for drug abuse and this is one reason I have expanded the VA's alcohol treatment program some 25 percent in the last 72 months. I've also expanded our research into the cause of alcoholism. It is such a devastating disease, and it is—unfortunately—such a pervasive disease in our culture. It is not only the single biggest health care problem in the VA system, it is the single biggest drug problem in the country (Cleland, 1980, p. 57.)

The overall incidence of alcoholism in the general population is conservatively estimated to be 8 percent. However, several local surveys and research studies indicated that alcoholism—at least for some subgroups of disabled people—may be much more prevalent than among the general population. The Rehabilitation Services Administration (RSA) reports approximately 5 percent of the people served by State-operated rehabilitation agencies last year were classified as multidisabled alcoholics, with either a majority or secondary disability of alcoholism in combination with an additional mental or physical disability (Hindman, 1980b, p. 5).

Although the precise numbers of multidisabled alcoholics served by federally supported alcohol treatment programs is not known, the National Institute on Alcohol Abuse and Alcoholism (NIAA) estimates that the rate of alcohol problems among the disabled is at least that of the general population. "Based on a conservative 8 percent prevalence rate, 2.8 million Americans are multi-disabled alcoholics" (Hindman, 1980, p. 5).

Isaacs, Buckley, and Martin (1979) wrote:

Alcohol usage is pervasive in our culture; Chafetz estimates that there are roughly 100 million users of alcohol in the United States, of which approximately 10% are heavy users or problem drinkers. A survey of the research literature, however, found no research studies on the use of alcohol among the deaf (nor any other handicapped group for that matter). It is a sobering fact that we know more about the alcohol use patterns of a few thousand Lepch of the Himalayas than we do about the estimated 13 million hearing-impaired persons in our country (p. 464).

In addition, the number of the learning handicapped, or as they are sometimes labeled, those with minimal brain dysfunction or attention deficit disorders is in the thousands. A computer search revealed that there were no studies regarding their use of drugs and alcohol. This is also true for the asthmatic population.

The Seed featured excerpts from the report of the Commission on California State Government Organization and Economy, known as the "Little Hoover Commission." The report stated:

Conservative estimates were used to determine the possible number of chemically dependent Californians with disabilities. Following the Department of Rehabilitation's figures, between 10 and 18 percent of the State's population has some form of significant disability—2.3 to 4.1 million people. Since most accepted estimates put the percentage of the general population with alcohol or drug problems at 20 percent, it may be assumed that at least 500,000 disabled Californians are chemically dependent (*The Seed,* 1987, p. 4).

The Commission cited the variety of identified barriers to effective treatment services as reported by the Darrell McDaniel Independent Living Center, which surveyed 27 treatment programs in Southern California. They were:

25 percent of the facilities they surveyed would not permit persons using prescription medication to enter their programs.

Only 7 percent of the facilities surveyed accepted Medi-Cal or Medicare as payment for treatment.

Only 59 percent of the programs would use a sliding scale according to the client's income.

40 percent of the treatment programs were not accessible to persons using wheelchairs.

30 percent of the treatment programs were in areas where there was no public transportation for persons in wheelchairs, even though all treatment programs receiving federal or California State funding are required by law to have facilities accessible to persons in wheelchairs.

In 99.7 percent of the treatment programs surveyed, American Sign Language interpreters for deaf persons were not available and would not be paid for by the treatment program or the person's insurance, even though 45 percent of the programs were required to provide such interpreters (*The Seed,* 1987, p. 5).

The Commission further reported that "the main issue is not new funding dedicated to special programs for the disabled, but rather to integrating the disabled community into existing substance abuse treatment facilities" (*The Seed,* 1987, p. 5). The issue of "isolation" of the disabled is an aspect of their alcohol abuse that needs to be addressed during the recovery process rather than dismissed by placing people with handicaps in greater isolation in treatment programs for the disabled only. The disabled need special treatment within a broad treatment program. The "one program fits all" approach is not good for anyone but is especially detrimental to people with handicaps.

Developing special aspects of a program necessitates looking at the individual needs associated with each disability, and then looking at the individual needs of each person with a handicap. Once the needs have been determined, an individualized treatment program can be developed. The National Council on Alcoholism recommends that a person suffering from alcoholism and another disability be labeled a multidisabled alcoholic person to reinforce the concept that alcoholism itself is a disabling and handicapping condition.

THE DEAF AND THE HEARING IMPAIRED

Are Drinking Patterns of the Deaf and the Hearing Impaired the Same as Those of the General Population?

In a study by Isaacs et al., (1979), the patterns of drinking among the deaf were found to be very similar to those of the general population: no significant differences emerged. There is a possibility that the frustration experienced by a person with severe disabilities in obtaining employment and gaining social acceptance may contribute to a higher prevalence of alcohol abuse in this group than would be found in the general population.

Although the goal in treating the deaf alcoholic is treatment in mainstream programs, there are special needs of the deaf that need to be addressed.

If the drinking patterns of the deaf do not appear to be significantly different than those for the general population, why aren't the deaf using mainstream treatment centers? Some of the reasons are:

- The deaf community is a closely knit community that opposes such a move because the deaf have just recently overcome the stigma of "deaf and dumb." Attempts to start rehabilitation programs for the deaf alcoholic have met with massive denial by the organized deaf community because they refuse to accept the existence of the problem (Isaacs et al., 1979). They do not want the stigma of "deaf and drunk."

- The deaf community shows a great mistrust of the hearing community (Watson, Boros, & Zrimec, cited in Boros, 1980-81).

- There is a lack of knowledge regarding available resources. This is due to the fact that much of the "general information held by deaf adults comes from personal contact with other deaf persons rather than from the media, therefore they are often unaware of existing agencies" (Isaacs et al., 1979).

- A lack of personnel to serve as interpreters to deaf alcoholics is a stumbling block. Most agencies surveyed by Isaacs et al. (1979) were at a loss as to what to do if a deaf person should enter their treatment program. Once in treatment the deaf person encounters many problems (Isaacs et al., 1979).

Problems the Deaf and the Hearing Impaired Encounter in Treatment

The main factor inhibiting treatment and recovery for the deaf person is the inability to communicate. Those who have other handicaps generally can communicate. However, the inability of the deaf person to communicate necessitates that the caregivers determine, before treatment, the level of communication of the deaf person and the type of interpreters needed. It is also important to determine the background of the deaf person. Factors such as "educational history, type of communication they have had with their parents, the onset of the hearing loss, the degree of hearing loss, are areas that need to be addressed with oneness and sensitivity" (Kannapell, 1980).

Another problem involved in the recovery of the deaf person is the attitude of the caregivers. Very often the caregivers find the disability a greater factor in recovery for themselves than for the deaf person because they tend to focus on the handicap and its causes rather than on the deaf person's self-image and family structure. In addition, caregivers may become "enablers" to the deaf alcoholic in that they may "patronize" the patient, deciding what the patient does or does not need to do rather than making sure that the deaf patient utilizes the program to the greatest extent, much as a person without handicaps would. On the other hand, caregivers very often tend to be "inflexible" and negative. They may require the deaf person to attend meetings without an interpreter because that is what everyone is "supposed to do." What the deaf person, as well as the person without handicaps, wants during treatment is to be treated as an equal with special needs and have a program designed to meet his or her special needs (Kannapell, 1980).

Barbara Kannapell, President of Deaf Price, Inc., an agency that provides advocacy services for deaf people, noted that caregivers are often at a loss to understand the predicament of the deaf. An example of this occurred when a staff member at a hospital called to ask Kannapell to speak to one of the deaf patients. When Kannapell arrived with her interpreter, they discovered that the patient could sign very well on a one-to-one basis but became lost in a group session because she needed an interpreter.

The communication problem does not lie in simply being unable to hear and thus to speak clearly. The communication problem leads to serious language problems. The combination of these two factors leads to a lower educational level for the average deaf person. Communication and language problems lead to serious social and psychological problems. Resulting feelings of low self-esteem, isolation, loneliness, and frustration contribute to the incidence of alcoholism among the deaf (Watson et al., cited in Boros, 1980). The language problem causes serious gaps in education and social situations, which leads to a lack of understanding and comprehension of situations and reading materials. The subtle and inferred aspects of communication are never learned by the deaf, as abstract and inferred terms are difficult to sign. Signing involves concrete materials. "25% of all communication is through words, the remaining portion must be through other means such as body language, voice inflection and facial expression" (Bormann, et al., as cited in Watson, 1972, p. 33). Thus the hearing impaired are multihandicapped insofar as they are unable to hear, unable to communicate with hearing people except through an interpreter, and are alcoholic. In working with the person with handicaps, the issues of the caregivers often get in the way because they focus on the deaf person's inability to communicate rather than focusing on the person.

When asked what could be done to improve outreach and early identification of the alcoholic person who is deaf, Scanlon offered the following answers:

- Caregivers need to acknowledge the alcohol abuse and not deny the handicap due to their own fear and feelings regarding disabilities.
- Caregivers need to view the chemical dependency and the underlying issues and not consider the alcoholism as a natural condition of the disabled person.
- Caregivers need to be aware of services available to treat the multi-disabled alcoholic.
- To avoid misdiagnosis, caregivers should be empathetic but not display pity toward the disabled.

Many find it difficult to deal with people with handicaps because of feelings of helplessness in regard to their handicap. It may be difficult to face the person with handicaps. To avoid discomfort, some avoid dealing with them. It is important for caregivers to examine their own motives and behavior. Is the caregiver helping to solve the problem or is the caregiver maintaining a status quo? It is important to look beyond the hearing impairment to the person and consider that 90% of deaf people have hearing families, and 90% of deaf parents have hearing children. Many of the hearing impaired reach an academic level of fifth grade, which is more a function of language difference than cognitive incapacity (Haley, 1985).

Myths Involved in Treating the Deaf and the Hearing Impaired

Haley (1985) discussed myths surrounding the deaf:
- *Myth 1: "A deaf person is a deaf person is a deaf person."* In other words, there is little else to consider regarding a deaf person, except that he or she is deaf. Except for some factors that make the deaf person unique, the deaf are generally like people found in a cross section of the population. The factors that make the deaf person unique are the time of onset of the deafness, the severity of the hearing loss, the mode of communication, and the quality of support and encouragement provided by the family.
- *Myth 2: "The deaf alcoholic drinks to escape his or her deafness."* Very often caregivers project their feelings and theorize that the deaf person is reacting to the deafness. They often overlook the fact that when the deaf person is drinking, he or she may feel much as a person without handicaps feels; i.e., closer to people, more expressive of feelings, more sexual, or

openly angry and hostile. For deaf people, deafness is a way of life and has become an integral part of their self-identity. The drinking comes much later (Haley, 1985).

❉ • *Myth 3: "All families of deaf alcoholics are alike."* In regard to the development of the family as a whole, there is the same amount of diversity found in the deaf culture as in the hearing culture. One will still encounter family rules, family roles, boundaries, family homeostasis, family values, and subsystems in families with deaf members (Haley, 1985). Of course, diversification among deaf families is found. The differences have to do with parental reaction to the deafness in the family as well as cultural, educational, and social backgrounds.

Debilitating aspects of child rearing occur in several forms, i.e., over-protecting, dominating, infantilizing, and scapegoating. In a family in which the deaf person is overprotected, the world is held at bay. The deaf person's most outrageous demands are met with little consideration to the development of a positive self-image in the deaf person or a sense of independence. Sometimes the overprotection, or "smothering mothering," is a mask or cover of the parent's real feelings of anger and hostility toward the child.

If the parent is dominating, the deaf child becomes dependent, passive, submissive, and withdrawn. If the parent is overly indulgent, the deaf child may be characterized by disobedience, temper tantrums, excessive demands, and generally tyrannical behaviors (Haley, 1985).

In the third type of family, the deaf member is infantilized. The deaf child has no chance to develop independence because he or she is kept in a "childlike" bond in which discipline and development are cast aside in the parent's need to keep the child "safe" and "childlike."

A fourth family type occurs when the family uses the deaf member as a scapegoat for family hostility. In this type of victimization and rejection, the deaf member's psychological scarring and sociological maladjustment are common results of this dysfunctional family system.

Scapegoating, infantilizing, and overprotecting often result in feelings of isolation and resentment on the part of the deaf person. This leads to a poor psychological adjustment, a low self-image, and the development of persistent denial and externalization tendencies (Haley, 1985).

❧ • *Myth 4: "The deaf adult alcoholic is not affected by her or his family."* Lawson, Peterson, and Lawson (1983) theorized, as have other researchers, that alcoholism is an outgrowth of dysfunction in the family structure. Because of this, the alcoholism needs to be treated within the context of the family structure (Haley, 1985). Deaf adults who come from a family that infantilized, overprotected, and scapegoated them will carry resentment and bitterness. In addition, they will find themselves unable to cope with daily living responsibilities, which embitters them even more because they feel that this training should have been provided within the family structure (Haley, 1985).

Treatment for the Deaf and the Hearing Impaired

Treatment for the deaf has been slow in coming. An article in the Alcoholics Anonymous (AA) newsletter *Grapevine* written by a recovering deaf alcoholic in 1968 raised the awareness for the need for services. However, it was not until the mid-1970s that the Hearing Society in the San Francisco Bay Area developed one of the first programs designed specifically for the hearing impaired person. The program provided interpreters to deaf substance abusers, aided the police in understanding the unique communication problems of the deaf substance abuser, and operated a 24-hour telephone service to facilitate communication between the staff of community agencies and deaf clients. Although this group is no longer in existence, it paved the way for similar groups to be established (Boros, 1980–81).

The Pathfinders' Service Center in San Diego, an outpatient, family oriented alcoholism treatment program, incorporates special outreach services for the deaf alcoholic. The program provides crisis telephone counseling via two portable TTY phones that are answered 24 hours a day. Additional services, including videotaped alcohol information presented in American Sign Language, are also provided by the agency (Boros, 1980–81, p. 26).

Watson et al. (cited in Boros, 1980–81) discussed eight basic requirements for adapting a treatment program that would be responsive to the needs of the deaf patient:

1. Develop an outreach program whose main goal is to develop the trust of the hearing people within the deaf community. Without trust, education of the deaf community is impossible. The next step is to obtain support of the program among deaf leaders.
2. An "influence leader who is a member of the hearing community, supportive, and communicative with the patient on the patient's level needs to be established. This person should be with the patient constantly to enhance effective communication with the communicatively impaired patient. The influence leader ensures that the patient understands all counseling sessions" (Watson et al., cited in Boros, 1980, p. 28).

3. Maintain therapy with a therapist who can communicate effectively with the patient at a level that is comfortable to the patient.
4. Establish a "counseling rapport." The counselor must have a thorough awareness of the other implications of deafness.
5. Integrate the deaf patient with hearing patients not only for socialization reasons but so that the deaf can realize that others have serious problems, too.
6. Place deaf patients in small groups in which they will discuss the aspects of lectures and diactic sessions to make sure that the material covered was understood.
7. Use visual aids to further understanding.
8. Develop an aftercare program in which interpreters are available.

Alcoholism Intervention for the Deaf (AID)

AID is an advocacy program funded by the nonprofit Cleveland Clinic Foundation. Its job is to deliver alcoholism services to deaf people in the area. This population consists of approximately 25,000 deaf people throughout Ohio (Boros, 1980).

The AID program offers

> interpreter services, inservice training on deafness, awareness to alcoholism program personnel, alcoholism education to both rehabilitation services personnel and deaf community groups, outreach to and confrontation with deaf problem drinkers, assistance to alcoholism counselors within the hospital treatment programs who need interpreters for deaf clients, followup visits to clients following discharge from treatment agencies, and ongoing evaluation of the effectiveness of AID advocacy services (Boros, 1980, p. 28).

The AID agency was founded in the hope of counteracting some of the barriers found in treatment of the deaf alcoholic patient such as denial and stigmatization, a lack of interpreters, an inability to comprehend reading material, difficulty in absorbing verbal lessons and lectures, and a lack of aftercare facilities for support. The agency's goals were to develop a program that would:

• establish a field office in an agency that was already working with deaf people

- employ staff that was fluent in sign language and knowledgeable about deafness
- provide ongoing alcoholism training for all staff
- implement procedures to locate untreated deaf alcoholic clients
- provide interpreters to agencies serving deaf clients
- provide educational services to agencies about deafness and to the deaf community about alcoholism
- provide information regarding barriers to successful treatment through a daily log
- appoint an advisory committee representing various agencies and groups of disabled consumers (Boros, 1980–81).

The first priority of AID was to help alcoholism agencies achieve these goals. Information regarding the treatment of deaf problem drinkers was supplied. Not only was information regarding alcoholism provided, but the psychological effect of deafness was presented as well as several weeks of basic sign language instruction to possible caregivers.

To dispel the deaf community's denial and unwillingness to work with alcoholism agencies, training sessions were provided. Programs on prevention and education were presented to deaf adolescents. In addition, AID's services were publicized. Soon, referrals were being made. Thus the AID staff became heavily involved in the treatment process in addiction to conducting prevention activities (Boros, 1980). Assessments of substance abusing clients for vocational rehabilitation agencies were provided. Some of the other developments were a network of half-way houses for aftercare treatment and a network of support people for AA, Al-Ateen, and Al-Anon meetings.

THE SPINAL CORD DISABLED

Are Drinking Patterns of the Spinal Cord Disabled the Same as Those of the General Population?

"Alcohol and drugs appear to be a major, but seldom discussed, factor in spinal cord injuries" (O'Donnell, Cooper, Gesner, Shehan, & Asheley, 1981, p. 27). A study conducted at the Montebello Center Spinal Cord Unit in Baltimore indicated that of 47 patients, 29, or 62% were identified as having alcohol or drug related injuries. However, a search of the literature of the past 10 years revealed "that no studies linking alcoholism or drug abuse to spinal cord injuries have been published" (O'Donnell et al., 1981–82, p. 27).

In 1973, spinal cord injury service wards were raided by "Federal marshals and the quantity of drugs and alcohol confiscated from the patients brought the problem to the attention of the Veterans Administration and other officials in Washington, D.C." (Anderson, 1980, p. 37). One of the results of this raid was the realization that drug abuse among the spinal cord disabled was a nationwide problem. This realization led to the development of the Drug Dependency Treatment Program, which was to serve as a model for other VA centers.

The problems associated with drug and alcohol abuse are not just a result of the disabling factors of the injury but were often factors in causing the injury. In addition, many disabled spinal cord patients led a life style fraught with great risk taking. These factors led to a continued use of alcohol and drugs after the injury. Very often prescription drugs are added to those previously used (O'Donnell et al., 1981).

Problems the Spinal Cord Disabled Encounter in Treatment

One of the major problems is that many programs are not physically accessible to the disabled due to the lack of wheelchair ramps. Another major problem is that there are countless psychological barriers to overcome in working with these clients, barriers most ambulatory programs are not equipped to handle. Many patient treatment centers are not equipped to provide the physical maintenance needs of these patients (Anderson, 1980).

The physical maintenance problems seriously affect many areas of an inpatient program: one is scheduling. The patient programs begin at 9 AM, a time considerably later than ambulatory programs. The reason for this is the time required for a quadriplegic patient to get out of bed and complete morning grooming chores. Generally, this takes from 2 to 4 hours. By the time the patient has been lifted from the bed, sometimes by a lift device; has accomplished bowel care; has showered and dressed, with the help of two attendants; a great deal of time has passed (O'Donnell et al., 1981).

The alcoholic spinal cord injury patient very often has physical problems exacerbating the spinal cord injury that are due to overuse of alcohol and drugs. For instance, many clients have decubitus ulcers, or bedsores, due to sitting in their wheelchairs for days while they were drunk. Poor nutrition also plays a role as the patient will neglect eating while she or he is using. In addition, a major complication occurs when bladder and kidney infections develop. This causes toxicity, further complicating health factors.

A fourth complication to substance abuse treatment is the fact that few of the clients have dealt with their injury, which may have been connected with or caused by substance abuse (Anderson, 1980):

> The battle wounded veteran often returns to the community after treatment somewhat intact, because prior to their injury they had their lives in pretty good order, and felt good about themselves. Others who became injured while under the influence of drugs and alcohol, were using alcohol and drugs before the injury to help themselves feel better about themselves, and this pattern has continued and possibly escalated after the injury (Anderson, 1980-81, p. 38).

Sometimes there is little motivation to leave a residential setting. Some clients may feel very comfortable in an institutional setting, and not wish to complete a successful treatment program. These clients are generally found in the VA programs in which clients may stay for an indefinite time. It is a clean, comfortable, no-risk environment. In addition, there is a "Catch-22" in that the

> paralyzed person is financially rewarded to remain institutionalized. A veteran with a service-connected injury who is a quadriplegic with loss of bowel and bladder function receives over $2000 per month tax free, so for many of these people there is little incentive to do anything but alcohol and drugs. Veterans with non-service-connected injury receive much less; $200 to $400 per month (Anderson, 1980, p. 38).
>
> If the quadraplegic obtains work, they may develop a urinary tract infection or a decubitus ulcer because they have been sitting too long. This may result in their being out of work for a long period to recuperate, but they may find it takes many months to process the necessary papers. Many find it easier to just remain on the benefit rolls (Anderson, 1980, p. 38).

In addition to the many physical problems of the spinal cord disabled, the psychological ones present special barriers. "Not unexpectedly the paralyzed person will try to use his disability to manipulate the treatment program, as an excuse to escape responsibility for his or her actions (Anderson, 1980, p. 38). In order to counteract this ploy, the treatment team needs to be very familiar with the subculture of the paralyzed person. An ambulatory addict goes into treatment to deal with his addiction. "The spinal cord injured have come into treatment to deal with their addiction plus a physical disability that may well have been a result of their drug or alcoholic abuse" (Anderson, 1980, p. 38).

Medical Problems Due to the Mixing of Alcohol and Prescription Drugs

Some problems result from the effect that alcohol and drugs have on the central nervous system. Since alcohol and marijuana are central nervous system depressants that interfere with motor activities, especially those that are learned, and the patient is depressed because of his or her injury, the likelihood that he or she will overcome the depression is very low. Because the patients are often "hung over," they do not participate in a motivated manner in the physical rehabilitation program (O'Donnell et al., 1981).

The use of alcohol and drugs interferes with prescribed medication, sometimes in dangerous ways. "The patient who drinks while taking warfarin compounds to prevent blood clot formation risks life-threatening internal bleeding because alcohol's interaction with blood-clotting substances may further decrease clotting activity" (O'Donnell et al., 1981, p. 28).

The sheer volume of urine produced by heavy beer drinking can ruin an intermittent catheterization program. "Men and women who have attained a level of reasonable control due to regaining bladder reflexes may blow this by drinking which causes large volumes of urine to stretch the bladder so that useful reflexes are lost and chances of getting off constant drainage are ruined" (O'Donnell et al., 1981, pg. 28). The distended bladder can trigger a reflex that causes blood vessels to constrict, resulting in excessive and in some cases life-threatening high blood pressure (O'Donnell et al., 1981).

Disulfiram (Antabuse) therapy must be either avoided or very carefully monitored because of the dangers of severe alcohol-disulfiram reactions in an already disabled individual. Suicide by this means could also be viewed as a "way out" by a depressed patient with a drinking problem (O'Donnell et al., 1981).

It is important to provide constant nursing surveillance to avoid adverse interactions with tranquilizers, sedatives, narcotics, and antibiotics, or anticoagulants in patients who may have been given a drug or alcoholic beverage by a well-meaning friend, relative, or staff member. Sometimes people perceive giving alcohol as a way to provide their loved ones with some "enjoyment" and "normalcy" (O'Donnell et al., 1981).

Psychological and Social Concerns

Many patients were very active before to their injury. They were risk-taking, daring individuals who often ignored possible consequences of their life style. This attitude often prevails after the accident. Very often they continue to run the "tightrope" between life and death by not heeding restrictions on drug and alcohol use while using prescribed drugs (O'Donnell et al., 1981).

The "devil may care" outlook that led them to activities of high risk and high mobility, often causing injury, makes rehabilitation difficult, as they are uninterested in intellectual pursuits and miss their thrill-seeking adventures. This causes greater depression, which leads to greater alcohol and drug consumption (O'Donnell et al., 1981).

> The continued use of alcohol impairs the patient's capacity to adapt to limitations and to plan for a return to the community. Energy, rather than being used to cope with reality, often is invested in maintaining defenses of fantasy, denial and projecting. For example, patients fantasize about walking or running again; they deny their own role in the accident or grimness of the prognosis; and they shift the responsibility for their feelings onto others. For example, they feel helpless, yet blame physicians who are unable to bring about recovery. The inadequacy of these defenses in warding off anxiety is often disguised by alcohol consumption (O'Donnell et al., 1981, p. 28).

Not only does the patient experience a need to adapt to both the physical and the psychological impact of the injury, but so does the family. Family members may be feeling guilt at not having taken better care of the injured person. They may be feeling anger and hostility toward the patient because the accident has impacted drastically on their lives, too. Both of these attitudes may lead to family members being in a position in which they will be supportive, or enabling, of the injured person's alcohol and drug consumption.

Hospital personnel also often fall into this trap. They too may have unresolved issues regarding people with handicaps: anger or guilt. These issues may lead caretakers to "overlook" the injured person's use of alcohol and drugs. At times personnel may participate in helping the patient obtain or consume drugs and alcohol (O'Donnell et al., 1981).

The study by O'Donnell et al. (1981) of 42 patients, 32 of whom used alcohol and drugs before the accident that caused their severe disability, indicated that all 32 of the patients continued to use and abuse alcohol after the study. The results clearly indicate that a majority of the patients had a common problem: alcohol and drug impairment (O'Donnell et al., 1981). The trauma of the injury to the patient and the family is difficult enough, but when the abuse of alcohol and drugs is added to the injury, it is devastating. Education and preventative measures can be developed. Alcohol and drug education of the caregivers of the spinal cord disabled is a must.

Treatment for the Spinal Cord Disabled

Locating the drug and alcohol treatment unit in the spinal cord injury rehabilitation center allows caregivers to accommodate the needs of the patient while ongoing physical and occupational therapy continues. Thus, in addition to the regular services provided for patients, they will receive drug and alcohol treatment. The treatment focuses on "community living and on encouraging patients to learn to assume responsibility for their behavior as well as educating them to the reasons they are relying on alcohol and drugs to cope" (Anderson, 1980, p. 39).

In such a setting, each day begins with a staff meeting in which shifts touch base on how the patient has been progressing over the past 24 hours. Once a week the staff meets with the client to discuss his or her progress and to get input from the client as to his or her particular concerns. Treatment planning is done together at this time. The staff also meets twice a month to make major decisions about where the program is going (Anderson, 1980).

A community meeting is held much like a town hall meeting, where staff and patients discuss aspects of the program and its progress. At this time plans of short- as well as long-term plans are made. Topics of discussion range from promotions of patients from one phase to another to demoting patients for not complying with the rules of the community. Upcoming events are discussed and planned. Most meetings are held with staff and patients getting equal time to discuss and vote. In this way the division between staff and patients is minimized.

The patients are encouraged to plan and implement as many events as possible in order to give them a sense of power and to eliminate the feelings of hopelessness and powerlessness. The goal is to develop total independence in patients (Anderson, 1980).

In addition to the varied activities and physical rehabilitation, all patients receive counseling to help with psychological problems. This is continued by the staff even after the patient has moved into the community. This is done on a crisis basis as well as support.

Assertiveness training is incorporated into the activities. Group therapy using a Gestalt therapy model is also offered. Occupational therapy is provided that develops skills such as communication, assertion, manual dexterity, and a sense of responsibility and accomplishment. Spirituality, from a universal perspective, is concerned about developing "good feeling" (Anderson, 1980).

The patients are required to keep a journal in which they write down their daily feelings and how they affected their thinking and behavior. At times these are shared with the group, and the group responds by helping the patient examine his or her coping mechanisms (Anderson, 1980–81).

Volunteers are a vital part of the program because they bring into the treatment community someone who can help establish contact with the community at large, i.e., the community outside the hospital. The volunteers offer many kinds of activities, from information on finance to general education on anthropology, history, and psychology.

The patients learn to establish networks in the community before discharge. This is done by encouraging the patient to attend Narcotics Anonymous and AA meetings in the community (Anderson, 1980–81).

PEOPLE WITH EPILEPSY

The rate of epilepsy of onset in early childhood is approximately 3.1 in 1,000. Another increase of incidence rates occurs after the age of 50, and it occurs primarily in men. Although there are no large-scale studies as to the number of people who develop epilepsy from the use of alcohol, the numbers from small regional studies are enough to cause some concern. At present there is no demonstrated safe level of alcohol use for persons with epilepsy (Little & Gale, 1980). In discussing epilepsy and alcoholism there are several factors involved: (a) those who develop childhood epilepsy from organic origins or falls, (b) those who develop epilepsy later in life from organic origins other than drinking, and (c) those who develop epilepsy from abuse of alcohol and/or drugs.

Those with epilepsy may seek relief in alcohol from psychological and social problems they face, exacerbating their condition and making those conditions they were worried about worse. Those who develop epilepsy from heavy alcohol abuse may bring on withdrawal or brain damage leading to epilepsy. At this time treatment opportunities for persons with both problems are very limited. In fact, there appear to be no programs designed specifically to help the individual suffering from both alcoholism and epilepsy (Little & Gale, 1980).

THE BLIND AND THE VISUALLY IMPAIRED

Problems the Blind and the Visually Impaired Encounter in Treatment

As with other disabilities, one of the basic problems in treatment is that the caregivers tend to focus on the dominant characteristic, i.e., the lack of visual acuity or the blindness. Because of this the clinician tends to overlook the long history of learning experiences and adaptive behaviors to life problems learned and experienced by the individual.

Glass (1980) discussed two types of visually impaired problem drinkers: the person who drank prior to the onset of the visual disability, type A, and the person who drank after the onset of the disability, type B. The type A individual is characterized by a history of life problems, anxiety, tension, depression, and stress, with which he or she has never been able to cope effectively. Type A's principal problem-solving technique is drinking. Because of the deficiency in problem-solving and coping skills, the onset of the disability serves only to intensify and magnify the inability to cope effectively.

The type B person's problem drinking began after the onset of the visual disability. Although type B's coping and problem-solving skills may be somewhat limited, the drinking had not become habitual prior to the disability. "Both type A and type B tend to share an absence of preparation for the stress experience that all will surely encounter during the process of adapting to the severe physical disability of blindness (Glass, 1980, p. 20). The disability of blindness impacts on "the individual in terms of emotional feeling states, interpersonal social interactions, cognitive functioning in terms of thought structure, and its verbal expression and physical function in terms of performance of skills necessary to daily activity" (Glass, 1980, p. 20). The individual experiences stress as he or she learns to adapt to the handicap. The feelings of powerlessness and frustration become full blown as one realizes that his or her independence has been drastically curtailed.

Patients develop psychological barriers due to images of what they are becoming or have become due to the visual disability: the worry that they will become a burden to others, the worry of becoming less than a whole person, the worry that they will be rejected by the opposite sex, the worry that they will not be able to live up to expectations of others and themselves, the worry over the inability to use power tools or participate in sports (Glass, 1980).

Very often the visually disabled begin to experience less and less activity, less stimulation, increased social isolation, and sometimes, depression. "If alcohol has been a part of their lifestyle, there is an increased likelihood of its becoming a more and more dominant part of their daily living" (Glass, 1980, p. 21).

Since the type B person's drinking was not habitual prior to the onset of blindness, alleviating the underlying problems of stress related to the disability and developing concrete supportive coping skills may serve to stop the alcohol abuse. Type A problem drinkers require specific treatment for alcohol abuse (Glass, 1980).

Treatment for the Blind and the Visually Impaired: The VA System

VA medical centers throughout the United States send referral applications to rehabilitation centers for the blind and visually impaired within the VA. These are sorted out into type A and type B categories.

> The type A individual is generally referred to a psychiatric clinic for treatment of the blind where the underlying life problems and problem drinking are the focus of therapy. The psychiatric clinic also emphasizes development of such skills as limited mobility, and personal management (Glass, 1980, p. 21).
>
> In this program emphasis is on learning, lifestyle change, and strategies of relaxation. Behavior change techniques include social skills training, assertiveness training, aversion therapy, and observation/concentration training. The type A problem drinker must resolve his life problems—including alcohol dependence— as a condition for transfer to the VA system's full scale blind or low-vision programs (Glass, 1980, p. 22).
>
> The type B person is usually admitted directly to the rehabilitation center as regular applications, under the condition that their drinking problem be managed either through total abstinence or though controlled drinking (Glass, 1980, p. 22).

The rehabilitation process for type B patients consists of developing survival skills to help them cope with the world as it is with a visual disability. The development of independence is generated by being responsible for the upkeep of oneself and one's lodgings. A program of physical conditioning is begun after 2 weeks of evaluation. This program takes into account nutrition and excessive weight. With this program, patients with visual handicaps are taught to integrate recreational activities into their life style. In addition, various forms of therapy are utilized. They range from group therapy to general assertiveness training, relaxation training, social skills training, and hypnosis.

The patient develops more independence by learning to travel safely and efficiently in a wide variety of urban and rural travel situations. In addition, the use of skill tools is developed, which allows the patient to regain much of the feeling of power, mobility, and communication skills. With the growing sense of accomplishment, the self-esteem returns.

THE DISABLED IN REHABILITATION CENTERS

Are the Drinking Patterns of the Disabled in Living Centers the Same as for the General Population?

"Persons with disabilities run a high risk of developing alcohol and drug abuse on several different levels" (Hepner et al., 1980, p. 11). The first aspect contributing to this problem is the availability of or easy access to drugs through prescriptions. Physicians are likely to prescribe medications because the need is often based on pain or severe spasms. In addition, many physicians share general societal attitudes toward disabled persons, including feelings of pity, guilt, and fear. The physicians often feel that it is the best they can do (Hepner et al., 1980).

Another reason the disabled run a high risk of developing drug abuse patterns is that the disabled often take the "path of least resistance" to assuage feelings of frustration and anxiety about being disabled and being thrust into an often unproductive and dependent role (Hepner et al., 1980).

A third reason is that the disabled are an oppressed minority in our society. The promise of relief, highs, and numbness that alcohol and drugs provides eases the oppressed feeling and provides an immediate and attractive alternative (Hepner et al., 1980).

A fourth reason stems from the result of medical intervention and the rehabilitation process. "Statistics revealed that 41 percent of disabled clients at the Center for Independent Living had drugs prescribed for them that they felt were unnecessary. Often these drugs are taken in combination with alcohol" (Hepner et al., 1980, p. 12). This is different than the first reason, in that in this instance the drugs were not requested by the patient but were administered at the doctor's direction. The Center for Independent Living in Berkeley reported that "25 percent of their clients were abusing alcohol and other drugs that cause social, mental or physical dysfunction" (Hepner et al., 1980, p. 12).

Problems the Disabled in Rehabilitation Centers Encounter in Treatment

One of the problems encountered is that centers are not available to treat disabled persons who are substance abusers. As mentioned earlier, access to treatment centers if often difficult, and personnel generally are not trained to treat people with disabilities. In addition, the disabled are excluded from "professional substance abuse agencies by a wide variety of physical, cultural, attitudinal and communications barriers" (Hepner et al., 1980-81, p. 13).

A study conducted at the State Technical Institute and Rehabilitation Center in Michigan of 273 adults with handicaps with a mean age of 26.3 years who were enrolled as trainees in trade and technical departments indicated that alcohol was widely used. "The patterns of social use of alcohol indicates that a high percentage (36.95 percent) of respondents were sometimes or predominately solitary drinkers" (Rasmussen & DeBoer, 1980, p. 49). "The data indicate the more frequently clients drink, the more frequently they drink alone" (Rasmussen & DeBoer, 1980, p. 50). In addition, the "data indicates that 36.9 percent of the clients receive medicines from a physician, but do not specify whether prescription medications were for chronic or temporary conditions" (Rasmussen & DeBoer, 1980, p. 51). There was also a positive correlation between drinking and family alcohol problems, feelings of boredom, and feelings of unhappiness and general dissatisfaction with life, as well as a positive correlation between alcohol use and the use of nonprescription medicines, tobacco, caffeine, marijuana, and cocaine.

Treatment for the Disabled in Rehabilitation Centers

The Center for Independent Living in Berkeley, California, which has served more than 6,500 people over a period of 7 years in a wide range of services, found that "the emphasis on peer support interaction is effective in overcoming initial hesitancies of potential clients in approaching human service agencies" (Hepner et al., 1980, p. 13). The counselors in the program need to be sensitively trained in the treatment of the disabled. In the center, a network of independent living programs is essential for the disabled substance abuser.

The first phase of recovery is spent exploring new ways of being in social situations. "Because of the general isolation and discrimination experienced by disabled people, several negative characteristics are prevalent; low self-esteem, self-hatred, and low motivation, all reinforced by an overall lack of successful experiences" (Hepner et al., 1980, p. 15). These issues need to be the focus of attention during treatment. In addition, the disabled have often had to endure long periods of isolation during childhood from others their age due to institutionalization or recuperation. For those who became disabled later in life, as a result of injury or illness, "they have had to spend long recuperative periods in medical and rehabilitation institutions where they were often subjected to impersonal and alienating treatment as 'objects.' In both instances the disabled have incorporated into their self-image society's general perception of the disabled as being 'less-than-whole'" (Hepner et al., 1980, p. 13).

Since alcohol and drugs "were 'easy' ways to avoid the difficult and painful work necessary to develop appropriate social skills and overcome social isolation" (Hepner et al., 1980, p. 13), as the disabled become less isolated and more independent they may develop a co-dependent. The co-dependent is someone who "needs to be needed." This person is available to the disabled person for support during crisis periods. Because the co-dependent, or co-addict, "needs to be needed," he or she may impede the progress of the disabled person. Conversely, disabled persons, as they grow less isolated and more independent, may become co-addicts themselves due to the fear of being unable to make satisfying relationships. "Co-addicts attempt to be responsible for the substance abuser's life at the expense of their own. An important part of recovery, then, is learning to discriminate between selfishness and genuine self-interest" (Hepner et al., 1980, p. 14).

Education concerning the mixture of prescription drugs with alcohol and nonprescription drugs is an important part of the first phase of treatment. For instance, a patient taking medications for control of epilepsy may not be aware of the effect when these drugs are mixed with alcohol, nonprescription drugs, or pain-killing drugs. The Center for Independent Living found Valium to be the "most frequently prescribed drug among the disabled community" (Hepner et al., 1980, p. 14). Although it takes 3 months of taking 80 to 120 mg of Valium daily to become physically addicted, an emotional addiction can occur immediately (Hepner et al., 1980).

One of the clients at the Center for Independent Living had become disabled at age 14. Six years of taking Valium followed. She also started drinking heavily during this time. She entered therapy complaining of severe depression, lethargy, and suicide attempts. A month after attaining sobriety, her symptoms lessened greatly. She attended support groups, as all patients do as a part of their treatment, in addition to therapy. She was eventually able to talk about her feelings for the first time since her accident.

The second phase of treatment focuses on learning new ways of dealing with feelings such as loss, anger, and sexuality. During the rehabilitation process the client is encouraged to develop independent living skills and means of dealing with anxiety, expectations, and low self-esteem. Training in independent living skills, as well as peer counseling, medical counseling, and counseling about sexuality and the disability, is a part of the rehabilitation process.

THE DEVELOPMENTALLY DISABLED

Are the Drinking Patterns of the Developmentally Disabled the Same as for the General Public?

Although there are no statistics regarding whether or not the developmentally disabled use alcohol and drugs to a greater extent than does the general population, there is considerable evidence that they use it for about the same reasons. Those reasons are to "feel like everyone else" to "hang out at bars where people are friendly" "to overcome loneliness" and "to be liked" (Wenc, 1980). "As more states deinstitutionalize residence in public psychiatric hospitals and more developmentally disabled persons attempt to integrate into the community, it is expected that the incidence of problems with alcohol and other drugs among this special population will increase" (Wenc, 1980, p. 43).

A developmentally disabled person is someone with an IQ between 60 and 85. The disability is severe, chronic, and attributable to a mental or physical impairment or to a combination of mental or physical impairments. Developmental disability is manifested before the person attains the age of 22. It is a disability that is likely to continue for the rest of the person's life. The developmentally disabled have substantial limitations in three or more areas of major life activity, such as self-care, receptive and expressive language, learning mobility, self-direction, capacity for independent living, and economic self-sufficiency. Being developmentally disabled does not mean that the person cannot learn, it means that the person will need more time to learn and that learning will need to take place in concrete terms, as abstract learning is extremely difficult. The developmentally disabled are readily manipulated and have difficulty learning from previous experiences (Wenc, 1980).

This disability will not be "arrested" or cured. Learning focuses on developing or modifying behavior. "Many developmentally disabled persons have marginal adaptive skills. Their work history is sporadic. They may be on general relief or receiving Supplemental Security Income. Their physical health varies based on their degree of permanent physical disability" (Wenc, 1980, p. 43). The developmentally disabled who live outside institutions generally live in urban areas. There they tend to blend into the general population. However, in rural areas they are highly visible and generally known by a nickname to the police and social service agencies (Wenc, 1980).

Treatment for the Developmentally Disabled

The developmentally disabled generally participate in drinking because it allows them to socialize in situations that would not otherwise be available to them. Caretakers need to keep in mind that a developmentally disabled person's capacity to take in and understand information and then act on it is very limited. When the detoxification facility becomes aware of a developmentally disabled person, it needs to have a specific person who acts as a liaison to the developmentally disabled community who will act as an advocate for the developmentally disabled person. "There is a necessity for a team consisting of law enforcement, alcohol treatment, developmental disability advocacy, and the medical personnel to develop a realistic, comprehensive treatment plan for the alcohol impaired person" (Wenc, 1980, p. 45). If the client is able, he or she should be allowed to participate in and contribute to the treatment plan. The advocate for the developmentally disabled person should act as the coordinator of this team.

Often a referral to AA meetings is made. However, the "individual may lack the verbal and motivational skills needed to voluntarily attend a self-help meeting. It is better if the disabled person attends the meeting with a volunteer, and the two attend the self-help meetings, and not the testimonial. This provides an alternative to the social scene of the bars" (Wenc, 1980, p. 45). There is a particular need for AA groups for those who are disabled.

Emotions Anonymous is a group that borrows heavily from AA but is primarily for the developmentally disabled. The AA format is followed, and educational and relaxation techniques are incorporated into this format. James Voytilla founded this group with the goal of providing a range of services, within a group setting, for the mentally retarded substance abuser. It is a long-term group that is sensitive to the "pervasive social isolation and high anxiety levels among this population" (Small, 1980, p. 46).

"Emotions Anonymous uses the Twelve Steps of AA but substitutes the word 'emotions' for 'alcohol.' The emphasis on group problem solving techniques is maintained and group members are taught to listen closely to the stories of others. Basically, we try to boil down the Twelve Steps into practical, do-it-yourself exercises that people can do during the week" (Small, 1980, p. 46).

Every week members set goals and report on how they did the following week. When they succeed, the group gives them a lot of social reinforcement. The social reinforcement is probably the most important part of the group process (Small, 1980). The goal of the group process is to teach the participants to relax and reduce their anxiety. To do this they are educated in the effects of alcohol abuse and what it means to be alcoholic. Relaxation techniques, group exercises, and movement with music are aspects of the relaxation development. "Voytilla says, 'They hold a lot of tension in. We believe that by helping them learn to control this tension and anxiety, we can help them control their drinking problems' " (Small, 1980, p. 46).

THE MENTALLY ILL

Are Drinking Patterns of the Mentally Ill the Same as for the General Population?

The Director of the Apollo day care program in St. Paul, Minnesota, reported that "there is a substantial number of chronically mentally ill people who have problems with mood-altering chemicals, especially alcohol" (Hindman, 1980a, p. 47). Some of the clients at the day care center have serious drinking problems. Often the mentally ill experience many more problems while drinking as they are unable to think clearly, hallucinate, and have delusions. Very often the alcohol problem is not diagnosed by professionals because of the propensity of the mental illness. However, the director of the day care center noted that when abstinence occurred the staff noticed a marked change in the clients, and many of the "signs of mental illness disappeared" (Hindman, 1980a, p. 47).

Problems the Mentally Ill Encounter in Treatment

"One of the major stumbling blocks to sobriety among mentally ill alcoholics is widespread reluctance of professionals to recognize the need to treat alcohol problems" (Hindman, 1980a, p. 47). John Honebrink, the director of the day center, believes that

the care homes of the mentally ill need to value sobriety. The professionals need to recognize chemical dependency as a problem for the chronically mentally ill. Very often the focus is on the mental illness, while omitting treatment of the alcoholism, feeling that once the mental illness is cured, so the alcoholism will be. Yet, the drinking has to stop in order for the exacerbation of the mental illness to stop (Hindman, 1980a, p. 47).

CONCLUSION

Statistics indicate that there is a large number of people with disabilities who are substance abusers. NIAA estimates that the rate of alcohol problems among the disabled is at least that of the general population. The Commission on California State Government Organization and Economy stated that a conservative estimate of disabled Californians who are chemically dependent is around 500,000. The California commission also reported that the main issue is integrating the disabled community into existing substance abuse treatment facilities, as the issue of "isolation" due to their disability is also an aspect of their alcohol abuse. Integration also helps them to relaize that everyone has problems.

It is important for caregivers to see the total person and not just the handicap. Although people with handicaps need special treatment within a program, they also need to be integrated into the mainstream, or general population, during the treatment program.

The deaf have difficulty in treatment programs because they do not want the stigma of "deaf and drunk" to be coupled with "deaf and dumb." In addition, the deaf need special interpreters and a knowledge and trust of community resources. The communication problems of the deaf lend themselves to problems in educational development. The subtle and inferred aspects of communication are never learned by the deaf, as abstract and inferred terms are difficult to sign.

The spinal cord disabled often have difficulties in getting treatment in the mainstream because the facilities are not wheelchair accessible. Often, treatment programs begin before the person is able to function, as getting ready for the day takes a long time. In addition, some of these patients have led lives of risk taking prior to their disability. Some of this risk taking may have included drug use coupled with a life style of bravado physical acts. Very often prescription drugs are added to the drugs used before the injury. Those patients whose lives were intact prior to the injury have less difficulty in making a transition than those whose lives were "helter skelter" prior to the injury. At times the "paralyzed person may use his disability to manipulate the treatment program, as an excuse to escape responsibility for his or her actions" (Anderson 1980-81, p. 38). Sometimes hospital staff and family members exacerbate treatment by believing that the use of alcohol is a way to provide their loved ones with some enjoyment.

The purpose of this chapter was to give an overview of handicapping conditions. All people with handicaps who abuse drugs and alcohol need to develop coping skills, assertiveness, and self-esteem as well as establish a supportive network in the community at large. Behavior and life style change techniques need to be developed as well as strategies for relaxation.

REFERENCES

Anderson, P. (1980–81). Alcoholism and the spinal cord disabled: A model program. *Alcohol Health and Research World, 5*(2), 37–41.

B.J. (1968). AA and the deaf mute. *The Grapevine* (December), 32–33.

Bormann, C.G., Howell, W.S., Nichols, R.G., & Shapiro, G.L. (1969). *Interpersonal communication in the modern organization*. Englewood Cliffs, N.J.: Prentice Hall.

Boros, A. (1980–81). Alcoholism intervention for the deaf. *Alcohol Health and Research World, 5*(2), 26–30.

Clelawn. (1981). Perspectives: An AH&RW interview feature. *Alcohol Health and Research World 5*(2), 57–63.

Dean, J., Fox, A., & Wesley, J. (1985). Drug and alcohol use by disabled and nondisabled persons: A comparative study. *International Journal of the Addictions, 20*(4), 629–641.

Glass, E.J. (1980–81). Problem drinking among the blind and visually impaired. *Alcohol Health and Research World, 5*(2), 20–25.

Haley, T. (1988). The deaf alcoholic: Six misconceptions. Paper written for the University of Nebraska-Lincoln.

Hepner, R., Kirshbaum, H., & Landes, D. (1980–81). Counseling substance abusers with additional disabilities: The Center for Independent Living. *Alcohol Health and Research World, 5*(2), 11–19.

Hindman, M. (1980–81a). Group treatment of the mentally ill substance abusers. *Alcohol Health and Research World, 5*(2), 47.

Hindman, M. (1980–81b). NIAA announces initiative on multidisabled persons. *Alcohol Health and Research World, 5* (2), 2–10.

Isaacs, M., Buckley, G., & Martin, D. (1979). Patterns of drinking among the deaf. *American Journal of Drug and Alcohol Abuse, 6,* 463–476.

Kannapell, B. (1981). Perspectives: An AH&RW interview feature. *Alcohol Health and Research World 5*(2), 57–63.

Little, R.E., & Gayle, J. (1980–81). Epilepsy and alcoholism. *Alcohol Health and Research World, 5*(2), 31–36).

Murray, J., *L.A. Times,* Sunday, Sept. 27, 1987, p. 1.

Newsnotes: The multidisabled. (1980–81). *Alcohol Health and Research World, 5*(2), 64–67.

O'Donnell, J.J., Cooper, J.E., Gesner, J.E., Shehan, I., & Asheley, J. (1981–82). Alcohol, drugs and spinal cord injury. *Alcohol Health and Research World, 6*(2), 27–29.

Perspectives: An AH & RW interview feature. (1980–81). *Alcohol Health and Research World, 5*(2), 57–63.

Rasmussen, G.A., & DeBoer, R. (1981–82). Alcohol and drug use among clients at a residential vocation rehabilitation facility. *Alcohol Health and Research World, 5*(2), 40–56.

Scanlon (1981). Perspective: An AH & RW interview feature. *Alcohol Health and Research World* 5(2), 57–63.

The Seed. (1987). Summer, pp. 4–5.

Small, J. (1981). Emotions anonymous: Counseling the mentally retarded substance abuser. *Alcohol Health and Research World* 5 (2), 46.

Watson, E.W., Boros, G., & Zrimea. (1980). Mobilization of services of deaf alcoholics. *Alcohol Health and Research World* 4(2), 33–38.

Wenc, F. (1980–81). The developmentally disabled substance abuser. *Alcohol Health and Research World,* 5,(2), 42–46.

Chapter 5

Substance Abuse Problems of the Elderly: Considerations for Treatment and Prevention

Ann W. Lawson

INTRODUCTION

The geriatric population is often overlooked and sometimes hidden in American society. Yet it is a rapidly growing population with increasing needs. Of the estimated 250 million people in the United States, 20 million are older than 65. It is predicted that 35 million people will be in this age bracket by 1990. Offer (1974) predicted that by the year 2000, one half of the population will be older than 50 and one third will be older than 65. Brotman (1980) reported that life expectancy for men is 70 and for women is 77. With advances in technology and medical care, these estimates may rise even higher, and the life expectancy could increase. Even though the elderly population is increasing, their problems continue to be overlooked or misdiagnosed.

Although it may seem that the elderly have more physical problems than other populations, they are rarely thought of as drug abusers. Yet the elderly are at high risk for misuse and at considerable risk for abuse of legal drugs, and there is a small group of elderly opiate addicts (Glantz, 1983). These misuses and abuses include alcohol, prescription drugs, and over-the-counter drugs. These problems are often complicated by mental disorders or are confused with the symptoms of aging. Furthermore, the elderly use 3 times as many prescription drugs as all other groups combined (Hanan, 1978). This puts them at risk for drug interactions that often go undiagnosed because of the similarity between drug interaction symptoms and the symptoms of old age (forgetfulness, weakness, confusion, tremor, anorexia, and anxiety).

PHYSICAL, SOCIAL, AND PSYCHOLOGICAL RISKS FOR SUBSTANCE ABUSE

The aging process creates new physical, social, and psychological stresses that increase the risk level of drug abuse and misuse for the elderly. Physical aging processes promote a dependence on drug use for symptom reduction that can lead to overmedication and drug misuse. The physical changes of aging alter the way in which a drug is absorbed and distributed through the body, metabolized, and then excreted. The elderly experience decreased tolerance for drugs, and drugs stay in the body longer and have prolonged biological activity. They have more clinical and toxic effects, and they tend to accumulate in fatty tissues (Shader, 1975). Additionally, the elderly have increased physical illnesses and complaints, some from the physical aging process and some from psychosomatic origins. They have more contact with physicians who prescribe medications, and they may be less concerned with the prevention of illness and more concerned with medication of symptoms. They are often victims of self-neglect, falls, and aggressive and violent behavior, sometimes at the hands of their relatives.

Loss also plays a part in physical risk; the loss of body functions and attractiveness is a problem for some of the elderly. They may lose teeth and hair, develop dry skin, and lose muscle tone. The senses are also affected. Vision and hearing losses can lead to reduced communication or misunderstandings that create paranoid ideas. Ultimately, these physical limitations may reduce the availability of hobbies and sports that provided identity and self-worth.

Psychologically, the elderly face a number of late-life stresses including bereavement from the loss of family and friends, loss of occupation because of retirement, loneliness, boredom, and impaired health and physical abilities. Many of these losses occur within short periods of time. Stresses mount one upon the other, and the elderly can find themselves constantly dealing with loss. Kinney and Leaton (1987) reported that the elderly can react to these losses in several ways. They commonly use denial to avoid facing the reality of the losses. They may pretend that the problems do not exist or are just temporary. The emotional pain may be expressed by somatization, or complaining of physical pain that is an outward expression of hurt from the loss. This may be seen as socially more acceptable, and it may be reinforced with attention from medical personnel, whereas emotional problems may be ignored. If the elderly respond to the losses by restricting their emotional responses, they may begin to withdraw from their environment in an attempt to shut out further "bad news." Unfortunately, this creates more of a problem with depression and lack of support systems.

Depression is prevalent among older people. It may be environmentally or physically caused or a manifestation of a physical problem. Suicide is also a problem in the elderly population. "Twenty-five percent of those who commit suicide are over age 65. The rate of suicide for those over 65 is five times that of the general population. After age 75, the rate is eight times higher" (Kinney & Leaton, 1987, p. 306).

Sociologically, loss plays a part in increasing the risk of substance abuse for the elderly. With aging come the illnesses and deaths of family and friends. Isolation becomes more of a problem to those left surviving. These deaths also bring about thoughts of one's own death, which can cause considerable anxiety. Geographical separations are also a part of the family life span. Children leave home for school and marriage and often move far away. The grandchildren that should provide comfort and stimulation to the elderly may visit only once or twice a year.

Retirement changes the social environment of the elderly in many ways. The loss of income affects the elderly by decreasing purchasing power, fixing income, and often reducing comfort and luxury. Along with the financial losses are the losses of status, identity, and sometimes self-worth. Even the gain of spending more time with spouses can become a problem: adjusting to the change of routines and making allowances for the other person's needs.

The sex life of the elderly is often affected, not physically but sociologically. If the elderly are physically healthy, they are usually interested in sexual activity and are physically capable. The biggest problems lie in the availability of a partner and society's belief that the elderly should not be sexually active. Rarely are the elderly encouraged to date, and sexual activity may be discouraged even in married couples.

Considering the difficulties of aging, it becomes more understandable how they could be at risk for drug abuse. If self-esteem is reduced by the losses and changes of aging, the elderly are at risk for drug and alcohol abuse that attempts to relieve this pain. This risk can be further increased by the need for medications and the frequent contacts with the medical profession.

It is interesting to compare this aging population with adolescents, an age group that is more easily recognizable as drug abusing. The similarities include uncertain and changing roles and self-concepts, lower social status, disadvantages in employment and income, shifting and uncertain social supports, and limited resources for coping. Both groups also find drugs readily available. One difference is that adolescents use illicit drugs more often, whereas the elderly use licit drugs (Mandolini, 1981). This difference is understandable for people who grew up in the Prohibition era, which colored their views of alcohol consumption and the use of illegal substances.

This same group spent a lifetime learning to trust physicians and to use medications when they were sick. Often their physician is an important social contact who gives them drugs to relieve symptoms and stresses.

Drugs most often prescribed for elderly patients are cardiovascular medication (22%), tranquilizers (10%), diuretics (9%), and sedative-hypnotics (9%) (Mandolini, 1981). These drugs are prescribed for heart disease, hypertension, arthritis and rheumatism, and mental and nervous conditions. It is common for the elderly to combine their prescription drugs with over-the-counter drugs, increasing the potential for harmful interactions.

In addition to prescription drug misuse, the elderly have alcohol problems, psychiatric disorders, and reduced resources. These difficulties are hard to diagnose, and they overlap. The elderly may not seek psychological care or drug and alcohol rehabilitation, and they may have lost many of the social contacts who could intervene and get help for them: the threat of job loss is no longer there, and they may be living alone with little contact with family and friends. To complicate the picture further, the elderly may be experiencing new physical limitations. Busse (1983) pointed out that two in five men aged 65 and over have restricted activity, and one in four is unable to carry on some major activity. Those over 75 years of age are even more limited.

This chapter focuses specifically on drug misuse and abuse, alcohol problems, and the best methods of helping the geriatric client. There is limited literature on the problems of the elderly and the kinds of therapy most beneficial to them. As Glantz (1983) noted, "Research in this area is really just beginning and the relevant literature is limited, often inconclusive and sometimes contradictory" (p. 1). It is, however, important for therapists to be aware of potential problems and the symptoms of these problems in their elderly clients.

ABUSE AND MISUSE OF LEGAL DRUGS

Because of their physical problems and reliance on the medical profession, the elderly are at risk for overmedication by their physician, drug interactions, erratic drug use, and misuse of over-the-counter drugs (Whittington, 1983b). Their unique life situations and the presence of chronic illnesses contribute to the misuse. The aging who are most at risk are alcoholics, the chronically painfully ill, and those who are troubled with chronic anxiety states, somatization disorders, and insomnia (Kofoed, 1985).

How common is substance abuse in late life? Use of illegal drugs such as marijuana, LSD, and opiates is usually found only in aging criminals.

Older opiate users often switch to more readily available drugs such as hydromorphone (Dilaudid) and reduce their intake, or they use barbiturates or alcohol as substitutes on occasion. The abuse of cocaine and amphetamines is rare mainly because of the decreased effect of these drugs with aging and changing neurochemistry (Kofoed, 1985). Although this is a small problem with the elderly now, as the younger population currently abusing illicit drugs grows older, it will probably increase.

More frequently, the elderly abuse prescription drugs. They comprise 10% of the population, yet they use 25% of all prescribed drugs (Basen, 1977). Prescription drugs are more available than illicit drugs to the elderly and are often prescribed for pain or insomnia. Sedatives and narcotics are the most common drugs of abuse, followed by narcotic analgesics (Kofoed, 1985). Women, twice as often as men, abuse analgesics (including opioids), antianxiety agents, and sedative hypotics (Atkinson, 1984). Twenty-five percent of the drugs prescribed for the elderly are psychoactive. Stephens, Haney, and Underwood (1982) found that 18% of the elderly receive psychoactive drugs. However, two thirds were taking them as prescribed; those who were not were underusing them. The major problem with prescription use among the elderly is omission (Schwartz, Wang, Zweitz, & Gross, 1962). This can be as much of a problem as overmedication. Medications taken properly can improve the quality of life for the elderly and may be needed to allow independent living.

It is important to distinguish between drug abuse and misuse with the elderly: this distinction helps to locate the area in which intervention is needed. There are two major differences between abuse and misuse. First, abuse is intended, or the inappropriateness of use is known, whereas misuse is inadvertent. Second, abuse has psychoactive or psychosocial consequences and may involve licit or illicit drugs, including alcohol (Glantz, 1983), whereas misuse does not.

To elucidate further, drug abuse is the nontherapeutic use of drugs, including alcohol, that adversely impacts the user's life. The drug may be obtained from legal or illegal sources and used occasionally or habitually. As Glantz (1983) outlined, abuse entails some or all of the following:

- using an illegal drug
- using an illegally obtained drug (i.e., by falsified prescription)
- using multiple prescriptions of the same or similar drug
- using a drug prescribed for another person
- hoarding drugs and taking them all at one time
- knowingly using a drug for purposes other than those for which it was prescribed

- violating prescription directions, deviating in quantity or frequency, or consuming with other contraindicated drugs
- using alcohol excessively
- consuming caffeinated beverages excessively
- smoking more than is considered safe
- taking more of an over-the-counter drug than recommended by directions
- combining over-the-counter drugs with alcohol or a prescribed drug (or both).

Drug misuse is the inappropriate use of drugs that were meant to be used therapeutically. Glantz (1983) described misuse as the inappropriate prescription of drugs due to:

- the physician's lack of knowledge
- errors in the physician's judgment
- lack of supervision of a physician or not following instructions
- excessive use of over-the-counter drugs.

Misuse of drugs usually takes four forms: overuse, underuse, erratic use, and contraindicated use (Peterson, Whittington, & Beer, 1979). The most common misuse of drugs among the elderly is underuse. This occurs most frequently when prescribed drugs are expensive, are used mainly to control symptoms, and are likely to produce side effects (Hemminki & Heikkela, 1975). Most often, misuse of drugs among the elderly is due to errors by the physician and in the prescription process. According to Whittington (1983a), problems include:

- selecting an inappropriate medication
- prescribing too high or too low a dosage
- prescribing too many different drugs at a time
- failing to check the potential for side effects or interaction
- failing to check the patient's drug history, including over- the-counter drugs, current prescriptions, and alcohol intake
- prescribing over the telephone
- providing inadequate oral or written instructions for taking the medications or inadequate information about possible reactions
- allowing too many automatic renewals.

Physicians may hold stereotypes of the elderly. They may feel that aging is synonymous with disease and that there is little that can be done to help the elderly. This may cause physicians to rely on medical (drug) solutions to nonmedical problems. This process is further complicated by the following problems of the elderly (Whittington, 1983a):

- They may have several simultaneous problems and medications.
- They experience a slower rate of drug absorption, distribution, metabolism, and excretion.
- They are at greater risk for side effects.
- They often have cognitive deficits and may view their physician as a powerful authority whom they will not question.

Given this dilemma, it is difficult to know where to intervene. Do physicians need to be educated about the unique pharmacological and psychological needs of the elderly, or do the elderly need to be self-advocates? The answer, probably, is both, but therapists who work with elderly patients can also be teachers and advocates once they understand the risks that are inherent when a such a patient seeks medical help.

Several investigators have studied the misuse of prescription drugs among the elderly to determine the reasons for the problem. Doyle and Hamm (1976) studied 405 people in Florida who were 60 years of age or over. When questioned about the process of receiving prescription drugs, 72% said they did not usually inform physicians if they were using drugs; only 13% saw the physician in person, and the rest received the prescription over the telephone. Furthermore, 75% did not question the pharmacist about the drug's action, possible side effects, or its cost. The Michigan Office of Services to the Aging and Michigan Office of Substance Abuse Services (1979) surveyed 371 persons aged 60 or older to discover why they stopped taking or varied their prescription drugs. The responses indicated that 43% felt better when they stopped or varied their prescription drugs, 18% reported side effects as the reason, and 10% forgot to take the medication. Stephens, Haney, and Underwood (1981) found that their subjects stopped their medication or varied it for several reasons: 48% "did not like it" (or possibly did not like the physician), 23% used medication only when they needed it, 6.8% said that they got better results their way, 4.1% experienced bad side effects, 9.4% felt the drug was too expensive, and 2.7% forgot. Although it is reported that the elderly hold physicians in high esteem, they often appear to make medical decisions themselves that are often against the physician's advice.

Another area of prescription drug misuse is institutions. Often there is overuse of psychoactive medication, particularly sedatives and tranquilizers, because of the staff's desire to control agitated, unruly, or demanding patients (Gubrium, 1975; Learoyd, 1972). Misuse can include errors in the administration of drugs in nursing homes (too much, too late, or with the wrong liquid); this is due to a lack of staff training, poor controls, overloaded staff, and the use of unlicensed nursing aides to distribute medications (Gubrium, 1975).

The main reason that abuse and misuse of prescription drugs by the elderly and those attending them are dangerous is their unique biological changes that cause the elderly to react differently than younger adults. With aging comes a decline of protein and an increase in fat. Moreover, the metabolic rate declines 16% between 30 and 70 years of age, and caloric requirements decrease by one third. The loss of brain cells may also make the elderly more sensitive to drugs, and enzymes and neurotransmitters are altered. The activity of monoamine oxidase increases, and dopamine, norepinephrine, serotonin, tyrosine hydroxylase, and cholinesterase activities decline. Furthermore, absorption of drugs is slow and erratic because of the low acid level in the stomach. Fat-soluble drugs (phenobarbital, diazepam, and chlorpromazine) tend to be stored for longer periods in the elderly. For these reasons there is a decrease in the intensity of the drug but a prolonged duration, which ultimately produces a toxic effect. Circulatory changes also alter drug absorption; drugs may accumulate in the brain and heart because these organs are the first to be supplied in the presence of a decreased cardiac output. The liver's capacity to metabolize drugs decreases with aging; this may be due to a reduced protein intake, which reduces available metabolizing enzymes, and may cause prolonged effects of some drugs. Other drugs that need to be metabolized for full effect are reduced in their effectiveness (Hanan, 1978). The kidneys also lose their functioning: there is a 30% glomerular filtration rate in individuals older than 65 so that drugs are excreted less efficiently.

Because of the potential for misuse of prescription drugs by the elderly, the therapist working with this population should be alert to signs of psychological reactions and behavior changes that could be due to toxicity or drug interaction. Antipsychotic drugs may cause oversedation, restlessness, withdrawal, and depression. Antidepressants may elicit confused states and exacerbate schizophrenic and manic symptoms. Antianxiety drugs may lead to oversedation and occasionally disinhibition or uncontrolled rages. Antimanic drugs such as lithium can cause confused states that can mimic organic brain syndrome if the drug level becomes toxic. This distinction is particularly crucial.

ABUSE AND MISUSE OF OVER-THE-COUNTER DRUGS

One of the most dangerous practices among the elderly is self-diagnosing and self-medicating with over-the-counter drugs. Kofoed (1984) reported that 69% of people 60 years of age and older use such drugs, and 40% use them daily. This is due partly to economics and possibly to bad experiences with health professionals. Over-the-counter medications can cause the elderly many problems, so it is important to screen for them routinely when working with these clients.

In large doses, analgesics such as aspirin and acetaminophen can cause acute metabolic disturbances and organic mental disorders. Aspirin can cause stomach bleeding. Acetomenophen elevates serum alkaline phosphatase levels, and overdoses can cause liver damage (Stewart, Hale, & Marks, 1982). Laxatives are used by 10% of the elderly and can cause diarrhea and malabsorption syndromes. Antihistamines and anticholinergics, which include cold and allergy medications and sleeping aids, interact with alcohol and other drugs to enhance sedative effects. It is possible to develop toxic psychosis or delirium from anticholinergics. Antihistamines may be used by the elderly as sedatives and can produce acute toxic delirium resembling atropine psychosis (Shader, 1975). Sympathomimetics or decongestants can have a stimulant effect and produce psychoses similar to those induced by amphetamines, although this is rare in older persons. Alcohol-containing drugs, such as night cold medicines, are often used for the alcohol effect, but some elderly consider them medicine and deny that they have alcohol related problems. Antacids and bromides have been known to cause psychiatric symptoms; bromide toxicity can resemble schizophrenia.

Although caffeine and nicotine may not seem dangerous because they are in common daily use, they can be problematic for the elderly. Caffeine overuse can contribute to anxiety and panic disorders, cardiac dysrhythmias, gastric disease, and osteoporosis. Caffeine is often found in over-the-counter medications as well as in beverages. Nicotine contributes to oral and lung cancer, osteoporosis, weight loss, decreased muscle strength, and decline in pulmonary functions. Heavy cigarette use in older men may indicate high alcohol consumption and should be investigated (Schuckit & Miller, 1976).

ALCOHOL ABUSE AND ALCOHOLISM

Research has indicated that alcohol abuse and alcoholism do exist among the elderly. An estimated 2% to 10% of the elderly suffer from alcoholism

(Glantz, 1983). The subgroup with the highest risk is widowers over age 65 (Kinney & Leaton, 1987). There is a higher than average incidence in widows, nursing home residents, patients on medical wards, and psychiatric patients (Schuckit & Miller, 1976; Zimberg, 1979).

Three factors contribute to the reported low rate of alcoholism among the elderly: (a) the early mortality of alcoholics; (b) "spontaneous recovery" attributed to substitute dependencies (67%), medical problems induced by alcohol (48%), membership in Alcoholics Anonymous (AA) (38%), or a new love relationship (38%); and (c) underdiagnosis and underreporting (Vaillant & Milofsky, 1982). Alcoholism among the elderly is often hidden by family members or through isolation, or it is sometimes confused with normal aging, because trembling, confusion, and mental lapses can be seen as symptoms of alcohol abuse and dependency or aging.

Elderly alcoholics differ from younger alcoholics in several ways. They do not drink as much on each occasion, but they are likely to drink more frequently. They rarely reach the point of needing detoxification and rarely have withdrawal symptoms (National Institute on Alcohol Abuse and Alcoholism, 1978). They may be more psychologically dependent than physically dependent on alcohol.

Investigators have distinguished two types of elderly alcoholics: early onset and late onset (Zimberg, 1974a). Approximately two thirds of the elderly alcoholics are early onset, and one third are late onset. The early onset alcoholics are those who began to have drinking problems early in life and have survived into old age. They may or may not have developed physical problems as a result of their drinking, and they may have personality characteristics similar to those of younger alcoholics.

Late onset alcoholics have recently begun to experience alcohol problems, usually in response to stress in their lives. They do not have the personality characteristics of younger alcoholics, but they do experience the stresses and problems of aging: depression, bereavement, loneliness, retirement, marital stress, and physical difficulties (Rosin & Glatt, 1971). Most late onset alcoholics begin drinking in an attempt to alleviate life stresses; the behavior is therefore seen as reactive. Because the alcohol enhances the feelings of isolation and boredom that led to the drinking in the first place, a destructive cycle of more isolation and more alcohol to relieve it becomes established. Late onset alcoholics are generally responsive to treatment and have a good prognosis, but they often go unnoticed and untreated. In a study conducted in Baltimore, Rathbone-McCuan, Lohn, Levenson, and Hsu (1976) found that 85% of those who could be diagnosed as alcoholic were not receiving treatment for their alcohol problem.

Although many of the alcohol problems of the elderly are stress related or hidden, older people who drink experience problems similar to those of younger alcoholics, including hangovers, blackouts, memory loss, shakes, psychological dependence, health problems and accidents due to existing health problems being exacerbated by alcohol use, financial problems, family and marriage problems, problems with friends and neighbors, job related problems (if they are still employed), attitude problems, and legal problems (Carruth, 1973) .

In a study of lifetime drinking patterns aimed at elucidating the drinking patterns of the elderly, Dunham (1981) interviewed 310 persons 60 years of age or older living in low income housing in Dade County, Florida. Only 100 of those interviewed reported any drinking in their lifetime. Subjects were placed in five drinking categories: heavy drinkers, moderate drinkers, light drinkers, infrequent drinkers, or abstainers. Six life patterns were discovered: rise and fall (25%), rise and sustained (28%), light drinking throughout life (21%), light drinking with late rise (7%), late starters (11%), and highly variable (8%).

In the rise and fall pattern, the subjects' alcohol consumption began at age 21, increased at age 24, was heavy for 17 years, decreased at age 61, and terminated (complete abstention) at age 68. These subjects usually were women with low levels of education and an alcohol related illness. In the rise and sustained pattern, the subject's alcohol consumption began at age 17, increased at age 25, and was heavy for 36 years. The subjects were usually white or black men with average education, and they were the least likely to have alcohol related illnesses. Those who drank lightly throughout their lives began at 30 and usually returned to abstinence at about age 72. These subjects were most often Latin women with less than a high school education; they had a moderate chance of alcohol related illnesses. Subjects who reported light drinking with a late rise in alcohol consumption began at age 31 and started drinking heavily at age 74; these were usually Latin men with a low incidence of alcohol related illness. In the late starter pattern, subjects began drinking at age 54 and continued for 17 years or began at age 49 and continued for 3 years and stopped. These subjects were mostly black or white (not Latin) men; those who stopped early were mostly women. The alcohol related illnesses were moderate. Those characterized as variable drinkers began at age 22, increased their drinking at age 30, crossed the light-moderate boundary 3 times, reached the first peak after 9.6 years, and decreased at ages 56 and 65. The subjects were usually black men with alcohol related illnesses.

Dunham (1981) pointed out that at least four of these drinking patterns can be problematic for the elderly: rise and sustained, light drinking with late rise, late starter, and variable patterns. Findings also indicated that women are likely to return to abstinence, whereas men often continue heavy drinking. Blacks often follow variable patterns and have many alcohol related illnesses, and whites most often follow the rise and sustained pattern. People following these two patterns are most likely to become early onset alcoholics, while those who follow the light drinking with late rise or the late starter pattern are apt to become late onset drinkers. This information may be useful to the therapist when obtaining drinking and drug use histories from patients; it helps identify those who are in high-risk groups and indicates treatment strategies.

There are additional risk factors for elderly alcoholics. Family and genetic factors play a part: there is an inverse relation between reported family alcoholism and the age of onset of alcoholism (Atkinson, 1984). Older alcoholics in treatment have a lower rate of family alcoholism than younger patients (Jones, 1972; Penick, Read, Crowley, & Powell, 1978). This is probably due to a complication of environmental factors in alcoholic families that produces early alcohol abuse among children of alcoholics. Late onset alcoholics (after age 40) report familial alcoholism 41% of the time, and early onset alcoholics report a family influence in 86% of the cases (Atkinson, 1984). This underscores the role of late-life stresses and adjustments as a risk factor for late onset alcoholism. Not all stressed elderly people become alcohol abusers late in life, however, and stress may not be a factor in early onset alcoholism.

One of the most dangerous problems for the elderly who drink is the interaction of alcohol and other drugs. As discussed earlier, the elderly use many prescription and over-the-counter drugs that can cause problems when combined with alcohol. States of confusion or sedation out of expected proportions can occur: "Unexpected response to prescribed medication may be the clinician's first clue to undisclosed substance abuse" (Atkinson, 1984, p. 12).

Because environmental stresses and psychological reactions to aging play an important part in the etiology of substance abuse in the elderly, they respond well to treatment that considers alleviating some of the environment problems. Therapies that have been helpful with the elderly substance abuser are socialization, group therapy, case work, and cognitive therapy. Zimberg (1974b) recommended psychosocial interventions with the elderly. Antidepressant medications are sometimes necessary, but often cognitive therapy is more effective. Elderly alcoholics view their alcoholism differently than younger alcoholics; they feel that they do not need detoxification and are reluctant to undergo inpatient treatment. They may also feel out of place if they are admitted to a program with younger alcoholics. Feelings of stigma are greater among the elderly, probably because they grew up before and during the Prohibition era, when little was known, mentioned, or done about drinking problems. These same people were conditioned to feel guilty and ashamed when they drank. As a result they use a strong denial system to hide their drinking (Buys & Saltman, 1984).

TREATMENT OF THE ELDERLY

The elderly are underrepresented in treatment populations. They do not seek assistance from traditional treatment sites and are often embarrassed to ask for help. Therapists may be reluctant to treat elderly clients because they think the treatment will be unsuccessful in making major changes in their lives, or they lack hope for the future of the elderly. Inpatient alcohol wards may be reluctant to treat the elderly because of other physical problems that put them at high risk for injury with some treatment methods. Cardiovascular impairments in the elderly make it risky to use Antabuse. Aversive therapies, such as shock or nausea-producing medications, are also not recommended. Lack of hospitalization insurance keeps some elderly patients out of treatment centers, and some detoxification centers reject older people because they fear medical dangers. Yet when the elderly get help, they respond well.

The elderly need to be treated in places that they are already frequenting. Senior citizen centers in neighborhoods with a high population of older people are good places to work with the elderly. AA groups in these centers are helpful. Efforts can be made to combine the expertise of the therapists who specialize in geriatric populations and those who specialize in substance abuse. Many elderly citizens may need help in their homes. Home visits are a good way to see the elderly person in his or her safest environment. This helps with evaluation of his or her level of functioning and provides information about family and home life.

Therapists who want to work with the elderly need more than just a liking of old people. They must have a genuine respect and a deep sense of caring for the elderly; a history of positive experiences with the elderly; an ability and desire to learn from them; a conviction that the last years of life can be challenging and fruitful; knowledge of the biological, psychological and social needs of the elderly; a healthy attitude regarding their own eventual old age; an understanding of the developmental tasks of each period of life; an ability to deal with extreme feelings of depression, hopelessness, grief, hostility, and despair; personal characteristics such as humor, patience, enthusiasm, courage, endurance, hopefulness, tolerance, nondefensiveness, freedom from limiting prejudices, and a willingness to learn; and the ability to be both supportive and challenging and the sensitivity to know when each is needed (Corey & Corey, 1982).

In working with the elderly it is essential to obtain a complete history and to perform a comprehensive assessment. The history should include information about the client's social history, financial status, emotional well-being, medical condition, and self-care status. In doing the assessment, therapists should look for the client's strengths and remember that the elderly are survivors. When creating treatment plans, therapists should use all possible social networks. Family, social services agencies, senior citizen centers, special senior programs, transportation programs, medical help, public health nurses, and recreation and education programs are just a few possibilities. The therapy environment and materials need to be customized for the elderly. The room should be well lighted, easily accessible, and in a safe place, and there may be a need for vocal amplification and large print. The pace of the therapy should be slow.

Goals for working with the elderly should be realistic and small. Therapists need to see small changes as important and not expect quick, radical changes. Therapists may have to take an active role and meet survival needs of food and shelter before proceeding to other needs. Therapists' attitudes are also important: the elderly should be viewed as having dignity, intelligence, and something to contribute. They should not be talked to as if they were children or treated oversolicitiously.

An important resource for the elderly is the elderly themselves. Peer support and help are valuable assets. They provide help for others and improve the self-esteem of the one who is helping (Lawson & Hughes, 1980). An example of peer help can be seen in group work. Shere (1964) found in a group of people 85 years of age or older who met 47 times that feelings of loneliness and depression lessened, self-respect was regained, old pleasures were revived, social drives were reactivated, intellectual interests were reawakened,and community life was resumed. For the chemically dependent elderly, referral to AA, Narcotics Anonymous, or Al-Anon may provide additional support and networking if there are other elderly at the meetings. The therapist making this kind of referral should investigate the age levels of the groups before referring.

Group therapy for seniors with the goal of making life more meaningful is especially beneficial. The groups need to take a positive approach and have clear goals; task-oriented groups work best. The sessions should go at a slow pace and be supportive. It is not advisable to mix regressed clients with those who are at a high level of functioning. Group themes can include loneliness, social isolation, loss, poverty, feelings of rejection, the struggle to find meaning in life, dependency, feelings of uselessness, hopelessness and despair, fears of death and dying, grief over others' death, sadness over physical and mental deterioration, depression, and regrets over past events (Corey & Corey, 1982). Life review is healthy and often helpful to group members. The elderly are a heterogeneous group and do not all need the same kind of treatment. There are a variety of groups that may be helpful, including groups with special emphasis on reminiscing, physical fitness, body awareness, grief work, occupational therapy, reality orientation, music and art therapy, combined dance and movement, preretirement and postretirement issues, remotivation, preplacement to prepare people to move from an institution to a community setting, attention to organic brain syndrome patients, educational seminars, creating and sharing poetry, health-related issues, and family therapy.

Marriage and family therapy should not be overlooked in working with the elderly. The elderly may need help in negotiating their new status as retired and increased time with marital partners, which may put a strain on the marriage if old marital problems were not resolved and surface after retirement or when the children have left home. Couples may have to renegotiate old contracts of relating and role behavior. Multigenerational family therapy may be very useful in making changes in family systems that reinforce, hide, or protect substance abuse in the elderly. Because alcoholism is a multigenerational illness, it is likely that others in the family may have similar problems, especially early onset alcoholics.

Although clinicians are just beginning to learn about the needs, problems, and life tasks of the elderly, it can be a rewarding experience to work with this population. Therapists need to look at their own issues with aging because they too are aging and will someday join an even larger group of senior citizens. The therapist who learns to help the elderly will undoubtedly assure himself or herself of a job for life.

PREVENTION OF SUBSTANCE ABUSE IN THE ELDERLY

Prevention can be seen as keeping people without problems from getting them (primary prevention), or keeping high risk people from developing problems (secondary prevention), or keeping problems from becoming worse (tertiary prevention). In preventing substance abuse in the elderly population, all three strategies apply. There is a long time between birth and old age for prevention activities. Some activities need to occur in childhood to impact on early onset alcoholics, whereas other activities should be directed at the stresses of the late onset alcoholic.

Early onset alcoholics could benefit from all of the prevention activities from education campaigns to intervention with high risk populations. Prevention and treatment programs for children of alcoholics would impact on these early onset alcoholics with a very high rate of familial alcoholism. Better methods of identification of children at high risk, better interventions, and improved treatment programs with higher success rates would reduce the number of elderly who arrive at old age with a long-term substance abuse problem.

Late onset alcoholism appears to be a response to the increased stresses of late life. Prevention activities that reduce these stresses or help the elderly cope with them could reduce the incidences of drug and alcohol use as a coping tool. These prevention activities can be broken down to impact on all three areas of stress: physical, social, and psychological.

Physical stresses will occur as the body wears down with age, but the medical responses to this can be changed to reduce the risk of overmedication, drug interaction, or drug misuse. Physicians must be educated about the special needs and problems of the elderly. They should be aware of the possible misunderstanding, misuse, and self-diagnosing that often occur when they prescribe drugs. Good drug histories can be taken initially and kept current, including questions about alcohol use. Telephone prescribing can be reduced, and physicians can spend more time with the elderly patient explaining the possible problems of not following directions or the effect of drug interactions. Pharmacists are beginning to check for possible drug interactions by referring to computer records of medications that have been prescribed for each person. Over-the-counter medication companies need to educate the public about the existence of alcohol and other ingredients in their products that can be addicting or cause problems when taken with other medications. This information should be given in a way that the elderly person could hear or see it; writing should be large and prominent.

Social risks can be reduced by increasing the social contact of the elderly person. Volunteer work can replace some of the losses of retirement. Social centers can provide activities that are meaningful and create a place for the elderly to meet others and even begin dating. Social isolation can also include the isolation of being involved only with older people. The elderly need contact with young people and especially children. Day care centers could begin a volunteer program for the elderly to teach skills to the children.

As isolation is reduced, so is psychological risk. Prevention strategies might include increased retirement planning that includes a second career or volunteer work in the first career. The elderly are a wealth of knowledge, and creative programs that put to use the skills learned by the elderly in a lifetime will benefit from this knowledge. Recreation that is designed with the limitations of the elderly in mind can provide a healthy leisure time activity. This can include learning new skills like folk dancing or yoga or finding a way to use an athletic talent in a less stressful way. Many people are not skilled at using leisure time constructively. This skill can be taught to the elderly before it becomes a problem.

Counseling can be a prevention method as well as a treatment approach. Losses are a natural part of the life cycle, but unresolved grieving can be helped with grief counseling in an individual or group setting. Marriage enrichment programs can provide new ways for elderly couples to communicate and establish new patterns for living together.

It is important for the therapist who is working with the elderly either in prevention activities or in treatment to remember that the elderly respond to most of the treatment approaches that work with younger people if they are given a few special considerations and if the therapist views the elderly as valuable and able to change.

REFERENCES

Atkinson, R.M. (Ed.). (1984). *Alcohol and drugs: Abuse in old age.* Washington, DC: American Psychiatric Press.

Basen, A.B. (1977). The elderly and drugs: Problem, overview and program strategy. *Public Health Report, 92,* 43–48.

Brotman, H. B. (1980). *Every ninth American: Development in aging* (rev. ed.). Report to the Special Committee on Aging, United States Senate. Cited in Benjamin B. Wolman (Ed.), *International encyclopedia of psychiatry, psychoanalysis and neurology: Progress, volume 1.* New York:

Busse, E. W. (1983). Geriatric psychiatry: Recent developments. In Benjamin B. Wolman (Ed.), *International encyclopedia of psychiatry, psychoanalysis and neurology: Progress, volume 1* (pp. 182–186). New York: Van Nostrand-Reinhold.

Buys, D., & Saltman, J. (1984). *The unseen alcoholics: The elderly.* Public Affairs Committee.

Carruth, B. (1973). Toward a definition of problem drinking among older persons: Conceptual and methodological considerations. In E.P. Williams (Ed.), *Alcohol and problem drinking among older persons* (pp. 29–44). Springfield, VA: National Technical Information Service.

Corey, G., & Corey, M.S. (1982). *Groups: Process and practice* (2nd ed.). Monterey, CA: Brooks/Cole.

Doyle, J.P., & Hamm, B.M. (1976). *Medication use and misuse study among older persons.* Jacksonville, FL: Cathedral Foundation of Jacksonville.

Dunham, R.G. (1981). Aging and changing patterns of alcohol use. *Journal of Psychoactive Drugs, 13*(2), 143–151.

Glantz, M.D. (1983). Drugs and the elderly adult: An overview. In M.D. Glantz, D.M. Peterson, & F.J. Whittington (Eds.), *Drugs and the elderly: Research issues 32* (pp. 1–3). Rockville, MD: National Institute on Drug Abuse.

Gubrium, J. (1975). *Living and dying at Murray Manor.* New York: St. Martin's Press.

Hanan, Z.I. (1978). Geriatric medications: How the aged are hurt by drugs meant to help. *RN,* January, pp. 57–59.

Hemminki, E., & Heikkela, J. (1975). Elderly people's compliance with prescriptions and quantity of medication. *Scandinavian Journal of Social Medicine, 3,* 87–92.

Jones, R.W. (1972). Alcoholism among relatives of alcoholic patients. *Quarterly Journal of Studies on Alcohol, 33,* 810.

Kinney, J. & Leaton, G. (1987). *Loosening the grip* (3rd ed.). St. Louis: C.V. Mosby.

Kofoed, L.L. (1984). Abuse and misuse of over the counter drugs by the elderly. In R.M. Atkinson (Ed.), *Alcohol and drug abuse in old age* (pp. 50–59). Washington DC: American Psychiatric Press.

Kofoed, L.L. (1985). Substance abuse in the older patient. *Medical Aspects of Human Sexuality, 19*(2), 22–27.

Lawson, G. & Hughes B. (1980). Some considerations for the training of counselors who work with the elderly. *Counseling and Values, 24*(3), 204–208.

Learoyd, B.M. (1972). Psychotropic drugs and the elderly patient. *Medical Journal of Australia, 1,* 1131–1133.

Mandolini, A. (1981). The social contexts of aging and drug use: Theoretical and methodological insights. *Journal of Psychoactive Drugs, 13*(2), 135–142.

Michigan Office of Services to the Aging and Michigan Office of Substance Abuse Services. (1979). *Substance abuse among Michigan's senior citizens: Patterns of use and provider perspectives.* Lansing, MI: The Offices.

National Institute on Alcohol Abuse and Alcoholism. (1978). *Alcohol topics in brief: Alcohol and the elderly.* Rockville, MD: National Clearing House for Alcohol Information.

Offer, C. (1974). At sixty-five work becomes a four letter word. *Psychology Today, 7*(10), 40.

Penick, E.C.; Read, M.R.; Crowley, P.A.; & Powell, B. J. (1978). Differentiation of alcoholics by family history. *Journal of Studies on Alcohol, 39,* 1944–1948.

Peterson, D.M., Whittington, F.J., & Beer, E.T. (1979). Drug use and misuse among the elderly. *Journal of Drug Issues 9*(1), 5–26.

Rathbone-McCuan, E., Lohn, H., Levenson, J., & Hsu, J. (1976). *Community survey of aged alcoholics and problem drinkers.* Washington, DC: National Institute on Alcohol Abuse and Alcoholism.

Rosin, A.J., & Glatt, M.M. (1971). Alcohol excess in the elderly. *Quarterly Journal of Studies on Alcohol, 32,* 53–59.

Schuckit, M.A., & Miller, P.L. (1976). Alcoholism in elderly men: Survey of a general medical ward. *Annals of the New York Academy of Sciences, 273,* 558–571.

Schwartz, D., Wang, M., Zeitz, L., & Gross, M.E.W. (1962). Medical errors made by elderly chronically ill patients. *American Journal of Public Health, 52*(12), 2018–2029.

Shader, R. (Ed.). (1975). *Manual of psychiatric therapeutics.* Boston: Little, Brown.

Shere, E. (1964). Group work with the very old. In R. Kastenbaum (Ed.), *New thought on old age.* New York: Springer.

Stephens, R.C., Haney, C.A., & Underwood, S. (1981). Psychoactive drug use and potential misuse among persons aged 55 years and older. *Journal of Psychoactive Drugs, 13*(2), 185–193.

Stephens, R.C., Haney, C.A., & Underwood, S. (1982). *Drug taking among the elderly: National Institute on Drug Abuse treatment research report* (DHHS Pub. No. ADM 83–1229). Washington, DC: Government Printing Office.

Stewart, R.B., Hale, W.W., & Marks, M.G. (1982). Analgesic drug use in ambulatory elderly populations. *Drugs, Intelligence, and Clinical Pharmacy, 16,* 833–836.

Vaillant, G.E., & Milofsky, E.S. (1982). Natural history of male alcoholism: 4. Paths to recovery. *Archives of General Psychiatry, 39,* 127–133.

Whittington, F.J. (1983a). Consequences of drug use, misuse and abuse. In M. D. Glantz, D.M. Peterson, & F.J. Whittington (Eds.), *Drugs and the elderly adult: Research issues 32* (pp. 203–206). Rockville, MD: National Institute on Drug Abuse.

Whittington, F.J. (1983b). Misuse of legal drugs and compliance with prescription directions. In M.D. Glantz, D.M. Peterson, & F.J. Whittington (Eds.), *Drugs and the elderly adult: Research issues 32* (pp. 63–69). Rockville, MD: National Institute on Drug Abuse.

Zimberg, S. (1974a). The elderly alcoholic. *Gerontologist, 14*(3), 221–224.

Zimberg, S. (1974b). Two types of problem drinkers: Both can be managed. *Geriatrics, 29,* 135–139.

Zimberg, S. (1979). Alcohol and the elderly. In D.M. Peterson, F.J. Whittington, & B.P. Payne (Eds.), *Drugs and the elderly: Social and pharmacological issues* (pp. 28–40). Springfield, IL: Charles C Thomas.

Chapter 6

Alcoholism in the Black Community

Freida Brown and Joan Tooley

INTRODUCTION

Alcoholism is the number one health problem in the black community (King, 1982). The black community is composed of approximately 28.9 million people representing 12.1% of the total population of the United States (*Statistical Abstracts*, 1987). While underrepresented in the population, blacks remain overrepresented among the health statistics for life-threatening illnesses. The life expectancy for blacks continues to lag behind that for whites. The life expectancy for blacks is 69.5 years as compared with 75.3 years for whites (*Statistical Abstracts*, 1987).

Alcohol abuse is a primary health problem contributing to reduced longevity in the black community. High incidences of acute and chronic alcohol related diseases among blacks, such as alcoholic fatty liver, hepatitis, and cirrhosis of the liver; heart disease and cancers of the mouth, larynx, tongue, esophagus, and lung; and unintentional injuries and homicide, point to its endemic nature (Ronan, 1987). Curiously, rates for these alcohol related diseases began to soar after World War II. Why was there a marked upsurge in alcohol related diseases following World War II? An examination of the historical roots of alcohol in the black community provides some answers.

HISTORICAL ANTECEDENTS

Alcohol use among blacks began during the time of slavery. Slaves were given alcohol on holidays by their owners as a reward for obedience and hard work. Drunkenness was an acceptable norm for holiday celebrations and was viewed as a means for preventing insurrection. However, the danger of mass drunkenness and potential revolt was heightened following Nat Turner's revolt in 1830. Laws were enacted that placed tighter controls on drinking and even prevented blacks from owning stills. This prohibition was unenforceable during the Civil War, but following the Civil War, blacks were again prevented from owning alcoholic beverages and firearms in the southern states although they had been granted the rights of citizenship.

Political, social, and economic conditions for blacks worsened during Reconstruction. Political gains were quickly lost. In 1883, the Supreme Court outlawed the Civil Rights Act of 1875 and the doctrine of "separate but equal" was instituted. By 1910, most southern states had constitutionally disenfranchised freed blacks (Franklin, 1980). The failure to gain economic and political reform in the South along with maltreatment resulted in a mass migration of blacks into the northern industrial cities. In Philadelphia alone, the number of blacks rose from 84,000 in 1910 to 250,000 in 1940 (Ballard, 1984). A description of the conditions during that time is chronicled in an article in the *Public Ledger* on June 24, 1925. "A slum can be found strongly entrenched in this North Philadelphia neighborhood. Ignorance, dirt, overcrowding, disease, sloth, wine, drunkenness, corruption of youth all have their stranglehold" (cited in Ballard, 1984, p. 188).

The great majority of the migrants were forced into slum ghettoes because of discrimination, unmarketable skills, and economic instability. Moreover, family structures and relationships were disrupted and often dissolved as black men went to find work and housing in the industrial North and left their families behind in the agrarian South. Davis' (1984) theory is that for some, drinking became one means of coping with this change in environment, an environment devoid of support. An elite class had formed among blacks in the North. They were the educators, physicians, businessmen, the professionals who had been active in the movement to free the slaves in the South and had formed the major black institutions in the North. The elite did not welcome the throngs of poor and uneducated who merged from the South. Even the black church, which had always functioned as a spiritual healer, social welfare provider, and educator, was now overwhelmed with the influx of migrants from the South. A class structure quickly emerged: the black middle class and the black poor.

Statistics maintained by the U.S. Census Bureau since 1910 reflect the incidence of alcohol related diseases following this migration to the North. Since 1940, there has been a rapid annual increase in the frequency of cirrhosis of the liver as a cause of death in blacks. Deaths rose from 5.8 per 100,000 in 1940 to 20.4 per 100,000 in 1974. Concurrently, there was an increase in the number of hospital patients (from 40% to 50%) with a secondary diagnosis of alcoholism (Christmas, 1978). While other factors such as the high rate of hepatitis B virus among blacks could contribute to cirrhosis morbidity, alcohol is considered the primary contributing agent (Herd, 1985).

Herd's (1985) cohort analysis pointed to the importance of this migratory period and the temperance movement on the cirrhosis mortality rates among blacks. The 19th century temperance movement affected drinking patterns among all ethnic groups. At that time blacks had the lowest mortality rate due to alcoholism of any ethnic group. The 1880 U.S. statistics for alcohol related mortality revealed 6.7 per 1,000 deaths for the Irish, 2.7 for Germans, 2.5 for whites, and 0.7 for blacks. Chronic drunkenness among blacks was so rare that they were considered immune. Blacks strongly aligned themselves with the temperance movement because of its anti-slavery platform. The turn of the century saw a shift in the temperance movement's political base from northern abolitionists to poor rural southerners. The political ideology of the prohibitionists became white supremacy and black disenfranchisement. The prohibitionists urged protection of whites, particularly white women, from the "drunken debauches of half-crazed black men." Sex crimes were linked to alcohol, and racial violence ensued. Consequently, blacks detached themselves from the antiliquor movement and headed north to avoid the violence.

The prohibition era sparked the move to the "wet" North and simultaneously provided an economic base for the unemployed migrant, especially during the Depression. Alcohol became a central theme for the working poor, as manifested by bootlegging, speakeasies, and rent parties (Herd, 1985). Interestingly, death rates for cirrhosis of the liver began to increase for all cohorts born at the turn of the century. In general, black mortality rates tripled in the northeast while the rate for whites increased by 47%. There was a significant upsurge among blacks who had migrated to the North in comparison with their cohorts in the interior South. The rates for blacks in the South remained similar to those for their white counterparts. It was the urbanized black born in the early 1900s who contributed to the high statistics of the 1950s and 1970s.

Herd (1985) reported that there was a minimal increase in alcohol related deaths among later cohorts and even a sight decline. These later cohorts were born in the 1930s and 1940s. The 1940s ushered in the end to Prohibition and the great migration to the North. World War II began, but unlike after World War I, blacks did not return from Europe with illusions of equal participation in America's political and economic arena. Franklin (1980) described blacks as fighting against discrimination both at home and abroad. Historically, the next 30 years were replete with constant battles being fought on the home front for racial equality and a sense of black pride: the civil rights movement and desegregation, the black power movement and race riots, and the Republican era and severe cutbacks in social programs and high unemployment. The National Urban League reported that the black poverty rate rose to 31% in 1986, nearly 3 times that of whites. The median black income is still only 57% of that of whites (Staff, 1988). In the 1980s, both the black middle class and the black poor are growing, with implications for alcohol use.

Several causes of alcohol abuse and misuse in Black America have been identified. A primary factor is economics. Many black men drink due to unemployment, which leads to depression and frustration because of an inability to meet financial commitments. Williams (1986) also concluded that unemployment is correlated with a high risk for alcohol problems. Another explanation related to economics is availability. Liquor stores are readily accessible in black neighborhoods. For example, in Los Angeles, there are approximately three liquor stores per city block and other "mom and pop" stores that sell beer and wine. Parker and Harman (1978) found that the availability of alcohol, independent of other factors, appears to influence consumption rates (which is more closely linked with cirrhosis) but not rates of alcoholism. Black peer group pressure was also reported as a contributing factor: they expect members to drink and often times heavily. Brand names and quantity are often status identifiers. A final cause is use in an attempt to escape unpleasant feelings that are suppressed and repressed.

Stern and Pittman (1972) reported similar themes emerging from their review. They linked the pattern of weekend drinking in the black community to the idea that weekly pay and Saturday, historically, are primarily for relaxation, visiting, and drinking. A second theme was the prevalence of the use of the tavern in the black community as a social center. The third was the use of alcohol as an escape from personal problems.

Alcohol has served a consistent function for blacks in America. It rewards compliance and obedience, dulls the feelings of helplessness and rage, facilitates social functioning, and reflects economic trends. Reminiscent of its role during slavery, it may serve to maintain a particular class relationship (King, 1981). This historical pattern of alcohol use has played a significant role in influencing the current drinking patterns and attitudes toward drinking among blacks.

PATTERNS AND PRACTICES OF ALCOHOL USE

Alcohol use among blacks has not been greatly explored. Harper and Dawkins (1976) reported that of the 16,000 articles published in the 30 years prior to 1974, only 77 made reference to blacks, and only 11 were specifically about blacks.

King (1982) in his survey of the literature between 1977 and 1980 found that most studies on black populations were concerned with patterns of use, with social context being the central focus. Only one study (Stalls, 1978) explored racial differences in patterns of alcohol metabolism. Stall (1978) concluded that there was an increasing use of alcohol at an earlier age by youth and a growing intensity of use by women, with serious implications for fetal alcohol syndrome. Drinking reached its peak in the 16 to 23-year-old range as compared with the 18 to 25-year-old group of the 1960s. Among women, drinking was the highest for divorcées under 45; lower class women were more likely to be abstainers. Brisbane's (1987) profile of the black women in her study of adult children of alcoholics who were also alcoholics is consistent with this finding. The women were typically under 45, employed, and considered themselves middle class.

A community survey of drinking practices among 322 black adults (18 to 59-years-old) in two predominantly black San Francisco neighborhoods during 1979 and 1980 found that 37% of men and 63% of women were abstainers or infrequent drinkers, 17% of men and 8% of women were frequent drinkers who reported alcohol consumption on 17 days or more during the month, and 14% of the men and 3% of the women were heavy drinkers. The drinking related problems most often cited were marital (26%), job (23%), and family (21%) problems.

Fernandez-Pol, Bluestone, Missouri, Morales, and Mizruchi (1986) compared blacks and Puerto Rican alcoholics in the areas of psychological and social adjustments and benefits from drinking. Sex differences revealed that black women showed more personal adjustment symptoms related to drinking, were most likely to encourage their partners to drink with them, did not miss work or lose their jobs due to drinking, and depended more on alcohol for relaxation and to make friends. In contrast, black men had more fears after drinking, missed work and lost their jobs more frequently, and experienced more marital problems. When both partners are alcoholics, the family environment encourages alcoholism, and there is a lack of support for a sober life.

When Neff (1986) compared black drinkers with abstainers, there was a significant difference in psychological symptoms. Black drinkers reported more depressive symptoms than abstainers, and there was a tendency for quantity to be associated with depression. Neff cautioned against this interpretation because of the small sample size. He did conclude that drinking among blacks serves to reduce tension and distress and that the role of cultural factors needs further exploration. Sociodemographically, blacks had the lowest family incomes and the highest rate of broken marriages.

A correlational study by Schlenger et al. (1986) comparing blacks, whites, and Hispanics showed that blacks tended to fall in the extreme categories. They tended to be heavy drinkers (32%) or abstainers (35.4%) and reported no alcohol related problems (78.3%) and no need for treatment (79.9%); 91.4% indicated no prior treatment. The researchers cautioned that there are discrepancies in the cited data for middle class blacks. Middle class blacks are rarely represented in the statistics. When and if treatment is sought, it is short, at an ultraselective facility, and highly confidential. They are not found loitering but usually gather in groups at homes where excessive drinking is condoned by peers. Finally, the black community protects them due to their integration into highly visible positions.

Data from national surveys indicate that black youths between 14 and 17 years of age have higher abstinence rates and lower alcohol related social consequences than their white counterparts. Whites are more likely to report encounters with the police as a result of their behavior following drinking. Among white men, problem drinking is most likely to occur between the ages of 18 and 25. The high rates of heavy drinking and associated social problems in black men typically occur after age 30. This late onset of drinking may be a contributing factor to chronic alcohol related diseases (Ronan, 1987).

Williams' (1986) update of research on alcoholism in blacks pointed to the contradiction in the high incidence of alcohol related diseases and drinking patterns. When age and socioeconomic levels were controlled, blacks actually abstained more, drank less frequently, and consumed less alcohol than their white counterparts. Black women were the exception. Of the adult black women who drank, 11% drank heavily compared with 4% of the white women.

Several patterns surfaced from the literature that tended to distinguish black drinking practices from those of other populations: the late onset (around age 30) of drinking in black men coupled with the reluctance to seek treatment may contribute to the high rate of alcohol related diseases. Black men are overrepresented among the unemployed, which places them at high risk for alcohol abuse. There is an increase in drinking, generally as a social activity, by black women. Finally, blacks are more likely to encourage spousal drinking than are other ethnic groups. These differences and implications for treatment can be examined in the light of the psychosocial development of black men and women.

DEVELOPMENTAL ISSUES

King (1982) posed the questions: "Why is the consumption of alcohol (3+ drinks per day) most prevalent in the age decades 40-49 and 50-59? Is there a midlife crisis operating?" The literature suggests that most men go through some form of transition during midlife, but what precipitates the crisis is not often clear. Rosenberg and Farrell (1976) reported that the incidence of alcoholism, divorce, and suicide increased as a result of personal disorganization during the midlife years. Golembiewski (1978) also reported that both careers and marriages are at stake during the midlife years. Moreover, the death rate among men peaks between the ages of 35 and 40. Failure to attain career expectations is considered the primary factor contributing to depression and the subsequent physical illness that often results in death. The aspiration-achievement gap is the primary obstacle faced during the midlife transition (Brim, 1977). The two primary ingredients of adult life, work and love, are often the basis for the midlife crisis and may result in the use of alcohol as an escape mechanism.

It is not surprising, then, that the onset of heavy drinking by black men around age 30 is potentially exacerbated by the midlife crisis of the forties. Caetano (1984) suggested that this late onset of drinking reflects a stable pattern of midlife. If so, this would increase the risk of death related to cirrhosis in black men compared with white men regardless of the per capita consumption at any point in time (Herd, 1985).

Levinson (1978) maintained that there is also an "age thirty crisis" for every man and that it tends to be as severe and stressful as the one during the forties. He described it as "a man alone on a body of water trying to get from Island Past to Island Future" (p. 86). This is not merely a delayed adolescent crisis although many of the crises of adolescence may surface for resolution, especially identity issues. The developmental issues to be resolved are the same as those at age 40: family and work. According to Levinson, marital problems and occupational shifts are likely to occur around this time. Gould (1978) discovered similar issues at this age. This phase of development is characterized by increasing dissatisfactions, more self-reflection, dissatisfaction with marriage, and increasing investment in children. Sheehy's (1976) "Catch-30" also exemplifies a similar process around age 30. She stated that both men and women are feeling "too restricted and narrow" with the career and personal choices made in their twenties. This is a time for reassessing their choices and making new choices about career, marriage, and family.

While age 30 can be a crisis period for all men, Levinson (1978) remarked that it is especially difficult for black men. "The struggle to remain true to his dream is never easy for a black man in this society . . ." because of the "destructive forces of individual and institutional racism" (p. 89). The focal point of crisis resolution during both decades is the accomplishment of aspirations concerning occupation and marriage.

Resolving the major crisis of adulthood, which is the discrepancy between aspirations and goal attainment, is a difficult task for the black alcoholic community. It has been plagued by a history of being the last hired and the first fired, has been the subject of a matriarchal family structure, and has been enmeshed in families wherein there were either overdemanding requirements to succeed at all costs or a projection of unfulfilled needs of one of the parental figures: "I could not, you will." Overprotectiveness may have hindered the development of a true self-image, which was further complicated by the observation of excessive drinking by either or both parents, which in many instances led to verbal and possibly physical abuse. This type of modeling has led to a sense of mistrust, shame, and doubt with regard to interpersonal relationships. For the black male alcoholic, this may have readily transferred to his marital relationship.

Erikson (1982) maintains that the failed attempt at intimacy results in isolation: the core of adult pathology. For the black alcoholic this pathology manifests itself in succinct ways. King (1981) reported that dependency and depression were the most common disorders in the black population in the studies he reviewed. Steer and Shaw (1977) found the most meaningful dimensions of depression found in alcoholic black men were cognitive-affective impairment, retarded depression, and escapism. These symptoms are not uncommon in men who have failed to attain career choices and who at age 30 must evaluate their future within the context of their perceived failures.

Black male alcoholics also score lower on tests of personality integration, with a more passive and compliant coping style than other ethnic group male alcoholics (Carroll, Klein, & Santo, 1978). This passive and compliant coping style has its historical roots firmly planted in the slavery era. Black mothers had to socialize their male children to be passive if they were to survive the authority of the slave master; to be "uppity" meant possible physical punishment or even death. Today, the same survival skills are necessary; the authority figures have become the police, employers, and educators. Dependency and a passive coping style are also reported in the earlier literature on boys of father-absent homes (Barclay & Cusmano, 1967; Hetherington, 1966). Most studies suggested that boys of father-absent homes tended to be more dependent on their peer groups, displayed fewer aggressive behaviors, had lowered self-esteem, and were more likely to show overt masculine behaviors that were modeled upon age mates. Social class tended to be an intervening variable in most of the studies. The father's absence before the age of 5 tended to have a more deleterious effect on sex role orientation (Covell & Turnbull, 1982). The probability of a black child being in a female-headed household is high. Black women represent 59% of all female-headed households. Mothers encouraging masculine traits in their sons had more of an impact in father-absent homes than in father-present ones (Biller, 1969). This resulted in an increased likelihood of boys imitating masculine behavior observed among their peers. Implications for this are found in the distinct drinking patterns found among rural and urban drinking adolescents. Dembo et. al. (1978) found that rural youth were usually affiliated with a church that condemned alcohol use, had a close friend who drank and used alcohol as a way of rejecting adult standards. Urban youth, on the other hand, drank more if they perceived their neighborhood as tough, wanted to gain status in their peer group, and were less involved in school. The urbanized drinking youth was more likely to be from a female-headed household and more likely to use his peer group to establish his sex role behavior.

Historically, a different socialization process occurred for black women who had to be independent in order to care for their children. They could possibly lose them at a slave auction or trade and generally raised them alone. For unlike slavery in South America where the Spanish tried to preserve the family by permitting slaves to marry, slave holders in North America prohibited marriage and the creation of families.

Black mothers today continue to socialize their children differentially, instilling in their daughters traits that are typically viewed by the white culture as masculine and in their sons those traits that are considered feminine. For the oldest or only female child in the family, there is also the sex role of "second mother" who helps care for other male and female siblings and is in charge during troubled times. This helps prepare the female adolescent for adulthood.

According to Brisbane (1986) this same ascribed role is operating in the alcoholic family, except that the "family hero" is not receiving the nurturing she would in a healthy family. Most often the alcoholic parent is the father to whom the nonalcoholic mother generally directs most of her attention. The mother takes care of the essential needs of the children but is unable to provide for them psychologically; this responsibility falls on the parentified child (Brisbane, 1987).

During adolescence, when identity formation is the critical developmental task, the family hero has her sex role identity predetermined by her gender and birth order. Peer group formation may also be affected because her parental responsibilities may supersede age-appropriate activities. Moreover, she may wonder how she can take friends home when she doesn't know what to expect; she may also fantasize about the ideal, and accept the blame for the family's behavior, internalizing a "not good enough me." This identity foreclosure for the family hero means accepting the identity established by her parents and thereby increasing the probability of reliving their experiences, i.e., marrying an alcoholic spouse and/ or becoming alcoholic. She has an "isolation à deux" as a marriage model to emulate, in this case spouses living in a relationship mutually exclusive of their children. Erikson (1982) maintained that the isolation à deux serves to protect each partner from the necessity of facing the next critical phase of development. For alcoholic parents, this may be the raising of their children.

An examination of unemployment rates, the increasing number of female headed households, culturally distinct socialization practices, and historical influences in the black community point to the resilience and strength necessary for blacks to accomplish the developmental tasks of adulthood and adolescence. Erikson (1982) viewed the development of intimacy as a direct result of the resolution of the identity crisis of adolescence. Once a person establishes a sense of self, he or she can then share his or her life with someone while still maintaining his or her own identity. Being black in America means that an identity is not only established by the alcoholic's family and environment but is also affected by the institution of racism. Racism, identity, and intimacy are all crises to be resolved by the developing black alcoholic.

TREATMENT STRATEGIES

Blacks are less likely to seek treatment for problem drinking than any other group. The stigmas of the past still haunt the present, and some blacks have not forgotten the stereotypes in the field of mental health. Historically, blacks have justification for distrusting mental health professionals.

Sue (1981) provides a historical overview of the development of blacks' mistrust of the mental health profession. During the 1800s, psychological breakdowns were attributed to blacks not knowing how to handle their new-found freedom from slavery. The 1900s heralded in an era of misdiagnosis, with blacks more often diagnosed as schizophrenic. Counseling in schools began along with psychological tests and notions of what was good for minorities. Minority students were "tested" into vocations that led to dead-end jobs and unemployment. Both practices continue today. As late as 1930, it was believed that blacks should not be psychoanalyzed; the primary concern was freeing the black person's libido. Not surprisingly, these beliefs were held during the black migration to the North that resulted in the overcrowding of the cities and unemployment and fed into the fear of unleashing the black man's pent-up sexual energy into the white community. The genetic inferiority theory was replaced by the theory of social pathology in the 1950s. Again, blacks were felt to be beyond counseling because of the pathology of their community. The notion of keeping the pathology within the black community was fuel for segregationists and a way to feign off the inevitable civil rights movement. On the heels of the

black power movement, sensitivity to ethnic differences blossomed. The philosophy became that counseling for minorities must involve a poignant sense of their history, the present, and the future. Black coping skills were acknowledged; therefore, successful counseling must be a combination of "survival" and "change" mechanisms.

Treatment methodologies for the 1980s and the future must have a multimodal approach for black alcoholics. The research suggests several areas that must be addressed to increase the likelihood of successful treatment outcomes. The first step is getting the alcoholic into treatment. Programs should be located within the community, particularly for lower-income blacks who rely on public transportation and may not be able to afford transportation costs. The upwardly mobile black is more likely to seek private services outside the community where he or she resides. The black church can serve a dual role in this first step for not only can it provide a facility but can also act as a referral source. Most churches are centrally located in the black community and even as members relocate, they tend to maintain the "church home."

The church has been the mainstay of the black family. Rather than seek outside help for problems, the family has taken them to church in prayer and guidance from the minister or priest, who in many instances has not relied on mental health professionals. Black female alcoholics report that their children, usually an adolescent son, was responsible for motivating them to stop drinking and that their faith in God and church attendance helped them stop. Many reported that they stopped drinking prior to seeking professional help and that it was their spirituality that helped with the transition (Brisbane, 1987). Westermeyer (1984) found that recovering abusers returned to their former values, beliefs, and attitudes with renewed vigor or adopted new ones to replace the alcoholic subculture. Spirituality, religion, and the church are important life features for blacks (Hudson, 1986; Knox, 1986). The church can therefore be a viable resource in the treatment of black alcoholics by (1) becoming more aware of the substance abuse problems in their communities and congregations, (2) encouraging its membership to seek professional help, and (3) establishing chapters of Alcoholics Anonymous (AA), Al-Anon, and other liaison groups to assist with rehabilitation (Dembo et al., 1983).

According to Westermeyer (1984), ethnically sensitive programs do attract more people into treatment and consequently do help more minority alcoholics. Williams (1982) discussed the need for culture-specific approaches that involve understanding the client's frame of reference and incorporating it into therapeutic strategies to maximize their effectiveness. Matching the race of the therapist with the alcoholic can be a beginning step in achieving an ethnically sensitive program. However, black therapists must be cognizant of transference and countertransference issues with their black clients. The inculcation of black self-hatred is a part of black history. "If you're white, it's alright; if you're brown, step around; if you're black, get back" looms in the black psyche. This belief is evident in the consumer behavior of blacks: since integration, the patronage of black professionals has declined. Prior to that time blacks could obtain professional services only from other blacks. An approach-avoidance conflict often exists for the black mental health consumer. There is a need to talk with someone of like kind with whom they can relate and identify; and yet, there is often the notion that the black professional is not as competent. Helplessness, rage, and the stigma of racial inferiority are often projected onto the black therapist. Black therapists may see in their black clients those feelings that they have denied or repressed, such as inadequacy. Moreover, they may have identified with the white power structure that continues to oppress minority communities. The black client's paranoia about "white oriented" organizations within the black community are valid and may need to be surfaced. Black mental health professionals must deal with their own issues of alienation, validation, rage, and racial inferiority if they are to work effectively with the issues of the diverse subgroups being treated.

Black alcoholics are not a homogeneous group. The literature clearly points to social class and subcultural differences. The social class distinctions have been present throughout history: the degree of spirituality varies as well as self-esteem and racial pride. While racial discrimination may be an overriding causal variable in the equation of mental health for blacks, its impact remains different for each subgroup. For example, for the middle income black, the drinking related issue may be alienation on the job; for the lower income black, it may be unemployment; and both may be mediated by racism. Different issues require different intervention strategies with an underlying theme.

Rogan (1986) suggested that matching the ethnicity of the counselor and the alcoholic and developing culturally sensitive treatment programs are not enough to help the minority alcoholic recover. Moss, Edwards, Edwards, Janzen, and Howell (1985) contended that cultural sensitivity is not the crucial first step to recovery; the alcohol related factors must first be addressed. Eighty percent of their counselors cited three factors critical to sobriety: (1) recognition and acceptance of the problem, (2) awareness of the reasons for drinking, and (3) motivation to refrain from drinking. They further cautioned that placing personal/social factors first will be less successful than emphasizing the actual drinking factors. Personal and social variables important to the recovery process included gaining an appreciation for life, spiritual awareness, improved self-image, and pride in one's heritage. The drinking related factors the counselor must first confront are those related to the survival needs of the alcoholic. Employment, health, safety, housing, food, clothing, and court related and school related issues must all be considered before exploring other issues. Relief from these stressors can be a beginning step toward reducing the tension being alleviated by drinking. Exploration of the factors contributing to the alcoholism is important during the initial phase of treatment.

The involvement of the family is paramount in the treatment of the black alcoholic. The therapist must identify the nuclear family and the extended family network, which may include other than blood relatives. It is not uncommon for close ties to form with neighbors, church members, or social group members who acquire titles such as "grandma," "cousin," "aunt," or "uncle." These "relatives" often provide assistance in the form of shelter, food, money, or clothes during difficult times. They may also take on counseling roles that relatives find too painful, such as drug abuse or incest (Brisbane & Womble, 1986). The family hero should also be consulted for the contribution she can make to the treatment of her parent(s) and siblings; as well as making help available to her. The high incidence of spousal drinking among blacks also points to the need to assess the drinking behavior of both partners and their involvement in the treatment strategy. The function of the alcoholic's social group in the promotion of drinking behavior should also be considered, particularly among black women who drink to make friends. Lower income, urban adolescent men are more likely to be influenced by their peer groups to engage in heavy drinking. Group treatment strategies can help model more effective ways to acquire friendships and establish a sense of self. Harper (1984) suggested that the cultural styles of blacks and the drinking patterns of black alcoholics favor the use of group modalities. Group modalities to consider include AA, educational groups, family counseling, job orientation groups, and social skills groups.

Once the survival and social factors are addressed, then the psychological and cultural determinants become the key to long-term effectiveness. Effective treatment strategies in this area tend to be cognitive, directive, and action oriented (Harper, 1984). Gore and Maultsby (1986) devised a cognitive treatment method that is comprehensive, short-term, and culture-free. The method involves an emotional self-help technique called "rational self-counseling" that teaches clients an effective way of relieving emotional tension without alcohol. Of primary significance for blacks is that treatment is placed under the control of the client.

In summary, there must be an awareness of the socioeconomic context and its impact on the intrapsychic processes. The elimination of stereotypic biases by both staff and clients and the inclusion of cultural mores, values, and traditions are necessary to maximize intervention and treatment. Essential in the treatment process is the involvement of the black community, which includes the church, the nuclear family, the extended family, and social groups.

PREVENTION

The church can be a prevailing force in the prevention of alcoholism by establishing educational programs designed to inform its members of the causes, intervention, and prevention of alcoholism and ensuring that policy makers and planners recognize that ethnic minorities, because of their cultural heritage and socioeconomic status, experience problems in context very differently from the nonminority society (Dembo et al., 1983).

Prevention of alcoholism begins with the young. Preschoolers can learn about the dangers of alcoholism through the use of puppets, stories, and songs. Equally as important for black children is the development of a positive racial identity, which generally begins to form around age 3 or 4. Racial pride coupled with a strong positive self-concept can only fortify the black child for combating the destructive effects of racial discrimination. Coping skills must be taught to the school-age child and adolescent to help them minimize the pressure to get involved with alcohol and other chemical substances, particularly during adolescence when peer group formation is so important and peer pressure is at its highest.

Because of the late onset of heavy drinking among blacks and their reluctance to obtain treatment, it is important to form a coalition composed of clergy, mental health professionals, and physicians. More research needs to be conducted on the biological basis of alcoholism among blacks as well as the negative health related complications. This can help with the development of appropriate referrals, diagnosis, and treatment.

The data suggest that cultural issues are operating in the etiology and treatment of black alcoholism. Research should begin to explore intraracial differences to identify effective coping strategies of blacks for treatment implications.

This chapter examined historical, cultural, and psychological factors contributing to alcoholism in the black community. The studies reviewed clearly indicated the role of history in the use of alcohol in America. Both the role of the temperance movement and the migration to the North in the early 1900s served as a turning point in alcohol consumption by blacks. Racial discrimination did and continues to play a critical role in the etiology of drinking among blacks. Needless to say, it is not the only culprit in this endemic problem. Prevalent in the literature is the need to examine cultural, social, and psychological factors as they influence the drinking behaviors of blacks and still recognize the diversity of the black experience.

REFERENCES

Ballard, A.B. (1984). *One more day's journey.* New York: McGraw-Hill.

Barclay, A., & Cusumano, D.R. (1967). Father absence, cross sex identity, and field-dependent behavior in male adolescents. *Child Development, 38,* 343–350.

Biller, H.B. (1969). Father absence, maternal encouragement, and sex role development in kindergarten boys. *Child Development, 40,* 539–546.

Brim, O.G., Jr. (1977). Theories of the male midlife crisis. In N. Schlossberg & A.D. Entine (Eds.), *Counseling Adults.* Monterey, Cal.: Brooks/Cole.

Brisbane, F.L. (1987). Divided feeling of black alcoholic daughters. *Alcohol Health and Research World,* 48–50.

Brisbane, F.L., & Womble, M. (1986). Afterthoughts and recommendations. *Alcoholism Treatment Quarterly, 2*(3–4), 249–270.

Caetano, R. (1984). Ethnicity and drinking in Northern California: A comparison among whites, blacks and Hispanics. *Alcohol and Alcoholism, 19,* 31–44.

Carroll, J.F.; Klein, M.I.; & Santo, Y. (1978). Comparison of the similarities and differences in the self-concepts of male alcoholics and addicts. *Journal of Consulting Clinical Psychology, 46,* 575–576.

Christmas, J.J. (1978). Alcoholism services for minorities: Training issues and concerns. *Alcohol Health and Research World, 2*(3), 20–27.

Covell, K., & Turnbull, W. (1982). The long term effects of father absence in childhood on male university students' sex-role identity and personal adjustment. *Journal of Genetic Psychology, 141,* 271–276.

Davis, F. (1974). Alcoholism among American blacks. *Addiction, 3,* 8–16.

Dembo, R., Burgos, W., Babst, D.U., Schmeidler, J., & Le Grand, L.E. (1978). Neighborhood relationships and drug involvement among inner city junior high school youths: Implications for drug education and prevention programming. *Journal of Drug Education, 8,* 231–252.

Erikson, E.H. (1982). *The life cycle completed.* New York: Norton.

Fernandez-Pol, B., Bluestone, H., Missouri, C., Morales, G., & Mizurichi, M. (1986). Drinking patterns of inner-city Black Americans and Puerto Ricans. *Journal of Studies on Alcohol, 47,* 156–160.

Franklin, J.H. (1980). *From slavery to freedom: A history of Negro Americans.* New York: Knopf.

Gary, R. (1985). Treatment needs of black alcoholic women. *Alcoholism Treatment Quarterly, 2*(3–4), 97–113.

Golembiewski, R.T. (1978). Mid-life transition and mid-career crisis: A special case for individual development. *Public Administration Review, 14,* 215–222.

Gore, T., & Maultsby, M. (1986). The rational alcoholic relapse-prevention treatment method: A new self-help alcoholism treatment method. *Alcoholism Treatment Quarterly, 2*(3–4), 243–247.

Gould, R.L. (1978). *Transformations: Growth and change in adult life.* New York: Simon & Schuster.

Harper, F.D. (1984). Group strategies with black alcoholics. *Journal for Specialists in Groupwork, 9*(1), 38–43.

Harper, F., & Dawkins, M. (1976). Alcohol and blacks: Survey of periodical literature. *British Journal of Addiction, 71,* 327–334.

Herd, D. (1985). Migration, cultural transformation and rise of black liver cirrhosis mortality. *British Journal of Addiction, 80*(4), 397–411.

Hetherington, E.M. (1966). Effects of paternal absence on sex-typed behaviors in Negro and white preadolescent males. *Journal of Personality and Social Psychology, 4,* 87–91.

Hudson, H.L. (1986). How and why Alcoholics Anonymous works for blacks. *Alcoholism Treatment Quarterly, 2*(314), 11–29.

King, L.M. (1982). Alcoholism: Studies regarding Black Americans: 1977–1980. *Alcohol and Health Monograph No. 4 : Special Population Issues,* 385–407.

Knox, D. H. (1986). Spirituality: A tool in the assessment and treatment of black alcoholics and their families. *Alcoholism Treatment Quarterly, 2*(3–4), 31–43.

Levinson, D.J. (1978). *The seasons of a man's life.* New York: Knopf.

Moss, F., Edwards, D.E., Edwards, M.E., Janzen, F. V., & Howell, G. (1985). Sobriety and American Indian problem drinkers. *Alcoholism Treatment Quarterly, 2*(2), 81–96.

Neff, J.A. (1986). Alcohol consumption and psychological distress among U.S. Anglos, Hispanics and blacks. *Alcohol & Alcoholism, 21*(1), 111–119.

Parker, D.A., & Harman, M.S. (1978). The distribution of consumption model of prevention of alcoholic problems: A critical assessment. *Journal of the Study of Alcohol, 39,* 377–399.

Rogan, A. (1986). Recovery from alcoholism: Issues for black and Native American alcoholics. *Alcohol Health and Research World, 11*(1), 42–44.

Ronan, L. (1987). Alcohol-related health risks among Black Americans. *Alcohol Health and Research World,* 36–39.

Rosenberg, S.D. & Farrell, M.P. (1976). Identity and crisis in middle-aged men. *International Journal of Aging and Human Development, 1,* 153.

Schlenger, Hubbard, Rachal, Bray, Scaddock, Cavanaugh, & Kinzburg. (1986). Patterns of alcohol and drug abuse in drug treatment clients from different ethnic backgrounds. *Annals of New York Academy of Science, 472,* pp. 60–74.

Sheehy, G. (1976). *Passages: Predictable crises of adult life.* New York: Bantam.

Staff. (1988, March 7). Black and white in America. *Newsweek,* pp. 18–23.

Statistical Abstracts of the United States (1987). U.S. Department of Congress, Bureau of the Census.

Stalls, F.A. (1978). Racial differences in alcohol metabolism. *Alcohol Clinical and Experimental Research, 2*(1), 19.

Steer, R.A., & Shaw, B.F. (1977). Structure of depression in black alcoholics. *Psychological Reports, 41,* 1235–1241.

Sterne, M., & Pittman, D.J. (1972), *Drinking practices in the ghetto.* St. Louis: Washington University, Social Science Institute.

Sue, D.W. (1981). *Counseling the Culturally Different, Theory and Practice.* New York: John Wiley & Sons.

Westermeyer, J. (1984). The role of ethnicity in substance abuse. In B. Stimmel, (Ed.), *Cultural and sociological aspects of alcoholism and substance abuse.* (pp. 9–18). New York: Haworth Press.

Williams, M. (1982). Blacks and alcoholism: Issues in the 1980s. *Alcohol Health and Research World, 6*(4), 31–40.

Williams, M. (1986). Alcohol and ethnic minorities: Native Americans—an update. *Alcohol Health and Research World, 11*(2) 5–6.

Chapter 7

Substance Abuse and the Physician

Nancy P. Moore and Gary R. Lewis

INTRODUCTION

The 1980s have seen an enormous growth in substance abuse awareness, education, treatment, and research. The *Diagnostic and Statistical Manual of Mental Disorders* (DSM III) recognizes that everything from tobacco and caffeine to heroin can be addictive and that the addiction can be treated. Substance abuse was once viewed only in terms of "street junkies" and skid row bums, then in terms of teenage experimentation as a developmental stage, and then in terms of the professional community. One segment of society in which substance abuse is still somewhat in the closet, at least as far as the general population is concerned, is the substance abusing health care worker.

There has always been a certain mystique surrounding those people that society thinks of as "professionals." Physicians are endowed with almost omnipotent and godlike powers because the knowledge and expertise they have is to a great extent outside the knowledge and experience of the general public. Physicians and other medical and mental health personnel are thus placed upon the proverbial pedestal by the consumers of their services. This has created a rather closed fraternity among these professionals. When they become stressed, ill, or otherwise impaired, their fellow professionals form a tight circle around them to protect them and keep their impairment from the general public. This places the impaired professional in a difficult position when it comes to seeking the help they may need.

It is estimated that 5% to 6% of the professional medical population of the United states is impaired, either by drug or alcohol use or abuse and/or mental illness (Arboleda-Florenz, 1984). Rick, Ferris, and Pitts, in a study conducted between 1967 and 1972, concluded that the suicide rate for psychiatrists is twice the rate of other physicians in different specialties (cited in Arboleda-Forenz, 1984). Blachly found that 100 to 300 physicians commit suicide each year (cited in Arboleda-Florenz, 1984). Smith and Strindler estimated that between 1% and 1.5% of physicians suffer from psychiatric disorders (cited in Arboleda-Florenz, 1984). Blachly found that suicide is the second most common cause of death among medical students and that this trend continues into middle age (cited in Arboleda-Florenz, 1984).

When confronted by statistics of this nature, it becomes very clear that there are definite needs that have to be addressed concerning the physical and emotional needs of this particular segment of the population. Not only is their personal health and happiness at stake, but there are consequences of the behavior of impaired physicians:

- lawsuits brought by patients
- liability of the impaired doctor's partners in practice
- liability of a referring physician, if the doctor who got the referral is impaired
- liability incurred by the hospital in which the impaired physician has practicing privileges
- liability of medical staff committees for granting staff and practice privileges to impaired physicians.

PREDISPOSING FACTORS AND PERSONALITY VARIABLES

Studies of predisposing factors and personality characteristics associated with substance-abusing physicians have brought to light several issues regarding why a physician, trained to alleviate pain and suffering, would become trapped in an addiction. This is interesting research because the first and easiest answer to this question is that physicians have easy access to drugs. But this was not found to be a paramount reason physicians indulged in controlled substances or alcohol. It became necessary to look at personality, life history, life style, and other physician vulnerabilities.

A joint study by the American Medical Association (AMA) and the American Psychiatric Association (APA) on physician suicides found that these physicians were more depressed, more worried about finances, and had suffered recent personal or professional losses. These physicians were found to be less satisfied, overall, with their careers and felt and acted less responsibly toward their patients and colleagues (Arboleda-Florenz, 1984).

Another study concluded: "Doctors who abuse alcohol or drugs show a tendency toward an 'isolated personality pattern,' described as high on denial, low in impulse expression, and very high on social introversion" (Arboleda-Florenz, 1984, p. 56). These vulnerabilities were associated with the demanding training that physicians go through that contribute to or exacerbate these already present personality traits. The physicians identified themselves with the "overworked" senior physicians who trained them and in fact modeled themselves along these behavioral patterns because being "stressed out" and overworked were seen to be side effects of being a physician. In effect, a "that's the way the profession is" attitude was passed on in training. Physicians were found to have few outside interests. They were interested only in their jobs and were obsessively oriented to success, but only in the job arena.

A study by Wallot (1984) examined the similarities between physician addicts and the so-called street addict. He found that physician addicts were generally older, had more marital and occupational stability, and generally had a much better prognosis that did the street addict. Additionally, it was found that physician addicts (be it drugs or alcohol) are labeled differently than street addicts. Physicians are often viewed as "therapeutic addicts," or people who become addicts through the therapeutic prescription use of various substances, mostly opiates, because of reality-based illness, pain, or surgery. Thus, physicians are felt to have the "disease" of addiction, a sort of occupational hazard, as opposed to the street addict, who is labeled a criminal.

Valliant, Sobowale, and McArthur (1971) conducted a study of the childhoods of 47 physicians, comparing their childhoods with the childhoods of 79 socioeconomically matched subjects who were in occupations other than medicine. The study was carried out over 30 years, beginning when the subjects were sophomores in college. Three factors that suggested psychological vulnerability were seen in the physician group: (1) bad marriages, (2) drug abuse, and (3) a tendency to use psychotherapy. From this same study the following emerged:

- There was no difference in intellectual aptitutde between the groups studied.
- Half of the physicians reported bad marriages.
- One third of the physicians reported drug/and or alcohol abuse.
- One third of the physicians had sought psychotherapy.

When these factors (which were often considered to be occupational hazards) were examined in the socioeconomically matched group it was found that only a minority of the physicians studied actually experienced these difficulties, as did a minority of the matched group. However, those that did experience these problems were found to have vulnerabilities that contributed to these problems that predated their entrance into medical school.

The following emerged in the physician group:

- There was no difference in intellectual aptitude between the two groups studied.
- Half of the physicians reported bad marriages (20% were divorced as opposed to 14% of the matched group).
- One third of the physicians reported drug and/or alcohol abuse.
- One third of the physicians had sought psychotherapy.

It is difficult for the physicians who are dependent on a mind- and mood-altering chemical to acknowledge their illness or seek treatment without encouragement. Usually, it is not until progressive behavioral deterioration becomes obvious to family or colleagues that the individual seeks assistance. Even then, through misjudgements related either to the toxic effect caused by any of various chemicals or to addiction to the chemicals, many physicians continue their substance abuse. Such physicians often will either leave or curtail practice rather than seek help.

Although continued recovery after treatment for chemical dependency is not certain, physicians who follow a structured rehabilitation program with continued participation in a self-help recovery group such as Alcoholics Anonymous (AA) or Narcotics Anonymous (NA) have a 77% to 100% chance for recovery (Gallegos & Norton, 1984). Thus, the rate of recovery for physicians exceeds that for treated populations in general.

There are several other factors that may interfere with a physician seeking treatment for substance abuse. Dependent physicians deny that their illness has reduced their ability to practice medicine or interact socially. Part of the psychological dysfunction from the illness is the increasing inability of the physician to conceptualize and think in an abstract manner. This in turn leads to rumination and self-recrimination as the illness progresses, making it difficult for the physician to seek treatment for the dependency. Over time, the responsibility of obtaining treatment for an impaired physician often shifts to family, friends, and concerned colleagues.

Confronting an ill colleague, spouse, or parent is a difficult task. However, a physician's hope for rehabilitation usually lies with someone in the family or a close colleague. The success of an initial confrontation depends on the respect and concern for the impaired individual shown during the confrontation. By moralizing or being judgmental, one lessens the chances for a successful outcome for an intervention. Although the initial confrontation by someone close to a chemically dependent physician often fails to result in immediate treatment, it may eventually lead to the beginning of recovery. It is wise to follow an initial confrontaton that has failed with a more structured and formal confrontation conducted by an individual qualified by training and experience. The second intervention will also most likely lead to treatment and recovery.

The following is a list of characteristics that may indicate impairment in a physician:

- disruption in family life
- the development of legal problems
- neglect of practice routines
- social isolation
- driving while intoxicated
- intoxication while attending social events
- noticeable odor of alcohol at the work site
- making hospital rounds at unusual times
- canceling office appointments without obvious conflict of time
- giving unusual or dangerous orders over the telephone, particularly from home during the evening or night
- disruptive behavior at meetings or failure to complete committee assignments
- forgetting social appointments
- holding telephone conversations with slurred speech or tangential conversation
- dressing sloppily or in a noticeably different style.

Referral to a treatment program is often delayed by those closest to the physician because of a concern that the physician may lose his or her anonymity. Unless a physician is in imminent danger to patients, or has already injured a patient, treatment programs are usually careful about protecting the physician's anonymity from any person or agency outside the treatment program, unless he or she personally requests the release of that information.

If left untreated, chemical dependence is a progressive and destructive illness. Early intervention prevents the accumulation of increasingly severe and potentially irreversible consequences for the physician's physical health, mental health, and social welfare. The most caring and constructive act for any true "friend" is an early referral to a treatment program. An almost universal reaction of physicians in recovery from chemical dependence is gratitude for intervention, regardless of how much they resisted diagnosis and treatment during their illness.

There are other special problems that have a bearing not only on why a medical professional might abuse drugs and/or alcohol but also on problems unique to treating the substance-abusing medical professional:

- *Professional image:* It is difficult for a physician to admit and accept that he or she is in need of help.
- *Finding help:* Medical personnel often find it difficult to decide where to turn for help because of concern about othe professionals finding out about their drug use or abuse.
- *Patient role:* It is very difficult for this group of professionals to accept the role of being a patient. It is often difficult for physicians treating impaired physicians to treat a member of their own profession.
- *Finances:* There is a risk of tremendous loss of income due to the impairment. However, it is often the threat of the loss of financial stability that encourages an impaired physician to enter a treatment program.

Treatment is much more acceptable now that all states have an impaired physician statute that is applied to the drug- or alcohol-dependent physician. The AMA, APA, and the American Psychological Association all provide ethical guidelines for the identification and treatment of members who are impaired due to drugs and alcohol.

The Council on Mental Health (1973) recommended that professionals first approach each other when there is suspected substance abuse. The ethics committee of the AMA, APA, and American Psychological Association also recommend this as a first step. If this is undertaken and the physician continues to refuse to seek treatment, then the appropriate licensing boards and committees must be notified. As has been stated, the spouses and families are often the best first step in any intervention process. The seriousness of the problem and the need to report these impaired individuals are not only for the protection of the public but for the physician. The 1973 statistics on physician suicides showed that approximately 100 physicians a year commit suicide (Concil on Mental Health, 1973).

Many of the same psychological mechanisms and underlying addiction that are found in the overall population are also found in addicted physicians. There are, however, a few additional factors of which the clinician needs to be aware: (1) drugs are much more available and untraceable for the physician; (2) it appears that among physicians, the defensive structure of denial is much more common and more difficult to overcome; (3) rationalization and justification of using the drugs or alcohol to allow them to continue functioning as professionals. This is generally said to be due to fatigue, chronic pain, or a variety of other somatic concerns. In actuality, this is a method they employ to prevent them from having to admit to themselves that they are addicted; (4) in this same manner, substance abuse often begins as an attempt at self-medication rather than soliciting care from another physician; (5) there is a pervasive lack of knowledge among doctors about the preaddictive psychological states (i.e., depression is often used as a reason for the first usage of a drug); (6) there appears to be a significantly higher incidence of dual diagnosis of substance abuse and personality disorder than for the general population (Little, 1971).

REFERENCES

Arboleda-Florenz, J. (1984). The mentally ill physician. *Canadian Journal of Psychiatry, 29,* 55–59.

Blachly, P.H., Disher, W., & Roduner, G. (1968). Suicide by physicians. *Bulletin of Suicidology, 4*(1), 1–18.

Council on Mental Health. (1973). The sick physician: Impairment by psychiatric disorders, including alcoholism and drug dependence. *Journal of the American Medical Association, 232,* 684–687.

Gallegos, K., & Norton, M. (1984). Characterization of Georgia's impaired physicians' treatment population: Data and statistics. *Journal of the Medical Association of Georgia, 73,* 755–758.

Harris, B.A. (1986). Not enough is enough. *New York State Journal of Medicine,* 2–3.

Herrington, R.D., Benzer, D.C., Jacobson, G.R., & Hawkins, M.K. (1982). Treating substance abuse disorders among physicians. *Journal of the American Medical Association, 247,* 2253–2257.

Laliotis, D.A., & Grayson, J.H. (1985). Psychologist heal thyself. *American Psychologist,* 84–98.

Little, R.B. (1971). Hazards of drug dependency among physicians. *Journal of the American Medical Association, 218,* 1533–1535.

Morse, R., Martin, M.A., Swenson, W.M., & Niven, R.G. (1984). Prognosis of physicians treated for alcoholism and drug dependence. *Journal of the American Medical Association, 251,* 743–746.

Silby, H.D., Kruzich, D.J., & Hawkins, M.R. (1984). Fentanyl citrate abuse among health care professionals. *Military Medicine, 149,* 247–248.

Stimson, C.V., Oppenheimer, E., & Stimson, C.A. (1984). Drug abuse in the medical profession: Addict doctors and the home office. *British Journal of Addiction, 79,* 395–402.

Valliant, G.E., Sobowale, N.C., & McArthur, C. (1972). Some psychologic vulnerabilities of physicians. *New England Journal of Medicine, 287,* 372–375.

Vogtsberger, K.N. (1984). Treatment outcomes of substance-abusing physicians. *American Journal of Drug & Alcohol Abuse, 10*(1), 23–37.

Wallot, H. (1984). Characteristics of physician addicts. *American Journal of Drug & Alcohol Use, 10*(1), 53–62.

Chapter 8

Special Issues of Adult Children of Alcoholics

Yvonne Kress

INTRODUCTION

According to the National Association for Children of Alcoholics (NACoA), about 25 million Americans have at least one alcoholic parent, and 52% of those alcoholic parents come from alcoholic families themselves (Fox, 1968). Therefore, the children of alcoholics (CoA) are considered to be at high risk for developing alcoholism and related problems. In 1945, the first paper on the subject of CoAs was published (Roe & Burks). In recent years, there has been a substantial amount of research that has examined and identified the special problems of CoAs.

Contrary to the general perception of the public, only 3%-5% of all alcoholics fall into the category of "skid row bums" (see Chapter 14). Adult children of alcoholics (ACA) come from all areas of the population: professionals, housewives, husbands, single people, athletes, politicians, etc. The prevalent view today suggests that ACAs have certain commonalities: family dynamics, personality traits, coping mechanisms, communication styles, and substance abuse patterns. As a result, the number of educational programs, support groups, and books on the subject of CoAs has mushroomed.

In the past, most treatment approaches for alcoholism have focused on the alcoholic person and the drinking behavior itself. Only recently have some treatment programs and therapists included family therapy and therefore shifted the focus of treatment away from the "disease" and the alcoholic onto the underlying dysfunctional dynamics in the family. To identify such dysfunctional dynamics, the roles of each individual in the family, their communication styles, and the adaptive functions of the symptoms need to be examined.

Some of the most widely used treatment approaches for alcoholics are the self-help groups of Alcoholics Anonymous (AA) and its charter groups for family members, Al-Anon and Al-Ateen. AA is based on the disease model as described by Jellinek (1960) and uses 12 steps to help members attain and maintain abstinence from drinking (see Appendix A). Since AA members believe that alcoholics suffer from an incurable disease, the goal must be total abstinence in order to control this illness. The pursuit of this goal may occur without any changes in the underlying dynamics of the individual and her or his family, which may result in the phenomenon of the "dry drunk." As research has shown, the cessation of drinking does not appear to reduce familial problems nor improve the nondrinking alcoholic's behavior (Booz-Allen and Hamilton, cited in Lawson, Peterson, and Lawson, 1983).

When dealing with an individual with a problematic drinking pattern, it is vital to explore her or his drinking history and the dynamics of the family concerning the alcoholism. The psychological problems of ACAs stem largely from the chaotic, confusing, and unpredictable family environment, which accompanies the alcoholic behavior of the parent(s). Whether the causes of alcoholism are hereditary or environmental remains an unanswered question since research has yielded contradictory results.

For the purposes of this chapter, Lawson's model of high-risk determination is used (Lawson et al., 1983). These authors considered three major factors to be the causal or contributing factors in the development of alcoholism: (a) physiological, (b) sociological, and (c) psychological factors. Consequently, this model gives justice to the nature versus nurture argument by including both factors and therefore allowing the clinician to determine an individual's risk for developing a dysfunctional drinking pattern (for details on this model, see Chapter 1). Despite contradictory results, it appears that genetics play at least a contributing role in the development of alcoholism, which puts ACAs into a high-risk group. In addition, growing up in an alcoholic family exposes CoAs to models of inappropriate drinking behavior and all related problems, therefore placing them both sociologically and psychologically into a high-risk group.

PHYSIOLOGICAL FACTORS IN THE DEVELOPMENT OF ALCOHOLISM

At the turn of the century, researchers had already become fascinated with the nature/nurture question pertaining to the development of alcoholism, and others have picked it up again in recent years. All researchers and clinicians agree that alcoholism runs in families. Goodwin (1971), after an extensive review of available research data, concluded that alcoholism, "irrespective of country of origin," occurs at much higher rates among relatives of alcoholics than in the general population (p. 545).

With regard to the issue of a genetic predisposition for alcoholism, twin and animal studies appear to yield the most reliable results. Assuming that monozygotic twins have an identical genetic makeup, it could be hypothesized that the concordance rate for alcoholism should be higher for them than for dyzygotic twins. Kaij (cited in Goodman, 1971) found a 58% concordance rate of alcoholism for monozygotic twins vs. a 28% rate for dyzygotic twins. These results included drinking patterns and the frequency and amount of drinking. In addition, he found that alcoholic deterioration occurred independently of alcohol consumption and assumed that a genetic contributor was responsible for that outcome. In contrast, Partanen, Bruun, and Karkkanen (cited in Goodwin, 1971) found no statistically significant within-pair variance between monozygotic and dyzygotic twins with reference to their alcohol abuse. Consequences of drinking behavior also did not differ between the two types of twins.

Roe and Burks' (1945) findings corroborated those of Partanen et al. The researchers compared adopted children of alcoholic biological parents with adopted children of nonalcoholic biological parents and found no significant differences in their consumption of alcohol. These results may lead to the conclusion that the fostering away from the biological alcoholic parent influences the children's development positively so that alcoholism and related problems were comparable to those of the controls.

Schuckit (1982) conducted a study with young men with alcoholic close relatives and found a higher alcoholism rate than for controls. An earlier study by Schuckit (1972) supported the genetic view. Children with at least one alcoholic biological parent who were raised in nonalcoholic families with half-siblings were compared with children without alcoholic biological parents who were raised in alcoholic families with half-siblings. The results revealed that the half-siblings of the alcoholic biological parents had a higher alcoholism rate than the half-siblings of the children of nonalcoholic, biological parents.

However, Lawson et al. (1983) suggested critical evaluation of data concerning careful differentiation of sociocultural influences and hereditary predisposition.

Additional research has been done in an attempt to prove a genetic basis for the development of alcoholism. In 1982, Gabrielli et al. tested the brain activity of children with alcoholic fathers using an electroencephalogram (EEG) and found it to be excessive. Furthermore, the boys of alcoholic fathers showed a specific EEG pattern, while the girls did not, thus suggesting that boys are genetically at a higher risk for developing alcoholism than are girls. As Kiloh (1961) suggested, slow brain activity is related to relaxation and drowsiness, while high activity seems to be related to tension and anxiety. Consequently, it can be postulated that alcoholics attempt to slow down their brain activity, i.e., achieve relaxation, by drinking (Propping, 1977).

Animal research offers another valuable source of data for genetic research. In an attempt to determine the genetic factors of alcoholism in rats, Rodgers and McClearn (cited in Goodwin, 1971) conducted self-selection experiments by crossbreeding rats that had different levels of alcohol consumption. The level of alcohol consumption in the progenies was found to average exactly that of the parental consumption. These findings suggested that the preference for alcohol over water is hereditary in rats and may allow an inference about humans.

Yet another kind of research also seems to suggest a genetic factor in alcoholism. In genetic marker studies, Cruz-Coke and Varela (cited in Goodwin, 1971) found a correlation between colorblindness and alcoholism. Specifically, male nonalcoholic relatives of alcoholics showed little difference in blue-yellow discrimination ability, while the female nonalcoholic relatives of alcoholics exhibited an effect on blue-yellow discrimination ability, and the controls did not.

The contradictory results provided by research on the biochemistry of the brain (Davis & Walsh, 1970), nutrition, and endocrine dysfunctions (Williams, 1959) confuse the inquiring clinician even further. Due to the difficulty in controlling variables and determining cause and effect, it has been impossible to satisfactorily answer the key question: Is it the genetic makeup of the alcoholic individual or the dysfunction in the family system that causes alcoholism and disruption in a family?

SOCIOLOGICAL FACTORS IN THE DEVELOPMENT OF ALCOHOLISM

Since genetic factors cannot be changed, it seems more beneficial to concentrate on those areas in the etiology of alcoholism that can be influenced: sociological and psychological factors. Alcoholic family systems represent the social environment for their children by modeling specific drinking behaviors and rules of the external world. Vaillant and Milovski (1982) postulated that the major contributors to alcoholism may be ethnicity and the number of alcoholic relatives. Other studies included the roles of sex, socioeconomic class, family of origin, religion, and age as the contributors or causes of alcoholism.

The strong impact of social attitudes on drinking behavior was experienced personally by this author when growing up in Germany. Although the Germans are known for a high consumption level of alcohol, drunken behavior is socially unacceptable and occurs much less than in the United States. Appropriate drinking behavior includes the control of rage and acting-out behavior. Lawson et al. (1983) offered a similar view. Mc-

Andrew and Edgerton (cited in Lawson et al., 1983) reviewed data from different sources and concluded that after the ingestion of alcohol, behavior does not necessarily change or involve a loss of control, as evidenced in other cultures. In addition, these authors interpreted drunken behavior in the United States as an excuse to act out angry impulses since the expression of negative feelings is not acceptable otherwise. Emoting is a more accepted form of relating between people in European cultures, and no excuse to do so is needed. This analysis, of course, contradicts the view that alcohol affects brain functions directly, thus causing the behavioral changes.

In reviewing many other sociocultural theories, multiple factors can be extrapolated as contributing to or causing alcoholism. Calahan (1970) maintained that a person's alcohol drinking is determined by her or his external support for heavy drinking, the type of social control, the attitude toward drinking, and levels of adjustment, conformity, and impulsivity. In the American culture, there are two extreme attitudes toward drinking alcohol: one rejects alcohol altogether, and the other condones indulgence or abuse. Neither extreme provides an appropriate drinking model for children. As a result, children may engage in rebellious drinking behavior in response to a teetotalling parent or identify with and copy the alcoholically drinking parent (Lawson et al., 1983). Bales (1946) postulated another sociocultural view, perceiving alcohol consumption as a means of tension release in a society that produces tensions and anxieties without providing the necessary outlets.

The absence of specific sociocultural factors in alcoholic or ACA families renders their offspring vulnerable to the development of alcoholism. O'Connor (1975) listed conditions that need to be present in a family in order to prevent the CoA from becoming sociologically at high risk for the development of alcoholism:

- Children are exposed early in life to alcohol in the family or during religious rituals.
- Parents drink moderately.
- Most beverages in the household are either nonalcoholic or predominantly nonalcoholic.
- Beverages are considered food and are consumed with meals.
- Drinking has no moral meaning.
- Drinking is not considered masculine or adult behavior.
- Abstinence is socially acceptable and drunkenness is not.
- All family members have the same standards for drinking behavior.

It is apparent that most alcoholic families lack some or all of these sociological characteristics.

PSYCHOLOGICAL FACTORS IN THE DEVELOPMENT OF ALCOHOLISM

Since the beginning of research in the field of alcoholism, clinicians and researchers have debated the question of the existence of the typical "alcoholic" or "prealcoholic" personality. Barnes (1979) postulated that the alcoholic functions as a stimulus augmentor. Due to the alcoholic's lack of ego strength, she or he cannot cope effectively with the overwhelming impact of internal and external stimuli and consequently tries to reduce the pressure by drinking. In his study of students who later became alcoholics, Barnes found a greater tendency to be nonconforming, impulsive, and outgoing than in controls who did not develop alcoholism. In addition, the Minnesota Multiphasic Personality Inventory (MMPI) was administered to a group of students before and after the development of alcoholic drinking behavior and to nondrinking controls. The results showed a persistently higher elevation on the psychopathic deviate (Pd) scale in the first group before and after the development of drinking behavior than in the control group. An elevation of the Pd scale may represent either aggressive or antisocial traits or intrafamilial conflict in an individual, therefore suggesting that certain underlying personality traits appear to be contributors to the development of alcoholism.

However, a study by Bohman (1978) did not yield a correlation between antisocial behavior and the development of alcoholism, as corroborated by Waters and Offord's study (cited in Adler & Raphael, 1983). Their results showed a correlation between the child's antisocial behavior and that of his or her parents and no correlation between alcoholic drinking and antisocial behavior. Such results suggest environmental influences rather then innate personality traits as the causes of or contributors to the development of alcoholism.

In assessing the psychological factors underlying the ACA's development of substance abuse and related problems, one must explore the family dynamics that produce such high-risk psychological factors. Lawson et al. (1983) maintained that the ability to solve problems and to identify with a role model are crucial factors in a child's development. They presented different parental types that affected that ability in children negatively, one of which is an alcoholic parent. Invariably, the alcoholic teaches drinking behavior as an acceptable coping mechanism. Although the child may have decided at some point never to be like the alcoholic parent, chances are that she or he will cope by drinking later in life when overwhelmed by stress. In addition, the CoA may feel guilty for the marital discord and for the drinking behavior itself. Family therapy addresses those issues, whereas individual treatment for the alcoholic tends to increase the child's feelings of guilt because of her or his feelings of anger toward a person who is "sick" (disease model). Adding to the child's dilemma is the drinking parent's emotional unavailability and unpredictability. When the child tries to elicit support from the nondrinking spouse, she or he is usually disappointed, since the co-dependent may be too angry or overinvolved with the drinking spouse.

Another parental type described by Lawson et al. (1983) that contributes to the development of alcoholism in children is the teetotaller. The teetotaller parent tends to teach rigid moralistic values and divides the world into good and bad, shoulds and shouldn'ts. This "black and white" thinking can be observed in most alcoholics or ACAs. In response to the teetotalling parent, the child can use drinking as a vehicle for rebellion against that parent. If there is a teetotalling and an alcoholic parent, the child may be very confused as to which set of values to follow and may either rebel and/or identify with one of the parents. The marital discord and underlying hostility in such families can be very disturbing.

Since adult problems can be traced to unresolved childhood problems, it is essential to explore the family dynamics of the family of origin in the ACA. Booz-Allen and Hamilton (cited in Lawson et al., 1983) stated that if children do not resolve their childhood issues concerning their parents' drinking and related problems, they will have to deal with them for the rest of their lives. Violence, sexual and emotional abuse, and inconsistent parenting are only a few of the traumatic occurrences CoAs must cope with. These symptoms, of course, also occur in nonalcoholic families.

Woititz (1983) presented a wealth of issues that CoAs must deal with and described how the upbringing in an alcoholic family affects all areas of the ACA's life. The roles the children played in the family system of origin largely determine the roles they play in their own lives as adults. The four different roles described by Woititz are (a) the overresponsible, (b) the scapegoat, (c) the clown or comedian, and (d) the withdrawn child. These role descriptions closely resemble those developed by Satir (1972). Wegscheider (1981) also identified similar roles played by CoAs:

- the dependent child, who appears charming and secure
- the chief enabler, whose successes provide the family self-esteem
- the scapegoat, who protects the family by allowing the parents to project their underlying negative feelings onto herself or himself
- the lost child, who withdraws and stays independent to avoid being a problem for the family
- the mascot (usually the youngest in the family), who distracts the family from their pain by being the clown.

Those role behaviors represent the CoA's defensive ways of coping with her or his underlying feelings of guilt, anger, loneliness, and sense of inadequacy. However, these role behaviors are not specific phenomena in alcoholic families but apply to most families, as described by numerous family therapists and theorists.

In order to fulfill a certain role, the child has to hide his or her own feelings and pretend to think, feel, and behave in a way consistent with that role. The price paid for that homeostatic function is apparent in the child's low self-esteem, caused by the denial of the real self. Although CoAs continue their role behavior throughout their adult lives, they may change the specific role that was assigned to them in childhood in accordance with the homeostatic needs of their present families. From a family systems point of view, drinking behavior represents an adaptive mechanism to maintain homeostasis in the family (Steinglass, Davis, & Berenson, cited in Jacob et al., 1978). The marital dyad may be stabilized by the controlled release of aggression that is possible because of the drinking and the role reversal that often occurs between the alcoholically drinking spouse and the child. In adult life, the ACA may take the role of the child, the alcoholic, or the co-dependent spouse, regardless of his or her role in the family of origin.

The ACA's ability to change her or his projected image in response to the family or relationship at hand is only possible with the existence of a denied, vulnerable, insecure self. Seabaugh (1984) postulated that the vulnerable self of the ACA is a result of the developmental failures in childhood that are typical of alcoholic families. Therefore, frustrations are dealt with as narcissistic injuries and further increase low self-esteem. Since CoAs were unable to get their needs met in a chaotic family of origin, they are is unable to recognize or meet such needs as an adult in themselves or others. Thus, their main issues in adult life are feelings of anger, need for control, and fear of abandonment. However, ACAs do not usually recognize these issues because of a lifelong practice of denial of feelings and thus are unable to ask for what they want (Cork, 1969). Since the expression of especially negative feelings were punished in the family of origin (Lawson et al., 1983), ACAs learned to protect themselves from or even alleviate psychological pain through repression (Gravitz & Bowden, 1984).

Unfortunately, due to denial, projection, rationalization, and other immature defense mechanisms, ACAs are able to cope with a "crazy-making" environment without recognizing the crazy-making nature of such an environment (Vaillant, 1984). In addition, they cannot recognize the causes of their often inappropriate, rigid coping mechanisms or their resulting anger and consequently tend to internalize such anger and become depressed and highly self-critical (Ingram, 1984). Ingram's study also revealed that ACAs tend to be preoccupied with reminiscing about the past and dreaming about the future rather than dealing with the present, which results in a lack of self-actualizing behavior. Tests of inner- and other-directedness showed a higher other-directedness in ACAs compared with controls. Obviously an adaptive way of being when reading and interpreting cues given by others is necessary to be prepared for the unpredictable situations in the alcoholic family of origin. The interpersonal relationships of the ACA are clearly colored by that tendency and seem to be very unstable and problematic, as evidenced in a higher divorce rate than in the general population. Goodwin, Schulsinger, Hermansen, Guze, & Winokur (1973) found no apparent correlation between the actual drinking behavior and the interrelational problems. Rather, the problems were caused by the dysfunctional underlying dynamics. As Woititz (1983) explained, ACAs want very much to have healthy, intimate relationships but have no frame of reference as to what healthy relationships look or feel like. In other words, they "don't know what normal is" (p. 26).

In the family of origin, the child learned the "push-pull" style of relationship, which entails the desire to be close and intimate at one point and rejecting at another. When the parent was drunk, the child was rejected, and when the parent was sober, she or he was pulled close, therefore creating either an enmeshed or a disengaged family system. As a result, the ACA's fear of abandonment is immense and is often coped with by counterdependent behavior and emotional distance.

Counterdependent behavior refers to that behavior that helps defend against one's own dependency needs. The defensively uttered words "I don't need anybody" may be evidence for such needs. The ACA's dependence on others for the provision and maintenance of self-esteem has been described by numerous researchers. Destructive and rigid family rules can be powerful contributors to low self-esteem; they suppress the development of the child's real self. Three such rules have been described by Black (1982): (a) don't talk, (b) don't trust, and (c) don't feel. Having learned these rules and abiding by them leave the ACA unprepared to relate intimately or to communicate truthfully with others. They often do not feel that anyone could ever meet their needs for love and support. Subsequently, they may not be able to recognize or accept loving care when they receive it (Leonard, 1982). In their attempt to elicit a loving response from others, ACAs often become very nurturing and pleasing themselves. Giving what they need provides some nurturance in their lives and fulfills the need for feeling needed. This is reflected in the ACA's career choices that lean toward helping professions, such as nursing, psychotherapy, physiotherapy, and social work.

Due to painful experiences with close relationships and faulty learning in their family of origin, ACAs are often unable to extend love and support to close family members (Rich, 1976). Showing love to a close family member exposes one's own vulnerabilities, which is experienced as a threat to the self and is translated into the loss of control by the ACA. The fear of loss of control creates the need for control and self-protection in all aspects of life, including intimate relationships.

Being prepared, ready, and alert at all times for the unpredictable external world deprives the ACA of spontaneity, the ability to express affect appropriately, and worst of all, the ability to have fun (Cermack, 1984). Woititz (1983) agreed with that assessment and stated that the ACA's tense alertness was learned in childhood to prepare for the alcoholic parent's unpredictable behavior or even abusive rage. Instead of being carefree children, ACAs learned how to control their own feelings and how to at least attempt to control the feelings of others.

The controlling maneuvers of ACAs have been compared with those of the passive-aggressive, dependent, narcissistic, and avoidant personality styles. If the defenses were very rigid and maladaptive, they would resemble those of the personality disorders. Typically, power struggles between family members, specifically spouses, are symptomatic of control issues, which remain even after the cessation of drinking (Gorad, 1971).

It appears that there may be differences in the coping skills and defense mechanisms of male and female ACAs despite similar underlying dynamics, depending on the number and sex of alcoholic parents and birth order. The male ACA seems to employ more narcissistic defenses, while the female ACA, drinking or nondrinking, tends to defend in a more dependent manner. Both seem to use passive-aggressive means of maintaining this "one up" position in relationships. Werner's (1985) research illuminated some of the differences in men and women in reference to their drinking behavior and development of psychological problems. Her study showed that sons of an alcoholic mother appear to develop greater psychological problems than the daughters of alcoholic fathers. Furthermore, sons of alcoholic fathers were at great risk for the development of alcoholism and related problems, while daughters of alcoholic fathers were not. It seems that the lack of adequate mothering from the alcoholic mother traumatizes the child greatly, especially if the father is unable to take over the mother's role, since most fathers are not socialized to nurture. Sons of alcoholic fathers, on the other hand, often did receive adequate mothering while identifying with the father by copying his coping mechanisms, i.e., drinking behavior.

Girls tend to marry alcoholics and become co-dependents, thus explaining the resemblance of their personality styles to those of the dependent or avoidant personalities (disorder). The co-dependent role usually represents an identification with the mother. The tendency to relive the situation of the family of origin over and over, even if that reflects self-defeating behavior, has been referred to as "repetition-compulsion" by Freud (1919).

Whether narcissistic or dependent, most ACAs report a sense of inner emptiness, which is caused by the denial of the real self (Kohut & Wolf, 1978; Woititz, 1983). In order to alleviate that sense of emptiness, ACAs and narcissistic personalities alike tend to abuse substances (Kernberg, 1985). Compounding the inclination toward substance abuse is the parental drinking model.

Because of the similarities between the co-dependent and the dependent personality style, Cermack (1984) proposed the addiction of the co-dependent personality disorder to the *Diagnostic and Statistical Manual of Mental Disorders* (DSM III). The co-dependent differs from the dependent personality in that the co-dependent is preoccupied with maintaining or gaining control; the dependent is more submissive. Taking over more and more of the everyday responsibilities in the family represents such need for control. Ironically, the prize for gaining that kind of control is the maintenance of a destructive family system that often includes abuse. The co-dependent's pattern perpetuates the alcoholic's immaturity and irresponsibility.

If anyone, it is usually the co-dependent who seeks help in order to alleviate pain or depression. According to Greenleaf (1981), depression is one of the major problems in alcoholic families. Having learned in their families of origin that their behavior does not have much impact on outcome, ACAs tend to display "learned helplessness" as a form of depression (Seligman, 1975). However, Katunich (1984) argued that ACAs employ learned helplessness only as a means to receive secondary gains. In her study, learned helplessness ceased when the secondary gains were eliminated.

Depressive moods have often been related to low self-esteem and a history of abuse, which is frequently the case in ACAs. Another contributor to depression in ACAs may be their skewed perception of reality. From the denial of real feelings and behaviors in the family of origin to the projected Pollyanna-like image, ACAs have been primed to distort reality, which is perpetuated by continuous lying and denying (Woititz, 1983). Woititz (1983) and Greenleaf (1981) agreed that ACAs do not know what "real" is and therefore maintain rigid, maladaptive defenses even when they are no longer required or effective. The result of reality misperception and the use of subsequent inappropriate defenses may be major factors in the development of depressive states.

Greenleaf (1981) proposed that ACAs can become as addicted to their depression as to the drinking in order to escape the real world and their own recognition of having to make adaptive changes. The fear of finding out what this mysterious, denied "self" is all about may explain the remaining depression after the ACA's own or spouse's recovery from alcoholism.

All of the seemingly dysfunctional behaviors of the ACA happen in the context of relationships. In examining the ACA's peer relationships as well as familial relationships, it becomes apparent that there is a lack of intimate friendships and support groups. Peer relations appear to be superficial and meaningless due to the ACA's projected image of superconfidence, superresponsibility, and/or delirious happiness that does not match his or her internal state. The denial of the underlying dependence and hunger for and fear of intimacy prevents the ACA from developing close, realistic relationships. In addition, ACAs' difficulties in recognizing their own responsibilities and impact on others cause them either to blame others or themselves indiscriminately, thus contributing to the distance in relationships.

When treating the ACA and the family, it is important to recognize that the Pollyanna-like appearance may represent a defense against underlying depression. Furthermore, ACAs' tendency to take themselves very seriously and personalize everything in their environment needs to be considered by the therapist when dealing with the issue of transference and the projection of blame and anger. In family therapy, it is likely that the relationships that the ACA tries to create closely resemble those of her or his life outside therapy. As a result, there may be a trend in therapy toward an enmeshed system with blurred boundaries or a disengaged system with rigid boundaries, according to the participant's own experiences.

CURRENT TREATMENT APPROACHES

At the time of this writing, Alcoholics Anonymous (AA) is the most widely used treatment approach for alcoholics and their families. Al-Anon, specifically designed for the family members of alcoholics, and Al-Ateen, for the teenagers of alcoholic families, provide a supportive environment for all individuals who are involved with an alcoholic. AA is a self-help group that was founded in 1935 and consists of group members whose common goal is the cessation of drinking.

As described by Lawson et al. (1983), AA is based on four fundamental beliefs:

1. Alcoholism is a progressive disease and is deadly without intervention.
2. The only remedy for alcoholism is abstinence.
3. Once an alcoholic, always an alcoholic: there is no cure.
4. No one can "treat" his or her own alcoholism without outside help.

With the help of AA's 12-step program (see Appendix A), group members are assisted through their recovery. Because of the anonymous nature of AA, reliable research as to the success rate of AA is impossible to obtain. However, researchers and clinicians estimate a 10% recovery rate, which is comparable to that of other treatment approaches. The advantages of AA are multifaceted, as described by Lawson et al. (1983). As discussed before, alcoholics and ACAs usually lack support groups and close friends. AA fills that void by promoting contact between recovering alcoholics and their sponsors. AA also provides the necessary structure for its members by offering frequent meetings. Finally, AA is nondiscriminating on issues such as sex, race, socioeconomic status, and religion. The goal of the AA members is a complete life style change. Clearly, membership in AA can be a useful adjunct to psychotherapy.

Nonetheless, there are some drawbacks to the AA concept. For example, AA's religious orientation may not be acceptable to some ACAs. Most important, however, is that the AA program perceives alcoholism in one way only: as a disease. Research has shown that there are many different types of alcoholism that must be considered in treatment. Calahan (1970) rejected the disease model on the basis of his research and his own experience.

The alcoholic's or ACA's tendency to project responsibility for feelings, thoughts, and behavior onto others or external causes is likely to increase when alcoholism is labeled a disease rather than a behavior. The behavioral consequences of the ingestion of alcohol can be blamed on the disease, therefore increasing the alcoholic's sense of lack of control. Secondary gains may also increase significantly when the alcoholic is labeled as "sick" instead of being held responsible for her or his behavior. Examples are the advertisements for treatment programs that claim: "It's not your fault. You have a disease." It could be postulated that the purpose of such advertising is merely to motivate alcoholics and their families to enter treatment. The disease concept promotes a treatment modality that focuses on the drinking behavior only and disregards the underlying dysfunctional dynamics. Obviously, alcoholism and its related problems are complex issues that extend well beyond a singular disease framework. Treatment programs must be designed to respond to those complexities.

In recent years, after the appearance of publications especially geared to the problem of ACAs and the formation of the NACoA (National Association for Children of Alcoholics), practitioners and treatment programs have been addressing this special population. Support groups structured much like AA are now available for ACAs all over the country. Some treatment approaches have started to include the family in the treatment process, therefore automatically reaching the children at high risk and the ACAs.

Inpatient treatment programs, designed for the detoxification of substance abusers, also offer group experiences to the recovering individuals. Most of the inpatient clinics are located in or somehow affiliated with a hospital and require a 1- to 8-week stay. The underlying medical model coincides with the concept of the disease model, and therefore, the groups provided by such institutions are based on AA. One of the drawbacks of inpatient treatment is the high cost, which prevents families of lower socioeconomic background from participating.

Unfortunately, most of these treatment approaches do not offer adequate aftercare to help the recovering person and his or her family maintain a healthier way of functioning. There is not much reliable data on the recidivism rate; however, it can be assumed to be high without appropriate aftercare or without a change in the underlying family dysfunction. When a recovering alcoholic returns to a family in which the drinking was adaptive, she or he will most likely resume drinking in a short time.

Individual therapy offers a variety of approaches. They include the transactional analysis (TA) model, the psychodynamic model, and various behavioral models. Often, only the nonalcoholic spouse seeks help in individual therapy in order either to motivate the alcoholic spouse to join at a later point or to deal with her or his pain or depression. When the nondrinking spouse goes through psychological changes during therapy by, for instance, disallowing role reversal in the family (Hecht, 1973) or not enabling the drinking behavior, the whole family system may change. Because of the fact that one family member's change has a great impact on the other members, individual or even family therapy without the drinking spouse can prove to be very helpful. In addition, groups for ACAs provide a supportive environment and are very useful as an adjunct to therapy.

Workshops and seminars that address the special issues of ACAs are available for individuals who want to learn and understand more about their difficulties. The support groups and workshops allow ACAs to express their feelings and to realize that they are not alone (Black, 1981). The groups along with individual or family therapy help the ACAs raise their self-esteem and learn new coping skills, thereby lowering the psychological and sociological risk for the development of alcoholism and related problems.

As discussed before, research has shown that cessation of drinking does not necessarily generate positive changes in the family (Cork, 1969). Therefore, it appears that either intrapsychic confict and/or family dynamics promote or contribute to the alcoholism and family disruption. This proposition has led to the introduction of family therapy into the world of treatment approaches for alcoholism.

Bateson (1959) established the concept of homeostasis in families. He postulated that whenever a system is threatened, it will move toward homeostasis (equilibrium). Therefore, heavy drinking and seemingly bizarre behavior can actually be seen as adaptive mechanisms to maintain homeostasis in the family. Cessation of drinking may pose such a threat. The more rigid the family system, the more fiercely the members will work toward homeostasis. Flexibility of interactional dynamics is necessary for a family system in order to adapt and cope with internal and external stressors.

Booz-Allen and Hamilton (cited in Lawson et al., 1983) recognized that alcoholism is not equally destructive in all families. It may be only a minor characteristic in the totality of the problem. A family does not have to be dysfunctional or pose a threat to the children simply because there is parental alcoholism. This may explain the 25% or more of CoAs who do not abuse alcohol or suffer from related problems. Such family systems must provide the crucial factors necessary to produce resilient, successful, and fulfilled offspring. Of course, the question of what was first, the alcoholism or the family dysfunction, cannot be answered with certainty. It is apparent, though, that the factors are interdependent. The discussion of resilient offspring and the development of a cohesive "self" will shed some light on what factors predispose a CoA to be at risk.

Resilient Offspring of Alcoholics

Werner (1985) conducted a longitudinal study to determine the differences between resilient offspring of alcoholic families and those who developed psychological problems and/or alcoholism. One of the significant differences found was the absence of marital conflict during the resilient offspring's first 2 years of life. Later in his or her development, the family conflict was comparable with that of the nonresilient group. In addition, the resilient children's mothers did not get pregnant again in the 20 months after the first child's birth and were thus able to give more attention and care to their first child than could the mothers of the nonresilient group. By the time they reached adolescence, the nonresilient CoA group showed a significantly higher incidence of serious illnesses, handicaps, and problems in family relations than the resilient children.

Werner (1985) and others understood the development of relationship patterns in the family as a bidirectional process that generates the child's adaptive and maladaptive functioning. *Bidirectionality* refers to the interdependent nature of the parent's effect on the child and the child's effect on the parent. The primary caregiver's perception of the child's innate temperament determines his or her responses, which, in turn, determine the child's responses. Therefore, a specific behavior can operate as a cause and an effect simultaneously. This view seems to be validated by the characteristics of resilient CoAs found by Werner (1985):

- a specific, innate temperament that elicits positive attention from the caregiver
- at least average intelligence and average reading and writing skills
- achievement orientations
- a caring and responsible attitude
- positive self-regard
- internal locus of control
- belief in self-help

Apparently, the resilient CoAs were able to develop those adaptive characteristics in a caregiving environment that provided sufficient attention and peaceful family interactions during their first 2 years of life. The absence of sibling births, prolonged separations from the primary caregiver, and parental conflict in infancy contributed to such an environment (Werner, 1985). Again, the child's temperament and the parent's perception of that temperament are crucial in setting off a sequence of response events in infancy (Millon, 1981).

It appears that the first few years of a CoA's life are the most crucial for the development of a healthy self-concept and stress resistance. Children who do not receive adequate care in infancy become vulnerable to psychological problems and substance abuse. To compensate for this lack of attention, the child must increase his or her outside support system and decrease his or her exposure to the parental alcoholism and associated problems. Unfortunately, this is rarely the case. By the time the child is old enough to employ adaptive machanisms, she or he is already likely to lack self-esteem and resiliency.

The Development of Self

In order to deal adequately with the issue of self-esteem, its etiology needs to be explored. The wealth of literature on that subject consistently refers to the CoA's low self-esteem, depression, and alcohol abuse. Woititz (1983) showed that CoAs are struggling with the consequences of their self-demeaning behavior and their sense of worthlessness in all areas of their life. The degree of self-defeating behavior and low regard for one's self can be viewed as a representation of a person's level of personality pathology (disturbances of the self). Self disorders on a pathology continuum range from mild impairments of self-esteem in relatively well-functioning individuals to serious disturbances of the self in persons who suffer from personality disorders.

In terms of object relations theory, it is assumed that the child is born without a cohesive self. Kohut and Wolf (1978) postulated that the self develops from the interdependent exchange of the child's innate temperament and maternal responses. Infants relate to their parents as self-objects, i.e., they view their parents as providers for all their need fulfillment. When those basic needs are not met, the child develops an inner void that causes a continuous hunger for approval, strength, and comfort from others throughout her or his life. Since the child's hungry self cannot provide such soothing and approval, the child has to develop ways to cope with that vulnerability. Possible coping mechanisms may be counterdependent behavior and submissive pleasing of others in order to elicit their care, love, and approval. The first reminds one of the narcissistic personality's defense against narcissistic injuries to the vulnerable self (Kohut & Wolf, 1978), while the latter resembles the dynamics of the dependent personality. Seabaugh (1984) applied that concept to ACAs, describing their coping mechanisms as defenses against narcissistic injuries of the vulnerable self. Interestingly, narcissistic personalities tend to use and abuse alcohol and/or other substances in an attempt to alleviate their inner sense of emptiness and to provide comfort and soothing for themselves (Kernberg, 1985).

When comparing the dynamics of the ACA and those of the narcissistic personality, one must also discuss the etiology of narcissism in the family by exploring the family environment of the children, namely the parental types and/or their relationships. Lanski (1981) discussed "narcissistically vulnerable" couples that tend to raise narcissistic children. He differentiated between two types of vulnerable couples: in the first case, one of the spouses is prone to acting-out behavior, such as substance abuse, but avoids conflict. In the other case, the spouses engage in volatile fights to vent their infantile rage, while no conflicts are resolved. Blame and humiliation are a part of everyday life in both cases and create an unpredictable, chaotic environment for children. The narcissistically vulnerable couple is attempting to compensate for and fulfill unmet childhood needs for approval and care. As a result, it is very difficult for that couple to give to their children what they did not receive themselves, and the children will continue the cycle.

Similar dynamics can be observed in alcoholic families where faulty parenting is prevalent. Yet, adequate mothering in the first 2 years of life has been shown to produce resilient offspring in alcoholic families, and infantile narcissism in children will change into a strong sense of self if the child receives adequate mothering.

Kohut and Wolf (1978) agreed with Lanski (1981) that childhood narcissism that does not disappear in adulthood is likely to stem from a narcissistic mother (parent) who is unable to provide accurate empathy or mirroring for the child. For example, "the gleam in the mother's eye" is an accurate approving response to the child's need for approval. Lack of accurate empathy refers to the mother's inability to recognize and respond to the child's needs when she or he requires it. On the other hand, the mother may overindulge or overwhelm the child with affection and approval when the child does not want or need it. Often, ACAs describe such experiences in their childhoods and also in their relationships with their spouses and parents.

In addition to accurate empathy, Kohut and Wolf (1978) postulated that appropriate frustrations of the children by the parents are a necessary factor in the development of a cohesive self. In other words, the parents need to be able to limit the child's behavior appropriately and provide realistic mirroring of her or his thoughts, feelings, and behaviors. From the frustrations by the parent, the child learns to control her or his impulses, while the parent's realistic reaction to whatever the child expresses or does provides the basis for the formation of a realistic sense of self. The realistic and strong self can be formed only when its functions are reflected accurately to the child so that she or he can internalize the reflected image. It can be concluded that accurate empathy provides the validation while the correct mirroring creates a realistic self-perception in the development of a cohesive, strong self.

In the process of developing a cohesive self, a person usually shifts from an external locus of control toward a more internal locus of control. As Werner (1985) found, the resilient CoAs tended toward a more internal locus of control. That shift happens when a person has successfully internalized the ability to approve of and provide comfort for himself or herself, therefore decreasing the dependency on others to provide external validation; and the ability to evaluate realistically his or her own limitations and capabilities, thus relinquishing the need for the environment to be a mirror.

As described by Woititz (1983), the ACA has an insatiable need for approval and validation and an unrealistic, mostly negative, view of himself or herself. Since the behavior may be grandiose, the image projected onto the world does not reflect reality. As in narcissism, underneath the secure and happy facade lies a vulnerable, shameful self. This damaged self is the result of being raised by an erratic, chaotic, inconsistent, and unpredictable alcoholic couple who did not allow for internalization of the necessary components by the child (Philipson, 1982). Occasional failures in mothering do not necessarily predispose a child to develop a damaged self, but consistent failures do.

The ACA, like the narcissistic personality, does not usually derive intrinsic satisfaction from the attainment of goals without someone else's approval. Philipson (1982) stated that achievements are meaningless without the "elusive maternal smile" (p. 32). Like the narcissistic person, the abusive alcoholic may be using alcohol as an excuse to express infantile rage that probably stems from unresolved, traumatic experiences in childhood (Marlatt,1981). Due to the lack of ego strength, persons with a personality disorder, and ACAs, react to stress in various disruptive ways rather than adapting appropriately. Apparently, anger seems to be the most powerful and repressed underlying feeling in both personalities since it is unleashed in stressful situations. It is expressed in the form of passive-aggressive acting out, volatile explosions, and drinking. Furthermore, the ACA's and narcissist's hypersensitivity to criticism and the denial of problems add to the maladaptive responses. The author's own experience seems to indicate that the alcoholically drinking ACAs are more similar to narcissistic personality structures, while the nondrinking ACAs resemble more the dependent personality styles.

Family Treatment

Alcoholism can be viewed as a disorder in itself or as a symptom of character pathology and/or family systems dysfunction. In both cases, alcoholism and the related and unrelated problems are passed on from generation to generation. According to Pattison and Kaufman (cited in Lanski, 1981), it is insufficient, however, to view alcoholism as a problem in the nuclear family system only. It needs to be viewed as a reflection of a larger, alcoholism-generating family system. Because of the vital role the family plays in alcoholism, it seems only logical to use family therapy as a treatment approach (Lanski, 1981; Lawson et al., 1983). If the character pathology of a family member is too severe with rigid defenses, marital or individual psychotherapy may be indicated as an adjunct to family therapy. However, the therapist has to be careful to avoid the "identified patient" syndrome by possibly seeing other subsystems in the family also. This approach may have to be used frequently.

It appears that the "special problems" of ACAs are comparable with those of personality disordered individuals and their dysfunctional families. The disease model and the treatment of the alcoholism itself have provided a way to avoid responsibility for the hard work of adaptive changing and their own contribution to the dysfunction of the family and their drinking behavior. The resistance to entering family therapy is compounded by a multitude of factors:

- the homeostatic function of the alcoholism
- the impact of the drinking behavior on the family system
- parental modeling
- physiological factors.

There are, of course, cases in which resilient offspring are produced in spite of family or personality dysfunction and where the alcoholic spouse does not cause severe disruption in the family. This author does not believe that all alcoholics or ACAs suffer from a personality disorder. There are countless types of alcoholism, and each case needs to be examined carefully with an emphasis on the etiology of the alcoholism.

Pattison and Kaufman (1981) differentiated between the causes of symptomatic alcoholism i.e., when the drinking develops as a symptom of another problem in the individual or family. An individual may start abusing alcohol as a reaction to stress and anxiety, which in turn increases the stress and anxiety in the family, therefore causing an increase in drinking behavior, etc. Later, this cycle may become a chronic pattern or cause a family crisis. This crisis can also trigger further drinking (Bowen, 1974). Family systems mostly prone to this type of development are triangulating family systems. Conflict between two family members, most likely the marital dyad, may be projected onto the children and/or alcohol itself and serve as the rationalization for disruption. Consequently, homeostasis is maintained.

Another type of symptomatic alcoholism occurs in the psychosocial partner choice between, e.g., a male alcoholic and a female co-dependent (Paolino, McCrady, & Diamond 1978). Subconsciously, partners are chosen on the basis of their levels of differentiation and ego strengths (Bowen, 1974), which is another explanation for the self-perpetuating nature of the alcoholic system. Pattison and Kaufman (1981) suggested that a common match occurs between the obsessive and the histrionic personality. Both will engage in a power struggle in which one of the partners will eventually become "de-selfed" and therefore vulnerable to alcoholism.

Healthy persons may marry alcoholics to fulfill certain unconscious needs and later develop personality problems by attempting to adapt to the alcoholic. This marital relationship deteriorates quickly when sex and affection are withheld as a passive-aggressive means to express anger. Often, sexual relations cease completely. At that stage, the alcoholic husband relinquishes more and more of his role as a father, while the wife becomes overresponsible. Children often have to take care of themselves and take the role of "parentified children." The family develops into a place full of anxiety and painful silence. As the alcoholic becomes more infantile, the other family members may join against him, therefore alienating him even more. As a result, he may increase drinking and other maladaptive behaviors (Jacob, Favorini, Meisel, & Anderson, 1978).

The co-dependent usually neglects the children psychologically because of the preoccupation with the drinking behavior of the spouse and sometimes becomes alcoholic herself. In addition, she may develop somatic symptoms with secondary gains. The family's coping and defense mechanisms are so rigid that a change in one of the members will increase their efforts to maintain the status quo: thus, the family hints to resume drinking when the alcoholic stops his or her drinking behavior.

These complex family dynamics cannot be addressed or changed successfully through individual treatment or group membership, such as AA. The drinking behavior itself may cease but without changing the underlying dynamics. In family treatment, the whole family can learn new ways of coping with stress and relating to each other, therefore preventing future alcohol abuse.

PRIMARY, SECONDARY, AND TERTIARY PREVENTION

The model of primary, secondary, and tertiary prevention was first introduced by Caplan in 1974. Primary intervention refers to the concept of preventing the development of substance abuse and related problems in high-risk populations, such as ACAs. This can be accomplished through educational programs, governmental policies for alcohol use, and changes in peoples' attitudes and customs concerning drinking behavior (Lawson et al., 1983). Secondary prevention describes the recognition and treatment of persons who already have developed problematic drinking patterns. The goal of treatment would be the avoidance of further, chronic problems. Tertiary prevention includes the treatment of serious substance abusers in either inpatient or outpatient treatment settings in order to treat their problems and to protect the environment from the negative influences of their behavior.

Primary prevention as a way to prevent or stop alcohol abuse may include physiological and sociological components (Lawson et al., 1983). Physiological factors can be treated only with medication, such as Antabuse; sociological and psychological factors can be influenced by education and therapy. Ideally, governments and community resources should be involved in an effort to reduce the damaging effects of alcoholism and the accompanying problems of the individual, family, and society.

Since the family has the greatest impact on the developing child, it would seem to be the most effective area in which to apply primary prevention. ACAs are considered sociologically at high risk for developing drinking and coping patterns similar to those of their parents because of the specific modeling that occurs in alcoholic families. By participating in treatment or educational programs, parents can learn new ways of coping with stress in and outside of the marriage and family, thus modeling these newly acquired, more adaptive mechanisms. In addition, the social environment of the alcoholic usually consists of friends that share the same or similar values and attitudes concerning drinking behavior, therefore reinforcing the maladaptive dynamics even further. To reduce or eliminate that risk, it is recommended that such families choose an environment that is conducive to appropriate drinking behavior or abstinence, as well as the development of healthy family relationships. AA may prove to be very helpful in providing a supportive environment where the people involved share the same goals.

In order to prevent psychological damage to the children growing up in alcoholic families, family therapy would provide an excellent vehicle for the parents to become more adaptive, healthy, and fulfilled themselves, therefore becoming increasingly competent to raise self-confident, psychologically low-risk children. ACAs may also benefit from intergenerational family of origin therapy (Framo, 1976). Dealing with their parents directly can help them resolve their lingering feelings of anger and pain. That fact alone can reduce the risk of projecting those feelings onto the children. As discussed by Lawson et al. (1983), parenting classes can also effect such improvements in the family. The problem with these classes may be low parent attendance due to the parents' own faulty modeling in their family of origin. Preventative therapy or other measures can be very effective in breaking this generational cycle.

Naturally, parents cannot be forced to attend parenting classes or family treatment. However, another avenue to implement change in dysfunctional families may be to reach the children in the schools. Early in their development, possibly in the sixth or seventh grade, children could be required to attend classes about relationships and family dynamics. Also, as Lawson et al. (1983) suggested, children could babysit in a day care center for a certain amount of time during the week, as part of the curriculum, in order to gain a realistic perspective on child rearing. According to Blum (1972), children from healthy families are at no risk, while children from dysfunctional families are at high risk for the development of substance abuse later in life. If the parents do not provide this healthy family environment, school programs can represent a chance for high-risk individuals to avoid the parent's dysfunctional patterns.

Since alcoholism can be viewed as a symptom of a dysfunctional family system or as individual psychopathology, it appears that the reduction of such dysfunction or pathology would produce healthier families in the future with less symptomatic behavior. Secondary and tertiary prevention involves the treatment of moderate and severe substance abuse cases. This population would also benefit from family therapy, thus reducing the family's symptom-maintaining function for the user.

CONCLUSION

In recent years, the labeling and/or identification of the special group "COAs" seems to have taken on a life of its own. Unfortunately, that development seems to encourage further ACAs' tendency to blame their parents' alcoholism for their own individual and family problems. Often they do not recognize that some of their problems and stressors are normal and occur as healthy developmental or situational factors in everyone's life. When responsibility for one's own problems is relinquished, true change cannot happen. Thus, it is important to explore whether the person entering treatment is really motivated to change or interested only in removing the symptom. When the treatment of alcoholism focuses on cessation of drinking behavior, the underlying dysfunctional dynamics are neglected. In the application of the disease model, the alcoholic gives up control over his or her "disease." This may increase a person's sense of powerlessness, contribute to a helpless, blaming attitude, and encourage avoidance of dealing with one's own feelings, thoughts, and behaviors. Under such circumstances, lasting change is difficult or even impossible to achieve.

It is hoped that prevention and treatment in the future will concentrate more on dysfunctional families and psychopathology rather than on a single symptom manifested by such families or individuals. In the age of special groups (ACAs, COAs, Women Who Love Too Much, Daughters of Mothers, etc.), the birth of yet another special group is suggested by this author: ACodFA (Adult Children of Dysfunctional Families with Alcoholism).

REFERENCES

Adler, R., & Raphael, B. (1983). Review: Children of alcoholics. *Australian and New Zealand Journal of Psychiatry, 17,* 3–8.

Bales, R. (1946). Cultural differences in rates of alcoholism. *Quarterly Journal of Studies on Alcohol, 6,* 480–499.

Barnes, S.E. (1979). The alcoholic personality. *Journal of Studies on Alcohol, 40,* 571–633.

Bateson, G. (1959). Cultural problems posed by a study of schizophrenic processes. In Auerbach (Ed.), *Schizophrenia: An integrated approach.* New York: Ronald.

Black, C. (1981). Innocent bystanders at risk: The children of alcoholics. *Alcoholism*, 22–25.

Black, C. (1982). *It will never happen to me!* Denver: M.A.C.

Blum, R., (1972). *Horatio Alger's children: The role of the family in the origin or prevention of drug risk.* San Francisco: Jossey-Bass.

Bohman, M. (1978). Some genetic aspects of alcoholism and criminality. *Archives of General Psychiatry, 35,* 269–276.

Bowen, F.M. (1974). Alcoholism as viewed through family systems theory and family psychotherapy. *Annals of the New York Academy of Science, 233,* 115–122.

Calahan, D. (1970). *Problem drinkers: A national survey.* San Francisco: Jossey-Bass.

Caplan, G. (1974). *Support systems and community health.* New York: Behavioral Publications.

Cermack, T. (1984). Children of alcoholics and the case for a new diagnostic category of codependency. *Alcohol Health and Research World, 8*(4), 39–42.

Cork, M. (1969). *The forgotten children.* Toronto: Alcoholism and Drug Addiction Research Foundation.

Davis, V.E., & Walsh, M.J. (1970). Alcohol amines and alkaloids: A possible biochemical basis for alcohol addiction. *Science, 167,* 1005–1007.

Fox, R. (1968). Treating the alcoholic family. In R.J. Catanzaro (Ed.), *Alcoholism: The total treatment approach.* Springfield, IL: Charles C Thomas.

Framo, J. (1976). Family of origin as a therapeutic resource for adults in marital and family therapy: You can and should go home again. *Family Process, 15,* 193–210.

Freud, S. (1919). Das Unheimlich. In S. Freud (1982). *Psychologische Schriften.* Studienausgabe, Band ILV. Frankfurt am Main: Fischer Taschenbuchverlag.

Gabrielli, W.F., & Mednick, S.A. (1983). Brief communications: Intellectual performance in children of alcoholics. *Journal of Nervous and Mental Disease* 444–447.

Gabrielli, W.F., Jr., Mednick, S.A., Volavka, J., Pollock, V.E., Schulsinger, F., & Atil, T.M. (1982). *Electroencephalograms in children of alcoholic fathers.* The Society for Psychophysiological Research.

Goodwin, D.W. (1971). Is alcoholism hereditary? A review and critique. *Archives of General Psychiatry, 25,* 545–549.

Goodwin, D.W., Schulsinger, F., Hermansen, L., Guze, S.G., & Winokur, G. (1973). Alcohol problems in adoptees raised apart from alcoholic biological parents. *Archives of General Psychiatry, 28,* 238–243.

Gorad, S.L. (1971). Communicational styles and interaction of alcoholics and their wives. *Family Process, 10,* 475–489.

Gravitz, H.L., & Bowden, J.D. (1984). Therapeutic issues of adult children of alcoholics. *Alcohol Health and Research World, 8,* 25–39.

Greenleaf, J. (1981). *Co-alcoholic/para-alcoholic.* Paper presented at the National Council on Alcoholism Forum, New Orleans.

Hecht, M. (1973). Children of alcoholics are children at risk. *American Journal of Nursing, 73,* 1764–1767.

Hindman, M. (1975). Children of alcoholic parents. *Alcohol Health and Research World,* 2–6.

Ingram, C.R. (1984). Adult children of alcoholics: The issues in their lives. *Dissertation Abstracts International, 45.*

Jacob, T., Favorini, A., Meisel, S.S., & Anderson, C.M. (1978). The alcoholic's spouse, children, and family interactions: Substantive findings plus methodological issues. *Journal of Studies on Alcohol, 39*, 1231–1251.

Jellinek, E.M. (1960). *The disease concept of alcoholism*. New Haven, CT: College and University Press.

Katunich, K.L. (1984). Learned helplessness in children of alcoholics. *Dissertation Abstracts International, 45*.

Kernberg, D. (1985). *Borderline conditions and pathological narcissism*. Northvale, NJ: Jason Aronson.

Kiloh, L.G., & Osselton, J.W. (1961). *Clinical electroencephalography*. London: Butterworths.

Kohut, H., & Wolf, E. (1978). The disorders of the self and their treatment: An outline. *International Journal of Psychoanalysis, 59*, 413–425.

Lanski, M.R. (1981). *Family therapy and major psychopathology*. New York: Grune & Stratton.

Lawson, G., Peterson, J., & Lawson, A. (1983). *Alcoholism and the family: A guide to treatment and prevention*. Rockville, MD: Aspen.

Leonard, L.S. (1982). *The wounded women*. Chicago: Swallow.

MacAndrew, C., & Edgerton, R.B. (1969). *Drunken comportment: A social explanation*. Chicago: Aldins.

Marlett, G.A., & Demaris, J.R. (1981). The think-drink effect. *Psychology Today, 93*, 60–69.

Millon, T. (1981). *Disorders of personality*. New York: John Wiley & Sons.

Moos, R.H., Bromet, E., Tsu, V., Moos, B. (1979). Family characteristics and the outcome of treatment for alcoholics. *Journal of Studies on Alcohol, 40*, 78–88.

O'Connor, J. (1975). Social and cultural factors influencing drinking. *Irish Journal of Medical Science, 65*–71.

Olson, R.J. Index of suspicion: Screening for child abusers. *American Journal of Nursing, 76*, 108–110.

Paolino, T.Y., McCrady, B.S., & Diamond, S. (1978). Statistics on alcoholic marriages: An overview. *International Journal of Addictions, 13*, 509–511.

Philipson, I. (1982). Narcissism and mothering: The 1950's reconsidered. *Women's Studies International Forum, 5*, 29–40.

Propping, P. (1977). Genetic control of ethanol action on the central nervous system: An EEG study in twins. *Human Genetics, 35*, 309–334.

Rich, A. (1976). *Of women born: motherhood as experience and institution*. New York: Norton.

Roe, A., & Burks, B. (1945). Adult adjustment of foster children of alcoholic and psychotic parentage and the influence of the foster home. *Quarterly Journal of Studies on Alcohol*.

Satir, V. (1972). *Peoplemaking*. Palo Alto, CA: Science and Behavior Books.

Schuckit, M.A. (1972). A study of alcoholism in half siblings. *American Journal of Psychiatry, 128*, 1132–1136.

Schuckit, M.A. (1982). A study of young men with alcoholic close relatives. *American Journal of Psychiatry, 139*, 791–794.

Seabaugh, M.O.L. (1984). *The vulnerable self of the adult child of an alcoholic: A phenomenologically derived theory*. Dissertation Abstracts International, 45.

Seligman, M.E.P., and Maier, S.F. (1967). Failure to escape traumatic shock. *Journal of Experimental Psychology, 74,* 1–9.

Seligman, M.E.P. (1975). *Helplessness.* San Francisco: W.H. Freeman.

Valliant, G.E., & Milovski, E.S. (1982). The etiology of alcoholism: A prospective viewpoint. *American Psychologist, 37,* 494–503.

Wegscheider, S. (1981). *The family trap.* Crystal, MN: Nurturing Network.

Werner, E.E. (1984). Resilient children. *Young Child, 40,* 68–72.

Werner, E.E. (1985). Resilient offspring of alcoholics: A longitudinal study from birth to age 18. *Journal of Studies on Alcohol, 47,* 34–40.

Williams, R.J. (1959). Biochemical individuality and cellular nutrition: Prime factors in alcoholism. *Quarterly Journal of Studies on Alcohol, 37,* 494–502.

Woititz, J.W. (1983). *Adult children of alcoholics.* Hollywood, FL: Health Communications.

Wolin, S., Bennett, L., Noonan, D., & Teitlebaum, M. *Families at risk: The intergenerational recurrence of alcohol.* Unpublished manuscript.

Chapter 9

Treatment of the Gay or Lesbian Alcoholic

Gary R. Lewis and Susann M. Jordan

INTRODUCTION

Rev. Elder Troy D. Perry is the founder and moderator of the Board of Elders of the Universal Fellowship of Metropolitan Community Churches. The Fellowship had its beginnings on October 6, 1968, with a mission to give a church and a spiritual home to the members of the homosexual community. From 12 individuals on October 6, 1968, the denomination has grown to more than 200 congregations throughout the world.

Rev. Elder Perry related a conversation he had with a psychologist that had great relevance. The psychologist in his conversation said, "You know, Troy, I have dealt with a large number of people from your community. It never ceases to amaze me at the amount of gay people who are neurotic." Rev. Perry paused for a moment and replied

Doctor, there is something that really amazes me also about the mental health of the gay community. What with growing up being told that they are going to hell; knowing that they are an outcast from society; repressing their real selves for fear of losing their job, apartment, or loved ones; knowing that their country feels that they are unfit to serve it; facing arrest, jail, and public humiliation for enjoying an evening with others from the gay community at a public place; being called "queer," "fag," "dyke," "lessie," and risking physical harm, losing their children as unfit parents if their sexuality became known—when I think of all these things, and more, that people in the gay community have to face

every day of their life from the time they are small children, I
wonder why we're not all neurotic.*

It is essential that those who are going to involve themselves with counseling
individuals in the lesbian and gay community understand the stressors that
are included in the personality development of the individuals as well as
those they must live with on a daily basis no matter how "out of the closet"
they might or might not be (personal communication, May 20, 1980).

A HISTORY OF HOMOSEXUALITY AND ALCOHOLISM

It was the "new" field of psychoanalysis that began to broach the study
of human sexuality. It was approached with the same fervor as that of the
new convert or perhaps the new nonsmoker. Shortly, more and more
behavior and personality characteristics were being related to sex, and
theories proliferated based on one or at most a few studies, usually from
small, middle-class Western cultures. Deviation from this norm was
explained in relation to the psychoanalytic concepts of stages of sexual
development.

Homosexuality was first linked with alcoholism at the beginning of the
20th century by Karl Abraham, also known as the first German psychoanalyst. In 1908 he wrote a paper whose English title is "The Psychological
Relationship Between Sexuality and Alcoholism," which was "the first
psychoanalytical view of alcoholism, offering the theory of homosexuality
on the Freudian basis as the underlying cause. Even with the passage of
time, that paper remains the classical exposition of the subject" (Smalldon,
1933, p. 650).

Two statements of Abraham's (1926) became fundamental to much of
the psychoanalytic thought that followed: "Alcohol drinks have an effect
on the sexual instinct, for they dispel the resistances present and increase
sexual activity" (p. 3). "To a healthy minded man any kind of tender contact
with other men is repugnant. . . . These feelings are dispelled by alcohol"
(p. 4).

Psychoanalysts of the strict neo-Freudian school appeared to believe that
homosexuality caused or was in some major manner linked to alcoholism.
They argued that alcohol caused regression to various levels of psycho-

---

*This personal communication is used with the permission of the Reverend Elder Troy D.
Perry.

sexual development: to a level of lewdness, to one where sadistic and masochistic tendencies are released, or to a stage where latent homosexuality is released. "According to the amount of alcohol taken, different degrees of regression may occur, and at the level reached different conflicts may be unearthed" (Read, 1920, p. 236).

According to Read (1920), alcohol is originally taken "to promote the social instincts and alleviate and narcotize the many mental conflicts to which we must all to some extent be victims" (p. 242). However, if taken in excess "its effects tend to destroy sublimation and aid mental regression . . . and thus bring into active conflict with the personality different impulses and desires previously more or less successfully repressed. Of these the homosexual impulse is found by analysis to be most frequent" (p. 253). Clark (1919), an American physician, stated that alcoholic hallucinations, both acute and chronic, "can be found to be a form of persecution mania arising from unconscious and denied homosexuality" (p. 931). Delirium tremens, according to Riggall (1923), a British neurologist and psychoanalyst, accompanied the "fear of men and of attacks from men. This fear, of course, is projection of the desire for male companionship" (p. 166). He neglected to say if this applied to women as well. Clark (1919) went further, saying that the deliriums are accompanied by alarming hallucinations not only of men "but of animals—well known sex symbols" (p. 931). In 1918 Wholey stated that "homosexuality is a normal instinct and plays an important role in the development of the individual's heterosexuality" (p. 447). This is the same type of thinking that was evidenced by both Freud (1898/1953) and Juliusburger (cited in Jelliffe, 1917) in their theories of bisexuality and its ensuing sublimation or repression of the sexual attraction to one's own sex. Miller (1972) subscribed to the same views and made the connection between homosexuality and alcoholism in the following manner:

> Every individual, according to the Freudian psychology, passes through a phase of homosexuality in his attempts to deliver himself from the thralldom of his own oedipus complex. In most of us it survives as an aroma of friendships with members of our own sex, and blossoms furtively and momentarily in the exuberance of the taphouse and the bar. But in some who become social pariahs it continues to dominate not only the sexual life, but the whole of the character. Such persons may be happy in their inversion, and continue without overt disturbances of behavior. In others, however, the solution is only partly completed, and the struggle between homosexuality and other urges in the sexual life and in the life of self becomes the source of the deepest unhap-

piness, if not the incentive to neurosis and even such psychoses as paranoia.

In such apparently blessed anodyne as alcohol the patient, quite unaware of the inner battle between homosexuality and normal sex of the higher manifestations of the self, seeks escape. In this escape the homosexuality may assert itself either in actual invert behavior or in pseudomasculine truculence with one's own sex. On the other hand, the normal sexuality with which the patient is endowed wins through and the victim may have sexual successes of transitory character. And, again, the ideal of the self may conquer over both forms of sexuality and emerge in gradiloquence of sublime detachment from all calls of the flesh. Such escapes in alcoholism occur only to the poet and the painter. They are rare amongst ordinary men (pp. 110-111).

The American neurologist and psychiatrist Hart (1930), however, voiced a dissident opinion. Using a sample of 30 alcoholic patients, including 5 women, he examined them for personality factors that might authenticate the psychoanalytic doctrine that homosexuality is an important factor in alcoholism. Only one patient was an admitted homosexual and drank less and for an abbreviated period. However, on the basis of defining homosexuality as a tendency to associate with one's own sex to the exclusion of the opposite sex, 11 persons (2 women) showed such tendencies. The 9 men drank almost exclusively with men or else alone. Three said that their desire for women diminished under the influence of alcohol. Hart did not draw the conclusion that such persons had homosexual tendencies: "On considering the group as a whole, there seemed little evidence of any importance or overt homosexual tendency" (p.127).

In 1923 Riggall presented what was the most obvious and popular connection between alcoholism and homosexuality, that of oral eroticism. "The craving for sweets, alcohol or tobacco is often due to the desire to satisfy the erotogenetic zone of the mouth, and it is my experience that such craving very frequently accompanies fellatio, the desire for which has obvious unconscious reference to the mother's nipple, and is only another proof of the large part a mother-fixation can play in homosexuality and alcoholism" (p. 166). There was, however, no recognition of the physiologically addictive quality of alcohol nor any explanation why the homosexual preferred alcohol to milk.

In 1944 Bergler (1944/1977) wrote *The Basic Neurosis* in which he expressed his opinion of homosexuality and oral eroticism:

The perversion homosexuality is genetically an oral disease. The homosexual pervert is a person who has failed in overcoming the trauma of weaning. He identifies unconsciously the breast via identification with the penis and escape to man from woman as the source of original disappointment. Thus the homosexual is an oral neurotic. As alcohol addiction has an oral basis too . . . the coincidence of drinking and homosexuality is possible (p. 466).

He did not see homosexuality as the cause of alcoholism:

A person under the influence of alcohol . . . can . . . use that defense mechanism in his alibi in the battle with his inner conscience. Since every orally regressed person fights his losing battle with the image of the preoedipal mother, one of his techniques in denying that conflict can be the formula: "How can I be accused of *masochistic* submission to the mother, if I'm really interested in the man?" (p. 243).

While more ambiguous, Wholey (1918) also related anal eroticism to alcoholism and homosexuality: "The patient's overwhelming money complex revealing itself so dramatically in his psychosis, together with the marked obstinacy, orderliness, and punctiliousness characterizing the individual, present evidence of the relationship of chronic alcoholism with homosexuality and anal eroticism" (p. 442).

Riggall (1923) alluded to the relationship among masculinity, the power of creation, and alcohol:

Now, alcohol stimulates masculinity, and emphasizes the male ideas of greatness and power. Abraham deals with this characteristic in his work on creation myths. These myths, he finds, defy the male power of creation. And it is not difficult to understand how alcohol has come to be unconsciously identified with semen. So we get the "intoxification of love" idea, and a symbolic interpretation of the mythological nectar. The old-time libations to the gods probably embodied a similar unconscious idea, and today the common custom of drinking healths has a significant meaning (pp. 163).

Clark (1919) also discussed the drinking of alcohol in terms of manliness: "Man relies on alcohol because it gives him a feeling of manliness and flatters his manliness complex" (p. 93). Nevertheless, he contends: "Men drink, fall on one another's necks, feel themselves united by an inner bond and weep. In a word, their behavior is womanish" (p. 932).

Burton (1956) studied 87 male alcoholics of whom only 2 had histories of long-lasting homosexual behavior. This led him to agree with Clark about the "manliness complex," but he related it to the idea of *latent* homosexuality. "Many discussions of alcoholism paint latent homosexuality as a potent force in the genesis of the condition. The position is taken here that only if by latent homosexuality is meant a pattern of incomplete and distorted masculine identification are these discussions appropriate. The desire of these alcoholics is not to be a woman but rather to be a complete man" (p. 52).

When dealing with women, the entire issue becomes even more ambiguous. Riggall (1923) stated: "Such women as drink will frequently show strong homosexual tendencies. Whereas men, however, drink to overcome the repression of natural homosexuality, women are more likely to drink to bring out the male side of their bisexuality" (p. 163).

Clark (1919) agreed: "Women who have a strong desire for liquor are likely to prove homosexual" (p. 932). Clark maintained that women's social teas were sublimated expressions of feminine homosexuality, but that alcohol, formerly reserved for men, was more satisfactory. "The viral component of women is stirred today, and this helps explain the women's increased turning to alcohol" (p. 931).

In 1926 Abraham contended that alcoholism was principally a male problem; the psychosexual character of women incited them far less to take alcohol. Psychoanalysts appeared to have centered their work on the man. Women in general and lesbians specifically, even when included in the samples, were not usually taken into account in the conclusions regarding alcoholism and homosexuality (Levine, 1955). Then, as now, women alcoholics tend to make up a minority in the treatment setting. It is uncertain whether the nominal numbers, the predominant attitude in society that women did not "count," or that it was too bothersome to come up with separate conclusions drawn from women's case histories produced this lack of investigation.

Knight (1937) did report the finding of fewer women alcoholics. He accounted for this by suggesting that women, "although they may have in infancy experienced the same oral pacification and thwarting, having many more socially acceptable ways of indulging their passivity than men do . . . are not driven to drinking as the only solution" (p. 244). He added: "if there is a strong active homosexual component . . . they may drink to emulate masculinity." While many believed in the paucity of women alcoholics, the Psychiatric Division of Bellevue Hospital in New York reported that in 1935, 1,633 women were admitted because of alcoholism. This compared with 7,506 men during the same period with the same diagnosis (Curran, 1937). Curran's study was made up of 50 women aged 17 to 63 of lower socioeconomic status diagnosed as having "very severe alcoholism." Thirty of these women felt that drinking made them more socially acceptable. Two admitted to having had homosexual experiences, one when she was 12, and the other when she was 8. Only one "wanted to be a boy." Twenty felt they had satisfactory heterosexual relations, and in only 10 cases was sexual desire or pleasure increased by drinking. In hallucinations, homosexual remarks and threats were much less outspoken than in male alcoholics. The author summed up his findings: "The evaluation of homosexuality and promiscuity in men and women differs greatly in our present society" (p. 653).

Wall (1937), an American psychiatrist, studied 50 women patients, the total consecutive admissions over the years 1920 to 1933 of women at Bloomingdale Hospital "in which the immediate cause of hospitalization was alcoholic indulgence" (p. 943). Findings considered important by Wall were that many of the women (32) had frequent temper tantrums in childhood and showed no strong attachment to any family member. Five women had a history of overt homosexuality, but most said "I like men, but I despise women." Wall (1937) found unequivocal distinctions between men and women in their psychosexual development. The men showed considerable mother attachment and preferred the company of their own sex. The women, however, preferred male fellowship. In response to this finding Wall stated: "Concerning the psychosexual development of the alcoholic patient, much emphasis has been placed on homosexuality, particularly in the psychic sense. No one with psychiatric experience doubts its significance" (p. 1390).

Beyond the fact that there were 11 cases of overt homosexuality, that most of the patients indicated a preference for male drinking compatriots, and that those who developed alcoholic psychoses "revealed the homosexual conflict," it is difficult to ascertain just what light was placed on the problem. The most significant and interesting finding was the differences between male and female alcoholics. The women had highly individual problems and their alcoholism or excessive drinking was more intimately associated with a definite life situation than that of the men.

Wall (1937) reported that when he presented his paper in 1936 to the American Psychiatric Association, Karpman wanted to know what he had learned about jealousy in women. Karpman stated: "As one knows, alcoholics as a group are very jealous." He found a homosexual factor in a man's jealousy because, although the jealousy is apparently directed at a woman, "it enables him to preoccupy his mind physically with the man" (p. 953). Also at the meeting was Schilder, who attempted to indicate a homosexual aspect of women's alcoholism: "One may speak about a homosexual relationship between mother and daughter"; he did not develop this proposition.

Weijl (1944), an American psychiatrist, based on his perceptions rather than quantitative data, stated: "With the increasing masculinity of women, apparent in the choice of professions, in clothes, and in women's attitudes toward life, we find an increased inclination toward alcohol and drunkenness" (p. 203). This statement summarized what psychoanalysts who came before him thought about homosexuality and alcoholism. Weijl concluded, like so many others, that the latent homosexual drives are directly connected with the causes of compulsive drinking. This type of thinking dominated psychoanalytic thought as late as the 1960s.

In 1965 Cappon stated: "The natural history of the homosexual patient seems to be one of frigidity, impotence, broken personal relationships, psychosomatic disorders, alcoholism, paranoiac psychosis and suicide" (p. 126). Although this may be the case with the homosexual who seeks psychoanalytic help, the danger is that this "natural history" may be generalized to all homosexuals. Cappon added that "alcohol is used as an escape from conflict; to brave the world of abnormalcy, to gain Dutch courage, to anesthetize feelings of fear and inadequacy and, most of all, to numb one's perception and so escape from oneself, until the next morning" (p. 126).

Blum (1966) gave a clear account of how the basic concepts of psychoanalysis were applied to the development of the theory of alcoholism:

> In psychoanalytic writing the term addiction is not used in the strict sense of dependence upon a pharmacologically active substance. . . . Rather, in speaking of addiction, psychoanalysts refer to dependence on a substance, an activity or a person believed to provide pleasure on the one hand and relief from psychic pain (anxiety, etc.) on the other hand. Such dependence is conceived of as resulting from developmental failure (p. 263).

Addiction supposedly protects the individual from the "graver consequences of this failure: suicide, psychosis, asocial or criminal behavior" (Blum, 1966, p. 263). However, according to Cappon (1965), addiction does not protect the individual, or at any rate the homosexuality, from any of these behaviors except, maybe, the criminal.

Blum (1966) thought it would be an error to attribute a unitary theory of alcoholism to the psychoanalysts, that the framework of psychoanalysis is too complex for a single-factor explanation. It is this complexity that makes the experiments "disproving" psychoanalytic theory "regrettable" because they isolated a single facet out of this great complex structure. In her reading of the literature, she found that analysts related homosexuality only to the alcoholics fixated at the anal stage. Blum contended that the case studies of alcoholics have produced evidence of a third stage of psychosexual development: the phallic-oedipal state: "These patients have progressed beyond a homosexual love choice to a heterosexual one and have come to grief over the conflicts arising from their very progress. They have not been able to come to terms with the emerging sexual feelings toward their mother" (p. 267). Blum summarized: "psychoanalytic theory may be seen to have made a very considerable contribution to the developmental theory of alcoholism and to the differential classification of alcoholics" (p. 288).

The literature of the 1960s and 1970s began to evince a transition away from traditional psychoanalysis and the medical model it followed. This meant a movement from the view that both homosexuality and alcoholism were diseases to be cured. It was perhaps the humanistic movement more than others that first expressed a positive side of the personality and focused on the human potential (Rogers, 1961). The existential model as described by Laing (1967) stressed the uniqueness of the individual and the freedom of self-fulfillment. The emergence of labeling theory (Becker, 1962; Schur, 1971) had a noteworthy effect as well. It purported that behavior was criminal or sick only insofar as it was labeled as such by a given society.

Perhaps one of the most effective voices undermining the influence of the psychoanalytic model were those of homosexuals themselves. It was they who complained that the research and writings to date focused on the pathological side of the homosexual to the exclusion of the possibility of stability. They also reported the pernicious effects of psychoanalysis on the patient and the public as well (Altman, 1971; Weinberg, 1972; Ziebold, 1979). The determination of the gay liberation movement was heard in the 1950s (Cory, 1951) but became more blatant in the 1960s (Hoffman, 1968) and 1970s.

One result of these various forces was that homosexuality began to lose its "sickness" label. In 1973 the "official" classification of homosexuality by the American Psychiatric Association was changed from "psychiatric disorder" to sexual "orientation disturbance," and Socrides (1978) lamented the fact that homosexuality was not considered a disturbance in the 1974 printing of the American Psychiatric Association's *Diagnostic and Statistical Manual of Mental Disorders* (DSM III). It was listed as a sexual orientation disturbance in which "homosexuality in and of itself does not necessarily constitute a psychiatric disorder" (Bayer, 1981, p. 136).

In general, the study of the effects of alcohol on large samples and even whole populations was well under way by the 1970s, showing the diversity of both the causes of alcohol problems and the types of individuals involved. Thus speculation on and research into the causal relationship between alcoholism and homosexuality has all but disappeared over the past 10 years from the pages of psychiatric, psychoanalytic, and addiction journals.

In 1972, Miller wrote an article that provided an entirely different, and these authors believe more rational, interpretation on male companionship.

"Men's tendency to pursue ties to other men need not rest on a basic homosexual drive, as such. It seems much more likely that it rests on a society definition of women as a different and less significant order of being" (p. 156).

Homosexuality is less and less frequently considered a pathology (Clark, 1975), and the emphasis is shifting from changing the homosexual patient to fit into society to making him comfortable with himself (Gilbert, 1978). This is by no means an exclusive view. The *American Journal of Psychotherapy* seems to follow still the more traditional view that both homosexuality (Socrides, 1978) and alcoholism (Khantzian, 1980) are psychiatric disorders.

The importance of this psychoanalytic belief is in how it will affect the theories and choice of research topics. It can be seen that a great deal of effort was put into studying the homosexuality-alcoholism connection. Also of importance was how the theory and the research it fostered affected patients and the general public. Cory (1951) believed that the American public associated homosexuality with drunkards. An example of how the homosexuality-alcoholism theory filtered down to the layman is the novel *Lost Weekend* by Charles Jackson (1944). In this book, the traditional psychoanalytic association is made between homosexuality and alcoholism. As far as homosexuality and alcoholic patients are concerned, whether a therapist would see them as having a personality disorder or not would depend to a large extent on how much the therapist followed the views of the psychoanalysts.

CENTRAL ISSUES IN COUNSELING THE LESBIAN OR GAY ALCOHOLIC

The preponderant issue that affects all other issues was first identified by Weinberg (1972): "homophobia." He defined this as "the revulsion toward homosexuals and often the desire to inflict punishment as retribution . . . and in the case of homosexuals themselves, self-loathing" (p. 133).

Despite the massive evidence that homosexual people are as varied in their personalities as any other subculture, the public continues to hold many misconceptions, which in some cases are thought to justify discriminatory practices. Among these misconceptions is the belief that homosexuals seduce young children (in Fresno, California, in 1976, there were only two cases reported where a person was alleged to have seduced a same-sex child, and one of these was a man who seduced both a brother and a sister). There are the beliefs that the homosexual is untrustworthy, that homosexual men hate women, that lesbians hate men, that homosexual men are passive and effeminate in their actions, and that lesbians are all "dykes" and masculine in manner and attire. It is important for the counselor to examine his or her own attitude concerning the entire sphere of sexuality but most importantly that of homosexuality. The reason for this emphasis is that by best estimates gays and lesbians make up some 10% of the total population (Kinsey, Pomeroy, and Martin, 1948; Kinsey, Pomeroy, and Martin, 1953).

Some research seems to indicate a significantly higher percentage of lesbian and gay alcoholism than in the general population (Fifield, De-Creascenzo, and Latham, 1975). The report *On My Way to Nowhere: Alienated, Isolated, Drunk: An Analysis of Gay Alcohol Abuse and an Evaluation of Alcoholism Rehabilitation Services for the Los Angeles County* stated that 1 in 3 gays or lesbians had a "significant" drinking problem (cited in Fifield et al., 1975). When one compares this with the 1 in 10 in the general population, the large numbers become more obvious. Therefore, it is likely that an alcoholism counselor will encounter many lesbian and gay alcoholics entering treatment. Thus, if the counselor's morals, values, or belief system places him or her in conflict with those of the client, it will be extremely difficult if not impossible to intervene effectively in the addictive process. It is critical that the counselor understand that gay and lesbian clients have a full range of problems. They have the same or very similar sexual issues, dysfunctions, and anxieties as do heterosexuals.

For counselors to treat these patients in a constructive and effective manner, they must be able to focus on the alcoholism and ignore the client's sexuality unless and until it becomes a problem for the client. While the counselor needs to be aware of the client's orientation, there are times when sexual issues must be addressed forcefully and directly. Being able to make such judgments, to make them accurately, and objectively, and to carry out the treatment in a sensitive manner requires that counselors have significantly tempered their own homophobia and have acquired a fair amount of knowledge of the gay/lesbian life styles. Being able to do this also requires that counselors have a repertoire of methods that directly address the issues particular to lesbian/gay clients. The first of these is to develop a rapport in which the client feels safe enough to reveal his or her orientation.

If gays or lesbians had to contend only with the homophobia in society, that would be hard enough. But the irony is that homophobia does not stay only out in society. As children are born and raised principally by heterosexual parents in a homophobic culture, gays and lesbians learn almost by an osmotic process to be homophobic. As they first learn that they are "different" (and this is often as early as 5 or 6 years), they begin to introject and internalize these homophobic feelings. If the young child is male and effeminate, he begins to view the world as a hostile, abusive, finger-pointing environment. If he is a "typical" ball playing, rough and tumble type, then he denies that he is like "those" people and continues to be lost and alone in his feelings. When he gets older and decides that perhaps he is "one of them," he often attempts to adopt the mannerisms and life style that he believes will enable him to be accepted. Unfortunately this frequently leads to an identity dysphoria. If the child is female and a tomboy, she is felt to be cute until she is 10 or 11. Then the "cuteness" begins to leave and she is encouraged to become more "ladylike." She then, in an attempt to conform, begins to lose sight of who she is and what she is really like. If she is not a tomboy but is very ladylike, she will tend to experience many of the same feelings and denials as the "typical" boy. And frequently it is only after disastrous relationships with men that she will finally allow herself to begin feeling those "unacceptable" feelings. No matter which way it occurs, when they have internalized this homophobia, they learn to fear and hate that which makes up their identity and that which constitutes the very core of their being: not just their sexual orientation but their existential "way of being" in the world.

Internalized homophobia takes many forms and has many effects, some subtle, some blatant. Many people (including gays and lesbians themselves) think that heterosexuals are superior. The authors were once told by a client in a group therapy session that he experienced this in the following manner: He was working in an acute care setting in a major university hospital. He had to make decisions daily that meant the life or death of the patients under his care. He recalled going to a "straight" bar one evening after work, near the hospital. He said that it was one of those "red neck places that I only thought existed in the south." As he stood there, he looked down at his hands and realized that he had saved a life that day. But next to him stood a dirty, unshaven, overweight man dressed in filthy jeans and a torn T-shirt and he said, "I felt so inferior to him because he was 'normal.' "

Many gays and lesbians think that even though they are gay they should marry, have children, and live a heterosexual life style because to be gay is sinful or unnatural. They may even learn to think of themselves as not gay, as straight, because to think the other way is too painful, confusing, and/or too frightening. Hatred, loathing, contempt, fear, and many, many other negative feelings make up the personality of some homosexuals. The feelings generated by internalized homophobia have wide-ranging and often very negative ramifications for gays and lesbians. Self-hatred and self-loathing are destructive to ego-development and functioning; they can contribute to depression, suicidal thoughts or behavior, alcoholism, and drug abuse and addiction of many types. These feelings often serve to isolate one gay or lesbian from another. The resultant signs of denial, withdrawal, and isolation are all too familiar to the alcoholism counselor.

Fear, misbelief, mistrust, suspicion, anxiety, and wariness are also created by this internalized homophobia. If a person believes that the very essence of his or her makeup is contemptible and immoral, what chance is there for self-esteem in any aspect of his or her life? Instead, the person believes that he or she is unalterably inadequate and defective and unacceptable to God, society, and, most important, to his or her family. Of course, this can do little but to serve to foster the belief that he or she is unacceptable to even himself or herself. Accompanying this type of dystonia is a fear that has many of the symptoms of full-blown paranoia. This is characterized by the belief that people suspect or are whispering about the person's sexual orientation. However, the old joke holds very true here: "Just because I'm paranoid doesn't mean they're not out to get me."

For an individual to be subjected to this type of homophobia both externally and internally can be predictably overpowering. At best, this type of stressor can provide an opportunity for the gay or lesbian to learn from experience and survive it. They then become stronger and more resilient than those who have not had to encounter this type of stress. Unfortunately, what all too frequently happens is that the individual's ego structure is not adequate to counter the stress, and the stress destroys him or her.

When the alcoholism counselor ascertains that his or her client is lesbian or gay, whether just "coming out" or unabashed, he or she will discover that some basic decisions will need to be made if he or she is to intervene in the person's alcoholism effectively. There are four guidelines that these authors have found essential in their own experience.

1. *Homosexuality is only a part of a person's total sexuality.* Too often, the total sexuality of the homosexual client is believed to be expressed in relationship to those of his or her own sex. This is just not the case. Homosexual feelings and responses are a part of one's total sexuality and are not expressed only through what is termed "overt sexual acts."

A person's sexual identity is defined as a combination of his or her gender identity, gender role behavior, and sexual orientation (Hawkins,1980). Since this is not a chapter on sexuality, the discussion is limited to the component of sexuality most relevant here: orientation.

Sexual orientation refers to the *object* component of the psychological factor of the biosociopsychological mode. It is an attempt to identify the gender of the person's sexual and primary relationship partner. Simply stated, sexual orientation is usually defined by two factors: (a) the physical, which includes gender preference for sexual partners and sexual relationships (Hawkins, 1980); and (b) the affectional, which includes gender preference for primary emotional relationships (Shively & DeCecco, 1977).

This orientation has traditionally been labeled *homosexual, bisexual,* and *heterosexual* and has sometimes been presented as existing on a continuum, with *homosexual* at one end and *heterosexual* at the other (Kinsey et al., 1948). However, most research literature is inconsistent in establishing criteria for identifying the orientation of subjects, with the majority of studies that dichotomize into heterosexual and homosexual often based on physical activity alone (Masters & Johnson, 1979). Although certainly simplifying matters for the researchers, this dichotomy has done much to complicate further the acquisition of knowledge through research by ignoring the multiple components of orientation. From this dichotomy arise such statements as, "Well, you have to be either homosexual or heterosexual," or "If I engage in sexual activity with someone of the same sex, then I must be a homosexual." Neither statement is necessarily true.

Although the definition of *orientation* as involving only the two factors may be sufficient for simplicity, it is not sufficient for full understanding. In addition to the preference for a sexual and affectional partner, a historical perspective should be included, along with an exploration of partners in sexual fantasy. Thus, rather than a simple two-factor phenomenon, sexual orientation is composed of six parts. The counselor needs to consider both the historical and present partner preference for (a) sexual activity, (b) primary affectional relationships, and (c) fantasy; with each of the six parts consisting on a continuum from *exclusively homoerotic* to *exclusively heteroerotic.* This means that it is possible to develop a six-part orientation for an individual. This continuum is made up of the following areas:

- *exclusive homoerotic:* preference for same-gender partners
- *predominant homoerotic:* preference primarily for same-gender partners
- *ambisexual homoerotic:* usually preference not based on gender but occasional preference for same-gender partners
- *ambisexual bisexual:* preference not based on gender
- *ambisexual heteroerotic:* usually preference not based on gender but occasional preference for opposite gender partners
- *predominantly heteroerotic:* preference primarily opposite-gender partners
- *exclusively heteroerotic:* preference for opposite-gender partners only.

The fact that these points have been identified does not make them discrete categories. On any part of an orientation continuum, a person might be somewhere between two points. It is important to remember that this is a continuum, not a set of discrete points.

Identifying the orientation of the client is not too difficult when all of the components match. If someone prefers to engage in sexual activity with, to establish sexual relationships with, to form primary relationships with, and to fantasize about someone of the same gender and accomplishes all of these, then the orientation is clear. That person has a homoerotic orientation (Moses & Hawkins, 1982).

The counselor who works with sexual feelings needs to see sexuality as a part, not the total, of the personality. The word *sex* should not be limited to what a person does with his or her genitalia. When it is said: "John had sex with Mary," what is usually meant is that genital sexual intercourse took place. However, a broader view needs to be taken. Sexual response is a part of life almost from the beginning to the end. Even on first meeting, persons may have strong emotional, sexual feelings about each other, yet no involvement may take place. In some instances these friendships grow deep and last many years and still no physical relationship develops. Then, too, sexual feelings express themselves in sensual ways other than specific genital contact. All of the senses may become involved in one way or another but still without overt genital involvement. No matter where a person falls on the continuum, his or her life is filled with relationships that create sexual feelings of varying intensities that are not acted out in genital encounters. Even those men and women who accept celibacy as a rule for life do not give up their sexuality. They may learn how to control and inhibit their feelings so that there is never genital contact with another person; however, this does not mean that sexual feelings are not present.

2. *It is important to accept the fact that gays or lesbians are not pathological just because of their homosexuality.* Hoffman (1968) decided that before he made any pronouncements on the subject, he would leave the clinical atmosphere of his office and learn about the homosexual world. This meant being involved with homosexual organizations, knowing gay and lesbian individuals who worked for the "liberation" movement, visiting gay and lesbian bars as well as other places where men and women meet, and through all these contacts, encounter many persons who had never felt the need for professional therapeutic help. After 2 years he reported that the majority of persons he had met were functioning in life with adequacy and in a manner that would be considered "successful."

It is possible, in fact, given the numbers quite likely, that every person knows one or more successful homosexuals but is unaware of their sexual orientation. They are accepted as acquaintances or friends and function as adequate, productive members of society. Freedman (1971) stated:

> Empirical psychological research has proved that homosexuality is compatible with positive psychological functioning. The statement is based on research studies in many geographic locales, using a wide variety of psychological instruments and techniques. These studies suggest that most homosexually oriented persons (who are generally not visible to us as such) are coping efficiently with their life situations and are effective in environmental mastery. Many homosexually oriented individuals are in fact . . . self actualizing (p. 106).

3. *It is necessary to accept homosexuality as within the sexual norm and within the natural order.* The alcoholism counselor who views his or her client as "some kind of freak" may not manage to conceal those feelings or be very effective in the therapeutic process.

The argument that homosexuality is "unnatural" has been used for numerous years. This almost always refers to the genital act and not necessarily to emotional relationships. Close friendships, often long lasting, have existed between man and man, woman and woman, and have never been questioned. It is when genital contact exists that there is alarm.

Much research has been conducted on the sexual patterns of primitive societies. Ford and Beach (1951) studied 76 primitive societies and found that in 49 of them some form of homosexual activity was considered normal and acceptable. They also indicated that in their investigation of animals there were numerous instances of homosexual behavior and activity. Benson (1965) researched homosexuality and made this statement:

> Factually, what man does is choose which laws of nature, biological or non-biological, he wishes to operate within in a particular time and place. The more knowledge he accumulates the more he is able to change the "is" into whatever he decides. So the argument that homosexuality is against the law of nature, that it is perverse, has as much or as little logical or factual substantiation as the assertions that circumcision, bottle feeding, contraception, eating cooked foods, or mouth-genital contact are perverse. Perversity is a term used by those who do not approve of your way of changing or modifying a law of nature. All a person is entitled to say is: I do not like homosexuality because . . . and here he can supply a reason. However, he cannot say the reason is that it is against the laws of nature (because this is a personal choice of which of nature's laws he would like to be dominant) (p. 21).

4. *The genital act of homosexuality is not of itself immoral.* An alcoholism counselor who would deal with individuals about their sexuality must reconcile himself or herself to some position about the rightness and wrongness of the sexual act itself.

This need to develop a moral perspective in regard to an alcoholic client is not a new quandary. A close relationship has always existed between moral beliefs and medical, particularly psychological, diagnosis and treatment. Ancient and medieval beliefs influenced the diagnosis and treatment of the insane (Foucault, 1973). Halleck (1971) stated that even in present day medical treatments there is political implication.

American history provides examples of the politicization of psychological diagnoses. Benjamin Rush led the development of psychiatry and diagnosed a variety of behaviors as medical, including lying, drunkenness, and crime. A fierce advocate of independence from England and a signer of the Declaration of Independence, Rush diagnosed anyone opposing the revolution as suffering from the disease of "revolution." He was an early and active abolitionist, basing his convictions partly on the belief that blacks had a disease called "negritude," which was inherited from ancestors with leprosy and which had turned their skins black (Conrad & Schneider, 1980).

While Rush was the medical advocate for abolition, Samuel Cartwright represented the slavery side of the argument. In 1851 he wrote a paper describing the disease "drapetomania," a condition that only affected slaves "and whose major symptom was running away from the plantation of their white masters" (Conrad & Schneider, 1980, p. 35).

In the mid-1900s feminists opposed abortion as oppression of women. They then affiliated with a newly organized group called the American Medical Association (AMA) to lobby state legislatures to forbid abortion. This was a stroke of luck for the physicians who made up the new AMA and were struggling desperately for medical primacy over other medical and nonmedical groups. They saw the antiabortion statutes as a means of creating a medical monopoly (a view not unfamiliar today). The legislators (who were white, native-born Americans) believed that only middle and upper class women were having abortions, while waves of lower class immigrants were having large families, and they felt betrayed by their own women. What they wanted was more native, Protestant babies to "save America from the foreigners" (Mohr, 1978, p. 80).

Can the alcoholism counselor be neutral concerning morality when working with the homosexual client? At the asking of this question many counselors attempt to retreat by ascribing this to the role of the "pastoral counselor," not the "secular counselor." There is the assumption made that the pastoral counselor will provide answers to the client's questions concerning normative values and religious beliefs. In contrast, the secular counselor is assumed to take a neutral, pedantic role. As such, the secular counselor will not attempt to impose solutions but, maintaining a neutral standpoint, will attempt to draw emotional and moral solutions from the client.

This is, in reality, very misleading. In recent years many of the more insightful clergy are moving more and more toward the psychological model and keeping their own religious views in the background. Concurrently, the psychological community is recognizing that it is not dealing with a religiously or morally neutral process. Psychology, like religion, attempts to guide people who wish to change their lives. In assisting these clients to minimize their emotional torment, the counselor operates with certain images of "sin" (the causative agent in the stress's dynamics), of "salvation" (the movement away from the pain), and some general interpretation of human fulfillment and life's meaning (Browning, 1976).

No gay or lesbian can escape responding in some manner to the ways in which the Judeo-Christian tradition has dealt with homosexuality. Likewise, it is predictable that numerous gay and lesbian clients will be working on issues of self-worth and self-esteem stemming from preconceived condemnation by organized religion. Especially when working with the gay or lesbian alcoholic in a traditional setting, the need to complete the "steps" requires an involvement with spirituality. When they confuse this with the need for involvement with religion, a major stumbling block exists. Therefore, whether the biblical and theological arguments are of personal interest to the counselor is not the point. They do matter to the recovery process of the lesbian or gay alcoholic. Accordingly, it can be enormously helpful if the counselor is able to respond knowledgeably to the question: "But doesn't the Bible say homosexuality is a sin?" with "No, not as I understand it." A number of books exist on relevant biblical and theological issues (Bailey,1955; Boswell, 1980; Horner, 1978; Kosnick, Carroll, Cunningham, Modras, & Schulta, 1977; McNeil, 1976; Pittenger, 1967; Scanzon & Mollenkott, 1978; Woods, 1977). A brief summary of these issues is given here.

Any specific biblical reference relating to homosexuality needs to be evaluated with several things in mind. The most important fact is that homosexuality as an *orientation* is not mentioned in the Bible. This concept of orientation is a modern one beyond the thought of the day. The Bible's references are statements of condemnation toward certain types of same-sex sexual activities. The biblical authors felt that only heterosexuality was "natural." In fact, this concept is the basis for the infamous passage in Romans 1:26 that has long provided the strongest New Testament argument against homosexual activity as intrinsically unnatural. The normal English translation for the phrase has been "against nature." Boswell (1980) noted: "The modern reader is apt to read into that phrase a wealth of associations derived from later philosophical developments, scholastic theology, Freudian psychology, social taboos, as well as personal misgivings" (p. 88). It is difficult to ascertain what Paul meant by this phrasing. The phrase as it appears in the original is *ten phusken kresin*. However, in Romans 4:18 God acts as a *parà phúsin* in grafting a wild olive branch (the Gentiles) onto a cultivated tree (the inheritance of the Jews). This makes it clear that the phrase itself does not necessarily imply a moral judgment on the action as wrong.

If other examples are looked at, it can be seen that Paul most likely accepted the phrase from the popular Stoic philosophy of the day: one that referred to a religious and cultural heritage, not to a philosophical natural-law judgment. The Jews are Jews "by nature"; the Gentiles are uncircumcised "by nature." Except for one verse in Galatians the character referred to by *phusin* does not represent something inherent but is a matter of training or social modeling. A good example of this is in Corinthians, 11:14: "Does not nature teach you that, if a man has long hair, it is a shame unto him?"

When Paul used *ten phusken kresin,* he did not make a distinction between nature and Jewish custom. There seems to be a merging of two thoughts in Paul's mind of what is natural (*parà phúsin*) and the concept of *toevah* (or what is not proper according to Jewish law and custom). When looking at passages where Paul stated that pagans had "abandoned" the "natural uses" of their sexuality for that which is "beyond nature," it would seem that Paul was referring to the pagans who went beyond their own sexuality (heterosexuality) and indulged in new sexual pleasures (homosexuality) as a part of a cultic worship practice.

The remaining two verses in the New Testament that have been used to condemn homosexuality were also authored by Paul: I Corinthians 6:9 where the word *malakói* is used and I Timothy 1:10 where the word *arsenokóitai* is used. *Malakói* (literally translated as *soft*) seems to indicate a person of dissolute personality, not homosexuality, and *arsenokóitai* (couch-man) refers to homosexual sexual activity such as male prostitution, which in the Old Testament was associated with cultic worship practices.

In the Old Testament it is Genesis 19 and the story of Sodom and Gomorrah that are most frequently used to condemn homosexuality. However, this interpretation is only a relatively recent one. In the Old Testament itself the sin is one of inhospitality (Ezekiel 16:49-50; Wisdom 19:13-14; Ecclesiaties 16:8). Even in the New Testament Jesus speaks of the sin of Sodom and Gomorrah as one of inhospitality and not receiving the "Word of God" (Luke 10:10-13).

There are two additional Old Testament passages that are indisputably denunciations of homosexual acts. Leviticus 18:23 and 20:13 are a part of the "holiness code" or the code used to provide a separateness of God's chosen people from the surrounding tribes with their idolatrous practices. Many people who wish to use religion to condemn homosexuality use a literal translation of these texts and forget their historical content.

Rev. Troy Perry related a story in his book (1972) in which he had one of his first encounters with this type of person while demonstrating in front of the Los Angeles offices of State Steamship Lines, who had fired a young man for being homosexual

> Well, you know that thing about pride going before a fall. I looked up as proud as all get out, and I saw this lady coming determinedly up the street. I held out a leaflet and said, "Here, madam, would you take one of our leaflets?" She didn't say a word. She just hauled off and hit me as hard as she could with her purse. I didn't believe it. So, like a fool, I repeated myself. I said, "Madam, are you sure you don't want one of our leaflets?" So, she hit me again. She said, "If I had my way all of your perverted individuals would be locked up, in jail, and the key thrown away!" I said, "Madam, that's a wonderful Christian attitude you have." She looked me over, backed off a step, and I thought she was going to hit me again. She said, "Young man, do you know what the Book of Leviticus says?" I told her, "I sure do! It says that it's a sin for a women to wear a red dress, for a man to wear a cotton shirt and woolen pants at the same time, for anyone to eat shrimp, oyster, or lobster—or your steak too rare." She said, "That's not what I mean!" I said, "I know that's not what you mean, honey, but you forgot all of these other dreadful sins, too, that are in the same book of the Bible." She said, "Do you know what Saint Paul said?" Again, I said, "I sure do. He said for women to be silent, not to speak." She said, "That is not what I mean either." I said, "I know it's not, honey, but Paul disliked women: he said that women were not to teach, preach, and that they were not to have any sort of authority over a man. Where would our women's liberation groups be, if they had listened to the Apostle Paul? He didn't like women with short hair, or men with long hair. Are we going to close the doors of the church just because the Apostle Paul didn't like women with short hair, nor men with long hair?"*

---

*Source: From *The Lord is My Shepherd and He Knows I'm Gay* (p. 150) by T. Perry with C. Lucas, 1972, Austin, TX: Liberty Press, Inc. Copyright 1972 by Liberty Press, Inc. Reprinted by permission.

Alcoholism counselors, therefore, need to be aware that careful examination of biblical material renders no clear-cut scriptural word on homosexuality as a sexual orientation or upon homosexual genital expression of a relationship based on love and respect. Specifically, what the Bible does give is references to certain kinds of same-sex acts in quite different religious and cultural contexts from those faced by gays and lesbians today. Often forgotten, and a subject important to make the gay or lesbian alcoholic aware of, is the manner in which scripture celebrates instances of genuine love (including physical) between two men or two women—David and Jonathon, Ruth and Naomi, Jesus and the Beloved Disciple. But just as important is the Christian approach that counsels each person to assess every moral judgment in terms of a spirit of love for God, humanity, and oneself. The Bible conveys the message that human sexuality is one of the greatest and best of all gifts. It is to be integrated into the fullness of what it means to be a person: the very essence of a person's being expressed in ways that honor both the self and the other involved.

ALCOHOLISM TREATMENT AND GAY MEN

One of the most important issues necessary for the counselor to understand is that regardless of how "together" the gay client may seem, internalized homophobia is almost certainly a factor in his substance abuse. If these issues are not confronted, either because of fear of offending the client or because of one's own countertransference issues, then the likelihood of effective intervention and long-term sobriety is highly questionable. It is superfluous whether the counselor is an expert in the field of alcoholism. Even if he or she is adept, this does not automatically mean that he or she can treat the gay alcoholic. It is necessary to realize that the gay person is a unique individual with his own set of psychological dynamics shared, in full, with no one else. Gays can be found in all socioeconomic levels, in all ethnic groups, and in the majority of, if not all, occupations. Also unique to the gay alcoholic is his need to have engaged in a "coming out process." This process can be anywhere from a rigidly held "double life style" to a frank attitude of not caring who knows. It is imperative that the counselor understand this process of "coming out of the closet" and be aware of just where the client is in the process. Further, an awareness of the different subcultures in the gay community and the client's involvement in them is necessary to understand fully the dynamics of the individual.

When the heterosexual counselor treats the gay alcoholic, he or she needs to be very aware of the tendency of many gay alcoholics to play the "poor me" and "if only" games (Steiner, 1971). In both situations, homosexuality is used as a tool to manipulate the counselor into not looking at the real issue: his drinking. In fact he has spent much of his life (childhood and adulthood) learning to manipulate: first, an environment hostile to him because of "being different," and second, one that threatens to take away the only solution he had found to his problem: his drinking.

The counselor can expect the repeated use of: "You don't understand me" whenever real progress is being made. If the counselor is heterosexual an appropriate response might be: "You're right, I really don't understand much about you, but I want to. I really care about you, and you're getting sober. What do I need to understand to help you do that?" The counselor must repeatedly refocus the client onto his alcoholism. While in many, if not most, cases, his sexual orientation will be deeply intertwined with his drinking, the focus should always be on the drinking, not the sexuality. If he can be helped to discover that the drinking is only covering up and intensifying his negative feelings about himself, then he will have begun the road to recovery. If the client continues to focus only on his gayness and the heterosexual counselor is unable to effect a positive change, then a referral to a gay agency or counselor is the appropriate step. Gayness is not an excuse in a gay agency or with a gay counselor.

It is necessary for the counselor to recognize that there are certain issues that differ between the gay and heterosexual alcoholic. One of the major differences is the lack of places for social involvement that do not include alcohol and drug abuse. In most parts of the country, bars are one, if not the only, place where gay men may socialize freely. When individuals get together in a private setting there is usually a focus on alcohol and drug use to facilitate social interaction and sexual encounters. For many gay men, alcohol is synonymous with having fun and being able to engage in physical intimacy.

A second issue that is of particular import to the gay man is self-esteem. Some of the low self-esteem that will be found is relatively easy to counter. These are the individuals who are much more acceptable, in both personality and physical stature, than they believe. The only special referral that might be appropriate for these individuals is to gay Alcoholics Anonymous (AA) meetings where they can be "loved" back to health. In most other ways, they will respond well to the same groups and techniques used with heterosexual clients.

There is also the "vicious queen" who, usually as a result of a long drinking history and a very low opinion of himself, has developed the symptoms of a personality disorder. Much of the same treatment that is directed toward the "borderline" patient will be effective with this client.

The major focus of the counseling will need to be directed toward his underlying "oral" rage and fear of engulfment and loss of self. This client will almost always require intensive, long-term therapy using various techniques to help him separate and form a healthy new self-identity. In this client, it will often be found that the alcohol has provided him with a transitional object as he struggles to make himself into a whole.

Another very important aspect of counseling the gay man is an awareness of the importance of body image. The alcoholic will usually feel ugly and unattractive. In reality, the negative effects of alcoholism frequently produce physical unattractiveness. This is usually due to the lack of personal care and hygiene on the part of the alcoholic. With sobriety and a return to proper hygiene, a person's physical attractiveness can return to the same levels that existed prior to drinking.

When the gay alcoholic becomes sober, one of the most frequent complaints is the lack of a sex drive. Many gay alcoholics have a great deal of anxiety over penis size. These attitudes can have a direct bearing of the eventual ability of the gay man to have sex soberly. His fears of rejection because of small or oddly formed genitals are usually only the symptoms of underlying negative feelings about himself and his gayness (homophobia). Traditional sex therapy techniques such as self-pleasuring exercises, conjoint sexual exercises, affirmation, etc. will help the individual obtain a satisfactory sexual life, perhaps for the first time.

A major area the alcoholism counselor must address if he or she is working with the gay alcoholic is AIDS. Everyone involved in substance abuse counseling must avail themselves of the information that is becoming more and more readily available on the subject of AIDS.

When this epidemic first began there was little understanding that substance abuse had anything to do with AIDS. This, in large part, was due to alcoholism professionals not being involved in the field. However, today the number of substance abusers who are also HIV+ (the virus that causes the immunosuppression) causes counselors to be concerned for both their client and themselves.

Smith, Co-Chairman of the San Francisco AIDS and Substance Abuse Task Force stated:

> The good news is that the basic substance abuse counseling techniques are very effective in working with gay substance abusers who have AIDS or ARC [AIDS Related Complex]. Nevertheless, many of our cherished principles of substance abuse treatment do need to be modified in working with these people, and this is difficult for many workers in the alcoholism treatment field to

accept. It is commonly felt, for example, that when you start making alcoholics "special" you give them an excuse to drink. Another basic principle in alcoholism treatment is that the client has to take individual responsibility. In working with substance abusing AIDS patients we actually take over some of their responsibility. We even reach out to these clients when they are still drinking or taking drugs. For these individuals we also have to replace some of the standard outcome goals, such as going to work, with other goals such as developing a better social life or getting involved in their treatment for AIDS. (Cited in Acquired Immune Deficiency Syndrome, 1986, p. 54.)

These individuals are indeed different from the majority of the clients in treatment. They are different in that it would appear that they are under a death sentence and usually have only a short time left before they will die from one of the various infections with which they are afflicted. Thus, for the alcoholic with AIDS it becomes an issue of "quality" not "quantity" of life. Care needs to be taken to provide the person with AIDS (PWA) with clear-cut information about both AIDS and substance abuse of all types. That means that the alcoholism counselor must be up to date on the latest information concerning the signs and symptoms that the client can expect as well as the type of activities (including sexual) in which he may safely engage without harm to himself. Referral resources need to be available for the client, and he must be encouraged to use them.

Most people develop different behavioral mannerisms that they use in various environments, and this responsiveness, when accomplished rather than regressive, is considered a psychological strength. Problems arise when these personality states become dissociative, when amnesia between states, or a fugue state, develops. In many gay men there is a loss of spontaneity in public because their "straight" facade is ensconced. The need to keep the hidden self secret is evident in both alcoholic and gay men. The effect of a person having two secret selves (one alcoholic and one homosexual) is synergistic. The client becomes overly protective of himself to prevent anyone from finding out about his gayness or his alcoholism. His defensive structures become varied and, when successfully challenged, more primitive. Therapeutic intervention with this type of gay man is analogous to working with a dissociative disorder in which the intergration of the personality is the goal.

The stress on youth in the homosexual community can put many stressors on the gay alcoholic. The homosexual world abounds with myths concerning the older gay man: when they grow old they will be lonely and alone;

gay men become child molesters when they can no longer attract other gay men at the age of 40; older gay men commit suicide or go crazy; older gay men are all old queens or aunties; etc. Even though there is little evidence of any of these things occurring, these myths are widely held in the gay community.

The aging process is often accompanied by a reduction of the sex drive, premature aging of the body, and loss of status as employment, friends, and finances change. It is not unusual to find that the older gay alcoholic has become indifferent to new situations, no matter what pleasure they offer. It seems that nothing and no one can please him or influence him to take down his "walls" and share even a small part of himself. He feels first that his homosexuality has made him one of life's untouchables, and second, that the label *alcoholic* has made him even more unworthy (if that is possible). This defensiveness is the result of years of thinking, feeling, and behaving in a world through a bottle. Along with his sobriety, he will need to learn new ways to communicate with the world around him.

It is necessary for the alcoholism counselor to be aware that there exist several genres of the gay subculture. Some of the grouping surrounds sexual activity preference such as sadomasochism or "water sports"; others involve like fantasies. Several groups have to do with the time period in which the gay man entered the gay community. The subculture of the 1930s was very different from today's subculture. In the 1950s and 1960s the oppression produced secrecy and the need to keep one's sexual orientation hidden at all costs. The oppression faced in the 1970s resulted in just the opposite: gays and lesbians began to become militant and organize. The change in the APA's diagnostic manual (first DSM II and now DSM III) was in major part due to the organization and militancy of the lesbian and gay community. When working with the older gay man, a group composed of others of like age will be much more necessary than with a heterosexual of the same age. This will be helpful in reducing the isolation and in providing successful role models for the members so that they can see the possibilities that exist for them.

In conclusion, any treatment for a problem presented by a gay alcoholic needs to be based on the facts that (a) he is part of a gay subculture and an understanding of that culture will be essential to understand and intervene in the process, and (b) he almost certainly will have beliefs and behaviors that many in the general society might find questionable and some even distasteful. The alcoholism counselor needs to be able to place his or her own value system in the background when evaluating the client. If the counselor is convinced that the client's outlook is immature, destructive, or restrictive, then, and only then, is it permissible for the counselor to express his or her concerns about that behavior. He or she needs to present them in a clear manner that will allow the client to recognize that they are the counselor's subjective views.

The alcoholism counselor needs to be aware of the developmental stages of a gay man's coming out process. For example, it is these authors' experience that a preponderance of gay men develop homoerotic feelings early in life and feel a generalized anxiety over those feelings. These feelings of being separate, unequal, and less than others may intensify into paranoia, depression, denial, and the like. Alcohol is frequently discovered at a relatively early age to possess a wonderful quality of being able to "make the world" if not go away, at least manageable. This soon turns from an occasional adventure into continual self-medicating. For this reason, it is so very necessary for the alcoholism counselor to take a good psychological history and a drug and alcohol use history. This will allow the counselor to understand the formation and perpetuation of behaviors that affect the client in the "here and now."

In treatment of the gay alcoholic, counselors need to be aware of the many, many stresses on the gay client that arise from society at large, gay society, and from the client himself, not only because of his gayness, but also because of his alcoholism. The oppression faced by many gay alcoholics is experienced in many ways and assaults different aspects of the personality. Since the client many times is unaware of these stresses, it is the function of the counselor to be cognizant of what the client may be experiencing and authenticate the right of the client to have responded in the manner in which he did.

There is less oppression of gays and lesbians today than at any time in recent history. However, there are still forces at large that tell the gay and lesbian community that they are perverted and sick. And there are still thousands and thousands of young gay men and lesbian women sitting in churches, synagogues, classrooms, and around the family table hearing this. And as long as this oppression exists, gay and lesbian alcoholics will continue to exist as well.

ALCOHOLISM TREATMENT AND LESBIAN WOMEN

This population belongs to two groups not generally accepted by society: (a) homosexuals, and (b) alcoholics. In addition, they belong to a group further oppressed by society: women. The dynamics unique to each area are intertwined and cannot be separated into distinct categories. Therefore, it is relevant to address those dynamics related specifically to women (and therefore relevant to lesbians), to alcoholism, and to lesbians.

A good treatment program needs to address a multitude of issues. It needs to be flexible to allow for the individual differences of each client. It needs to be sensitive to the issues relevant to the lesbian population. A program that operates on the precept that alcoholism is concerned only with alcohol cannot provide an environment in which lesbians can thrive in the recovery process. An effective alcoholism counselor must be sensitive to all kinds of oppression and must identify related dynamics. Swallow (1983) eloquently stated this point:

> Often in alcoholism and addiction rehabilitation programs, all symptoms are attributed to the substance . . . low self-esteem, depression, anger, isolation, alienation, paranoia, distrust, self-hatred. For the lesbian, these are also symptoms of social, cultural class and racial oppression. From the point where a lesbian is drug/alcohol dependent she is at least triply oppressed . . . as an addict/alcoholic, a lesbian and a woman. Oppression escalates as she differs from the "establishment" . . . for example, if she's older, or working-class, or third world, or a mother. A good program needs staff who are sensitive to these issues (p. 80).

The following is a self-report (*The Way Back*, 1982) of a recovering lesbian that exemplifies one specific way in which issues related to alcohol intertwine with issues related specifically to lesbians: "I believe that when I opted for straight life, I opted for alcoholism, because that was the only way I could live and psychologically survive" (p. 66). "[I eventually closed] the door on the straight life that was untenable to me, and became gay—openly gay. I think that it was because I was sober that I could do it, but, also, because I was sober I *had* to do it—to assure that I was going to stay sober and live a comfortable life" (p. 72).

Research and literature addressing issues related to alcoholism in the lesbian community are limited. The drinking of lesbians per se was not reported or apparently specifically studied until the mid-1970s. In the past 10 years there has been a handful of reported research projects, first person accounts, and newspaper stories. Research is sorely needed to support a growing body of hypotheses, assumptions, theories, and observed characteristics regarding alcohol-abusive lesbians. For general information about working with lesbians (i.e., nonalcoholism specific), the reader is referred to the work of Woodman & Lenna (1980).

Though the treatment of alcoholic lesbians is in many ways similar to the treatment of alcoholic women in general (i.e., similar issues must be addressed), there are relevant dynamics specific to lesbians. It appears that levels of excessive drinking or alcohol dependence are greater in lesbians than in heterosexual women. Research studies estimate alcoholism rates to be between 25% and 35% among lesbians compared with 5% to 10% among heterosexual women (Diamond & Wilsnack, 1978; Keller, 1975; Saghir & Robins, 1973).

It is important to note that there is no particular psychotherapy for lesbians. Rather, there is psychotherapy for women who happen to be lesbian. Counselors "who work with lesbians need to have an understanding of the consequences of social, political, and economic oppression upon the psychological development of their clients and be able to help them understand the ramifications of this oppression" (Anthony, 1985, p. 53). This is a particularly important dimension to explore in terms of the client's use (abuse) of the self-medicating properties of alcohol to manage the feelings attached to these issues.

Diamond and Wilsnack (1978) studied alcohol abuse among lesbians. Though more research is required to extend their tentative conclusions regarding treatment, their work is offered here as an introduction to important variables that need to be addressed in the alcoholism treatment of lesbians. They proposed four possible motivations in the drinking behaviors of lesbians:

1. *Dependency:* This theory predicted that lesbian drinkers have strong dependency needs and that drinking enhances their sense of dependency gratification. However, Diamond and Wilsnack's study failed to support that drinking enhanced gratification of dependency needs.
2. *Power:* Drinking appeared to be associated with an increase in power related behaviors (assertiveness, sexual advances, verbal and physical aggression) that may act as a compensation for feelings of dependency.
3. *Sex role expectations and conflicts:* Drinking appeared to be associated with behavioral changes that were predominantly in the traditional masculine direction (greater assertiveness, dominance, activity).
4. *Self-esteem and depression:* Most subjects experienced increased feelings of self-esteem while drinking. They all reported that depression frequently precipitated their drinking.

An important feature supported by this study is that, in terms of sex role influences, most subjects perceived the masculine behavioral changes and the feeling of enhanced levels of power as desirable, and many used (or abused) alcohol as the instrument to produce these desired changes. "Thus, rejection of certain aspects of traditional femininity, including dependency, and the desire to compensate through enhancement of personal power may interlock as a syndrome that encourages dependence on alcohol" (Diamond & Wilsnack, 1978, p. 136).

Another interpretation of the dependency and power findings is related to issues of anger. Lesbians appear to experience higher levels of generalized anger than do heterosexual women, perhaps due, in part, to societal oppression of homosexuality. Drinking apparently facilitates the repression of this anger.

It is important to note that the four motivating factors are relevant in all aspects of alcoholism treatment. However, for the purpose of a concise, yet inconclusive, presentation of important dynamics in the treatment of alcohol abuse with lesbians, the following categories were arbitrarily chosen:

- alcoholism and gender
- lesbian relationships and alcoholism
- isolation and loneliness
- age of the lesbian
- Alcoholics Anonymous (AA) and lesbians
- homophobia, judgments, and prejudice.

Alcoholism and Gender

Research supports that, in the population as a whole, alcohol is often used as a self-corrective means of balancing gender role dysfunction. It is used as a self-medicating vehicle surrounding issues related to feelings of one's own maleness and femaleness. In its self-medicating fashion, it allows individuals to experience those aspects of themselves they would normally suppress, such as dependency, autonomy, power, and/or boldness. It appears that this trend may be exacerbated in the gay community because of the lack of defined sex-role behavior. "When people experience an incongruity between who they think they should be and who they really are in the context of gender role behavior, tremendous confusion, discordance and dysfunctional patterns of reciprocal feedback will result" (Bepko & Krestan, 1985, p. 52). In the general population, drinking is often a response to a failure or conflict in living up to prescribed role expectations. Without these expectations lesbians may be more inclined to use alcohol as the means to attain some degree of sex-role identity.

Current societal trends are toward more androgynous gender roles, and these trends particularly affect lesbian relationships where there exist undefined sex-role barriers. In a study by LaTorre and Wendenburg (1985) exploring the psychological characteristics of bisexual, heterosexual, and homosexual woman, it was reported that the proportion of androgynous and undifferentiated individuals was much greater among lesbians. Lesbians and bisexual subjects also possessed more socially desirable masculine traits than did heterosexual subjects. Therefore, it is important for the counselor to be aware of his or her possible prejudice against women who display independent and autonomous ideas and behaviors. Relevant also is the possibility that the client may be experiencing some underlying dissension (resulting in dysfunction) related to self-identity issues in balancing feminine and masculine characteristics. These individuals may have opted to deny femininity in the pursuit of desired masculine traits. Others have integrated both, thereby attaining a more complete whole.

A woman with predominately feminine personality traits finds it difficult to stand up to another individual (Bem, 1975), let alone an entire society. Bisexual and homosexual women may have character traits that allow them to do so.

> Some succeed by repressing or suppressing both their masculinity and their femininity (i.e., undifferentiation); others are able to develop both sets of attributes to high degree (i.e., androgyny). If this speculation is true, we may . . . expect that undifferentiated lesbians experience more anxiety about their erotic preference because of their repression or suppression (LaTorre & Wendenburg, 1985, p. 96).

This creates a greater susceptibility to alcoholism and a poor prognosis in recovery unless these issues are addressed and the client is able to develop coping strategies more characteristic of an androgynous lesbian.

"Alcoholism may be a marker of the inability to achieve an adrogynous integration of sex role behavior within the individual and with the relational system. It is also a marker of the constriction imposed by a larger social context in which such integration has been explicitly defined as nonnormative" (Bepko & Krestan, 1985, p. 52). This is further exacerbated by the nonnormative nature in the special population of lesbians.

> If heterosexuals experience a need for self-correction based on their perception that they fail to meet social requirements for adequate maleness or femaleness, this conflict may be significantly intensified in a lesbian relationship where no clear rules exist for defining who operates in what mode. . . . It is important to acknowledge in a discussion of sex roles that differences and similarities in role conflict between heterosexuals and lesbians do exist (Bepko & Krestan, 1985, p. 53).

In summary:

> In many, if not all, families in which alcoholism is a factor, an inability to acknowledge or act on feelings that run counter to traditional sex role expectations is always present to a greater or lesser degree. . . . It seems clear to us that no lasting effective clinical work can be accomplished with families [and individuals] unless family members [and individuals] are helped to develop an awareness of the constricting nature of sex role stereotypes, and are also helped to negotiate new expectations of self and others within the family context (Bepko & Krestan, 1985, p. 57).

Therefore, it is of utmost importance in the treatment of lesbians to explore thoroughly feelings of femaleness with the client. This can be effectively accomplished in the context of exploration of sex-role identity and feelings of self-worth.

Lesbian Relationships and Alcoholism

Anthony (1985) reported that the most common presenting problem of lesbians seeking counseling or psychotherapeutic services is difficulty with a lover relationship. Some of these difficulties stem from lack of social and personal support systems available to lesbians, who often remain closeted to varying degrees because of societal oppression. The day-to-day need for secrecy and discretion has monumental effects in established relationships as well as in developing relationships. For the single lesbian there is neither a defined courtship ritual nor a large variety of meeting places in which to enhance the development of social skills. Typically, lesbians are unskilled in initiating social contacts. Learning how to court and be courted is not something they learn easily while still in the closet. "Even though a woman does not acknowledge her lesbian identity until she is 30, 40 or 60 years old, she may then go through a form of 'adolescent dating anxiety'" (Anthony, 1985, p. 50). As alcohol is sometimes a central part of lesbian social activities (e.g., gay bars) and drinking is often felt to decrease anxiety, increase self-esteem, and release inhibitions, this aspect of the lesbian subculture enhances alcohol abuse.

Isolation and Loneliness

Historically we haven't had many places outside of the barroom setting where we could gather, socialize and be who we are. I

don't think most women go the bar scene intending to drink. I
think they go there mostly to socialize. At least in the beginning,
that's the gathering place, that's the place to go. Essentially, that's
how it's set up right now; there's where we go. But the whole
setup pushes the drug called alcohol. So to take alcoholism out
of its community base, we as a community have to build alternative structures to the bars to fulfill what the bar provides, which
is socializing and networking (Swallow, 1983, p. 85).

This above report of a recovering alcoholic lesbian exemplifies one component of the tremendous isolation and loneliness that predominate in this
community. In addition, societal oppression (both homosexual and heterosexual), the lack of community resources, and the isolation from neighbors, work peers, and even other lesbians (due to the limited availability
of meeting places) further enhance the isolation of the lesbian. The result
is a lack of support systems, without which one is more likely to make
alcohol a central part of life. In addition, the lack of social support systems
lessens the chances of success in recovery. Counselors can be a great asset
to the client if they avail themselves of resources such as gay book stores,
lesbian organizations, gay AA meetings, lesbian counseling services and
support groups, lesbian and gay community centers, and local lesbian and
gay switchboards and hotlines.

As isolated women, lesbians tend to hide their illnesses because the
treatment may feel far worse than the disease. It appears that an environment unconditionally accepting and supportive of their life style, and
thereby of them as persons who suffer from alcoholism, not lesbianism,
would enhance their chances of seeking treatment and their chances of
success in such treatment. Particularly relevant to successful treatment is
the development of social skills, social support systems, and feelings of
self-worth that would help convert feelings of estrangement and isolation
into feelings of connectedness and belonging. "Related to sobriety are
problems around loneliness and structuring leisure time activities. . . . [The
homosexual alcoholics] have isolated themselves by drinking, and the void
must be filled" (Colcher, 1982, p. 47).

Age of the Lesbian

Recent societal trends have had a monumental influence in all aspects
of women's lives (e.g., self-identity, self-esteem, sex-role behaviors, role
expectations). These trends have affected the lives of lesbians in some
areas specific to lesbian life styles. The old patterns of traditional role play

in lesbian relationships (i.e., "butch" and "fem") are no longer predominant in these relationships. There appears to have been a major shift to androgynous-oriented relationships. The age of the client is relevant in terms of her perceptions of sex-role behaviors and her own role in a relationship. Alcohol is sometimes used unsuccessfully as a transitional object in dealing with these changing trends and in coping with the ambivalence associated with lessening role boundaries. Exploration into related issues is essential in order to enhance the development of skills necessary to deal with the lack of defined role expectations.

Age is also relevant in the shaping of one's positive or negative identity as a lesbian. Those who have been actively lesbian for many years have experienced societal oppression that is qualitatively different than that experienced by younger lesbians. Some younger lesbians engage in a type of ageism where "there is ageism, dirty-old-women jokes and women who are prejudiced or have preconceptions about lesbians that really hurt" (Swallow, 1983, p. 70).

Alcoholics Anonymous and Lesbians

AA participation concurrent with counseling is often a good treatment plan. However, there are some issues specific to lesbians that the counselor needs to be aware of. The following story exemplifies one such issue. Stonedey (1983) was in her second year of sobriety when she and her lover moved to a different community as a result of harassment connected to their lesbian life style. This account begins with her first attendance at the new AA site:

> I looked around the room for somebody like me, a lesbian, a gay man. There were some possibilities. Statistics had it that there were four of us there, but no one I could immediately identify. . . . A man named Gary spoke. . . . "I was on my way here and I ran into an old girl friend who's a full-time teacher, a part-time ski instructor and a full-time lesbian." The room exploded in laughter. He then explained that it was probably his fault (he used the word fault) that she was a lesbian. . . . I felt my anger explode within me. . . . I remember the old neighborhood and knew I couldn't come out here. I might be revealing myself to a neighbor or the chief of police. . . . I walked home . . . feeling vulnerable, knowing there were enemies in each car that passed (p. 48).

Most major cities have lesbian and gay AA meetings. The counselor should be aware of such resources and make appropriate referrals. The advantages and potential power of homogeneous groups are exemplified by a lesbian's experience at a gay hospitality suite at the 1980 45th AA Aniversary Conference in New Orleans:

> I was healed in places I didn't even know were hurt, simply the magic of lesbians giving to one another, giving the one thing the world can't take away: the ability to be so in tune with others in our own kind that we pass the strength among us to weave the spell of overwhelming unconditional love (Swallow, 1983, p. 32).

Homophobia, Judgments, and Prejudice

Counselor

"Heterosexual therapists who downplay the importance of society's homophobia may fail to maintain empathy. A clear understanding of society's oppression is essential to keeping the consequences of such oppression in perspective" (McCandlish, 1985, p. 75). It is of utmost importance for lesbian alcohol abusers to work with counselors who accept the client's sexual orientation. Fear of rejection may keep many lesbians from seeking traditional services. "It is evident that when gay-identified therapy is available, clients will come, and they will come to gay identified services sooner that [sic] they will go to nongay services" (Driscoll, 1982, p. 79).

Several researchers have suggested that counseling for homosexual clients with drinking problems often becomes a power conflict because the heterosexual therapist may focus on the treatment of homosexuality and not on the drinking problem (Beaton & Guild, 1976; Small & Leach, 1977). Sobriety is the main issue of treatment. Usually sexuality is disturbing only if the counselor makes it so. However, sometimes the client will seek treatment for alcohol related problems but will later want to explore dynamics related to her homosexuality. It is important to explore issues related to sexual orientations with the clients who are experiencing ambivalence or difficulties, but it is not necessary to treat homosexuality per se—it is not a disease. In the treatment plan for lesbians, sobriety must be stressed first. "Until a person has achieved sobriety, it is difficult for the worker to discuss deeper issues and impossible for the patient to handle them" (Colcher, 1982, p. 46).

Client

The client's feelings of internalized homophobia were addressed in preceding sections and are not repeated here. They are mentioned again here to reiterate the importance of exploring this dynamic with the lesbian client as it is so often intertwined with issues of alcoholism.

Summary of Specific Treatment Implications

1. *Alcoholism and gender*

- Process the client's self-identity as a woman and the associated feelings of femaleness.
- Explore the client's tendency toward androgyny and undifferentiation.
- Explore the client's feelings about her own sex-role behavior and develop an awareness of the constricting nature of sex-role stereotypes.

2. *Lesbian relationships and alcoholism*

- Process the client's self-identity as a lesbian.
- Develop social skills related to courtship and explore the possibility of "adolescent dating anxiety."
- Develop relationships and communication skills relevant to committed relationships.

3. *Isolation and loneliness*

- Know resources and make appropriate referrals and recommendations.
- Develop real and effective social power.
- Develop effective support systems.

4. *Age of the lesbian:* Explore issues relevant to her specific age group.
5. *Alcoholics Anonymous and lesbians:* Know the differences between gay AA meetings and nongay AA meetings and be able to make appropriate referrals.
6. *Homophobia, judgments, and prejudice*

- Process countertransferential issues related to counselor homophobia, judgments, and prejudice.
- Process the client's possible internalized homophobia.
- Look for common denominators as well as differences as an aid to limit overgeneralizing about "lesbians," but recognize that she has distinct experiences that influence her alcoholism.

- Process the client's experience with homophobia, judgments, and prejudice that may have left wounds that have not healed.

7. General

- Be sensitive to issues related to societal oppression of lesbians and gays as well as of alcoholics.
- Aid in the development of confidence and self-esteem in the client.
- Consider assertiveness training if appropriate.
- Process "coming out" issues if relevant to treatment.
- Know the literature and use it selectively with clients.

REFERENCES

Abraham, K. (1926). The psychological relationships between sexuality and alcoholism. *International Journal of Psychoanalysis, 7*, 1–10.

Altman, D. (1971). *Homosexual oppression and liberation.* New York: Outerbridge and Dienfrey.

Anthony, B. (1985). Lesbian client–lesbian therapist: Opportunities and challenges in working together. In J. Gonsiorek (Ed.), *A guide to psychotherapy with gay and lesbian clients* (pp. 45–59). New York: Harrington Park.

Bailey, D.S. (1955). *Homosexuality and the western Christian tradition.* London: Longmans.

Bayer, R. (1981). *Homosexuality and American psychiatry.* New York: Basic Books.

Beaton, S., & Guild, N. (1976). Treatment for gay problem drinkers. *Social Casework, 57,* 302–308.

Becker, H.S. (1962). *The outsiders: Studies in the sociology of deviance.* New York: Free.

Bem, S.L. (1975). Sex-role adaptability: One consequence of psychological androgyny. *Journal of Counseling & Clinical Psychology, 42,* 155–162.

Benson, R. (1965). *In defense of homosexuality.* New York: Julian.

Bepko, C., & Krestan, J. (1985). *The responsibility trap: A blueprint for treating the alcoholic family.* New York: Free.

Bergler, E. (1977). *The basic neurosis: Oral regression and psychic masochism.* New York: Grune & Stratton.

Blum, E.M. (1966). "Psychoanalytic views of alcoholism." *Quarterly Journal of Studies on Alcohol, 27,* 259–299.

Boswell, J. (1980). *Christianity, social tolerance and homosexuality.* Chicago: University of Chicago Press.

Browning, D.S. (1976). *The moral context of pastoral care.* Philadelphia: Westminster.

Burton, A.D. (1956). The psychodynamics of alcoholism: A survey of 87 cases. *Quarterly Journal of Studies on Alcohol, 17,* 443–460.

Cappon, D. (1965). *Towards an understanding of homosexuality.* Englewood Cliffs, NJ: Prentice-Hall.

Clark, L.P. (1919). Some psychological aspects of alcoholics. *New York Medical Journal, 109,* 930–933.

Clark, T.R. (1975). Homosexuality and psychopathology in nonpatient males. *American Journal of Psychoanalysis, 35,* 163–168.

Colcher, R. (1982). Counseling the homosexual alcoholic. *Journal of Homosexuality, 7,* 43–51.

Conrad, P., & Schneider, J.W. (1980). *Deviance and medicalization: From badness to sickness.* St. Louis: C.V. Mosby.

Cory, D.W. (1951). *The homosexual in America: A subjective approach.* New York: Breenberg.

Curran, F.J. (1937). Personality studies in alcoholic women. *Journal of Nervous and Mental Disorders, 86,* 645–667.

Diamond, D., & Wilsnack, S.C. (1978). Alcohol abuse among lesbians: A descriptive study. *Journal of Homosexuality, 4,* 123–142.

Driscoll, R. (1982). A gay-identified alcohol treatment program: A follow-up study. *Journal of Homosexuality, 7,* 71–80.

Fifield, L., DeCreascenzo, T.A., & Latham, J.D. (1975). *Alcoholism and the gay community.* Los Angeles: Gay Community Services Center.

Ford, C., & Beach, F. (1951). *Patterns of sexual behavior.* New York: Harper & Row.

Foucault, M. (1973). *Madness and civilization: A history of insanity in the Age of Reason.* (R. Howard, trans.) New York: Vintage/Random House.

Freedman, M. (1971). *Homosexuality and psychological functioning.* California: Brooks/Cole.

Freud, S. (1953). Sexuality and the etiology of neurosis. In E. Jones (Ed.), *Collected papers.* London: Hogarth.

Gilbert, A.L. (1978). Psychosocial considerations in treating adolescents. *American Journal of Psychoanalysis, 38,* 355–358.

Halleck, S.L. (1971). *The politics of therapy.* New York: Science House.

Hart, H.H. (1930). Personality factors in alcoholism. *Archives of Neurology, 24,* 116–134.

Hawkins, R. (1980). The Uppsala connection: The development of principles basic to education for sexuality. *SIECUS Report, 8*(3), 13–14.

Hoffman, M. (1968). *The gay world.* New York: Bantam.

Horner, T. (1978). *Jonathan loved David.* Philadelphia: Westminster.

Jackson, C. (1944). *Lost weekend.* New York: Farrar.

Jelliffe, S.E. (1917). The Mentality of the alcoholic. *New York Medical Journal, 105,* 629–635.

Keller, M. (1975). Problems of epidemiology in alcohol problems. *Journal of Studies on Alcohol, 36,* 65–79.

Khantzian, E.J. (1980). The alcoholic patient: An overview and perspective. *American Journal of Psychotherapy, 34,* 4–19.

Kinsey, A., Pomeroy, W., & Martin, C. (1948). *Sexual behavior in the human male.* Philadelphia: W.B. Saunders.

Kinsey, A.C., Pomeroy, W., Martin, C.D., & Gebhard, H. (1953). *Sexual behavior in the human female.* Philadelphia: W.B. Saunders.

Knight, R.P. (1937). The dynamics and treatment of chronic alcohol. *Bull, Minninger Clinic 1,* 233–250.

Kosnick, J.A., Carroll, W., Cunningham, A., Modras, R., & Schulta, J. (1977). *Human sexuality: New directions in American Catholic thought.* New York: Paulist.

Laing, R.D. (1967). *The politics of experience.* New York: Pantheon.

LaTorre, R., & Wendenburg, K. (1985). Psychological characteristics of bisexual, hetero-sexual and homosexual women. In M.W. Ross (Ed.), *Homosexuality, masculinity and femininity* (pp. 87–97).

Levine, J. (1955). The sexual adjustment of alcoholics. *Quarterly Journal of the Studies on Alcohol,* 675–680.

Masters, W., & Johnson, V. (1979). *Homosexuality in perspective.* Boston: Little, Brown.

McCandlish, B.M. (1985). Therapeutic issues with lesbian couples. In J.C. Gonsiorek (Ed.), *A guide to psychotherapy with gay and lesbian clients* (pp. 71–78). New York: Harrington Park.

McNeil, J.J. (1976). *The church and the homosexual.* Kansas City: Sheed, Andrews, and Mcmeel.

Miller, J.D. (1972). Sexual inequality: Men's dilemma (a note on the oedipus complex) paranoia–other psychological concepts. *American Journal of Psychoanalysis, 32,* 148–155.

Mohr, J.C. (1978). *Abortion in America.* New York: Oxford University Press.

Moses, A., & Hawkins, R. (1982). *Counseling lesbian women and gay men.* St. Louis: C.V. Mosby.

Perry, T., with Lucas, C. (1972). *The lord is my shepherd and he knows I'm gay.* Los Angeles: Nash Publishing.

Pittenger, N. (1967). *Time for consent.* London: S.C.M.

Read, C.S. (1920). Psychopathology of alcoholism and some so-called alcoholic psychoses. *Journal of Mental Science,* July, pp. 233–244.

Riggall, R. (1923). Homosexuality and alcoholism. *Psychoanalysis Revised, 10,* 157–169.

Rogers, C.R. (1961). *On becoming a person.* Boston: Houghton Mifflin.

Saghir, M.T., & Robins, E. (1973). *Male and female homosexuality.* Baltimore: Williams & Wilkins.

Scanzon, L., & Mollenkott, V.R. (1978). *Is the homosexual my neighbor?* New York: Harper & Row.

Schur, E.M. (1971). *Labeling deviant behavior: Its sociological implications.* New York: Harper & Row.

Shively, M., & DeCecco, J. (1977). Components of sexual identity. *Journal of Homosexuality, 3*(1), 45.

Small, E.J., Jr., & Leach, B. (1977). Counseling homosexual alcoholics: Ten case histories. *Journal of Studies on Alcohol, 38,* 2077–2086.

Smalldon, J.L. (1933). The etiology of chronic alcoholism. *Psychiatry Quarterly, 7,* 640–641.

Smith, T.M. (1986). Counseling gay men about substance abuse and AIDS. In *Acquired immune deficiency syndrome and chemical dependency: Report of symposium sponsored by the American Medical Society on Alcoholism and Other Drug Dependencies, Inc. and The National Council on Alcoholism.* (1986). MD: U.S. Department of Health and Human Services.

Socrides, C.W. (1978). The sexual deviations and the *Diagnostic Manual. American Journal of Psychotherapy, 32,* 414–425.

Steiner, C. (1971). *Games alcoholics play: The analysis of life scripts.* New York: Grove Press.

Stonedey, S. (1983). Reminders. In J. Swallow (Ed.), *Out from under: Sober dykes and our friends* (pp. 46–49). San Francisco: Spinsters.

Swallow, J. (1983). *Out from under: Sober dykes and our friends.* San Francisco: Spinsters.

Wall, J.H. (1937). A study of alcoholism in women. *American Journal of Psychiatry, 93,* 944–955.

The way back. (1982). Washington, DC: Gay Council on Drinking Behavior.

Weijl, S. (1944). Theoretical and practical aspects of psychoanalytic therapy of problem drinkers. *Quarterly Journal of Studies on Alcohol, 5,* 200–511.

Weinberg, W. (1972). *Society and the healthy homosexual.* New York: St. Martin's Press.

Wholey, C.C. (1918). Revelations of the unconscious in a toxic (alcoholic) psychosis. *American Journal of Insanity, 74,* 437–447.

Woodman, N.J., & Kenna, H.R. (1980). *Counseling with gay men and women: A guide for facilitating positive lifestyles.* San Francisco: Jossey-Bass.

Woods, R. (1977). *Another kind of love.* Chicago: Thomas More.

Ziebold, T.O. (1979). Alcoholism and recovery: Gays helping gays. *Christopher Street, 3,* 36–44.

Chapter 10

The Hispanic Chemically Dependent Client: Considerations for Diagnosis and Treatment

Stanley L. Eden and Robert J. Aguilar

DEMOGRAPHICS

There are approximately 15 million persons in the United States who are of Hispanic (or Latino) descent. These figures do not include the estimated 6 million undocumented Hispanic aliens who are predominantly Mexican. As a group, Hispanics are the youngest and fastest growing minority in North America. Approximately 44% of the total U.S. Hispanic population is under the age of 18.

It is estimated that by 1990, Hispanics will be the largest minority group in the United States, with California's Hispanic population greatly increasing and Texas showing its population of Hispanics to have increased significantly by the year 2000. (1980). The Hispanic group is composed of individuals from many diverse racial and national backgrounds. They are Mexican (69%), Puerto Rican (16%), Cuban (6%), Central and South American (8%), and Spanish (13%). Racially, Hispanics are white, black, or Indian, or combinations of these groups. This fact may explain the social and cultural differences, when they exist, among the Hispanic subgroups.

It is estimated that in the United States, Spanish is either the sole language spoken or is the preferred language of at least 50% of the Hispanic population.

The income of approximately 22% of Hispanic Americans is below the poverty level, compared with about 11% for non-Hispanics (U.S. Bureau of the Census, 1980).

Education

There appear to be educational variations among the subgroups in the Hispanic American population. Puerto Rican and Mexican Americans have the least number of years of education of the larger Hispanic subgroups, and Cuban Americans have a college education rate that is almost 3 times the rate for other Hispanics. These discrepancies in educational levels may be attributable to the various socioeconomic backgrounds from which the different subgroups migrated. Many Cuban Americans have middle class and upper–middle class origins, whereas most Mexican and Puerto Rican Americans have rural agricultural backgrounds (U.S. Bureau of the Census, 1979). These and other differences in educational levels should be taken into account by substance abuse therapists since they can have a marked effect on the content and process of the therapeutic situation.

Employment

Census figures show that Hispanics in general have a high rate of unemployment and that Hispanic men have an unemployment rate that is approximately one-third higher than the national average. It is estimated that 30% of Hispanic youths between the ages of 16 and 19 are unemployed (U.S. Bureau of Labor Statistics, 1978). Higher paying technical/professional jobs are held by Hispanics at one-half the rate at which the larger U.S. population holds them. Based on these employment figures, it seems very likely that Hispanic substance-using clients may be having problems of employment and the subsequent and added problems of low income and/or poverty.

The Hispanic Family

Twice as many Hispanic families have five or more members than does the non-Hispanic U.S. population. About 25% of all Hispanic American families with children under 18 years of age are below the poverty level. Fifty-one percent of these are headed by women with no husband living in the household (U.S. Bureau of the Census, 1979). Hispanic families may be 3 times more likely to experience alcohol related difficulties than families in the general non-Hispanic population.

Many researchers have presented information supporting the idea that a strong relationship exists between the high level of alcohol oriented problems and the high number of low economic level families in the Hispanic population. These findings suggest that alcohol for many Hispanics may at least partially be caused by the stress of poverty (Alcocer, 1977).

Sexual, parental, and spousal roles in more traditional Hispanic families are usually clearly defined, with the husband being seen as the household head. Child and youth behavior is closely monitored and guided by the parents. These family behaviors are reinforced by cultural, social, and religious beliefs that play a strong role in more traditional Hispanic household environments. However, when acculturation to American society occurs within the Hispanic family, these traditional roles can break down, and the use of alcohol and/or drugs can become a method for reducing the stress caused by these changes in family interaction.

ALCOHOL AND DRUG USE

Research on substance abuse among Hispanics indicates that alcohol is the most frequently abused intoxicant. Marijuana appears to be the second most used drug, with heroin and cocaine being third. Inhalants seem to be a substance very frequently abused among young Hispanics.

Alcoholism has been found at higher rates for Hispanics than for non-Hispanics. Edmondson (1975) suggested that Mexican adult men have an alcoholism rate that is significantly higher than the national norm for other American men. Other researchers have also reported high levels of alcohol related difficulties within the American Hispanic community (Alcocer, 1975; Blum, 1973; Garcia, 1976; and Ruiz, Vasquez, & Vasquez, 1973).

Reliable data showing the usage rate of heroin among Hispanics are difficult to obtain, but Desmond and Maddox (1984) presented research that indicated that Mexican Hispanics may be second only to blacks in heroin abuse. Lukoff (1972) suggested that Puerto Rican Hispanics were second in rank after blacks in heroin use. Bell and Chambers (1970) found that approximately 56% of the Hispanics they studied were under the age of 18 when they began to use heroin. They found also that teenage Hispanic men began heroin use earlier, on the average, than Hispanic women.

Other research on teenage Mexican Hispanics in an East Los Angeles barrio indicated that approximately one of four of those teenagers questioned had used or were using inhalants as an intoxicant (e.g., model glue). Marijuana use was double the national rate, and alcohol use was almost even with national statistical norms (Padilla, Padilla, Morales, Olmeda, & Ramires, 1979).

This same research suggested that substance abuse by Mexican teenage men exceeded Mexican female usage and that the prevalence of substance use among the Hispanic substance-abusing teenagers in this study increased in variety with age. The substance abuse usually progressed sequentially with age from inhalant use, to marijuana, and then to alcohol. It should be kept in mind, however, that the validity of this study may be limited geographically to similar barrio situations. But for those therapists working mainly with Hispanics from barrio environments, this information could prove to be of great value. In general, the literature suggests that among older teenage Hispanic substance abusers, alcohol is the most frequently abused chemical, with marijuana second, stimulants third, and all other intoxicants, such as hallucinogens, barbituates, etc., about evenly distributed in percentage of use (Guinn & Hurly, 1976; Wellisch & Hays, 1974).

Hispanic women have the lowest rate of alcohol abuse of the entire U.S. Hispanic population. But even though alcohol is less frequently abused by female Hispanics, it is still the most often used intoxicant for those Hispanic women who have substance abuse problems. Chambers (1971) and Lukoff (1972) found that only about 20% of the Hispanic heroin users they studied were women. It has been suggested that the traditional social and cultural values among Hispanics, which have formerly helped keep Hispanic female alcohol and drug use at such low rates, gradually break down as Hispanic women undergo acculturation to American society and as larger numbers of Hispanic women obtain more years of education. These findings indicate that alcoholism may be much more prevalent among moderately to highly acculturated Hispanic women. (See Gilbert 1978; Holch, Warren, Smith, & Rochat, 1984).

Cultural and Historical Factors

Alcohol drinking has been used in the past by many pre-Hispanic Mexican and Central and South American cultures as a social behavior that served as a communally binding act, an act that helped to add social cohesion to their societies (Madsen & Madsen, 1969).

Alcohol problems arise when the stress of social and cultural adaptation is added to the Hispanic client's life. When drinking is seen as a socially accepted behavior by the community, family, and friends, alcohol may be seen as an accepted way of dealing with these added stresses. There is also the cultural concept of "machismo," which historically has been an accepted form of behavior for Hispanic men. Panitz, McConchie, Sauber, & Fonseca (1983) and Abad (1974) presented ideas that suggested that the consumption of alcohol may be viewed as an accepted male behavior well in line with the Hispanic concept of machismo. It is very possible that even second and third generation American Hispanic men are still influenced by cultural alcohol/drug consumption with the display of machismo (i.e., "macho" behavior).

In the past, pre-Hispanic cultures in Central and South America also employed drugs, such as mescaline, in their religious ceremonies. Even today, peyote and other herbs are used by some Mexican and Central/

South American society subgroups for spiritual and curative purposes. This cultural acceptance of herbal/drug use may help Hispanics accept the use of alcohol and/or drugs as a means of self-medicating psychological, sociological, and physiological stresses when they arise. These cultural and historical aspects can cause Hispanics to be sociologically high at risk for substance addiction, and when they are added to the stresses Hispanics encounter as they acculturate to American society, the sociological risk for substance abuse becomes even higher.

Diagnostic Considerations

In attempting to ascertain the etiology of Hispanic clients' substance abuse problems, three important risk factors should be closely examined: psychological, sociological, and physiological (Lawson, Ellis, & Rivers, 1984). Sociological factors will often present themselves more obviously as etiological determinants in the formation of the Hispanic client's chemical dependency. But as the Hispanic client's identification with his or her more traditional Hispanic cultural origins declines, these traditional sociological factors will change to sociological risks caused by the effort to adapt to American culture and society. These issues of cultural values, social adaptational stresses, socioeconomic level, and the acquired acculturational level will all combine to complicate and raise the sociological risk for Hispanic clients. This could also put Hispanic clients at higher psychological and physiological risk since the three risk factors are interrelated.

It will become the therapist's task to evaluate the way in which any extremely high risk factor will affect the remaining two risk factors. An evaluation of all three risk factors will help ensure a thorough diagnosis of the Hispanic client's substance abuse problem.

Sociological Risk Factors

Some of the sociological issues that tend to raise the chemical dependency risk level of Hispanic clients are very often related to the traditional social values the Hispanic client may hold. A particular Hispanic client (especially a man) might not see the relationship between his or her alcoholism/drug dependency and the use of these substances as social enhancers when interacting with friends.

This culturally accepted use of alcohol means also that many of the Hispanic client's friends may rely heavily on alcohol or drug use as a socially binding behavior. This behavior on the part of friends, or the acceptance by friends of drinking/drug taking behavior, may be openly or inadvertently reinforcing the client's chemical dependency. This social behavior raises the client's sociological risk.

The issues of cultural adaptation to American society and the accompanying new social values learned can often cause problems in the Hispanic client's family of origin and in the nuclear family. These intragenerational and intergenerational problems are often caused by the differences in educational and acculturational levels that may exist between the Hispanic client and his or her family members. As these sociological and cultural changes take place, feelings of guilt, self-doubt, and betrayal may occur as individual members perceive a cultural distancing taking place between themselves and other members of the family. If the changes in social and cultural values cause extreme emotional uneasiness in a particular family member, alcohol or drugs may be used to help him or her deal with these psychological stresses. An example of this would be when Hispanic youths become more culturally and socially Americanized in their values and orientations than their parents. Difficulties can arise as the parents and children attempt to adjust to the cultural differences that appear to be separating them.

Adolescence is a difficult time for both child and parent. Within families such as American Hispanic households when there may possibly exist great differences in education, speech, and social values between parent and child, the stresses these differences cause may lead the parent or child, or both, to begin to rely on alcohol or drugs in order to cope.

There has been some evidence that suggests that nuclear family problems can also arise when a more sociologically and culturally adjusted Hispanic marries a less well-adapted person of Hispanic descent or marries an individual of a completely different ethnic background (Gilbert, 1980). The emotional and psychological difficulties that can arise in these types of situations due to the differences in acculturational levels can also raise the sociological risk for some Hispanic clients.

There may also be problems regarding the ability to obtain and maintain employment due to language differences and the lack of vocational and educational training. This problem also helps to put Hispanic clients at high sociological risk for substance abuse. Satisfying work or gainful employment has long been associated with one's sense of self-esteem. Alcohol and/or drugs may be helping the Hispanic client deal with the loss of self-esteem caused by unemployment. The low income level among American Hispanics puts them, as a group, at high sociological risk. The emotional and psychological effects of poverty or near poverty may be part of a particular Hispanic client's substance abuse etiology.

These sociological factors put Hispanics at very high risk for chemical dependency. Any one or all of these sociological factors may be contributing to a particular Hispanic client's substance abuse problem. A close examination of the client's acculturational level and the degree to which he or she identifies with more traditional Hispanic social values will give the therapist very good clues as to the etiology of the client's chemical dependency. These sociological factors also often raise both the psychological and physiological risk levels for Hispanics.

Psychological Risk Factors

With Hispanic clients, as with any person or group of persons who are attempting to overcome cultural and social differences between themselves and others, there will be comparisons made between the Hispanic client's social and personal abilities and those of more socially adept individuals in the larger population. If the Hispanic client is in some way relating his or her self-esteem to being accepted or rejected by more socially acculturated Hispanics and non-Hispanics, and if the client sees himself or herself as being socially rejected, this lowered social self-image may serve to lower the client's personal level of self-esteem. If a particular Hispanic client already psychologically suffers with very low self-esteem, as many substance abusers do, this added negative social self-image, especially for newly immigrated Hispanics, can help maintain and often increase the psychological risk. This socially caused decrease in self-image, if combined with other personal problems such as sexual dysfunctions, family of origin issues, shame of poverty, etc., will mean that Hispanic clients who have these problems are at extreme psychological risk for substance abuse.

Hispanic clients use psychological care facilities less frequently than do members of the larger U.S. population, often due to cultural, social, and language differences. This suggests that perhaps many Hispanic substance abusers may be medicating themselves in order to lessen the effects of neurosis and psychosis by using alcohol or drugs (Kuanert, 1979). Chemically dependent Hispanic clients may have increased feelings of inadequacy because of a real or perceived loss of control over social situations, also due to language and cultural differences between themselves and the mainstream American society. Hispanic clients may also have feelings of inadequacy, if they have little or no opportunity to change their social and economic conditions due to a lack of education and/or training.

The feeling of being in control of oneself socially, and of being in control of one's environment, may depend a great deal upon the Hispanic client's degree of acculturation. If particular Hispanic clients find themselves in a vastly different culture, one they have difficulty relating to and one that has difficulty relating to them as well, this social/cultural shock, and the stress it creates, can increase the psychological problems that many Hispanic clients face. If the client is already chemically dependent, the issue of personal control will likely be important to the client. When a feeling of loss of social control is combined with the more personal control issue, this very often complicates the Hispanic client's psychological problems and substance abuse difficulties even further (Lawson et al., 1984).

Due to social and cultural differences between themselves and the larger American society, Hispanic clients may feel a sense of social isolation that can increase any personal feeling of isolation they may have. Alcohol or drug taking behavior may be helping the Hispanic client deal with the increase in this psychological problem.

Awareness by the therapist of both the socially created psychological problems (e.g., poor social self-image) and the more personal psychological problems unique to the individual Hispanic client (e.g., sexual dysfunctions, low self-image) will give important information for diagnosis and treatment design that will help the therapist lower the client's psychological risk.

Physiological Risk Factors

It has been shown that stress of any kind can alter human physiology and that the sociological stress which Hispanics often encounter, such as low income, unemployment, acculturation difficulties, etc., can raise the physiological risk for Hispanic clients. Some studies have suggested that Hispanics may be at higher physiological risk, at least for alcoholism, due to inherited genetic predispositions. But the studies done to date have not taken into account the specific sociological stress Hispanics may be undergoing that could alter the outcome of any biochemical research done regarding Hispanics. There has been research reported that indicates that children who have alcoholic parents or grandparents are at higher risk for alcoholism due to the fact that these children are physiologically related to parents who display substance abuse behavior (Lawson et al., 1984).

When individual Hispanic clients come from an alcoholic family, they are already at high physiological risk. When this high physiological risk is added to an already high level of risk caused by sociological stressors, this puts Hispanic clients at an even higher physiological risk level.

The actual physical availability of alcohol and/or drugs should be considered when working with Hispanic substance abusers since community, recreational, and other social functions may put Hispanic clients in close proximity to alcohol.

TREATMENT CONSIDERATIONS

Treatment of chemical dependency in Hispanics is a major challenge. Three central factors contributing to this challenge are the intergration of alcohol consumption in the Hispanic culture, the psychology of the Hispanic, and the family dynamics of the traditional Hispanic.

So inculcated is drinking behavior in the Mexican culture that social functions ranging from baptisms to funerals include the availability of alcoholic beverages. Drinking occurs when the individual is coping with negative feelings and is experiencing positive feelings as well. The use of alcohol and/or drugs among Hispanics has been well documented and predates the Spanish conquest. However, its use today goes well beyond the models provided by the Aztec (inebriation was reserved for elders and priests) or the image of the contemporary macho man. Exacerbating the problem is the relative ignorance of the connection between alcohol consumption and the social dysfunctions it causes. The problems that drinking causes are seen not as distinct problems related to drinking behavior but as an integral component of family problems.

The fatalistic element of the Hispanic psychology helps to incorporate the drinking problem. When the drinking problem is described, in an intake interview for example, it is often followed by the client saying: "that's life" or "this is our cross to bear." This external locus of control blocks both the identified alcoholic and the family from assuming a more active role in the recovery process.

Another significant contributing element is the infrastructure of the Hispanic family system. Very often the classic patrilineal or father/male–dominated family is a facade. The macho myth serves as a cover for the covert reality of a matrilineal or mother/female–dominated family system. Patterns of interdependence (enmeshment) in the immediate and extended families and exaggerated hierarchial roles (dominance/submission), coupled with the fiction of the male-dominated family, all present a pattern that can lead to alcoholic dysfunction.

This pattern of "dysfunction" is played out in the alcoholic family system. Co-dependency is demonstrated through the self-sacrificing wife and mother whose worth is gauged by her ability to endure and overcome life's perennial hardships. Chemical dependency of the spouse or children is a problem to be overcome with prayer, cajoling, or a visit to the priest. The thought of confronting the alcoholic (intervention) or setting limits is experienced by the nonalcoholic spouse as potentially destructive to the family unit. This double bind keeps the nonalcoholic spouse in check and allows the drinking behavior to continue. In the alcoholic co-dependent dyad, the nonalcoholic partner assumes a certain element of control of the family.

The difficulty in dealing with these issues in the Hispanic family is that the assumed roles in the alcoholic family are embedded in cultural norms. The interactions, with or without the introduction of alcohol, provide fertile ground for the establishment of the "classic alcoholic family" and are reinforced through cultural norms. This makes it difficult to intervene in this system.

Other factors that have complicated the effective management of chemical dependency have to do with the psychology of the Hispanic. This is expressed in patterns of interacting both in and outside the family. One example of this is the low incidence or underutilization by Hispanics of mental health services. Confronting the problem of chemical addiction may often be experienced by the Hispanic as a moral weakness or failure, thereby engendering feelings of guilt. The chemically dependent individual then has to face the fact that he or she is weak, a direct contradiction to his or her need to appear in control of his or her life (machismo).

Even though more facilities are available to treat Hispanics, the utilization of these facilities varies. Successful models, those that include mental health services within medical clinics, may not place emphasis on identification, referral, and/or treatment of chemical dependency. One of the social realities that has affected treatment pertains to economics. There is typically an underrepresentation of Hispanics in private chemical dependency treatment facilities. This is counterbalanced by an overrepresentation in public treatment programs (e.g., court referrals). Statistics vary; however, general trends support this observation (De Luca, 1981).

TREATMENT

Treatment of chemical dependency with Hispanics must necessarily take into consideration the many facets of the Hispanic culture. Treatment, to be effective, must attend not only to the language or communication needs of the clients, but also to the cultural factors that dictate to a large extent their psychology (Moustafa & Weiss, 1968).

Alcoholics Anonymous

AA is a viable treatment modality for alcohol abuse among Hispanics. But it should be kept in mind that often due to the adherence to the cultural concept of machismo, many Hispanic men may have difficulty admitting that they have a dependency on alcohol they cannot control. This admission of dependency is a required tenent of AA as a condition of treatment.

This need for admission of loss of control and dependency before treatment can progress may cause many Hispanic male clients to reject AA as a form of therapy. If and when necessary, Hispanic clients should be referred to Spanish speaking AA organizations to help reduce the effects of cultural differences during treatment.

Group Modalities

Psychodramatic, Gestalt, psychoanalytic, educational, and inspirational group techniques have all shown themselves to be effective in the treatment of chemically dependent persons. However, it should be noted that the degree of the Hispanic client's acculturation and language barrier may pose a problem that should be taken into consideration before a Hispanic client is encouraged to participate in a group therapy situation.

If the Hispanic client's level of acculturation and social adaptation is low, then "culture shock" may be increased if the client is put into a heterogeneous group environment. If the group is vastly different from the Hispanic client's social and cultural background, the normally desired effects of group therapy, such as a sense of cohesiveness, interpersonal learning, and universality, may not occur. The more difficult it is for Hispanic clients to see themselves as a part of the group process, the more difficult it will be for a group therapy situation to be effective. It has been reported that Hispanics verbally interacted at lower levels when put into groups that included persons of other cultural and ethnic backgrounds (Shera, Sanchez, & Huang, 1984). These ideas suggest that for perhaps some Hispanic clients with chemical dependency problems, a more culturally similar group should be used. Spanish speaking group leaders in many cases would greatly facilitate group interaction involving Hispanic clients.

Family Therapy

In the more traditional Hispanic culture, the family plays an important part in the life style of Hispanic individuals. Family therapy could therefore be put to great advantage when working with chemically dependent Hispanic individuals. The initial purpose of using family therapy with substance abusers is to attempt to evaluate the family's influence on the formation of the client's chemical dependency problem. Both the family of origin and the nuclear family can be used to evaluate and then alter the Hispanic client's substance problem since it is the family in many cases, through habitual dysfunctional behaviors, that has set the stage for the chemical dependency behavior of the client (Levant, 1984).

When acculturation to American society occurs in the Hispanic family, traditional roles can break down, and this complicates the family interactions even further. The use of alcohol and/or drugs can become a method for reducing the stress caused by these changes in family interactions. Family therapy can also help with the intrafamily acculturational problems that may be complicating the Hispanic client's substance dependency.

When using family therapy with Hispanic clients, it should be remembered that the feelings of isolation from the mainstream American society may complicate the problem of overenmeshment found in many ethnic minority families (Panitz, McConchie, Sauber, & Fonseca, 1983). This overenmeshment may make family therapy with Hispanic families somewhat more involved than with more mainstream American families. But this should not mean that family therapy with Hispanics should be avoided. If anything, this overenmeshment, when found, should make family therapy even more valuable.

A thorough assessment of the family structure is critical and cannot be sressed enough. Time is needed to allow the family to accept the therapist and to allow the therapist ample opportunity to assess the structure of the family (i.e., patrilineal vs. matrilineal).

Inpatient Care

Many Hispanics may not see inpatient care as a treatment of choice due to language and cultural differences between themselves and the predominantly non-Hispanic inpatient substance abuse facilities available to them. Other Hispanics, for cultural or personal reasons, may prefer to have their chemical dependency problems treated by a family physician. Some Hispanics may still prefer to have spiritual and herbal treatment done by a folk healer (e.g., Curendero). For these reasons, inpatient treatment does not show itself to be greatly accepted by Hispanic clients (Alcocer, 1975; Karno & Edgerton, 1969).

In some cases it may be necessary to use inpatient treatment procedures to help rid the Hispanic client of any physical dependencies he or she may have. Often drug aversion therapy employing Antabuse for alcoholism can be done safely only on an inpatient basis. Barbiturate addiction often requires hospitalization in order to ensure safe detoxification. It may also be necessary to place cocaine- and heroin-dependent Hispanic clients into an inpatient environment in order to remove the client from easy access to the particular drug being used.

If the client's attitudes toward institutionalized care are negative or if inpatient care is not feasible due to language barriers, etc., then, if hospitalized detoxification is not absolutely necessary, outpatient treatment can be recommended at half-way house facilities that might be more culturally and personally suited to the Hispanic client's needs (e.g., a Spanish speaking half-way facility) (Roth & Fernandez, 1980).

Individual Therapy

Individual therapy may be a useful approach; however, caution is necessary to ensure that this approach does not allow the client or the family to avoid appropriate treatment. The decision to use individual treatment is best if it comes out of the family assessment. If there are cultural differences between the therapist and the Hispanic client (e.g., Oriental therapist and Hispanic client), cultural flexibility and sensitivity are necessary. With Hispanic clients who are seen by non-Hispanic therapists, language comprehension and fluency will have a great impact on the therapeutic process. The effect of the language problems must be dealt with before any therapy can begin. If the language barrier is insurmountable, the client may have to be referred to a therapist who is more able to meet the client's needs (e.g., Spanish speaking therapist).

As much information should be obtained by the therapist regarding Hispanic culture as is possible. It should be emphasized that a great deal of subtle social and cultural variation can be found among Hispanics that needs to be considered when working with Hispanic clients. Cuban Hispanics, as an example, may not hold the same social and cultural values a Hispanic person from Puerto Rico might hold. But as with other minority individuals, as well as persons from the larger population, the therapist must first see the chemically dependent Hispanic client as a unique individual who is personally influenced by the dynamics of life, such as family, sex, race, social class, education, and culture. It does the Hispanic client very little therapeutic good, and it also limits the direction and outcome of the therapeutic experience, if the therapist strictly defines and categorizes the client solely in terms of his or her Hispanic culture and ethnic background.

Therapists are no more immune to stereotypical thinking than anyone else, whether they are Oriental, Anglo, or even Hispanic. Therapists have been trained and educated to place their thoughts into logically related categories. But the tendency to categorize should not cause therapists to place all Hispanic clients into a cultural/ethnic box. Once an individual client is seen as a "type," the therapist limits the interactional process.

This categorization and typing can occur even between Hispanic therapists, who may be better educated, and less well-educated Hispanics, such as many migrant workers.

The therapist should try to evaluate the Hispanic client's self-perceptions in order to ascertain the degree to which the client identifies himself or herself with his or her ethnic background. Once this is done, the therapist will have a better idea of how cultural aspects will affect the therapeutic situation. The therapist will then know how to structure the therapy in order to maximize therapeutic sessions.

In regard to specific individual therapy modalities, there is very little research that would indicate that one particular theoretical approach works better with Hispanic clients than another. But it has been indicated that Hispanic clients may prefer individual therapy over group methods for substance abuse problems (Desmond & Maddox, 1984). A role-structured therapeutic situation may have better outcomes than more freely interactive therapy methods when working with more culturally traditional Hispanic clients.

Present-time (i.e., existential) therapies may also be more useful with Hispanic substance abusers than the more historically oriented therapies (e.g., psychoanalysis, etc.) since self-disclosure may be difficult for many Hispanic clients (Sue & Zane, 1987). The reframing of the Hispanic client substance problem into medical terms (i.e., medical model) may help reduce "resistance" within the client, especially the male Hispanic, since this way of presenting the substance problem reduces the issue of emotional dependency and self-control.

Behavioral therapeutic methods might work well with relatively unacculturated Hispanic clients, especially if the behavioral therapy is presented in an existential manner. This would allow the behavioral goals to be more easily accepted into the Hispanic client's psychosocial frame of reference.

When formulating therapeutic treatment for individual Hispanics, the therapist should again remember that Hispanics are very often at high sociocultural risk for chemical dependency. Changes in personal attitudes regarding the reliance on alcohol or drugs as a social coping behavior or as a social enhancer may have to be made. With male Hispanic clients, sociocultural values that may be maintaining (macho) behavior, which often includes the use of drugs and/or alcohol, will have to be dealt with. Machismo characteristics may also present difficulty in the therapeutic situation with Hispanic male substance users in that machismo behavior often requires Hispanic men to react to verbal confrontation as a personal challenge. Alterations in the therapeutic process that keep confrontation to a minimum may have to be made by the therapist when working with Hispanic male clients.

Individual chemical dependency therapy with Hispanic women often must center on the newly acquired sociocultural values that have replaced or altered the traditional Hispanic cultural values that previously helped minimize Hispanic female drug/alcohol use. Changes in educational level and sex roles and the breakdown of traditionally held religious beliefs should also be considered in therapeutic situations that involve Hispanic women.

Hispanic youths are perhaps at higher sociological risk than Hispanic adults since adolescents are in a stage of development where drug and alcohol experimentation often takes on the characteristics of rites of passage. When one adds to this fact the already existing sociocultural risk factors for Hispanics in general, the need for increased therapeutic consideration and client evaluation become even more important in cases involving Hispanic youths.

The therapist, in assessing the personal issues of negative self-image, guilt, shame, etc., should keep in mind that if the Hispanic client displays these high psychological risk factors, then the therapist will have to encourage not only changes in the client's personal self-perceptions but also changes in social attitudes and values that accept the use of chemical intoxicants for social enhancement and/or the use of intoxicants as self-medication for social stress.

If the Hispanic client displays a high physiological risk factor (e.g., alcoholism in the family of origin), specific therapeutic efforts will have to be made that deemphasize and change social attitudes and values in the family that condone and accept drinking/drug taking for social or self-medicating reasons. Personal psychological attitudes and orientations have to be changed also (e.g., improvement of self-image). These personal/social changes will help decrease the physiological risk.

The therapist working with individual Hispanic clients or with groups should pay particular attention to the evaluation and reduction of the sociological risk because it is in the area of cultural attitudes and values, and acculturational difficulties (e.g., low employment, low income), that Hispanic clients are more vulnerable to chemical dependency. If the therapists can reduce any of the risk factors mentioned, whether sociological, psychological, or physiological, they will also be reducing the other factors since these factors are interrelated and do not exist in isolation. If one factor is decreased, it will reduce to some degree the other two.

Although Hispanics share many cultural similarities, individual substance users come from many walks of life and represent a multitude of personality types. No matter which therapeutic approach is used in individual treatment, it should fit the individual Hispanic client's needs and acculturational level. It may very well be that even after a thorough assessment of the sociological, psychological, and physiological risk factors, the efficacy of the therapy modality used may be determined to a very large degree by the motivation of the Hispanic client and the substance abuse therapist's desire to help.

SPECIAL PROBLEMS

Hispanic migrant agricultural workers are a group within the larger Hispanic American population that has a great need for chemical dependency services and treatment. Migrant Hispanic farm workers often represent the least acculturated group of all Hispanics. This means that the stress of social adjustment, isolation, and low income will be very high among this group, possibly even more so than for nonmigrant Hispanics. With Hispanic migrant workers, the often low level of acculturation means that substance abuse facilities in order to be effective will have to be staffed by Hispanics or at least Spanish speaking therapists.

PREVENTION

Whether substance abuse prevention is aimed at primary, secondary or tertiary stages or is aimed at the interplay of host, agent, and environment as in the community health model, the application of prevention efforts will have better effects when directed at Hispanics if bilingual communication methods are employed for presenting substance abuse information.

Prevention methods that include and are directed at the entire Hispanic family can also increase the effectiveness of prevention efforts. Among Hispanics there is a strong traditional religious heritage, and involving the church leadership in the presentation of prevention education could help increase the number of Hispanics reached.

Hispanic community groups and unions can also be used not only to present prevention information and education but to add peer group persuasion and role modeling to help reduce substance abuse behavior.

The content of prevention information, whether on a community level or on an individual basis, should be focused on educating the individual(s) regarding the cultural, social, and personal values and attitudes that may be directly or indirectly causing or maintaining substance use behavior, such as acculturation and social stressors, cultural traditions, and social and personal self-image.

REFERENCES

Abad, V. (1974). *Machismo and alcoholism among Puerto Ricans.* Paper presented at the Fourth Annual Alcoholism Conference of the National Institutde of Alcohol Abuse and Alcoholism, Washington, DC.

Alcocer, A.M. (1975). *Chicano alcoholism.* Paper presented at the First Regional Conference of the Coalition of Spanish Speaking Mental Health Organizations, Los Angeles.

Alcocer, A.M. (1977). *Alcohol abuse and alcoholism among the Spanish speaking: An overview.* Paper presented at the National Drug Abuse Conference, San Francisco.

Bell, J.D., & Chambers, C.D. (1970). *The epidemiology of opiate addiction in the United States.* Springfield, IL. Charles C Thomas.

Blum, R. (1973). Alcohol: The user. In J.F. Lotterhos & M.E. McGuide, (Eds.), *Selected readings for nurse care planning on alcoholism: A resource guide* (pp. 13–22). Greenville, NC: Alcoholism Training Program, East Carolina University.

Business Week. (1980). June 23, p. 86. The world's poor flood U.S.: Economic consequences of a new wave.

Chambers, C.D. (1971). *An assessment of drug use in the general population.* New York Narcotic Addiction Control Commission.

DeLuca, R. (Ed.). (1981, January). *Alcohol and health.* Rockville, MD: National Institute on Alcohol Abuse and Alcoholism.

Desmond, D., & Maddox, J. (1984). Mexican American heroin addicts. *Journal of Drug and Alcohol Abuse, 10,* 317–346.

Edmondson, H.A. (1975). Mexican American alcoholism and deaths at L.A.C. and U.S.C. Medical Center. Testimony before the Subcommittee on Alcoholism to the California State Health and Welfare Committee, February 7.

Garcia, L. (1976). Spanish speaking alcoholism problems and needs. Testimony before the Subcommittee on Alcoholism and Narcotics of the U.S. Senate, Washington, DC, February 4.

Gilbert, M.J. (1978). *Five week alcoholism enthnography conducted in three Spanish speaking communities.* Sacramento, CA: State Office of Alcoholism.

Gilbert, M.J. (1980). *Los parientes: Social structural factors and kinship relations among second generation Mexican Americans in two Southern California communities.* Unpublished doctoral dissertation, University of California, Santa Barbara.

Guinn, R., & Hurly, R. (1976). A comparison of drug use among Houston and lower Rio Grande Valley secondary students. *Adolescence, 11,* 455–459.

Holck, S., Warren, C., Smith, J., & Rochat, W. (1984). Alcohol consumption among Mexican American and Anglo women: Results of survey along the U.S.–Mexican border. *Journal of Studies on Alcohol, 45,* 149–154.

Karno, M., & Edgerton, R.B. (1969). Perception of mental illness in a Mexican American community. *Archives of General Psychiatry, 20,* 233–238.

Kuanert, A.P. (1979). Perspectives from a private practice. The differential diagnosis of alcoholism. *Family and community health—alcoholism and health,* Part II, 2, 2 (pp. 1–11). Rockville, MD: Aspen.

Lawson, G.W., Ellis, D.C., & Rivers, P.C. (1984). *Essentials of chemical dependency counseling.* Rockville, MD: Aspen.

Levant, R.F. (1984) *Family therapy: A comprehensive overview.* Englewood Cliffs, NJ: Prentice-Hall.

Lukoff, I.F. (1972). *Some aspects of the epidemiology of heroin use in a ghetto community: A preliminary report*. Washington, DC: Government Printing Office.

Madsen, W., & Madsen, C. (1969). The cultural structure of Mexican drinking behavior. *Quarterly Journal of Studies on Alcohol, 30*, 701–718.

Moustafa, A., & Weiss, G. (1968). Health states and practices of Mexican Americans. Graduate School of Business, Unpublished manuscript, University of California Mexican American Study Project, Los Angeles.

Padilla, E., Padilla, A., Morales, A., Olmeda, E., & Ramires, R. (1979). Inhalant, marijuana and alcohol abuse among barrio children and adolescents. *International Journal of the Addictions, 14*, 945–946.

Panitz, D.R., McConchie, R.D., Sauber, S.R., & Fonseca, J.A. (1983). The role of machismo and the Hispanic family in the etiology and treatment of alcoholism in Hispanic American males. *Journal of Family Therapy, 11*, 31–44.

Roth, R., & Fernandez, D. (1980). Historic accord between Hispanic alcoholism community and N.I.A.A.A. *Alcoholism, 2*, 20–33.

Ruiz, P., Vasquez, W., & Vasquez, K. (1973). The mobile unit: A new approach in mental health. *Community Mental Health Journal, 9*, 18–24.

Shera, W., Sanchez, A., & Huang, T. (1984). Verbal participation in group therapy: A comparative study on New Mexico ethnic groups. *Hispanic Journal of Behavioral Sciences, 6*, 277–284.

Sue, S., & Zane, N. (1987). The role of culture and cultural techniques in psychotherapy: A critique and reformation. *American Psychologist, 42*, 37–45.

U.S. Bureau of the Census. (1979). Population characteristics: Persons of Spanish origins in the United States. *Current population reports*, Series P-20, 339. Washington, D.C.: U.S. Census Bureau.

U.S. Bureau of the Census. (1980). *Current population reports*. Washington, D.C.: U.S. Census Bureau.

U.S. Bureau of Labor Statistics. (1978). *Employment and earnings*. Washington, D.C.: U.S. Bureau of Labor.

Wellisch, D., & Hays, J.R. (1974). A cross-cultural study of the prevalence and correlates of student drug abuse in the United States and Mexico. *Bulletin on Narcotics, 26*, 35.

Chapter 11

Adolescence: A Physiological, Cultural, and Psychological No Man's Land

David Archambault

INTRODUCTION

Adolescence is first a matter of biology, that is, an intrinsic developmental process in a strictly physiological sense. It is also a matter of psychology insofar as it involves the resolution of internal issues around oneself, one's relationship to others (particularly the opposite sex), and one's place in the world. Finally, it is a matter of culture: this is when rites of passage, ideals, values, and cultural norms or expectations enter the child's life in a new and more accountable manner.

The model of adolescent drug abuse presented in this chapter deals with the special problems of adolescents in these three areas. Adolescents are a special population that is composed of representatives from every other special population. The therapist treating an adolescent population must be aware of issues that are important to each ethnic, social, and economic group.

Adolescents in our society are individuals in the process of change in every area of life. These changes are not of their own choosing. They are forced upon them by biology and culture. They are expected to make these changes without regard to how well their environment (i.e., family, education, cultural background, etc.) has prepared them for change. Physiologically their body often seems out of control in terms of growth, acne, and sexual development. This happens at a time when adolescents could be in desperate need of an anchor in their life. Yet their body changes in ways they do not understand, cannot control, and do not desire (e.g., acne, lumps in the breast, menstruation). Adolescents do not have the experience to know what they are becoming. They are unsure of their worth to others, to society, and to themselves.

Culturally, adolescents are individuals in a no man's land. They are somewhere between the relative safety of childhood where structure and

223

simplicity were the order of the day and the unfamiliar complexities and expectations of adulthood. Their body is maturing sexually, and yet sex is often taboo for the teenager in our society. They are no longer accepted as a child. They are told (and expected) to act like an adult. Yet most of the adult activities that are most visible to adolescents and children (sex and drug and alcohol use) are still considered off limits and even punishable. As a society, we stress the good life of alcohol, purchasing power, and the sexual conquest. Unless adolescents have been exposed to learning experiences in the home (or elsewhere) that enable them to be realistic and insightful regarding their goals, timetable for development, progress, and relationships with others, they are likely to be dissatisfied with themselves and feel anger toward those around them and the world in general.

Undoubtedly, some adolescents are well prepared for the transition to adulthood. They have had consistent culturally appropriate adult models who gave them clear realistic messages about what to expect from themselves and others. They have been encouraged to set goals and develop the skills needed to achieve those goals. At the same time, they are taught how and encouraged to enjoy their youth and life in general. All things considered, they feel good about themselves and others. Their fortunate learning history has given them the confidence that they can smoothly make the transition to adulthood (indeed most of the children in this category have had increasing responsibility and achievement as they grew older such that the transition to adulthood is natural and with few surprises).

The other extreme are adolescents who must sort through almost total chaos and inconsistency to find an identity and purpose. Their principal caretakers and role models often provide them with a maze of double messages, hypocrisy, neglect and abuse (often physical and mental). For these children, and many others who fall between the two extremes, a drug (which produces consistent pleasure or relief from stress or anxiety and allows them to forget those problems they are unable to understand, unprepared to solve, and often not responsible for) becomes a powerful reinforcer and friend.

WHY DO ADOLESCENTS TAKE DRUGS?

Many of the reasons for adolescent drug use have just been discussed. *The* reason for adolescent drug use probably does not exist. No single reason and no list of reasons will apply to all adolescents. Drug use results from a complex interaction of genetic endowment, behavior patterns, motives, and social and psychological determinants. Reasons for use may be extremely complex or as simple as availability.

Segal, at the University of Alaska, examined self-reported reasons for drug use among a group of adjudicated juveniles (Segal, Cromer, Stevens, & Wasserman, 1982). The results of Segal's investigation indicated that reasons for drug use could be summarized under at least three motives. The first was an expanded awareness-insight motive. Drugs were used to achieve greater understanding about oneself and things in the environment. The second was a drug effect motive. This motive involved the use of drugs to produce a "high" to achieve a feeling of mellowness and a high sense of ease with friends and to feel more creative. The third motive was to increase activity. Here the goal was to "obtain new and exciting experiences to satisfy curiosity and for the high drug use can bring" (Segal et al., 1982).

The patterns of self-reported reasons in this study indicated that the need to achieve altered states of consciousness is an important element in drug taking. Furthermore, different drugs are used selectively to achieve the desired state of altered consciousness. Marijuana use is primarily associated with obtaining a state of mellowness, stimulants are associated with a desire to increase energy. It seems evident that expectations associated with the use of certain drugs may help relieve anxiety or at least cope with it.

No relationship was found between drug use and type of offense. This suggested that different motives for drug taking and committing an offense may exist. For instance, criminality may be more related to sociological processes, while drug use could be more significantly related to personality factors and less related to social factors. Treatment would then need to focus on personal development and achieving a positive self-concept along with alternatives to drugs.

Beshner and Friedman (1979) reviewed research and offered several reasons for drug use among adolescents. First, drugs are readily available; second, drugs provide a reliable, quick, easy, and cheap way to feel good; third, peer groups become increasingly important as a socializing influence during adolescence and drugs offer one way of gaining peer group acceptance; fourth, drugs are used as a coping mechanism to deal with unpleasant feelings and emotions, relieve depression, reduce tension, and cope with pressure.

Research (Segal et al., 1982) indicates that alcohol is often used and perceived as a means to deal with personal needs and problems by detained and adjudicated juveniles. Findings by Cahalan, Cisin, and Crossley (1969) indicated that alcohol is used by people who are anxious or depressed to help with their problems. To some extent it seems that alcohol has become a self-prescribed tranquilizer for our stressful society. Children see their parents come home from a hard day at work and declare "I need a drink."

It seems that adolescents have learned early in life that alcohol use has a special function as a means to deal with problems and unpleasant feelings. Segal's research also indicated that beer drinking, in particular, may be seen as a reward for hard work or a means to cool off in hot weather. This could be a result of advertisement: "It's Miller Time;" "This Bud's for you for all you do."

Segal (Segal et al., 1982) did not find any reports of drinking just to be sociable among adolescents. This finding was in contrast to the self-reports of college students (Segal, Huba, & Singer, 1980). Those in Segal's research had not arrived at culturally sanctioned alcohol use due to their young age. It is also logical to assume that this was an unusually troubled sample and that alcohol was used as a means to cope. For the troubled adolescent, alcohol (or drug) use may be a way to feel better (as opposed to "high") by relieving stressful emotions. This type of use simply models the perception of society that associates drug and alcohol use with mood change.

Though one may not care to accept it, there are probably positive reasons why some adolescents use drugs. It may be that in our society drug experimentation has become a normal part of growing up, just one component of a rite of passage. Peer acceptance and curiosity can also contribute positive motives for substance use.

Beschner and Friedman (1985) separated adolescent substance abuse into two types. The first type is the experimental, situational, or recreational user. The second type is the user with serious personal problems, a compulsive and dedicated user. They found that this second group composed approximately 5% of the teens aged 14 to 18; this group has serious drug and drug related problems and is likely to be the group most in need of treatment.

Social bond theory purports that most individuals will deviate if the bonds of conformity are weakened or broken. The most consistent extralegal factor affecting marijuana use is peer or social support.

The social bond theory was tested in a study done by Peck (1983). Peck hypothesized that people with large numbers of friends who did not use marijuana would also not use marijuana. Peck found that of those people who reported having no friends who used marijuana, 95% were nonusers themselves. Of those people who reported having only a few friends who smoked marijuana, 66% were nonusers. Conversely, of the people who reported that almost all of their friends used marijuana, 92% also used marijuana, and of those who reported that all of their friends smoked marijuana, 96% also smoked marijuana. These findings support other literature that consistently suggests that people are more likely to behave in accordance with the expectations of significant others rather than generalized expectations of a society. These findings contribute significantly to the understanding of drug use by adolescents whose peer groups are becoming increasingly important, especially when one considers that marijuana use is likely to be widely practiced and accepted by this peer group.

A non-marijuana-using peer group would seem to be crucial to the deterrence of marijuana use. It does not seem unreasonable to speculate that these findings would be valid for drug use in general, especially in the early stages of use.

SCOPE OF USE

The greatest focus of recent drug research has been on youth (particularly adolescents) and drug abuse. Drug abuse does not usually occur before adolescence. Traditionally, youth are seen as the key to the successful future of any society. Drug abuse is considered a threat to the healthy development of youth and therefore a threat to society.

Results of the National Survey on Drug Abuse in the household population of the United States (Fishburne, Abelson, & Cisin, 1980) provided strong evidence that there has been a steady increase in adolescent substance abuse since the beginning of the survey in 1972. Almost one third of all youth aged 12 to 17 have used marijuana, and more than half of that group has used it within the past 30 days; 10% and 7% of 12- to 17-year-olds have used inhalants and hallucinogens; approximately 7% have used alcohol, and more than 50% have used tobacco.

According to the Drug Abuse Warning Network System (Glynn, 1981), one third or more of the drug related emergency room visits in 1980 for marijuana use, PCP use, and quaalude use were by youths 10- to 19-years-old. One quarter of amphetamine related visits were by youths from this same group as well as 10% or more of visits due to cocaine, barbiturates, antidepressants, and antianxiety substances.

The University of Michigan's annual survey of high school seniors (aged 16 to 18) from 1975 to 1981 showed an increased use for this age group compared with the youth population in general. The data showed that 33.37% had used marijuana within the last 30 days, 3.9% had used cocaine within the last 30 days, 10.2% had used stimulants, and 70% had used alcohol. Regarding alcohol use, more than 40% reported binge drinking (over five or more drinks in a row) during the 2 weeks prior to the survey. "Compared to the heroin addiction epidemic of the 60's and 70's adolescent drug abuse today is more broadly based; it cuts across all socioeconomic strata and involves a wider array of chemical substances" (Beschner & Friedman, 1985).

The teenage driver is responsible for 44% of all fatal crashes at night where alcohol is involved. Drunk driving accidents are the leading cause of death in people aged 16 to 24. Alcohol was found in the blood of 58% of teens killed in traffic accidents (43% of those were legally drunk).

Seven percent of high school seniors reported daily use of marijuana (Johnston, Backman, and O'Mally, 1981). Twenty-five percent of elementary school children feel pressure to try marijuana, beer, wine, and liquor. "Typically, persons who have a degree of experience with marijuana (used more than 10 times) will become involved in the use of another illicit drug" (Beschner & Friedman, 1985). The most often-abused drugs by adolescents are tobacco, marijuana, and alcohol. These are often called "gateway drugs" because their use frequently leads to the use of other drugs.

Adolescents who use drugs usually use alcohol also. Alcohol is often used in combination with other drugs, particularly marijuana. Because of this combined usage, it will often be misleading to label adolescents as having a drug *or* an alcohol problem. Research has shown that drug abuse treatment programs often neglect alcohol use. A more realistic approach for most adolescents entering drug treatment is a three-part diagnosis of drug, alcohol and psychological problems (Hubbard, Cavanaugh, Graddock, & Rachel, 1983).

PATTERNS AND CONSEQUENCES OF USE

In 1984, Holland and Griffin compared adolescent and adult drug treatment clients as to patterns and consequences of drug use. They found that adults were more likely to have used cocaine, heroin, and methadone, while adolescents were more likely to have used amphetamines, hallucinogens, and marijuana. Most adolescents in treatment had begun using drugs other than alcohol before the seventh grade. The average age of onset of drug use for adolescents was 11.8 years, and for adults, 15.1 years. Adults were more likely to have begun using alcohol; adolescents were equally likely to use other drugs before alcohol as alcohol before other drugs. Both adolescents and adults reported using an average of seven drugs other than alcohol. Adolescents began using a variety of substances earlier than adults and progressed to regular polydrug use more quickly than adults. Both groups were similar regarding the number of drug classes used, the number of drug classes used regularly, and the highest frequency of use. Four of 10 (37%) adolescents reported having been physically addicted to drugs. Adults were almost twice as likely to report having been physically addicted.

Adolescent self-reported alcohol use was greater than adult self-reported use. Fifty percent of the adolescents described their drinking as frequent or daily as opposed to 40% of the adults. Thirty-four percent of the adults rated their drinking as a moderate or serious problem, while 50% of the adolescents rated it a moderate or serious problem. Adolescents were also more likely to have experienced negative consequences of alcohol use (74% vs. 48%). Twenty-nine percent of the adolescents and 23% of the adults had previously received treatment for alcoholism.

Much of the research regarding substance abuse and family or psychological problems is etiologically inconclusive. However, from a clinical and treatment perspective, this does not seem to be a critical issue. It is important to recognize the often severe problems associated with the substance abuser and provide the services they need.

Both adolescents and adults reported growing up in families with many problems. Serious illnesses usually resulting in unemployment of the main wage earner and the need to go on welfare were reported by 28% of both groups. Fifty-seven percent of the adolescents and 40% of the adults reported violence as a frequent occurrence in their home. Thirty percent of the adults and 40% of the adolescents reported being physically abused. Given the type of family environment described by many of the clients in this study, deviant substance abuse is not so surprising. These environments appear to be poorly structured and lacking in a role model for appropriate parental identification. Family life seems to have been frequently volatile and unpredictable. Thus, feelings of inadequacy are to be expected, as well as poor relationship and communication skills. Peer acceptance, approval, and identification, which can be obtained through drug use seems to be a reasonable solution to an intolerable environment.

A modeling effect was supported by many of the subjects in the study. Deviant behavior was commonplace in many of the respondents' homes. Adolescents reported a 65% incidence of drug use compared with 46% for the adults. Family drinking problems were reported by 61% of the adolescents and 52% of the adults. Fifty-three percent of the adolescents reported that a family member had an arrest record, as compared with 42% of the adults.

The sample also scored high on several objective measures of psychological distress. Forty-eight percent of the adolescents and 28% of the adults had received treatment for psychological problems other than drug abuse or alcoholism. Twenty percent of the adolescents had received inpatient psychiatric care and 36% had attempted suicide.

Ninety-four percent of this sample admitted illegal activity other than illegal drug use. The average age of the first illegal activity was 12 for adolescents. Their first arrest took place (on an average) at age 14. For adults, the comparable ages were 16 and 17.7 years. Virtually all measures of criminal activity increased with age.

The adolescents in this sample were similar in many ways to adults who had used drugs, on the average, twice as long. The adolescents seemed to have more severe problems than the adults in the areas of alcohol use, family, psychological difficulties, and acting out behaviors.

Current age was not a reliable predictor of problematic drug use. Many clinicians and agencies use current age and primary drug use to describe involvement and select treatment approaches. However, there is a large body of data that suggests that age of onset of use, the number of drugs used, and the frequency of use are better indicators of the degree of involvement with drugs than is the type of drug used. Treatment should be predicated on these factors as well as on current age and primary drug of choice. The more frequently drugs are used, the more likely the client is to use a number of drugs. The probability of eventual abstinence decreases as the number of drugs used increases.

A summary of the analysis done by Holland and Griffin (1984) illuminates several useful relationships regarding ethnicity, sex, age of onset of use, duration of use, and age at admission to treatment.

1. *Lifetime prevalence:* The best predictor of heroin use was duration of life. So one might expect that a larger percentage of adolescents will use heroin as they grow older if their substance abuse continues. Other significant predictors of heroin use were race (non-white), age at admission (older), sex (male), and age of onset of drug use (older). The best predictor of amphetamine and/or hallucinogen use was race (white), age at onset of drug use (younger), and age at admission (younger). When other variables were controlled, age at admission to treatment was still a significant predictor of differential preference for these drugs. Duration of use was the only significant predictor of cocaine use. "While public opinion tends to focus on the type of drug used, the number of drugs used and the frequency with which they are used may be better predictors of problematic use" (Holland & Griffin, 1984, p. 87). In the Holland and Griffin (1984) study, duration of use (longer), age of onset of use (younger), and race (white) were significant predictors of frequent use of multiple substances. So a client who began to use drugs early was equally likely to be a high-frequency multiple-drug user as a client who began later but had been exposed to drugs for a longer period of time.

2. *Problems associated with use:* Addiction and treatment for abuse, medical problems, and psychosocial problems were examined as indicators of personal and social cast. Older and younger clients were equally likely to experience psychosocial and/or medical problems. Race (white), age of

onset of use (younger), and duration of use (longer) were all significant predictors of these consequences. The likelihood of prior treatment for substance abuse varied as a function of duration of use (longer), race (white), sex (female), and age at admission (older). It is interesting that, in this sample, women were more likely to have undergone prior treatment even though female involvement with drugs was less severe than male involvement.

3. *Alcohol use:* "After controlling for demographics, age of onset and duration of use, those who entered treatment early in their lives were still more likely than older clients to have been heavy drinkers, to have experienced psychosocial and/or medical problems resulting from alcohol abuse and to have had prior treatment for alcohol abuse" (Holland & Griffin, 1984, p. 88). There are, of course, many factors that affect the long-term success of treatment; however, this finding seems to indicate that the early treatment these people received was unable to alter their life pattern at best, and it is conceivable that poor treatment may have worsened the problem. Other predictors of negative consequences and patterns of alcohol use were race (white), age of onset of alcohol use (younger), and sex (male).

4. *Family problems:* Age of onset of use (younger) was the best predictor of family problems in this sample. Race (white) and sex (female) were also significant predictors of family problems. Duration of use had no association with family problems. This last finding seems not to support the hypothesis that drug use causes the types of family problems examined in this study (e.g., violence and alcoholism in the family). If these problems had been caused by drug use, one would expect an increase in the incidence of these problems with continued and increased drug use.

5. *Psychological problems:* Race (white) was the best predictor of psychological problems. Age of onset of use (younger) and sex (female) were also significant predictors. Duration of use was correlated with the severity of psychological problems in this sample.

6. *Criminality:* All factors were significantly associated with criminality. In order of significance they were sex (male), duration of use (longer), age of onset of illegal activities (younger), race (non-white), and age at admission (older).

In a recent study, Gonzales (1983) looked at age at the time of first drink, the place where the first drink was consumed, and whether the first drink was taken under parental supervision. The variables were then used to predict the amount of alcohol consumed and alcohol related behavioral problems when the students were in college. Gonzales found that college students who began drinking during the elementary and middle school years had significantly higher levels of use and alcohol related problems than those students who started drinking during the high school or college years. Students who had their first drink at a school related function had a significantly higher incidence of use and related problems than those students who had their first drink at home or at a bar, whose results showed a significantly lower incidence of use and related problems than any of the other groups. Gonzales also found that while having the first drink with parental knowledge or parental supervision did not significantly predict alcohol use while in college, it did significantly predict the incidence of alcohol related problems the students experienced in college. Students who were introduced to alcohol with parental consent (the majority of this study) experienced significantly fewer behavioral complications from their use of alcohol in college than those whose parents did not know about their drinking or those who were not sure whether their parents knew about their drinking.

SIGNS OF ABUSE

The following behaviors are possible indicators that an adolescent is experiencing problems (possibly substance abuse):

- quick drop in grades
- change in circle of friends
- emotional highs and lows
- defiance of rules and regulations
- frustration and giving in to peer pressure
- sleeping more than usual
- many excuses for staying out too late
- withdrawing from family functions
- change to worse physical hygiene
- not informing parents of significant events concerning school and social activities
- intercepting the mail
- isolating self—spending a lot of time in own room
- suspicion of things missing—money, prescription drugs
- selling possessions

- playing parents against each other—divide and conquer
- drastic weight change
- short temper
- defensive attitude
- calls from school—missing class, abusive to others, etc.
- legal problems
- coming home drunk or high
- drug paraphernalia
- abusive behavior

These behaviors are to some extent normal in many adolescents at certain times. The list is not exhaustive as there are as many different behavior patterns and behaviors as there are adolescents. Frequency of occurrence (more often) and clustering of behaviors are indicative of possible substance abuse and should be investigated.

Classroom behaviors to watch include:

- bloodshot eyes (marijuana)
- smell
- lack of responsiveness
- skipping class or school
- lots of talk about drugs or alcohol
- absenteeism
- sudden drop in grades
- defensive behavior
- tardiness or leaving the room a lot
- incomplete assignments
- jewelry (roach clips, t-shirts with slogans about drugs, etc.)
- verbal abuse toward teachers and classmates
- vandalism
- forged notes from home
- giving in to peer pressure

The list could be endless. One should watch for changes from the norm, several behaviors going on at once, and frequency of occurrence.

ASSESSMENT

Early in treatment it is important to determine the level of risk for substance abuse for the client. Lawson, Peterson, and Lawson (1983) proposed several questions that aid in determining the level of risk in each of three areas: psysiological, sociological, and psychological:

1. *Physiological*

- Do you have a parent or grandparent who was or is alcoholic?
- If you have started drinking, are you or were you able to drink larger amounts of alcohol than most of your friends with fewer physical consequences (i.e., hangover)?
- Did you drink large amounts of alcohol from the first time you started drinking?

2. *Sociological*

- Did (do) one or both of your parents have strong religious or moral views against drinking alcohol (or using drugs)?
- Are either or your parents alcoholics?
- Do you come from an ethnic background that has a reputation for a high rate of alcoholism?
- Do you consider your friends to be heavy drinkers?
- Does your social status match your concept of where you feel you should be in society (school, etc.)?

3. *Psychological*

- Did you have a parent who was alcoholic or chemically dependent?
- Were one or both of your parents teetotalers (chose not to drink and condemned those who made a different choice)?
- In your opinion, were your parents overly protective of you?
- Were your parents, in your opinion, overly demanding of you, in words or needs?
- Do you have something to do in life that makes you feel worthwhile (school, sports, hobby, job, etc.)?
- Do you have someone who loves you and someone who you love?

These questions provide a good starting point for the assessment of the client's risks and needs.

Physiological Factors

Children with alcoholic parents have more problems with alcohol than children who come from nonalcoholic homes. This statement has been supported by virtually every family study of alcoholism. For children who have alcoholic parents, 30% are alcoholic, 40% are moderate drinkers, and 30% are abstainers. For children whose parents drink moderately, 5% are alcoholics, 85% are moderate drinkers, and 10% are abstainers. For children whose parents are abstainers, 10% are alcoholics, 50% are moderate drinkers, and 40% are abstainers (Lawson et al., 1983).

Though heredity alone has not been shown to cause alcoholism, it does seem to be a significant contributing factor. Heredity and the learning that takes place in the environment created by alcoholic parents account for a great deal of the risk children of alcoholics experience.

The physiological risk for adolescents is also increased by normal changes and rapid growth. Any condition that threatens the self-image and for which the adolescent is unprepared and unsupported puts the adolescent at risk. Voice changing, rapid skeletal growth, hair on face/chest/genitals, acne, and menstruation are all new experiences for the adolescent. These changes increase the adolescent's awareness of new sexual roles, which can be both exciting and frightening. This area cannot be overstressed in its effects on a positive self-image.

Growth will make some adolescents feel awkward. Growing too fast, too slowly, or not at all can be equally threatening. Problems with coordination due to growth can have a negative effect on athletic or social (e.g., dancing) skills. Body image is extremely important to most people, and adolescents are no exception. The increased importance of peer acceptance makes acne, lack of musculature for the man, and failure to develop a classic feminine form for females other sources of disappointment.

Sociological Factors

Social factors that increase the risk for substance abuse begin with the family. Parental modeling of coping styles and substance use has a strong influence on the behaviors selected by their children.

Peer groups also exert a strong influence. Adolescents are more likely to act according to the norms of their peer group than to the norms of society in general. If drug use is accepted in the peer group, the risk for substance use is generally high.

Drug use was at one time (during the 1960s and 1970s) largely associated with the poverty and social deprivation of the inner cities. It is now evident that social deprivation can occur anywhere; it is not restricted to ghetto areas. Adolescent multiple substance users are found in all social economic levels. Data from household surveys show white adolescents as having a higher lifetime prevalence of illicit drug use than black or Hispanic youth. They also tended to use a wider variety of substances than their non-white counterparts as well to report more drinking and smoking in the month prior to the survey (Beschner & Friedman, 1985).

Schools are an important part of the adolescent's social environment, and drugs have become readily available on many campuses. Schools provide an area away from parental supervision where experimentation is accepted by and often encouraged by peers. Location is no longer a reliable indicator of drug availability in schools. Schools in upper-class urban areas are almost sure to have drugs easily available, just as on inner city campuses.

Psychological Factors

The family is certainly the crucible of psychological development for adolescents. Parents create an environment (positive or negative) based on their own learning history and skills, which they acquired from their parents. Parental absence may result in an emotionally unsupportive environment for which drug use may be a coping mechanism.

Parental approaches that use reasoning are generally more successful than approaches based on strictness of rules and limits. Parental styles that are overdominating or underdominating are common in families with substance abuse problems.

Parental styles should be investigated thoroughly, as they offer much etiological information about the adolescent's problems. Parents in dysfunctional family systems are likely to be products of dysfunctional families themselves. Lawson et al. (1983) described four parental types. These researchers found that each alcoholic almost always has one or both parents in one or more of these four identifiable categories: (a) alcoholic, (b) teetotaler, (c) overly demanding, (d) overprotective.

1. *alcoholic parents:* Alcoholic parents can foster alcoholism in their children in a variety of ways. Children learn by watching those around them (particularly significant others) and model the behavior they see. If a parent deals with problems or feelings by drinking or using drugs, the child will also learn that drinking is an option in similar situations.

In general, the alcoholic parent is in no position to promote the mental and physical health of his or her children. In his or her uncomfortable, guilt-ridden state, it is not likely that the alcoholic parent will have a loving, supporting, meaningful relationship with his or her children. If there is one nonalcoholic parent in the family, he or she is usually too angry and frustrated to be of much comfort.

Besides the breakdown in the parental relationship, there are many other factors that contribute to the high risk for children with alcoholic parents. Disruptions of family rituals (e.g., holidays, dinnertime, weekends) due to drinking, fear, or embarrassment about what will happen when friends come over all contribute to a poor self-image.

2. *teetotaler parents:* The term *teetotaler* is used to describe parents who have made a decision not to drink and who condemn those who have made a different choice. They feel that drinking is immoral or indecent. The teetotaler, therefore, is different from someone who chooses not to drink but has a live-and-let-live attitude concerning the choice others make.

The teetotaler is characterized by a rigid moralistic approach to life. Children are given black or white, right or wrong solutions, which often prove inadequate in a gray world. The child's life is full of "shoulds" and "should nots." Intolerance is the attitude toward the world that the children see modeled. "In short, the teetotaler parent gives the child a set of rules and expectations that are inconsistent with basic human needs and impossible to live by. In turn, the child has the perfect opportunity to graphically show contempt for those rules by abusing alcohol, usually during adolescence or early adulthood" (Lawson et al., 1983, p. 81). To complicate matters further, the children usually have guilt feelings due to not being able to live up to the expectations their parents have set. This last characteristic crosses over into the domain of the other parent type: the overly demanding parent.

3. *overly demanding parents:* Generally, the overly demanding parent makes it quite clear to the child what it is he or she expects. The problem is that the expectations are unrealistic. By trying to live vicariously through their children, overly demanding parents ask their children to succeed in all the areas in which they wish they had succeeded (e.g., sports, college, business). Parents who choose careers for their children often fit in this category.

Overly demanding parents may model a seemingly unattainable high degree of success as viewed by the child. The success they have achieved may have been at the expense of a close relationship with their family. Even though their intention is to help their children be happy, the children find it difficult to feel good about themselves when it appears that their parents care more about their careers than them. This is particularly tragic when the parents believe what they are doing is for the good of the family. They are only responding to their own significant models and upbringing.

This type of competitive family environment often results in siblings competing with one another and comparing themselves with each other.

Family rivalry does not necessarily stop with siblings. Parents may also compare themselves with each other. Regardless of who compares themselves with whom, the results are the same. "When people compare themselves with someone they see as better, they will perceive themselves as less than they want to be or should be, and their self-image will suffer as a consequence" (Lawson et al., 1983, p. 82). Sons and daughters of famous people often graphically illustrate these dynamics.

4. *overly protective parents:* Overly protective parents never give their child a chance to develop a sense of self-worth and a positive self-image. The child is not given the opportunity to master his or her environment. Overly protective parents can be the result of two dynamics. First, the parents may be overinvested in their children. They use their children to meet their own ego needs and to attain a sense of self-worth. Second, the parents may suffer from a reaction formation. The parents may have some doubt in their minds if they even really like their children. This thought is so unacceptable that they react by showing their children, as well as the rest of the world, how much they care through their overprotective behavior (Lawson et al., 1983). As a result of overprotective parents, children have no chance to develop coping skills. Children who do not have the skills needed to master their environment will not have a positive or secure self-image.

The four parental types are not necessarily pure types. A parent or parents may have qualities of more than one type. The common element for all of the parental types is that the children do not develop a positive self-image. It is important to remember that even though research shows parental type is important in the development of alcoholism, it is likely that many other factors also contribute.

When assessing why an adolescent is using drugs to cope or provide pleasure and excitement in his life, we often ask the wrong questions. Instead of asking why drug use is so addicting and reinforcing, perhaps one should ask why the rest of the client's life is so unreinforcing that he or she is willing to sacrifice everything else in his or her life for the opportunity to use drugs.

If one were to postulate a "feel good scale" numbered from 0 to 10, 0 being suicidal and 10 being complete ecstasy; the average person would probably usually feel like a 6 or 7, but there are things in his or her life that would periodically allow him or her to jump up the scale to an 8, 9, or even 10. Given the "feel good" status, a drug that enabled one to feel like 8, 9, or 10 would not be such a powerful reinforcer because there would be other things in life that would enable one to feel very good—at least part of the time. One would probably not be willing to risk all the other things for the sake of a drug that did little to improve his or her situation. A confused adolescent from a dysfunctional family that offers little emotional support probably feels like a 2, a 3, or maybe even a 1. For this individual, because of his or her state or deprivation, a drug that enabled him or her to feel like an 8 or better would be an extremely powerful reinforcer. If this individual also had few if any other alternative behaviors that would bring about such good feelings and peace of mind, the drug would take on even greater importance.

Psychological assessment should look closely at the client's "feel good" status. Until the client can find a way to meet his or her psychological needs in a more appropriate manner, drug or alcohol abuse is likely to continue.

Family issues are critical. A family with dysfunctional communication where parents may be largely absent or abusive when they are present is a poor environment for psychological growth. Social and communication skills are often deficient in children from such families. Children whose feelings have not been validated in the past when they tried to express them may not feel that they are important and will not develop the confidence or skills needed to express themselves clearly.

Adolescents who grow up in homes where education is not valued may see little need to work in school and may receive little encouragement when they do work hard. The counselor needs to encourage and give import to the adolescent's efforts. As a counselor in a juvenile detention facility, this author once had a minor client who was quite intelligent but did terribly in school and had done so for many years. This author told him that because school was so important, his first treatment goal would be to attend school each day and maintain a C average. During the first week after setting this goal, this author checked with him often and praised his attendance and effort. Within 2 weeks, he was making "straight As." When asked why he thought he had not done this in the past, he simply said: "No one ever told me it was important before." This minor also had many other problems that were less responsive to intervention, but his case does illustrate a point: one should not overlook the obvious or underestimate the power of encouragement and an enthusiastic interest in the client's achievement. School work can also have an impact on peer relationships and acceptance or rejection by certain peer groups. Adolescents who do poorly in school may not have access to groups that would be a more positive influence.

The therapist should also be alert to the adolescent who is under great pressure to excel and measure his or her self-worth solely by achievement (academic, athletic, musical, etc.). This is a precarious position for anyone and creates a great deal of anxiety for which substance abuse may be a coping mechanism or a means to relax.

Adolescents who use drugs to relieve depression have a particularly high probability of continuing to use drugs when compared with adolescents who use drugs for other reasons. For this group of adolescents, drug use probably has a negative reinforcing effect in that it removes an unpleasant emotion (depression). It should be pointed out that depression does not cause drug use but may be one reason for continued use. "In a study of high school students, drug users were found to have significantly more psychological symptoms—anxiety, obsessive compulsive reactions, hostility reactions, agitation, excitement and violent reactions—and less 'maturity' than students who do not use drugs" (Geckman & Utada, 1983, p. 63).

Adolescents in residential treatment often identify difficulty in expressing feelings, feeling bored, and getting angry as problems. Adolescents with these problems are psychologically at risk for substance abuse and will need treatment that addresses these problems to lower that risk.

Labouvie and McGee (1986) investigated personality variables and their effects on drinking behavior. Adolescents who started drinking early and proceeded quickly to heavier levels of use tended to score lower on achievement, cognitive structure, and harm avoidance while at the same time scoring higher on affiliation, autonomy, exhibitionism, impulsiveness, and play. They were more detached from the adult world and more involved with peer groups or themselves.

Sexual identity is also an important component of the adolescent's psychological health. Adolescents from an alcoholic or substance abusing family may not have learned the skills needed to relate sexually to their peers. They are likely to lack confidence and feel unattractive. This can be an especially important issue for adolescents who see sexuality as an integral part of the adult world.

Assessment is useful only if it in some way affects treatment and thereby benefits the client. If the same treatment or "shotgun" approach to treatment is given to everyone regardless of what assessment has shown, it is a pointless procedure. Assessment should explore the client's needs, and treatment should address those specific needs.

TREATMENT

For some youth early intervention has been found to increase the probability that the very behaviors one intended to change become stable. This is the source of the idea of 'radical nonintervention' (Sehur, 1971) with its sources in labelling theory.

The idea expressed in the quotation is that some behaviors will go away if the person is left alone. Certainly, this will not happen in all cases. As a chemical dependency therapist, one must decide whether to intervene or wait. This is possibly a more important question than the one usually asked: how to intervene. Three issues may be pertinent:

1. It seems reasonable to postulate that within our society substance abuse is increasingly a potential component of normal exploration and the development of ego identity.

★ 2. When working with adolescents, it is the maturity of the drinker more than the pattern of drinking that should be the focus for understanding adolescent substance abuse.

3. The opportunity to explore and experiment is thought to be crucial to the development of adolescents. Intervention early in the process can prevent the adolescent from coming to terms with the chemicals in his own manner.

Calling an adolescent an "early-stage drinker" or encouraging him or her to see himself or herself as an alcoholic in the AA perception as someone who cannot and never will be able to drink without losing control over his or her drinking will certainly threaten the development of a positive self-image. The premature self-definition imposed by treatment prevents the adolescent from becoming who he or she might become. It is probable that any given youth who drinks in a certain way will not become an alcoholic. One does not know for sure how the individual will develop. Thus, there is the paradox that early detection may result in a negative label and self-concept. On the other hand, it is an unquestionable fact that large numbers of adolescents abuse chemicals and get into trouble when they do.

There is a solution to this paradox. Treat the individual and the behavior. If treatment meets the need of the individual, labeling the client is unimportant. In fact, it may be possible to provide the very best treatment without labeling the client. Substance abuse may be an issue, but it is very likely only one of many issues. Family problems, social and work skills, impulsiveness, ability to deal with change, sexual identity, and role models are all issues of potentially equal or greater importance. As professionals, the first duty is to do no harm. With this concept clearly in sight, one can then proceed to help.

Few treatment programs in the United States are designed specifically to treat adolescents. "Approximately 20.6% of all drug clients in treatment (N = 173,479) are 19 years and under (NIDA, 1983a). Of the 3,018 substance abuse treatment facilities in the National Drug and Alcoholism Treatment Utilization Survey in September, 1982, only 155 (5.1%) had adolescents as their main clientele" (Beschner & Friedman, 1985, p.

152).Of the adolescents in treatment, 15.1% entered residential programs. When these clients were compared with clients in drug-free outpatient programs they were found to be "1) lower in educational level; 2) more likely to have been referred to treatment by the criminal justice system; 3) more likely to have had previous treatment episodes; and 4) more likely to have been using drugs other than marijuana, such as heroin, other opiates, cocaine, hallucinogens, barbiturates, and inhalants (NIDA, 1981)" (Beschner & Friedman, 1985, p. 154).

DeLeon and Deitch (1984) found that, compared with adults, adolescents in treatment had more disorganization in the family, received psychological treatment at an earlier age, and responded more to pressure exerted by family and fear of jail when deciding to stay in treatment and that educational needs and assistance and the need for family support played a greater role in their treatment.

In studying residential and day treatment programs, Beschner & Friedman (1985) found that counselors' attributes were one of the major factors affecting the effectiveness of the program. Three major attributes were found to be most important, especially in residential settings: "They were: l) natural ability and ease in relating to adolescents; 2) an ability to project a positive model; and 3) several years of counseling experience" (p. 160). These researchers concluded that there is a high level of alcohol and marijuana use that continues after treatment, indicating that current treatment methods have insufficient impact on adolescent clients. He also concluded that most adolescent clients and their families have multiple social and psychological problems that predate the substance abuse problem. This last conclusion seems to lend support for the use of family therapy as a crucial part of any treatment program dealing with substance abuse.

In a comparison of drug-free outpatient programs and residential programs, Beschner and Friedman (1985) identified what counselors considered to be the most effective counseling approaches:

1. An understanding and empathetic attitude.
2. Confronting the client with his/her self-destructive/maladaptive behavior.
3. Providing emotional support.
4. Providing practical assistance in solving the client's real-life problems (Beschner & Friedman, 1985, p. 163).

Intense involvement with drugs that began at an early age is indicative of many personal deficits and problems. A holistic approach to treatment that addresses more general deviance as well as attempting to instill a sense of personal adequacy and accomplishment is needed. Evidence regarding the relative effectiveness of any one treatment approach is inconclusive. There is reason to presume that residential drug-free treatment programs are effective with seriously involved drug abusers. "The amount of time spent in a program was found to be a powerful predictor of all post-treatment criterion behaviors for therapeutic community residents, irrespective of age" (Holland & Griffin, 1984, p. 88).

Because family issues are so pervasively interwoven in all areas of our lives, family therapy would seem to be the therapy of choice. The study by Holland and Griffin (1984) pointed out the high incidence of dysfunctional families among serious drug abusers. Because of the highly dysfunctional nature of some of the families, the therapist may be unable to enlist their cooperation. In these cases, family issues and the hurt, anger, and resentment fostered by the family environment should still be major treatment issues.

PREVENTION

Lawson et al. (1983) offered a philosophy of viewing the family system as the client. They felt that this approach went beyond the remedy of current substance abuse problems and offered a way to stop the intergenerational cycle of substance abuse by treating the abusers of the future (the children). Research studies have often documented the powerful learning of coping styles and modeled behavior in the homes of alcoholics and other substance abusers. A healthy home environment can buttress an adolescent in a relatively sick society. It is much more difficult to counter the effect of a dysfunctional home with school and community programs (though these are also needed).

It has been estimated that as many as 60% of alcoholics in treatment were raised in a home where there was at least one alcoholic parent (Lawson et al., 1983). Many of the children from these families continue to struggle with issues of (a) intimacy, (b) control, (c) responsibility, (d) identification and expression of feeling, and (e) trust (Black, 1979) even if they are not substance abusers themselves.

Primary prevention is intended to prevent a disorder before it occurs. Primary prevention can take the form of information or family therapy. It can include family skills training, parent education programs, and media messages ("Just Say No"). There is little research on prevention, and in the case of education, there are some indications that it can have an effect opposite to the one desired. Secondary prevention is an attempt to detect and halt the progress of a disorder early in its development. Therapeutic intervention is then used to restore health and, it is hoped, prevent future problems.

Primary prevention plans have typically had a goal of total abstinence. Informational scare tactics were often used to achieve this goal. Adolescents today (especially those already using drugs) question the credibility of these programs when the information runs counter to their own experience. They may also be unwilling to totally give up a substance whose use has become a rite of passage to the adult world, where use is not only permitted but encouraged.

Carroll (cited in Beschner & Friedman, 1986) thought that a more realistic approach to prevention was to shift efforts from primary to secondary prevention. Because no prevention strategy can hope to stop adolescents from experimenting with drug or alcohol, Carroll thought one should try to disrupt substance abuse behavior early before serious damage occurred. Carroll offered three objectives in order to achieve this secondary prevention: (a) teach adolescents to identify the early signs of abuse (how to distinguish between use and abuse), (b) teach adolescents how to assist peers and family members with substance abuse problems by helping them recognize and accept that they have a problem, and (c) teach them where they or their substance abusing friend or family member can go for help.

Whatever the prevention strategy, it is clear that in American society there is a perceptual link between chemical use and mood change, coping with unpleasant feelings and feeling better. One must continue to work to break this link. Realizing that adolescents use chemicals to feel better as well as "high," one must strive to make adolescents feel better through improved family systems, personal and educational achievements, and activities other than drug and alcohol use.

REFERENCES

Baizerman, M. *Youth and alcohol: Is there really an epidemic?*

Beschner, G.M., & Friedman, A.S. (Eds.). (1979). *Youth drug abuse: Problems, issues and treatment.* Lexington, MA: D.C. Heath.

Beschner, G.M., & Friedman, A.S. (1985). Treatment of adolescent drug abusers. *International Journal of Addictions, 20,* 97–993.

Beschner, G., & Friedman, A. (Eds.). (1986). *Teen drug abuse.* Lexington, MA: D.C. Heath.

Black, C. (1979). Children of alcoholics. *Health and Research World,* 23–27.

Cahalan, D., Asin, J.H. & Crossley (1969). *American drinking practices.* (Monograph No. 6.) New Brunswick, NJ: Ruther Center of Alcohol Studies.

DeLeon, G., & Deitch, D. (1984). Treatment of the adolescent abuser in the therapeutic community. In *Treatment services for adolescent drug abusers.* Rockville, MD: National Institute on Drug Abuse.

Fishburne, P.M., Abelson, H.I., & Cisin, I. (1980). *National survey on drug abuse: Main findings, 1979* (Pub. No. ADM 80-976). Washington, DC: Government Printing Office.

Glickman, N., & Utada, A. (1983). *Characteristics of drug users in urban public high schools.* Unpublished manuscript.

Glynn, T.J. (1981). *Adolescent drug abuse: Review of research based preventive intervention efforts.* Rockville, MD: National Institute on Drug Abuse.

Gonzales, G.M. (1983). Time and place of first drinking experience and parental knowledge as predictors of alcohol use and misuse in college. *Journal of Alcohol and Drug Education, 27*(1), 1–13.

Holland, S., & Griffin, A. (1984). Adolescent and adult drug treatment clients: Patterns and consequences of use. *Journal of Psychoactive Drugs, 17*(1).

Hubbard, R.L., Cavanaugh, E.R., Graddock, S.G., & Rachel, J.V. (1983). *Characteristics, behaviors and outcomes for youth in TOPS study.* Unpublished manuscript, Research Triangle Institute, Research Triangle Park, NC.

Johnston, L.D., Brockman, J.G., & O'Malley, P.M. (1981). *Highlights from student drug use in America, 1975–1981.* (PHHS Pub. No. ADM 82-1208) Rockville, MD: National Institute on Drug Abuse.

Labouvie, E.W., & McGee, C.R. (1986). Relations of personality to alcohol and drug use in adolescence. *Journal of Consulting & Clinical Psychology, 54*, 289–293.

Lawson, G., Peterson, J., & Lawson, A. (1983). *Alcoholism in the family: A guide to treatment and prevention.* Rockville, MD: Aspen.

Pattson, S., Kessler, R., & Hondell, D. (1977). Depressive mood and illegal drug use: A longitudinal analysis. *J. Genet Psychology, 131*, 267–289.

Peck, D.G. (1983). Legal and social factors in the deference of adolescent marijuana use. *Journal of Alcohol and Drug Education, 28*(3).

Segal, B., Cromer, F., Stevens, H., & Wasserman, P. (1982). Patterns of reasons for drug use among detained and adjudicated juveniles. *International Journal of Addictions, 17*, 1117–1130.

Segal, B., Huba, G.J., & Singer, J.L. (1980). *Daydreaming and personality: A study of college youth.* Hillsdale, NJ: Lawrence Earlbaum.

Chapter 12

Treatment and Prevention of Alcoholism in the Native American Family

Audry Hill

INTRODUCTION

The abuse of alcohol and its effects and consequences are without exception the major problems of the Native American family today. The effects are spiritually, physically, mentally, and emotionally tragic, and the consequences are found in the increasing rates of suicide, accidental deaths, criminal arrests, family violence, family breakdown, birth defects, and a multitude of medical problems. According to recent studies, as many as half of the 10 leading causes of death are directly or indirectly related to the effects of alcohol (Cohen, 1982). However, the effects are not uniform (Stratton, Zeiner, & Pardes, 1978), and the drinking patterns and behaviors vary throughout this culture (Levy & Kunitz, 1974). It does appear that where heavy drinking patterns occur, the effects on the native family are the same and the consequences occur consistently. In order to provide effective treatment and prevention strategies for this problem, it is necessary to focus on the development of a framework that addresses the spiritual, physical, mental, and emotional areas of Native American culture and examines the role the family plays in the development, maintenance, progression, treatment, and prevention of alcohol abuse and alcoholism.

It has been recognized that efforts to treat the individual are enhanced when it is possible to provide family treatment (Lawson, Peterson, & Lawson, 1983). Family treatment efforts are aimed at a total systems approach in the field of alcoholism today. Current literature in the field has combined three main theories into one central theory and has integrated the role of the family with the concept of familial alcoholism (Goodwin, 1983). Special populations have been identified, and the physiological, social, and psychological factors relevant to each culture have been explored. The purpose of this chapter is to discuss the ramifications of recent advances in alcoholism and family treatment for Native Americans.

CONCEPTUAL FRAMEWORK

In addition to incorporating a family systems approach that is based on a biopsychosocial framework for Native Americans, five reasons support this approach to treatment and prevention.

✦ 1. *Past efforts to treat the Native American alcoholic have been ineffective.* In a recent study of detoxification recidivism among this population, alcoholics were found to continue to experience serious alcohol related problems in spite of detoxification and treatment. The recurring episodes of severe alcohol abuse have been generally viewed as the "revolving door process" and indicate a need for more appropriate strategies and alternatives for treatment (Kivlahan, Walker, Donovan, & Miscke, 1985). Ineffectiveness has been attributed to a lack of a cultural context for drinking behavior, which refers to the beliefs, attitudes, social relations, and behaviors regarding drinking that are shared by individuals in a drinking group, family, community, and culture. There are dominant drinking patterns, and there are culturally deviant styles of drinking. Identification of alcohol abuse, treatment, and prevention require defining the principles underlying the deviant drinking styles. Indigenous forms of management for the use, abuse, and consequences of alcohol use have provided the method of treatment that has been shown to be most effective. This seems to be true in the relations between Native Americans and the white society in all institutional areas: politics, law, education, medical services, and social services. For example, Lewis and Ho (1975) recognized that sympathy for the social problems has not enabled the social work profession to serve this population effectively. They attributed this lack of success to (a) a lack of understanding of the cultural context of the social problems, (b) retention of stereotyped images of the culture, and (c) the use of standard techniques and approaches.

Attempts to work with Native Americans may be difficult for both the Native American and the white service provider. While the white worker often relies on stereotypes rather than facts, the native person, through education and acculturation, may have conflicting ideas of how to help. Ineffectiveness is directly related to the approach, method, and technique employed, and unless these helping tools are based on the cultural concepts of the Native American culture, they will meet with little, if any, success. The development of alternatives requires the integration of contemporary methods of service and common cultural principles. As there is a vast diversity of tribes and subpopulation segments within the Native American culture, it is necessary to gain an understanding of the cultural concepts common to the culture that address the etiology of alcoholism within the family.

2. *Treating the individual and returning him or her to the same dysfunctional family and environment where the drinking behavior took place perpetuate the process.* From the family systems perspective, the alcoholic is not the cause of the dysfunctional relations in the family unit. Alcoholism is viewed as a symptom of a dysfunctional family system. Treating the individual within a structured support program enables the alcoholic to gain insight into the nature of his or her problem. When replaced into the dysfunctional sets of interrelated behaviors of the family, the alcoholic most often reverts to drinking behavior patterns.

3. *Family members are in as much need of treatment as the alcoholic.* According to the family systems perspective, family members suffer from the same dysfunctional relations without the buffering effects of alcohol. Treatment often identifies earlier stages of alcoholism that may be manifesting in younger family members.

4. *Participation by all members of the household is essential for effective rehabilitation.* Treatment appears to be more effective when the alcoholic family member recovers in a family unit that views alcoholism as a family disease and pursues recovery as a group.

5. *Native people themselves view alcoholism as a community-based problem that requires a community-based solution.* Various statements addressing the problems of Native American families support these reasons for a family treatment approach that is based on the physiological, social, and psychological factors that have made alcoholism and its effects and consequences the major problems for Native American families (Select Committee on Children, Youth and Families, 1986).

Some problems?

Demographics

Estimates of the original population of the Native American culture at the time of the European contact range from 1,152,950 (Mooney, 1928) to 90 million (Dobbyns, 1976) to between 50 and 100 million prior to 1600 (Jacobs, 1974). Currently, there are 1.4 million Native Americans living in the United States, including Aleuts and Eskimos. Since the 1905 census, there has been a slight increase; however, a return to cultural prosperity would be a hasty conclusion. Native Americans continue to have the highest rate of alcohol abuse (Mason, 1985).

The U.S. government has separated Native Americans into three categories: (a) federally recognized tribes and bands, (b) non-federally recognized, and (c) urban Native Americans. Generally, there are 10 major cultural areas: the Northeast, Southeast, Plains, Arctic, Subarctic, Northwest Coast, Plateau, Great Basin, California, and Southwest. It is important to identify the cultural group to which the Native American family adheres to in the provision of treatment. One final subgrouping within this population is the context of urban or reservation life style. While current statistical information may be administratively functional, the important factor for a treatment approach for the family rests in how the native family views itself and in which cultural context it places itself and the life style to which it aspires. For example, in California, there are approximately 200,000 Native Americans from various cultural areas throughout the United States. An estimated 81% live in urban areas. However, it is not known whether all of these families live in urban areas by choice or by necessity due to housing, income, and services. It is necessary for the native family to define itself.

Confusion exists regarding the actual rates of alcohol abuse, and recent studies have led to an examination of the various tribes and bands. The problems encountered in studying the prevalence of alcohol abuse are compounded by the diversity within the culture. Recent studies do reveal that alcohol use and abuse vary from tribe to tribe and from urban to reservation communities. Levy and Kunitz (1974) found that acceptable drinking behaviors and alcohol related effects such as homicide and suicide rates varied widely among the tribes in Arizona. The Hopi had the lowest rate of alcoholism and the Apache had the highest rate. The reasons for these variations are not understood.

An identification of the factors that influence the diversity of alcoholism rates and related problems would have important implications for the development of effective strategies for family treatment and prevention programs. These factors would facilitate the identification of high-risk segments within this population. Although the Native American population has generally been recognized as a high-risk segment of the total population, it appears that new evidence shows that the tribes also show a diversity in alcoholism and alcohol related problems. Some tribes may be found to be at higher risk than others, indicating the need for culturally specific treatment approaches for the family.

In this chapter, the factors that place the native family at high risk are explored from a biopsychosocial perspective with a focus on the role the family plays in the development of alcoholism. According to Lawson et al. (1983), there are specific factors that predispose a particular person to a high risk for alcoholism.

Biopsychosocial Factors from a Family Systems Perspective

The biopsychosocial perspective is a combination of the three main theories of alcoholism. It is an examination of the physiological, social, and psychological factors that are generally identified with alcohol use and abuse. Research in these areas has been conducted to determine the specific factors that predispose Native Americans to such high rates of alcohol abuse and alcoholism. In each of these areas the current research is examined in relation to the role the Native American family plays in the etiology of alcoholism. At the end of each section, questions are presented that may be used to determine whether a family member is at high, medium, or low risk for alcoholism. This format has been prepared for determining the individual risk (Lawson et al., 1983) and is modified here for application to the Native American population, particularly the family.

PHYSIOLOGICAL FACTORS

The recent research on the physiological response to alcohol was examined to review ethnic differences in alcohol response, covering the literature from 1978 to 1984 and including nine areas of alcohol response: consumption rate, absorption rate, metabolism rate, alcohol dehydrogenase, acetaldehyde dehydrogenase, alcohol sensitivity (facial flushing and dysphoria), cardiovascular changes, psychological changes, and alcohol abuse. Evidence of ethnic differences was found for each category of alcohol response.

Ethnic Differences in Metabolism

Native Americans were found to vary greatly in alcohol consumption rates. Utes and Ojibwas considerably exceeded the total U.S. percentages for the proportions of current and heavy drinkers; other tribes, such as the Standing Rock Sioux, had similar rates of alcohol use; and the Navajo had lower rates than the total U.S. rate of consumption (Reed, 1985). It is important to know that variations in alcohol consumption do exist in the Native American culture.

Reed (1985) compared ethnic groups as to the average time to reach peak blood alcohol concentration or peak ear lobe flushing after taking a test drink. After fasting subjects were compared, and it was found that clear differences did exist: Native Americans showed the fastest rate of absorption. Faster rates usually produce a higher blood-alcohol concentration than do slow rates of absorption (Reed, 1985).

The metabolism rate of ethanol to acetaldehyde of Native Americans, measured as the rate of disappearance from the blood after a test dose, indicated a high average among the four tribes studied. Native Americans were found to have a higher alcohol metabolism rate, indicating a physiological difference. Although the data were based on the study of a small sample (four tribes) of the total Native American population, they do suggest further exploration for a possible genetic factor (Reed, 1985).

Alcohol dehydrogenase (ALDH) is the enzyme that catalyzes the initiation of alcohol metabolism, producing acetaldehyde. Native Americans were not included in this study; however, marked differences were found between whites and Orientals in the frequencies of genes at the five structural loci, specifically ADH_2 and ADH_3. These phenotypic frequencies do not differ between nonalcoholic and alcoholic whites. Ricciardi, Saunders, Williams, and Hopkins (1983) stated that there are no known physiological consequences of having two different phenotypes within the same ethnic population. To date, there are no similar studies that include Native Americans.

Acetaldehyde dehydrogenase, the enzyme that catalyzes the second step in alcohol metabolism from acetaldehyde to acetic acid and H_2O_2, has been found to exist in five isozymes whose structural bases are being investigated by Ricciardi et al. (1983). Native Americans were found to have deficient levels of ALDH, which is attributed to mutant variances in the structural gene for the enzyme, which has major consequences for alcohol use and abuse. According to Ricciardi et al. (1983), this deficiency explains the net alcohol response.

Facial flushing and dysphoria were the first established ethnic differences and were demonstrated by Wolff in 1972 (cited in Reed, 1985). He showed that marked facial flushing and dysphoria occurred in Orientals after they consumed one or two drinks, which has been confirmed by several studies. Reed (1985) noted that there is a similar response in Native Americans. With regard to ALDH-I, studies suggested that deficient levels of this enzyme would result in higher levels of blood acetaldehyde. Native Americans were not included in the study of blood acetaldehyde levels. However, in studies of Japanese alcoholics, the majority of the Japanese became too sick to drink enough alcohol to become dependent. If the social, physiological, or psychological situation encouraged such drinking, the Japanese would drink enough to become dependent. The deficient levels of ALDH-I seem to explain the low consumption rate in Orientals. For the Native American, however, the deficient levels do not predispose a low consumption rate of alcohol (1985) as they have a higher rate of consumption. It was noted by Reed (1985) that, like the Japanese, if the biopsychosocial factors encouraged a dismissal of the flushing and dysphoria, alcohol dependency would occur.

These observations on alcohol metabolism and ALDH-I deficiency provide the genetic basis for the clearest racial variation in alcohol response and have clear implications for the drinking behaviors of Native Americans.

Cardiovascular responses, such as the heart rate, systolic blood pressure, and diastolic blood pressure, following the consumption of alcohol have been extensively studied. The responses to alcohol of individuals in three ethnic groups were examined by Reed (1985). Native Americans were not included; however, the responses of Orientals to alcohol appeared to be largely due to the deficiency in the ALDH-I isozyme. Since Native Americans were also found to have similar deficient levels of ALDH-I, research in the area of alcohol response among Native Americans is warranted.

The psychological responses of Native Americans were studied by Farris and Jones (1978) who focused on the effects of alcohol on memory. A comparison of 15 white women and 15 Native American women revealed that both groups were equally affected. A study of Japanese men revealed that this group felt less fatigued after drinking, which was not related to the ALDH-I deficiency or to the facial flushing and dysphoria. Reed (1985) stated that there were too few studies in this area to draw any conclusions.

The final alcohol response examined by Reed (1985) was alcohol abuse and alcoholism. Reed found that it was difficult to compare ethnic groups due to the variations in definitions of "alcohol abuse," the lack of reliable data, and the diagnostic criteria used to define "alcoholism." However, the relative frequencies of alcohol related problems among Native Americans were used to compare this ethnic group to the total U.S. population. It was found that Native Americans had much higher rates of motor vehicle deaths (50% to 60% alcohol related), other accidental deaths (15% to 50% alcohol related), cirrhosis of the liver (85% alcohol related), and arrests for intoxication, which were extremely high by comparison. A similar disparity was found among Canadian native people. For example, in the province of Ontario in 1977, of a 2.1% native population, 26.4% of the offenses related to alcohol were committed by Canadian native people, according to Irvine in 1978 (cited in Reed, 1985).

Rates of alcohol abuse and the problems associated with these proportionately high rates have long been recognized. The variations from tribe to tribe and within the cultural areas require acknowledgment. It is important to note that a high level of alcohol abuse and alcohol related problems is experienced by both U.S. and Canadian native peoples; however, there is a variation within this population that seems to have some physiological basis, particularly in the area of alcohol response. The study of ethnic groups revealed that Native Americans are at a particularly high risk for alcohol abuse and alcoholism. However, further research is necessary to provide more information as most of the information was inferred from a small sample of the native population and from a comparison with the alcohol responses of Orientals. The identification of physiological differences within the Native American population seems to be necessary in order to determine the variations in alcohol response and other traits.

The implications for differences in alcohol responses based on a genetic predisposition have important implications for determining the level of risk for a particular family and tribe or native community, as it appears that alcohol responses vary within the cultural areas of the Native American population. The differences in alcohol responses require further examination in relation to the drinking behaviors and styles that differ from tribe to tribe.

Twin/Sibling Studies

Additional research support is based on the twin studies conducted to determine concordance rates of alcoholism for identical vs. fraternal twins and the stronger influence of the biologic family versus the adoptive family (Goodwin, 1979). Generally, the results have led to the conclusion that severe forms of alcoholism may carry a genetic predisposition, but heavy alcohol abuse reflects the importance of social and psychological factors. Similar studies by Schuckit (1972) found that half-siblings of one alcoholic parent were more likely to develop alcoholism as an early adult than those without an alcoholic parent.

Genetic predisposition for Native Americans is a hypothesis that has generally been considered nonexistent, or irrelevant (Lemert, 1982; Lewis, 1982); however, the evidence presented by Reed (1985) indicated a possible basis that warrants further investigation. A recent report by Weisner, Weibel-Orlando, and Long (1984) supported the claim that insufficient data exist to support or disclaim the genetic-physiological hypothesis. In addition, the variance of drinking levels and the possible association to alcohol response require further investigation. The discovery of a possible genetic-physiological basis for the transmission of alcoholism would have important implications for treatment and prevention strategies for the Native American population. Establishing a high-risk model to identify which of the cultural areas are at a particular high risk in terms of physiological factors would better the chances of effective, and earlier, prevention of alcohol abuse, alcoholism, and alcohol related problems.

Determining Risk Level

The following questions were developed by Lawson et al. (1983) to determine high and low risk for alcoholism based on physiological factors:

1. Do you have a parent or grandparent who was, or is, alcoholic?

2. When you started drinking, were you, or are you, able to drink more than your friends with fewer physical consequences (i.e., nausea, hangover)?
3. Did you consume large amounts of alcohol from the first time you drank?

According to Lawson et al. (1983), physiological risk is unlikely to change much in the individual. Age and medical problems are the only things likely to influence a change in a person's physiological risk. For example, physical risk is greater with increasing age as the body is not able to metabolize alcohol as efficiently as it could in earlier years. Younger people can consume large amounts without the same physical effects and consequences the amount would have for an older individual. A high-risk person would answer "yes" to any one of the questions, whereas a low-risk person would answer "no" to all three questions.

SOCIOCULTURAL FACTORS

A majority of the theories that account for the high rate of alcoholism for the Native American population are in this area. For example, a research review by Mail (1985) found that 295 studies supported a sociocultural explanation and noted that the 10 major theories lie in this category. These theories are based on causal or explanatory factors such as acculturation, anomie, recreation, deprivation, celebration, early exposure, gregariousness, affluence, poverty, role models, unemployment, learned behavior, and a lack of social norms. The review also indicated that the two main factors are (a) mass mourning for the loss of cultural tradition, and (b) a social response to the demands for integration and identification with the dominant culture (Lewis, 1982).

Theory of Cultural Relativity

Waddell (1981) presented a theoretical position that endorsed the principles of cultural relativity in the study and treatment of alcoholism in special populations. The main premises of this position are that interpretations of cultural behavior must acknowledge that the interpretations are being made on the basis of personal experience and assumptions from the cultural category of the interpreter. Findings and interpretations of cultural behavior must be made from within the frame of reference set by the cultural context under investigation. As a method of study, the theory of cultural relativity provides a framework that allows for a diversity of positions and techniques for gathering, ordering, and interpreting data. It is also a philosophical position that emphasizes the importance of cultural variables that shape the belief, attitudes, and behavior of the culture under study. Finally, it is practical in that individual interactions, i.e., adopting and acting on the basic propositions, have implications for the direction of human behavior, an important component for treatment and prevention in the field of alcoholism.

It would seem that the application of the theory of cultural relativity would provide a framework that would be sensitive to the cultural variations among Native Americans and Canadian native people when one attempted to identify specific risk factors.

evaluations of culture must come from a framework of that culture / not our white evaluation

Toward a Bicultural Family System

The attitudes, beliefs, and behaviors toward alcohol use are influenced by the family and maintained within the sociocultural context where the drinking behavior occurs. Parents are the primary contributors to the development of high risk factors for their children.

Cultural variations in each of the 10 major cultural areas can be examined in terms of language, ceremonial traditions, folk medicine, and worldview and in terms of alcoholism and drinking styles. In a study that compared western and eastern areas, it was determined that during a 4-year period from 1972 to 1975, western tribes had a higher rate of alcohol related deaths than did the eastern tribal areas. In a comparison of whites living in the same areas, the results were not statistically significant (Stratton et al., 1978). This would lend support to the theory that the duration of exposure to alcohol determines a cultural group alcoholism rate, which is based on an evolutionary premise. The physiological differences presented by Reed (1985) require further consideration here.

In terms of the native family, sociocultural factors that require examination in order to determine the risk for the development of alcoholism in one family member were provided by Kalicov and Karrer (cited in McGoldrick, Pierce, & Giordano, 1982). The family life cycle in its sociocultural context was described in terms of age, sex role expectations, value orientations, cultural traditions, and rituals in relation to expectable life cycle events, from courtship to later life experiences. The effects of acculturation, history, and change must be considered for their implications for the family life cycle within the cultural context. From a family systems perspective, each developmental stage requires an internal reorganization and elicits a different response from individual family members and as a family system that shares the same cultural beliefs, attitudes, and behaviors. Treatment approaches must take into account the family's historical perspective of acculturation, traditional cultural values, and the present cultural context. According to Weisner et al. (1984) cultural differences are predictors of various drinking levels, and as the family is also socialized within the particular cultural context, the family acquires the beliefs, attitudes, and behaviors inherent in that cultural area. Based on the findings that differences in drinking styles and levels vary according to cultural area and tribe, Levy and Kunitz (1974) gained support for their hypothesis that tribes vary in their response to interaction with the dominant society in ways that are determined by sociocultural factors that have a "remarkable persistence" over time.

These cultural variations in drinking style have implications for the native family as it is the family that is also socialized to the drinking styles that are dominant in its particular cultural area and tribal affiliation. Kalicov and Karrer's (cited in McGoldrick et al., 1982) examination of the cultural variations of the family life cycle provided important data that could be used for a similar examination of the Native American family. From the data provided by Weisner et al. (1984), the impact of different drinking styles developed in various cultural areas would provide implications for establishing risk factors from a tribal perspective and from a family life cycle perspective. Information on the drinking style developed by a family, how it developed and how it is maintained, has important implications for treatment and prevention.

It appears that the drinking style is maintained by entire families and not by individuals and, in a sociocultural context, is viewed as a social response that is culturally relative. Cultural affiliation and perceived psychological stress influenced by the dominant society and the relationship between the tribe and dominant society appear to be the most important predictors of alcohol consumption. The degree of traditionalism and cultural knowledge practiced by the family was associated with lower levels of alcoholism.

Determining Risk Level

Although many other sociocultural theories exist, the theory of cultural relativity has the value of allowing for the tribal diversity and the diversity of drinking behaviors practiced in Native American family systems. For the sociocultural factors, in terms of the role the family plays in the development of alcoholism, there are five questions that would establish a high, medium, or low risk. Each question is worth 1 point: a low score is 0, a medium score is 1 or 2, and a high score is 3 to 5.

1. *Do/did one or both of your parents have strong religious or moral views against drinking alcohol?* This question does not indicate a predisposition to alcoholism on this basis; however, it does recognize the eight characteristics of low rates of family alcoholism identified by O'Connor in 1975 (cited in Lawson et al., 1983).

2. *Are either of your parents alcoholics?* An individual growing up in an alcoholic home experiences an alcoholic role model. In the physiological section, this question addressed the physical environmental factors. This question, in a social context, addresses the hereditary factor.

3. *Do you come from a tribe or native community that has a high rate of alcoholism?* The reliability of this question will depend on the definition of *alcoholism* that is used by the individual. It will also depend on the reputation that the tribe, or native community, has for alcoholism. Generally, if alcohol abuse is a problem within the social context of the individual, he or she is aware of it. If unknown to the individual, it is possible to gain this information from other members of the group.

4. *Do you consider your friends to be heavy drinkers?* (This question could also be do you consider your family members to be heavy drinkers, as large extended family units are also sources of social relationships and drinking companions.) This question also depends on the definition of *heavy drinking* that is used by the individual, and his or her cultural context. One will need to consider the cultural relativity of drinking patterns. Generally, the norms are culturally defined and operate in the context of an extended family system. One should consider the social activities of the individual and the use of alcohol in these activities. Traditional ceremonies have prohibitions concerning alcohol, whereas the weekend drinking party does not.

5. *Does your social role and identity match your concept of what you should be doing and where you feel you should be within your family and native group?* The original question focused on social status. Generally, the status of Native Americans is equally low socioeconomically. There is also the cultural value for equality; therefore the question has been altered to focus on the role and identity of the individual. If the individual is aware of his or her cultural heritage and has been socialized in the traditional customs, values, and beliefs of the tribe, an understanding of his or her native identity and role in the family and community will be known. If not, this individual would be at high risk. Although cultural awareness by the individual does not necessarily eliminate the risk for alcohol abuse or alcoholism, the native individual who has no knowledge of cultural identity

and native family roles is at particularly high risk. Of course, one must also assess the degree of acculturation and the development of an identity and role outside the cultural context and extended family unit.

PSYCHOLOGICAL FACTORS

This section discusses what is considered to be the most important area in terms of treatment and prevention: the psychological area. The psychological factors that predispose an individual for high risk are examined in terms of a psychological response to the relationship of native people and the dominant society.

Studies of Psychological Factors

Psychological factors related to alcoholism include the level of depression, focus of control, and the overall psychological adjustment of the individual. These factors, developed within the family environment, have been considered as high-risk psychological factors for alcoholism by Jones-Saumty, Hochhaus, Dru, and Zeiner (1983). Their study investigated the drinking behaviors and psychological functioning of a group of Native American drinkers with a history of family alcoholism. Based on the study by Hoffman and Noem in 1975, it was determined that the incidence of alcoholism in Native American families was higher than among families of nonalcoholic Native Americans. However, no studies had been conducted that compared the incidence of familial alcoholism between Native American and whites. Also, the studies had been conducted with alcoholic subjects.

The study by Jones-Saumty et al. (1983) investigated group differences between Native Americans with a history of family alcoholism and a group without first-degree alcoholic relatives. Cross-cultural group differences between Native Americans and white social drinkers with a history of family alcoholism were also studied to determine the psychological factors identified with a high risk for alcoholism in the Native American family. The researchers hypothesized that due to the alcoholic environment, the Native American family would show lower levels of psychological adjustment and would report a more alcoholic drinking style than the group without a family history of alcoholism. In addition, they expected that the compound risk of family alcoholism and identification with an ethnic group with a high rate of alcoholism would result in the Native American families demonstrating lower levels of psychological adjustment and drinking behaviors more similar to those of alcoholics than did the white family groups.

Instruments used in this study included a background questionnaire that obtained information on demographics, the family history of alcoholism, and adaptation to the general society. Other tests included the Beck Depression Inventory, the Zung Self-Rating Depression Scale, Levenson's Locus of Control Scales, the Shipley-Institute of Living Scale, the Alcohol Use Inventory, and the Alcohol Consumption Survey.

In the first grouping, the comparison of Native American social drinkers with a history of family alcoholism and Native American social drinkers without such a history did not reveal any differences in psychological functioning measures. However, the group with a family history of alcoholism did report more symptoms of alcoholic drinking than did the other group. The symptoms of behavior were the loss of control of drinking and physical withdrawal, or hangovers. The lack of differences in psychological functioning between these two groups can be accounted for in two ways.

First, it may indicate that the family risk predictors relevant to white populations may not apply to Native American families. Second, a risk factor other than familial alcoholism may be stronger than family influences among this population (Jones-Saumty et al., 1983). It is possible that sociocultural factors that are specific to each cultural area, or specific tribe, are more important determinants of alcoholism than is the family. This makes sense due to the extended family system and close-knit interactions of various tribes and native communities. From the native perspective, the native tribe, or community, is the family. In the cases where tribes, or reservations, are small, a few large extended family systems comprise the community. The study may indicate the need to identify ways to determine the high-risk psychological factors by examination of the tribal influences on the individual and the native family.

The study by Jones-Saumty et al. (1983) further suggests that the Native American style of drinking is more escapist in nature and seems to stem from attempts to deal with the dilemma of acculturation to the dominant society while retaining the cultural identity. The psychological stresses of acculturation, the retaining of the cultural identity, and the alcoholic environment were identified as potent forces predisposing the Native American toward alcoholic drinking.

In the second grouping, matched comparisons were made between social drinkers in Native American cultures and the dominant society. Native American families reported more symptoms of depression, a stronger orientation toward chance control, numerous differences in drinking behaviors, and more symptoms of alcoholic drinking than did white families. Such drinking behaviors were reported as drinking for mental benefit, obsessive-compulsive drinking, guilt after drinking, drinking to change mood, loss of control of alcohol intake, physical withdrawal, and nonalcoholic drug use. Native Americans also viewed external causes (stressful events, environmental situation, etc.) as the most important influences for alcoholic drinking. According to a further study of the cultural and sociological factors in Native American alcoholism, Jones-Saumty et al. (1983) found that Native Americans gave primarily societal explanations for alcohol abuse and rated alcoholism as a disease more often than did whites.

The consistency of symptoms with both groups indicated a prevalence of depressive tendencies in Native American families with a history of family alcoholism. The families also assigned the cause for drinking to an external orientation, specifically to chance, on the locus of control measure. A psychological deficit found in the Native American group with a history of family alcoholism was in the level of cognitive functioning, specifically verbal and abstracting abilities; however, this is speculative when one considers the cultural differences in education, learning style, and language between the groups studied. In their conclusion, the investigators suggested that longitudinal studies of the offspring of social drinkers and alcoholics in the Native American culture who displayed the high-risk psychological functioning profile identified the development of alcoholism in adulthood.

With regard to the hypothesis regarding the drinking styles that resemble alcoholic drinking for Native Americans with a family history of alcoholism, the study found that they demonstrated a more pathological style of drinking, similar to alcoholic drinking. The white group reported a gregarious style of drinking. The results of the study provided evidence of cross-cultural differences. The drinking style of Native American families with a history of alcoholism involved escapist reasons based on the struggle for acculturation and the retention of cultural identity. This study did not consider the influence of the stereotyped identity of the Native American.

The psychological profile suggested depressive factors such as remorse and guilt after drinking, an inability to control drinking, external causal attribution with a chance orientation, and strong evidence of family influences toward alcoholic drinking. Psychological deficits suggested depressive symptoms prevalent in the Native American population including the families who exhibited an alcoholic style of drinking but reported no family history of drinking.

The question raised by the study is: Does the psychological deficit cause Native Americans to drink alcoholically, or does alcoholic drinking cause the psychological deficits that predispose them to depressive symptoms?

Many factors predispose an individual toward alcoholism in addition to the level of psychological functioning. According to Attneave (1982) the source of Native American family disturbance is influenced by the dissonance between native and white relations. Native American families suffer the same types of dysfunctions as other families: enmeshment, reenactment of abandonment, misunderstandings of self and others, effects of unfinished grief work, and the need to cope with anxiety. Of primary importance to the psychological functioning of the Native American family is the establishment of the value orientation held by the family and the cultural grouping of which they are a member.

A traditional Native American life style is not practiced by the majority of Native American families today. However, the value orientations are still transmitted by the family. These values are central to the way the Native American relates to the self, others, and the world. The data compiled by Attneave (1982) are summarized here.

Contemporary families have preserved the traditional time orientation to a degree. Present orientation and a reflection toward the past are combined to project a future image. A cyclical pattern of seasonal variations provides the rhythms for various activities, events, and ceremonies. Life cycle events are focused on the appropriateness of the current stage without a concern for the next stage. Future orientations are established for seasonable preparation and political alliances for the survival of the tribe. In general, a different time orientation continues to persist in the Native American culture. Native Americans struggle to adapt to the time orientation of the dominant society with ensuing stress. Resentment, confusion, rebellion, and apathy have resulted throughout the culture. Still, the future orientation is not a psychological motivating factor for this population.

In contrast to the prevailing orientation toward a control over nature, the Native American values a harmony with the self, others, and the environment; establishing a relationship in harmony with natural forces, with the total environment, is a way of life for the Native American family. Acceptance of natural events is an acceptance of the natural order of the world. The world exists as a spiritual force in the universe. The spiritual relationship to human and nonhuman elements is more important than gaining control or mastery to this culture.

Importance of Family Values

The relationship of the native individual to the cultural group of which he or she is a member requires an understanding of the value orientation toward social relationships. Value for the collective group supercedes the needs of the individual. Group consensus and preference for the collateral needs of the group provide the structural basis for group survival and cooperative efforts. Emergent leadership was a temporary role often reserved for elders whose lives represented wisdom and experience. "Pure" forms of democracy existed, and tribal matters required the slow process of consensus. Ostracism often occurred when consensus was not reached and operated for the good of the group. Rather than divide the group with differences held by the individual, voluntary parting was practiced. Communal values of sharing continue to persist. Accumulation of wealth is both impractical and often neutralized by tribal "giveaway" customs. Generosity is highly respected. The value of sharing is taught early to the young. The values that provide the basis of social relations in the Native American culture persist, yet the culture value preferences of the dominant society are a strong source of psychological stress for the Native American individual, family, and community.

The individuality and autonomy embedded in the collateral relations and the communal life style operated at a secondary level in the traditional native culture; however, the value orientation persists in two areas: individual autonomy as a way of being and the development of personality based on noninterference as a way of being.

Individual autonomy was respected as long as it did not harm the well-being of the group. Individual variability was appreciated for group enhancement. Competition was not adversarial but based on a desire to gain skills in social competence and personal competence and on a highly individualized rate of accomplishment and interpretation. For example, social competence would involve gaining skills in social relations: "being a good person" for the harmony of the self, others, and group. Personal competence would involve gaining skills in arts or sports or providing for the self and others: "being good to the self."

The value of noninterference as a way of being functioned in opposition to direct confrontation and has been described by Attneave (1982). As a means of social control and establishing acceptable boundaries for behavior, this value incorporated the use of shame, ridicule, and ostracism as a system of reward and punishment. Noninterference, at an extreme level, can operate as complete paralysis of social assertion and control; the innate potential forces within the individual are left to operate. Consequences are learned by making choices without outside interference or confrontation. The responsibility for the natural unfolding of the personality and the control of behavior from within is not assumed by any other person.

At times, this noninterference is confusing to an "outsider" as this also applies to self-destructive behaviors and situations where the behavior may harm the group as well. For example, a family therapist working with a family with alcoholism would be confused by the noninterference by family members. Direct confrontation would not be high on the list of ways of dealing with the behavior of the alcoholic (intervention and correction).

This applies to all but the very young children in the family. Native American families are viewed as "uncooperative" and uncaring rather than respectful of the individual autonomy of the individual and the innate, "positive" potential through which behavior operates. In contrast to white ethical problems surrounding human rights issues, Native Americans experience ethical conflicts between the value of noninterference and the need to protect, teach, and provide for their young.

Noninterference functions to embrace the traditional way of "becoming" and "being." A person is seen as continually "becoming" as a result of experiences in the past and present and is never hurried. Secondary values of "doing and being" are situational. "Doing" for the good of the group is commendable; however, it is also expected, and the individual functions without expectations of praise or special recognition. "Being" is considered the highest value of personal growth and is experienced as a harmonious relationship with the spirit, natural, social, and personal world of the native person.

For the contemporary native person, the value system based on "being and becoming" has deep cultural roots that are often the source of personal conflicts. Acculturation requires a set of values in direct opposition to the values of the native person. In summary, they are harmony versus control over nature, environment, and man; a present and past time orientation versus a future and present time orientation; collateral relations versus individual relations with others; "being and becoming" as the ideal mode of activity versus "doing" as the idealized mode of activity; and a belief in the innate nature of man vs. a "mixed" belief in the innate nature of man.

The conflicting values affect every family member, affecting the child from an early age. Parents struggle to rear their children in, and with, these conflicting value orientations with an awareness of how important it is to retain "the old ways" and the necessity to survive by conforming to the dominant society in an acculturative process. The young are raised to learn group sharing, responsibility, and individual autonomy at an early age. Children acquire the sense that each person is inherently good and that this potential is not to be forced. The consequences of choice and behavior have become remote in contemporary native families. An awareness of their conflicting values allows one to gain a sense of the psychological stress experienced by Native American families. According to Attneave (1982), from the native perspective, retaining cultural ties, and this is much a matter of retaining the extended family structure, is what is sensible to the native person and is vaguely incomprehensible to the dominant culture. What is acceptable behavior in one society is totally unacceptable in another, resulting in an existence that is in a constant state of transition and requiring psychological effort to travel back and forth between the "native world" and the "white world." Even though, as described by Attneave (1982), the level of subsistence is a marginal one in both worlds, it seems that the native person who is able to achieve a level of subsistence that is compatible with his or her sense of native identity and that allows him or her to function successfully between the native and white world is unlikely to abuse alcohol.

Recently, in contrast to the theme that tribal drinking behaviors are self-destructive, Lemert (1982) emphasized a positive use of alcohol as a focus for social behavior where traditional forms of social interaction and recreation were denied or no longer possible, e.g., Native American rituals and ceremonies. Vizenor (1984) found that some drinking styles can be viewed as a positive approach to social integration, a method of survival given the psychological stress of acculturation and cultural retention. The drinking style to which Native American families adapt, according to this view, functions to ease this stress. However, excessive drinking styles would serve to compound the stress, creating a dysfunctional Native American family system.

Models of Drinking within the Family

Early experiences of parent and child relationships play a critical part in the child's early development. In the Native American family, the extended family system enables other family members, such as grandparents, aunts, uncles, and friends, to share in the child rearing process. In determining the psychological risk factors for alcoholism in the family, it is necessary to identify the view toward alcohol held by older family members and the drinking style practiced by the extended family system. Consideration of the sociocultural context in which the drinking occurs must be given. Some of these styles have been identified by Weisner et al. (1984) as (a) serious drinking, (b) white man's drinking, (c) teetotaling, and (d) on the wagon. As parents model a style of drinking for their children, the experience of the child set by the parent's style of drinking is probably the most important factor in the development of alcoholism in later life. Although it is possible that one who is not alcoholic may have a parent or significant family member who fits one or more of these drinking styles, Native American alcoholics often have one or both parents or significant family member that role model one or more of the drinking styles.

Serious Drinking

This style is primarily practiced by younger men and women who are often unmarried; have lower socioeconomic backgrounds; and are not likely to participate in traditional ceremonial activities, use traditional medicine, or use the native language. Drinking is a shared social interaction, rarely practiced alone, and occurs in bars, hotels, or in the home. Drinking parties range from a day to a weekend to week-long binges that can go unchecked for months at a time, depending on the source of income shared among the drinking group. According to Weisner et al. (1984), the majority of the subjects in their study of drinking styles with 50% native ancestry fell into this category.

For the child, this style of drinking becomes a possibility in later life, even if the behavior is bewildering. For example, the early stages of the weekend drinking party appear to be fun, exciting, and pleasurable. Later on, a fight may break out or an accident or argument may occur; however, the drinking continues, and the child perceives "adult drinking fun" to be central to the group. Social interaction remains primary, but the context in which the behavior continues becomes strange. Children may vow never to act like that, only to find themselves being a part of this context in later life, perhaps even a participant in serious drinking. This style of drinking is an alcoholic style of drinking.

Young parents who are also serious drinkers are in no position to provide for the mental health and development of the child. In an alcoholic state, they are unable to establish a genuine, loving relationship that the child needs for healthy psychological development. In times of emotional need, the child is unable to receive the nurturance of the parent, who is too occupied with anger, frustration, and hopelessness. Although many other factors, physiological and social as well as other psychological factors, lead a child toward the development of alcoholism, the influence of the family is considerably high on the list of the most significant factors. One study found that the recurrence of alcoholism in families where family rituals were kept, in spite of alcoholic drinking, was low among the children. High alcoholism rates occurred for children whose families did not maintain family rituals, allowing the drinking behaviors to become more important than family interactions and celebrations (Wolin, Bennett, Noonan, & Tietelbaum, 1977).

White Man's Drinking

These drinkers tended to be middle-aged or older and from higher socioeconomic levels with more stable incomes and more formal education. There were slightly more women than men in this group. This could be due to a greater availability of jobs for women than for the male native person, who favors manual labor jobs in an increasingly technological society. Drinkers in this group tended to be either full-blooded or one-quarter blooded, in comparison with half-blooded in the previous group.

In contrast to the overdemanding parent presented by Lawson et al. (1983), the expectations are conflictual rather than unrealistic.

This type of drinking reflects the requirement of a bicultural life style that is characterized by a mixture of native and white values, a life style that is most often experienced by urban Native Americans. The acceptance of a bicultural life style often does not cause psychological problems for the child unless the parent is not resolved with this way of life. In that case, the child may be exposed to expectations to negate either the native or the white life style, making it difficult for the child to gain a positive self-image and cultural identity. If the parents are not happy with their own life style, it will be impossible for the children to feel good about themselves.

Where alcoholism occurs within this type of family context, it appears that treatment of the entire family is extremely important in order to help the native family become aware of the necessity underlying the need to adapt to a bicultural life style so that all family members can accept and gain a positive self-image and a positive sense of cultural identity.

Teetotalling

Teetotallers are basically abstainers. Lifetime abstainers are primarily older women of mid to low socioeconomic status who have never drunk or have only briefly experienced alcohol during childhood or adolescence. According to Weisner et al. (1984), this group is primarily affiliated with traditional or Christian religions. Native American abstainers tolerate the drinking behavior of other family members, maintaining the value of non-interference, which in non–Native American families is perceived as enabling. The persistence of traditional patterns of interaction has been interpreted as maladaptive in the acculturation process and as contributing to excessive drinking behavior (Redhorse, 1979). In contrast to the teetotaller in the dominant society, who feels that any drinking is immoral and indecent, the Native American teetotaller maintains a tolerant attitude toward the drinking behavior of others. The psychological implications are quite different for the child and other adults in their family context.

Traditionally, the role of elders, particularly the abstaining men and women, has a unifying role in the family, which is highly valued. In an examination of alcoholism, consideration of rights to heritage, tribal customs, and extended family is required. Historically, elders have defended the value of family life through deeds, not words or thought. Elders continue to sustain family strength by resisting white values. This is particularly so when the family is experiencing the devastating effects of alcoholism. However, this implies that the disintegration of the role that elders play in the maintenance of traditional family values will soon no longer provide the traditional source of strength needed by the family to overcome problems. If the abstaining elders can no longer perform their role, the young will not have the guidance and sense of direction needed to cope with their individual or family problems in later life. More respect is required for the role these abstaining elders play in the strengthening of family life.

Most Native American families firmly believe that people are not meant to be controlled and that one does not interfere in the affairs of others. From an early age, there is a passive attitude held toward the personal autonomy of another. This is often interpreted in the traditional methods of teaching and learning. The elder allows the child, or young adult, to make a mistake based on the inherent belief that the child will ultimately find the "right" way and that he or she will learn best that way. Learning through experience is viewed as necessary if the lesson is not to be forgotten. In terms of alcoholism, the traditional cultural values for teaching and learning can have tragic consequences for the entire family.

The abstaining elders, according to an examination of the role of elders in Native American family life (Redhorse, 1979), are the spiritual fabric that sustains family life and requires the interaction of young and old. For example, Mary Smith, 67 years of age, is a full-blooded Choctaw, speaks her language fluently, and has never had a drink in her life. She was raised to believe that drinking alcohol was "not good." Her social life is based on family life and her religion. She refuses to attend urban powwows because of the drinking she observed there. Mary models her beliefs by living by them. She is also a modest reminder of the role elders play in family and community life, which is significant to all family members.

On the Wagon

The second group of nondrinkers is largely composed of men, older and from lower and lower-middle socioeconomic backgrounds, who have had heavy periods of alcohol abuse and problem drinking throughout their lives. They are less likely to be married or to have any formal religious affiliations. Whether these men have been husbands and fathers, or not, they model a very confusing drinking style and life style to the children in the extended family.

The most dominant pattern of heavy drinking includes periods of heavy drinking interrupted by a family crisis, forcible incarceration, or involuntary commitment to a drug and alcohol treatment program, which is quickly abandoned by a return to heavy drinking. Usually, these returns are precipitated by feelings of boredom, loneliness, and a desire for contact with drinking family friends and family members. Within the extended family system, these members are accepted and tolerated without direct criticism of their behavior. They are not ridiculed, ostracized, or chastized by family members. Children may even view them as a "crazy fun" uncle or a rebel cousin. They may represent the uncle who has spent a lot of time in jail or who just doesn't go to work, which is also tolerated and rarely condemned in the extended family system. Regardless of the behavior, the individual is a member of the family first. On the wagon drinkers are neither encouraged nor discouraged; the value of personal autonomy and the belief that the person is inherently good predominate in the extended family system.

Weiser et al. (1984) found that abstinence that is associated with involvement in alcoholism treatment programs as a patient or counselor, membership in a church or Alcoholics Anonymous (AA), and the reintensification of traditional beliefs are the most significant factors in maintaining abstinence for this type of drinker. There appears to be a desire to attain and maintain abstinence on the part of these people; however, until these supports are provided, the revolving door process of the on the wagon drinker will continue and will continue to provide a confusing influence for the children in these family systems. These adults and the children for whom they model will develop maladaptive behaviors, poor coping skills, and low self-worth.

These parental types have one thing in common: their children do not develop a positive sense of self-worth. They also fail to adjust to their environment and have few interpersonal skills. This does not place the blame entirely on the parents. These parental types contribute to the development of alcohol abuse and alcoholism, but they do not cause it. The development of problems with alcohol for the Native American family is traced to its introduction by the white society on the one hand and to the contemporary cultural system that fails to teach effective parenting skills on the other.

Level of Risk

There are several questions that determine the psychological risk for alcoholism. Number values have been assigned to them. A score of 5 to 7 indicates high risk. Medium risk is indicated by a score of 3 or 4, and low risk by 1 or 2. The questions are:

- Do you have a parent who was an alcoholic or chemically dependent ? (*Yes* +1; *No* +0.)
- Were one or both of your parents a lifetime abstaining teetotaller? (*Yes* +1; *No* +0.)

- Were one or both of your parents an "on the wagon" teetotaller? (*Yes* +1; *No* +0.)
- Do you, or did you, have a close family relative that practiced "serious drinking"? (*Yes* +1; *No* +0.)
- Do you, or did you, have a close family relative that practiced "white man's drinking"? (*Yes* +1; *No* +0.)
- Do you have something to do in life that makes you feel worthwhile (e.g., job, sport, art, etc)? (*Yes* +0; *No* +1.)
- Do you have someone who loves you and someone you love? (*Yes* +0; *No* +1.)

The first question was used in the section on sociological reasons for alcoholism and is used here because of the psychological ramifications. Question 2 addresses the traditional life style of the Native American parent who adheres to the traditional belief that "we (Native Americans) shouldn't drink (alcohol)." This is an oral tradition based on the observations and teachings of the elders. Questions 3, 4, and 5 address the other parental and role model types in the family. The final two questions are obtained from the writings of William Glasser (founder of the Reality Therapy Institute) who believes that well-functioning individuals have met the essential human needs for love and power by attaining a healthy love relationship and doing something they feel is intrinsically rewarding and worthwhile to them. In summary, the lower the level of self-esteem, the higher the level of psychological risk for alcoholism.

IMPLICATIONS FOR TREATMENT AND PREVENTION

The importance of the three risk areas has been established in order to determine their implications for the treatment and prevention of alcoholism. The development of a framework that identifies factors that cause alcoholism in the physiological, sociological, and psychological areas is important in understanding how alcohol abuse and alcoholism are maintained and perpetuated in the Native American family system. Identification of the specific drinking behavior patterns requires an understanding of cultural behavior patterns, past and present, of the individual, the family, and the community in which they live. Identification of the drinking behavior patterns in the family helps the treatment provider gain a better understanding of how to provide effective treatment for alcoholism in the Native American family.

This information can provide a framework for understanding the development of alcoholism in the Native American family and for developing effective treatment strategies. It can also be useful in the development of prevention strategies for the problems of alcohol abuse and alcoholism for the individual, family, and native community.

SUMMARY

In order to develop effective prevention and treatment strategies to combat the devastating effects and consequences of alcoholism in Native American communities today, a conceptual framework that uses a holistic perspective is necessary. This framework must address the physical, social, and psychological influences involved. It appears that a biopsychosocial approach that considers the major factors of alcoholism can provide valuable insight into the development of alcoholism in the Native American culture.

Recent advances in the field of alcoholism have led to a family systems approach. This has revealed the importance of cultural norms regarding the use of alcohol, family role models, and the drinking patterns that have influenced the high incidence of alcoholism in Native American families.

The use of a biopsychosocial framework from a family systems perspective can identify significant influences in the development, progression, and maintenance of alcoholism in the Native American culture. This information is essential in the development, or modification, of techniques and strategies that are more effective for the treatment and prevention of alcoholism in the Native American population.

REFERENCES

Attneave, C. (1982). Native American families. In M. McGoldrick, J.K. Pearce, & J. Giordano, (Eds.), *Ethnicity and family therapy* (pp. 218–235). New York: Guilford.

Cohen, S. (1982). Alcohol and the Indian. *Drug Abuse and Alcoholism Newsletter,11*(4).

Dobbyns, H.F. (1966). Estimated aboriginal American populations: An appraisal of technology with a new hemispheric estimate. *Current Anthropology,7*, 395–416.

Farris, J., & Jones, B.M. (1978). Ethanol metabolism in male American Indians and whites. *Alcoholism: Clinical Experience, 2*, 77–81.

Glasser, W. (1976). New York: Harper/Colophon Books.

Goodwin, D.W. (1979). Alcoholism and heredity: A review and hypothesis. *Archives of General Psychiatry, 36*, 57–61.

Goodwin, D.W. (1983). *Alcoholism: The facts.* New York: Oxford University Press.

Hearing before Select Committee on Children, Youth and Families. *Native American Children, Youth and Families.* House of Representatives, 99th Congress, Seattle, Washington, January 7, 1986.

Hoffman, H., & Noem, S. (1975). Alcohol and abstinence among relatives of American Indian alcoholics. *Journal of Studies on Alcoholism, 36*, 165–171.

Jacobs, W. (1974). Tip of the iceberg: Pre-Columbian Indian demography and some implications for revisionism. *William and Mary Quarterly, 31*, 123–132.

Jones-Saumty, D., Hochhaus, L., Drug, R., & Zeiner, A. (1983). Psychological factors in familial alcoholism in American Indians and Caucasians. *Journal of Clinical Psychology, 39*, 783–790.

Kivlahan, D., Walker, D., Donovan, D., & Miscke, H. (1985). Detoxification recidivism among urban American Indian alcoholics. *American Journal of Psychiatry, 142*, 1467–1470.

Lawson, G., Peterson, J., & Lawson, A. *Alcoholism and the family: A guide to treatment and prevention.* Rockville, MD: Aspen.

Lemert, E. (1982). Drinking among American Indians. In E. Gomberg, H. White, & J. Carpenter (Eds.), *Alcohol, science and society revisited* (pp. 80–95). Ann Arbor: University of Michigan Press.

Levy, J.E., & Kunitz, S.J. (Eds.). (1974). *Indian drinking: Navajo practices and Anglo-American theories.* New York: Wiley.

Lewis, R. (1982). Alcoholism and the Native Americans: A review. In *National Institute on Alcohol Abuse & Alcoholism: Special population issues.* (Alcohol & Health Monograph No. 4, DHHS Pub. No. ADM 82-1193). Washington, DC: Government Printing Office.

Lewis, R., & Ho, M.K. (1975). Social work with Native Americans. *Social Work, 379–382.*

Mail, P. (1985). Alcohol and Native Americans. In *Alcohol topics: Research review* (pp. 1–8). Rockville, MD: National Institute on Alcohol Abuse and Alcoholism.

Mason, J. (1985). The body: Alcoholism defined. *Update,* January, pp. 4–5.

McGoldrick, M., Pearce, J.K., & Giordano, J. (Eds.). (1982). *Ethnicity and family therapy.* New York: Guilford.

Mooney, J. (1928). The aboriginal population of America north of Mexico. *Smithsonian Miscellaneous Collections, 80*(7), 1–40.

Redhorse, J.G. (1979, August). *American Indian elders: Perspective on cultural behavior and needs.* Paper presented at the Society for the Study of Social Problems, Annual Meeting, Boston.

Reed, T.E. (1985). Ethnic differences in alcohol use. *Social Biology, 32*(3–4), 195–209.

Ricciardo, B.R., Saunders, J.B., Williams, R., & Hopkins, D.A. (1983). Hepatic ADH and ALDH isoenzymes in different racial groups and in chronic alcoholics. *Pharmacology, Biochemistry and Behavior, 18*(Suppl.), 61–65.

Schuckit, M.A. (1972). Family history and half-sibling research in alcoholism. *Annals of New York Academy of Science, 190*, 121–125.

Stratton, R., Zeiner, A., & Pardes, A. (1978). Tribal affiliation and prevalence of alcohol problems. *Journal of Studies on Alcoholism, 39*, 1166–1177.

Vizenor, G. (1984). American Indians and drunkenness. *Journal of Ethnic Studies, 11*, 4–7.

Waddell, J.O. (1981). Cultural relativity and alcohol use. *Journal of Studies on Alcohol,* (Suppl. 9), 18–27.

Weisner, T.S., Weibel-Orlando, J.C., & Long, J. (1984). 'Serious drinking,' 'white man's drinking' and 'teetotaling': Drinking levels and styles in an urban Indian population. *Journal of Studies on Alcohol, 45*, 237–249.

Wolin, S., Bennett, L., Noonan, D., & Teitelbaum, M. (1977). *Families at risk: The intergenerational recurrence of alcoholism.* Unpublished manuscript.

Chapter 13

Alcoholism and Abuse: The Twin Family Secrets

Christine M. O'Sullivan

INTRODUCTION

The role of alcohol in violence, especially family violence, has been well known but little researched for many years—even centuries. The overwhelming majority of domestic disturbance calls, which are the single most dangerous kind of call to which a policeman can respond, involve alcohol in either the perpetrator or, less often, the victim. There are many reasons why alcohol is connected with domestic violence. Some of the reasons are chemical, such as the changes in the brain and its neurotransmitters, but some of the reasons are psychosocial. The cost of this violence in material damage is great, but the cost to the people affected by alcoholic violence is untold and uncounted.

There is a large population of people in this country who are the victims of the abuse that accompanies alcoholism. The abuse that this group has suffered, and is still suffering, is physical, emotional, and sexual. Included in the category of abuse is neglect, which is a form of abuse by omission instead of commission. Many of the victims of abuse have carried the scars of their abusive experiences secretly and shamefully for many, many years. This chapter discusses the cultural and historical background of the twin problems of abuse of people and abuse of alcohol, the relation of family violence to alcohol, the effects of alcohol abuse on the nonalcoholic members of the family, and the issues relative to the prevention, intervention, and treatment of the alcohol abuse.

CULTURAL ASPECTS OF ALCOHOL ABUSE AND FAMILY VIOLENCE

Culture can be a powerful influence on the definition of any kind of abuse. Since the family is set in a culture and is, in part, a product of the social current of the time, both have an impact on the functioning of the family. The cultural influences on the family, as well as the attitudes in the culture toward alcoholism and other forms of abuse, have a definite impact on the degree and scope of both problems. Since the family is the transmitter of cultural values for its members, parental attitudes toward alcohol and other abuse affect the culture as a whole. These attitudes, parental and cultural, deeply affect the way individuals perceive drinking, drunkenness, and the acts of an inebriated individual. The same cultural dynamics in action with alcohol are present in the abuse of one family member by another.

Cultural attitudes toward the family unit have for centuries helped perpetuate the family secrets of the abuse of chemicals and the abuse of people. In the United States, prior to the 20th century, the cultural view of the family was as a paternalistic unit with the husband/father having all privileges, responsibilities, and rights over his wife and children. In other words, wife and children lived under complete control of the husband. Legal rights for family members other than the men were nonexistent. The women and children were considered the chattel, or property, of the man. It was the man's right and, in some cultures, duty to discipline both his wife and children as he saw fit, with no interference from any person or institution. In some parts of the world, the man still has the power of life and death over his spouse and children.

Such attitudes have prevailed to a greater or lesser degree, with a few exceptions, throughout the major part of recorded history. The authoritarian attitudes toward family life began to change in the early part of the 20th century when women were granted the right to vote in the United States. However, women's (and children's) status as chattel had not appreciably changed because there was still economic and legal dependency on the husband/father. The right of women to vote became the first crack to appear in the wall of the paternalistic, authoritarian fortress called "the family."

Even though women were given the right to vote, both alcoholism and abuse remained family secrets. Nothing was done to protect the family members from an acting out, abusive, drunk or drug addict or from any other kind of violence that can be inflicted by one person in a family on another. In addition to, and consistent with, prevailing cultural attitudes toward women and children in the family setting, there was widespread exploitation of women and children in the work world. Both women and children (some as young as 7-years-old) worked long hours—up to 14 a day—under abominable conditions. Only gradually, and with the help of the trade union movement, were labor laws enacted that prevented the wholesale exploitation of women and children in the work force.

About 50 years after the enactment of the Fourteenth Amendment to the Constitution of the United States, which gave women the right to vote, another group that had been an impotent minority in American life began to agitate for power. This group was the American Black. From this movement, other relatively powerless segments of American society began to agitate for and to gain rights, privileges, and protections for themselves. The women's movement was the outcome of other movements (civil rights for minorities) to empower socially those with few or no rights prior to that time. Flanzer (1984) asserted that the rise of the women's movement of the 1970s is considered a major force behind the intolerance of further violence in the family. It could also be said that the phenomenon of the women's movement can be applied to the problem of alcoholism.

Lawson, Peterson, and Lawson (1983) presented three ways in which culture affects alcoholism: the degree to which a culture induces inner tension in its members, the attitudes a culture holds toward drinking, and the availability of substitutes for alcohol use. In other words, the acceptability of drunkenness and the diminished responsibility for the consequences of that drunkenness are defined by the larger society. Swanson (1984) suggested that a wife abuser may become intoxicated in order to carry out a violent act and then use his intoxication as an excuse for his behavior. Kantor and Strauss (1986) studied 3,250 families concerning the physical abuse of wives. They found that a combination of blue collar status, drinking, and approval of violence was associated with the highest rate of wife abuse. The cultural approval of violence by men had the strongest association with wife abuse.

An example of attitudes influencing perspectives on responsibility is found in research done by Carducci and McNeely (1981). In this study, both male and female alcoholics and nonalcoholics read an account of wife abuse and assigned percentages of blame to the man, the woman, and the situation. Nonalcoholics assigned less blame to an intoxicated husband than to a sober one and more blame to an intoxicated wife than to a sober one. However, alcoholics attributed more blame to the husband and decreased the blame attributed to the wife only when the wife was sober. For nonalcoholics, when the wife was drunk, the husband had a socially acceptable excuse for his abusive behavior. For alcoholics, alcohol consumption increased the amount of personal responsibility attributed to the intoxicated individual, especially when the other spouse was sober.

Although social movements have done much to bring the problems of abuse and alcoholism into public awareness, old attitudes still pervade large segments of society. According to a study done in 1970 by Stark and McEvoy, of a sample of 1,186 Americans surveyed, 1 in 5 approved of slapping a spouse, especially if he or she deserved it. This particular study mentioned another cultural myth that has been held for centuries—that family violence is a phenomenon of the lower class. The results found by Stark and McEvoy were not confined to the lower socioeconomic classes but were obtained from middle-class respondents also.

THE ALCOHOL-ABUSE CONNECTION

Historically, wife battering and child abuse were seen as lower-class phenomena as a result of drunkenness. In the late 1800s, the general consensus among police and judicial authorities was that the serious level of violent crime was due mainly to drink. In a National Society for the Prevention of Cruelty to Children report in 1897, more than half of the cases of child abuse were attributed to drunkenness (cited in May, 1978). During those times, the most common explanation for domestic violence was the heavy drinking of the working class. Observers of those times reemphasized the violence of drunken husbands, and a prison chaplain ascribed half of the cases of both wife and child battering to drunkenness. In Victorian and Edwardian times, the link between violence and alcohol was very much the focus of temperance workers. "Ex-wife beaters were prominent among the reformed drunkards regularly paraded at temperance rallies, and temperance workers did much to expose the problem" (May, 1978, p. 136).

Both alcoholism and family violence began to be studied quite seriously during the 1970s. Once alcoholism was destigmatized in 1957 by being declared a disease by the American Medical Association, treatment for a sick individual, rather than moral censure, became available for the alcoholic. Gradually, the public was educated to the idea of alcoholism as a disease rather than as a condition of moral turpitude, although there are some people who still adhere to the idea of the alcoholic as morally destitute. During the intervening years, the rate of research on alcoholism increased dramatically each year.

Family violence was an equally taboo subject prior to the 1970s: the family was considered a unit of nurturing and protection. The family was sacrosanct—not a place for the law or others outside the family to intrude. Therefore, the secrets of alcoholism, drug abuse, and abuse of family members remained "family business," not to be discussed outside the nuclear family. These secrets were closely held by the victims who considered it a shameful thing if anyone found out they were abused.

Within the past 10 years, research has begun to focus on the link between alcohol abuse and family violence. In a study of cases where there was the court-ordered removal of a child, 38% of the parents in the study were

diagnosed as alcoholics as opposed to 8% of the control group from the general population (Famularo, Stone, Barnum, & Wharton, 1986). Alcohol is said to be involved in more than two thirds of the nation's homicides, half of the nation's rapes and incidents of molestation, and up to 70% of the nation's assaults (Califano, 1986).

Within the family, an association has been noted between alcohol use and marital violence in just about all studies on the battered wife syndrome. Alcohol use preceded the violence in 93% of the cases in one study and in 60% in another (Swanson, 1984). Sedge (1979) and Block and Sinnot (1979) stated that alcohol is a contributing factor in violence in American society because it diminishes inhibitions against violence. Alcohol impairs one's ability to perceive anger or annoyance accurately in others. According to Borrill (1986), if people who have consumed alcohol have problems perceiving anger in others, they may behave in ways that are annoying or provoking to others. If alcohol depresses their mood and leads to an overreadiness to perceive disgust or contempt in others, they may themselves behave aggressively.

Krupp and Lehmann (1984), when studying 1,500 cases of domestic violence, found that 828 women, or 55%, reported that their husbands had a drinking problem and became abusive when they drank. Viken (1982), in a review of studies, found an association between alcohol abuse by the husband and wife beating. The correlations in these studies ranged from 22% to 93%. In an Austrailian study done in Adelaide, 60% of the respondents stated that heavy drinking preceded an attack (Parkin, 1982). A figure of 80% of all family violence where drinking is involved before, during, or after the critical event was found by Pelton (1982). Campbell (1986) found that while the majority of known alcoholics did not beat their wives, the percentage of batterers abusing alcohol ranged from 25% to 85%.

Population Characteristics

The demographics of the victims of abuse include all races, all ages, all religious groups, and all ethnic groups. Stacey and Shupe (1983) found that the ethnic proportions of battered women seeking shelter in the Dallas–Forth Worth area reflected the ethnic proportions of the general population. In the same study, it was found that these women were mostly high school graduates who did not receive Aid to Families of Dependent Children, or welfare. They were of the lower-middle and middle classes. It was noted that in research done by clinical psychologists in private practice, there were battered women from the upper-middle and upper classes.

The population of victims includes those children who are born with fetal alcohol syndrome (FAS) and those who are born addicted to drugs. Deutsch (1982, p. 3) stated that there are "at least fifteen million school age [sic] children living with parental alcoholism." Black's (1981, p. 141) research showed that 26% of children living in alcoholic homes had been incest victims: "This means that there are about four million children who have been subjected to an environment of alcohol *and* sexual abuse." Added to the children are those people who have grown up keeping the family secret of drug and alcohol abuse who are carrying around the result of all the various forms of abuse and neglect present in an alcoholic household. Certainly, the women who have married alcoholics and have been abused to the point where they demonstrate the battered wife syndrome are included in this population. Along with the physical battering, one can include those wives who are verbally abused and who live in fear of the batterer.

If 15 million school-age children are living with parental alcoholism, then there are at least 70 million adults, about one quarter of the U.S. population, who have been affected to some degree by an alcoholic environment in their formative years. The true measure of the particular population will not be known for many years to come because the twin family secrets of chemical dependence and abuse still exert a powerful influence on their victims. It is only within the past 15 years that alcoholism and family violence have been addressed as problems of great social magnitude.

Forms of Abuse

In any form, the term *abuse* is relative. What is abuse of alcohol to one person may be considered social drinking by another. A teetotaler might consider someone's having an occasional drink or two as alcohol abuse. However, when alcohol consumption causes one to lose control of his or her behavior constantly, it is safe to say that that person is probably a problem drinker. An active alcoholic would consider the fifth of whiskey or case of beer a day mere social drinking.

FAMILY DYNAMICS

Abuse of people is as relative a term as is abuse of chemicals. Some families believe in the injunction of "spare the rod, and spoil the child." These families believe in all manner of corporal punishment as means of child development and discipline. To them, a severe whipping in the woodshed is merely doing their duty as parents. To others who do not believe in corporal punishment, those families who use physical forms of punishment are considered abusive. For the purpose of this chapter, abusive behavior is that which would be considered excessive to any reasonable adult in the situation in which it occurs.

Other forms of abuse are relative also. Disciplinary actions in families vary widely. Some families never strike a child and can still be considered abusive because of the psychological methods they use to control a child's behavior. In many instances, parents administer various forms of punishment to children, fully believing that they are doing so for the child's "own good." Schatzman (1973) told of child-rearing practices promoted by a respected demagogue, Professor Shreber, in Europe during the end of the 19th century. Various and sundry medieval devices were invented by this teacher in order to train children in a proper manner. Some of these were restraints that held a child straight in bed, a rigid stick that was attached to a child's hair and to his or her waistband so that the child had to hold the head straight or have his or her hair pulled; and a prop that insured always correct posture at a desk. The general attitude toward the child was that the child had to be civilized by the parent and that the parent had to be strict and authoritarian at all times. The effects of this upbringing on this respected teacher's sons were that one committed suicide and the other was diagnosed to be a paranoid schizophrenic. While this kind of child rearing was considered normal, and even good, at the time, today one would consider these methods to be the height of cruelty to children. However, there is no lack for authoritarian parents in current 20th century society.

When one form of abuse in a family is uncovered, it is usually accompanied by manifestations of other kinds of abuse. When a child has been beaten severely, one can usually find emotional or psychological abuse and/or neglect as a part of the constellation of problems. In today's terms, abuse of one human being by another is something that needs to be assessed on a case-by-case basis. Abuse runs on a continuum, from mild where someone is slapped—maybe harder than the situation called for—to loss of life or loss of sanity.

There are no clear-cut divisions among the forms of abuse. Some instances of psychological abuse could be considered neglect. When a woman has been battered, there is usually coexisting verbal and psychological abuse. Certainly, sexual abuse can be considered in the categories of both physical and emotional abuse. The following categories are not intended to be all-inclusive for there have been volumes of research and hundreds of books written about each. They are intended to provide an overview only.

Neglect

Neglect is a form of abuse: abuse through omission of the actions that are necessary for the physical, mental, and sexual well-being of the victim. Some of the forms of neglect are physical: not attending to the physical needs of the victim, whether these needs are for food, clothing, clean shelter, or medical care. However, psychological neglect is far more common than physical neglect among the children of alcoholics and drug addicts. The nurturing and affirmation necessary for the healthy development of an individual are usually lacking as the addictive process continues its downward spiral. There is even sexual neglect, as there is little or no healthy role modeling or affirmation of the sexuality of the developing individuals. Information about sexuality and sex is generally lacking, usually as a result of parental confusion about sexuality.

Neglect causes problems, especially in the emotional sphere, that can be more devastating than the more overt kinds of abuse. In neglect, the individual is discounted and ignored. His or her presence or value as a human being is negated, whereas in the more acting-out kinds of abuse, the individual is acknowledged, even if it is in a negative, hostile manner. Much misbehavior on the part of a victim of abuse is to cause negative attention because the emptiness of no recognition at all is too frightening to the individual.

Prenatal Abuse

Abuse of an individual can begin even before birth. A mother's excessive ingestion of alcohol or drugs may result in her child being born with drug addiction or FAS. Babies born addicted to drugs or with FAS must then experience withdrawal and may further suffer mental and physical handicaps throughout life (National Council on Alcoholism, 1987). FAS presently occurs in 2 of 1,000 live births (Lipson, 1984). There are, therefore, thousands of children born each year with FAS.

Within the past few years, FAS has begun to be classified as prenatal child abuse. Condon (1986) presented the case history of a woman who had been a light drinker but became a heavy drinker toward the end of the second trimester. There was a strong impression that one function the abuse of alcohol served was to assault the fetus.

FAS has begun to appear in the courts as child abuse. In Canada, a woman who is the mother of an FAS child has already been brought up on charges of prenatal child abuse (Abel, 1984). The basic issue was in the general area of diminished life. In 1987, the County of San Diego brought a young woman to court who was charged with manslaughter. She had continued to take street drugs against her doctor's orders and gave birth to a brain-dead child. Alcohol and drug abuse in pregnant women is now being recognized as a predominant cause of preventable birth defects and is now finally being recognized for the child abuse that it is.

Sometimes, battering of the mother begins during pregnancy. Morgan (1982) stated that sexual frustration and stress, which may be compounded by the wife's pregnancy, may be determinants in wife battering. The battering endured by a pregnant woman can cause abuse of a child in utero. There are instances in which the beating is so severe that it causes a spontaneous abortion. Sometimes, the damage from a battering is enough to cause birth problems for the mother and, consequently, various problems for the child.

Physical Abuse

Physical abuse consists of hitting, biting, scratching, kicking, punching, or burning of another using either objects, such as paddles, belts, electrical cords, and other items that may be available in the area, or the hands, fists, or feet of the perpetrator. Included in physical abuse are also such actions as tying the victim into a chair, chaining the victim to other objects, and locking the victim in a closet or basement for a prolonged time. The author has had occasion to sit in Violence Court in Chicago and listen to police officers and medical personnel describe an incident of a 4-year-old child being held in scalding water, which gave the child second degree burns over 40% of the child's body. This was supposedly done to teach the child a lesson about hot water. Acts of this nature occur daily throughout the United States. The emergency rooms of hospitals have seen countless cases of children who "fell downstairs" but whose injuries, when examined, are not consistent with such an accident.

Morris (1985) stated that 46 million children aged 3 to 17 were living with their parents in 1975. Of those, 3 to 4 million had been kicked, battered, or punched by a parent at some time in their life. Between 1 and 2 million children had been beaten up while growing up, and as many as 2 million had been attacked by a parent wielding a gun or a knife.

Physical abuse is not just perpetrated on the children of the family; the spouse is the recipient of much of the battering that occurs in the family. There are men who feel that "a good beating" will keep their wife "in line." Physical abuse of family members can include very young infants. The author recalls a nurse discussing a 2-month-old infant being thrown against a wall and an 18-month-old boy being stomped to death by his mother's drunken lover. There is a constant stream of these kinds of injuries being seen by physicians and emergency rooms. Although sexual abuse and FAS are also physical abuse, because of other issues involved, they are treated as a distinctly separate kind of abuse.

Emotional Abuse

While physical abuse can cause damage that can last, and can even cause the death of the victim, emotional abuse, while leaving no visible scars or marks on the victim, can cause long-lasting damage to its victim's self-esteem, self-worth, and enjoyment of life. Emotional abuse can consist of either overt verbal attacks or ignoring the individual as if he or she were a nonentity. The alcoholic defenses of projection and denial, which are also operative in a violent family, can cause the recipients of those defenses to lose the ability to trust their own perceptions of the events occurring before their eyes. Verbal attacks tear down the victim's self-esteem by convincing the victim that he or she is worthless, that no one will ever want him or her, that it is his or her fault that the perpetrator of the violence is angry, and that if he or she were not the way he or she is, there would not be any violence.

A more insidious form of emotional abuse is that of the "silent treatment" where the victims are ignored and none of their emotional needs is addressed by the abuser. The victims then become nonentities, feeling as though they are unloved and unwanted. The perfectionistic projections of the abuser set up overdriven strivings in the object of the abuser's wrath. This sets up a perfectionistic life stance in the victims that permeates their every undertaking, robbing living of its joy and spontaneity. Double-bind communications set up a horrendous situation for the victims of these types of communication. The sufferers lose all confidence in their ability to make decisions, as whatever they do will be wrong. It is the lack of nurturing, affirmation, and self-identity, none of which is visible, that causes the internal scaring that will be carried with the victim throughout life until and unless treatment is obtained.

Sexual Abuse

Probably the first documented case of abuse due to drunkenness occurred in Genesis 19:31-38 when Lot's daughters seduced their father while he was drunk. Incest is one of society's strongest taboos in almost all cultures. However, in a home where alcohol abuse and violence are prevalent, the chances for incest to occur increase horrendously. As in emotional abuse, incest comes in two varieties. Overt incest includes rape, sodomy, fellatio, grabbing of the breasts or genitals, and any other physical sexual contact. These acts occur with or without nudity, which very often is a part of overt incest. Covert incest involves a patriarchal father acting seductively toward his daughter. Such fathers appear to be doting on their victims and can manifest very jealous behavior. The perpetrator will flirt with the victim and become quite jealous of the victim's contacts with other people of the opposite sex. In incestuous situations, only 10% of the victims are young boys (Carnes, 1983). The other 90% are female children.

The age of incest victims can range from children of less than 1-year-old to teenagers who are in high school. The author was told of a child of 13 months brought into the emergency room of a hospital with a ruptured larynx (voicebox) because the mother's drunken boyfriend had attempted fellatio with the child.

Incest is a particularly tragic crime not solely from the sexual perspective but from the fact that the very people on whom the child depends for protection and nurturing have betrayed the trust of the child. Many of these children grow up unable to have intimate relationships because their relationships have been sexualized to such a degree that they see other people as wanting them only for sexual purposes.

Both alcoholism and abuse in a family signal severe dysfunction in the unit. Whereas a healthy family is flexible and balanced, an alcoholic family, or one where abuse occurs, swings widely from overinvolvement with each other to distance, from rigidity to chaos, and maintains rigid boundaries to the public, while there are few or no psychological boundaries between the family members. The more severe the dysfunction of the family, the more isolated the family is from the community and support systems. There is also isolation of each family member from each other, with little or no communication occurring except at a superficial functional level.

Every family has themes. In a healthy family, these might be community service or excellence in athletics or education. An alcoholic and/or abusive family has themes also. The themes for these dysfunctional families are the same for alcoholic and abusive families: don't think, don't feel, and don't trust. Above all, don't talk about it (Black, 1981). The members of an alcoholic or violent family are discouraged from thinking about what they see in front of their eyes and what they hear being said because to think about them would be too painful. They are told how they "should" feel and indeed are discouraged from feeling since that is also too painful. All members of the family have difficulty trusting other people. The alcoholic family is so chaotic and unpredictable that there is no chance to believe that what is true for behavior today will necessarily be true tomorrow.

Vega and Vega (1986) stated that chemical dependence, family violence, and sexual abuse are seen as connected, yet separate, issues. Couples and families involved in these problems exhibit similarities and patterns: conditional acceptance; closed communications; blurring of roles; confusion over issues such as sexuality, sensuality, nurturing, affection, and intimacy; rigidity and enmeshment; and crisis—called the addiction connection.

The homeostasis, or balance, of an addictive family is very fixed and does not allow for growth or change, as the healthy family's balance does. The result of this lack of growth is the enmeshment evident among the family members. Some researchers have asserted that the use of violence and alcohol abuse serve to return the family to a previous homeostatic state. Flanzer (1984) suggested that the payoff for family violence and alcoholism may be their ability to help reassert control, to provide mastery over the moment, and to help reduce feelings of hopelessness, depression, and despair. One of the defense mechanisms that addictive families use in service to their homeostasis is denial. The members of a dysfunctional family try to present a front to the public or community at large of a "good" family. The children are cautioned not to discuss anything that happens in the family with anyone outside the family, and then they are told that everything in the family is normal—regardless of mother's black eye or dad's being drunk at the father-and-son school banquet. The members of these families tell themselves and others so often that everything is fine and that there are no problems that eventually everyone in the family believes these stories.

Because of the chaos in these families, the children assume adult re-sponsibilities at an earlier than appropriate age (Black, 1986; Deutsch, 1982; Woititz, 1983). The assuming of adult responsibilities then robs those children of age-appropriate development in addition to any other abuse that may have been inflicted upon them. Children become responsible for parental tasks, such as cooking and cleaning, at a much earlier age than what should be expected. The result is children who take themselves too seriously and have difficulty enjoying life.

The lack of boundaries among the members of addictive families extends to the boundaries between generations. The parents in these families are overly involved in their own parents' lives, as well as with their children's lives. Studies done recently (Carter, 1982; Julius & Papp, 1979; Middleton, 1984) have shown that addictive families beget more addictive families in the next generation. While there may be a genetic component to the trans-mission of both alcoholism and violence, the modeling done by the parents in a family along with the experience of growing up in the chaos of such a family transmits the alcoholism and/or violence down through another generation by teaching the children that these are normal family events. Middleton (1984) maintained that in a high percentage of families where father-daughter incest occurred, the mother was also a victim of sexual abuse in her family of origin. Carnes (1983) asserted that sexual addictions are also intergenerational, that children who are molested by their parents at an early age are at greater risk for molesting their own children. Sexual abuse of children generally occurs in those families that are experiencing marital problems and that are dominated by anxiety. In abusing/alcoholic families, privacy is not respected. There are fewer sexual restrictions, or excessive sexual restrictions, and little transmission of sexual information (Goodrick, 1983). Further, these families may be socially isolated and characterized by chronic brutality and alcohol abuse.

Strauss stated "The family is the most violent institution, group, or setting that a typical citizen is likely to encounter. There are exceptions such as the police or the army in time of war" (cited in Morris, 1985, p. 15). When a violent family is mixed with alcohol, the consequences are terrible and far-reaching. Clearly, the heart of the addiction problem is within the family system.

CONSEQUENCES OF ALCOHOLISM AND ABUSE

The consequences of living in or being brought up in an alcoholic or violent family vary according to the severity of the problem. Even in violent alcoholic families, not all the members are abused, or they are abused to differing degrees by the abuser. However, the results of being in an alcoholic family can be devastating to the point of loss of life: that of the victim and, sometimes, that of the abuser. At the least, children are affected in their relationships and school performance and must struggle with issues of self-esteem, fear, anger, and grief (Priest, 1985). Further, most children will suffer disabling emotional effects that they will carry to adulthood and that will adversely affect at least one more generation.

One of the more serious consequences of abuse is detailed in a book of case studies of children who killed either one or both of their parents. Morris (1985), in studying parricides, included 17 case histories of these children. Of the 17, 3 were mentally ill. In all 14 of the remaining cases, there was alcohol or drug abuse on the part of the parents.

Workers in the area of child abuse can describe the numerous outcomes of physical abuse: broken bones, brain damage, and burn scars from cigarettes and other hot objects. Cohn (1982) stated that 2,000 children die of abuse every year. She also maintained that if one finds fault with a child long enough, he or she will begin to find fault with himself or herself. She stated unequivocally that child abusers are the last generation's victims. Some of this abuse leaves noticeable scars physically and can damage a child developmentally. FAS, mental retardation, and other anomalies can sentence the child to a less than optimal life. Most of the damage done by abuse is that which cannot be seen. It is the scarring of the psyche and the lack of confidence and self-esteem that affect the child's functioning into adulthood.

The results of living in an alcoholic and/or abusive family can also be seen in other addictions and all manner of acting-out behavior. Numerous studies have found that abusive people have been abused as children, that batterers saw battering between their own parents, and that molesters were molested as children. Bottom and Lancaster (1981) asserted that childhood exposure to alcohol and drug abuse as well as addiction to gambling and crime among one or several family members often appears in the background of an abusive adult. It was also noted that a particularly high correlation has been found between wife battering and alcohol consumption by or prior imprisonment of an abusive husband. In a treatment program for the families of male sexual addicts, 70% of the families also had a chemically dependent member (Carnes, 1983). In other words, children who were abused, or saw abuse, when they were growing up are more likely to become abusers, as are the children brought up by alcoholic parents more likely to become alcoholic than are children who have neither abuse nor alcoholism in their background. Neidig, Friedman, and Collins (1985) maintained that the best predictor of violence is the individual's history of violent behavior and/or significant drug and alcohol involvement.

In cases of incest and molestation occurring in the family, the consequences lead to a life of fear and loneliness for the victim. As with all forms of abuse, self-esteem is affected, but with sexual abuse, the relationships the victim has with others are sexualized. This sexualization leads to wariness and suspiciousness of even social interchanges as the victim is waiting for the sexual aspect of the relationship to take place. This sexualization extends to the victim's children and, without treatment, will perpetuate another cycle of sexual abuse and incest. One incest victim told the author that she had a difficult time hugging her children for many years, as sexual feelings occurred. As a result of those feelings, she would tend not to touch her children. Fortunately, after some years of treatment she was finally able to hug her children without feelings other than maternal warmth.

Incest and molestation of children also result in post-traumatic stress disorder. This disorder consists of reliving the trauma by repetitive, intrusive remembering or dreaming of the events regularly and of emotional numbing and decreased environmental involvement in one's life. Additional symptoms include hyperalertness or an exaggerated startle response, disturbance of sleep, impaired memory, difficulty in concentrating, survival guilt, or avoidance of activities that could symbolize the trauma (Russell, 1985). Kovach (1983) found that of 117 recovering female alcoholics, 30% were survivors of sexual abuse. Of those, 40% had post-traumatic stress disorder, developed drinking problems earlier, and had a greater incidence of sexual dysfunction prior to abusive drinking. Both alcoholism and incest are often multigenerational. In many families where incest occurred, the mother was also a victim of sexual abuse in her family of origin (Middleton, 1984).

Alcoholism and drug abuse are often outcomes of being brought up in a family where alcohol abuse, battering, emotional abuse, and/or incest occurs. Child abuse, particularly sexual abuse, was prevalent in two groups of alcoholic women studied, those who continued drinking and those who achieved at least 1 year's sobriety. In these groups, parental conflict and alcoholism were common occurrences in their backgrounds (Lundy, 1986). In a study of alcoholic and nonalcoholic women, it was found that 74% of alcoholic women experienced sexual abuse, 52% physical abuse, and 72% emotional abuse. The nonalcoholic women reported rates of 34% for physical abuse, 44% for emotional abuse and 50% for sexual abuse. Comparing alcoholic with nonalcoholic women, there was a wider variety of sexual abuse perpetrated, with more incidents and longer periods for the alcoholic women (Covington, 1986). Schaefer, Evans, and Sterne (1985) found that sexual abuse occurred earlier for the chemically dependent as opposed to the general population of women. Over half the women in each sample reported having experienced sexual abuse in their childhood. The group of chemically dependent women was significantly more apt to go on to physically and/or sexually abuse a child than were the women in the control group.

Another term for the results of the neglect that is suffered by the children of dysfunctional parents, whether or not they are alcoholic, is *failure to thrive.* Oates (1982) stated that failure to thrive is caused by inadequate care and inadequate nutrition caused by adverse social circumstances and emotional deprivation. The children who manifest this syndrome are sad, apathetic, overly familiar with strangers, and indiscriminate in their seeking of attention and affection. While other problems can account for failure to thrive, alcohol and drug abuse are found in a large number of families where this phenomenon occurs.

Stacey and Shupe (1983) discussed the tendency to find abusers who were abused as children and alcoholics who had one or both parents who were alcoholic. This effect is called the "generational transfer hypothesis." The generational transfer works first by the parental modeling and by the children's imitating the parents' behavior. Second, the transfer of abusive behavior is accomplished by the children's experiences of being beaten. The victims then learn that being beaten by those who are supposed to love him or her is normal. Sandburg (1986) maintained that both physically and sexually abused children showed confusion over violence and nurturance. Those children consider violence the natural way to control family members. So the cycle continues on.

The emotional and psychological consequences of living in any kind of abusive family occur whether the abuse is physical, psychological, or sexual. Goodrick (1983) found that abused children showed signs of emotional damage, had a sense of isolation, experienced depression, and had physical complaints and low self-esteem. They were also involved in alcohol and drug abuse at an earlier age, especially the women who were victims of sexual abuse (Deutsch, 1983). These children lived in an atmosphere of fear and anger, never knowing when the violence would erupt. Many times they felt responsible for the drinking or abuse. Some children acted out their anger and became delinquent; others were "good" children.

Kaufman (1985a) found that the siblings in his study tended to fall equally into two basic categories: very good and very bad. The "bad" group consisted of drug and alcohol abusers and the children with delinquent behavior. The "good" group included children with parental family roles and who were quite successful, vocationally. A small number of the "good" siblings were quite passive, and some of those exhibited anger in disorders such as depression, tics, and headaches.

Children who are neglected because of the dynamics of the family grow up not knowing how to take proper physical care of themselves. Many children who are abused by neglect have poor dental hygiene and poor grooming. When they are ill, they may be discounted and told they are only bidding for attention. Their medical status may be suspect, as they generally are not examined regularly by doctors.

Women who are battered in a marriage may or may not show low self-esteem. They can, however, suffer any number of broken bones, burns, bruises, lacerations, and various forms of emotional abuse. Indeed, the abuse can lead to murder on the part of the battered wife. In general, the battered wife lives in fear and anger, as do the children.

The outcomes of both alcohol abuse and other forms of abuse are not confined just to the time of living in the dysfunctional family but continue on in the life of the victims. Woititz (1983) and Adult Children of Alcoholics, Chicagoland Area (1985) have developed a list of common themes in the lives of adult children of alcoholics. Some of these themes are: they guess at what normal behavior is, they judge themselves without mercy, they have difficulty having fun, they take themselves very seriously, they feel different from other people, and they are either super responsible or super irresponsible. Black (1984) presented the clinical profile of the children as isolated and unable to identify and express feelings and unable to trust, to be honest, or to form intimate relationships. The damage inflicted by either an alcoholic or violent family, or both, is deep and long lasting. Well, Rosen, Slater, McDonald, & Holden (1985) stated that children of alcoholics are at a greater risk of alcoholism because of child neglect.

INTERVENTION

Intervention produces the "significant emotional event" (Lawson et al., 1983) or "major outside experience" (Meagher, 1987) needed to stop the downward spiral of alcoholism. An intervention is the presentation to the alcoholic of the facts of what problems the abuse of alcohol has caused the people associated with the alcoholic. The alcoholic is then offered the opportunity of treatment, sometimes with the alternative of the loss of family or job as the only other option open to him or her. This technique is used with a high level of success in a number of situations. Meagher (1987) claimed that there is success (the alcoholic enters treatment) in 75% of interventions. A study of the mandated treatment of alcoholics who were abusers maintained that court intervention was justified because 47% of the offenders were at least partly rehabilitated (Sienkiewicz, 1983). In order to break the cycle of alcoholism and abuse, there must somehow be an intervention into the systems that produce the next generation's abusers and alcoholics.

An intervention or confrontation can be done at those points where the dysfunctional family must interact with the community in which it lives. There are many points of contact for the family with the community. It can be done at school, where the children, by law, must be; at an adult's place of employment; by medical and dental professionals; or by those people in the community who are in close physical proximity to the members of the family. In the case where law enforcement has entered the picture, there may well be court-ordered intervention.

Today, when a child is visibly physically abused, all states require that any health care or child care worker must report the child abuse to the appropriate child protective agency immediately for investigation. This action is, then, a forcible intervention under the guidance of the courts. There are various penalties associated with the failure to report, which include imprisonment and fines. The requirements for reporting vary from state to state, but all require a verbal report as soon as possible (Edwards & Gil, 1986).

In the case where the damage to the child is visible, reporting abuse is fairly clear-cut. However, most abuse is the kind that is manifested in the behavior of the child. Deutsch (1982) listed a number of indications that a child is living with alcoholism. Some of these included morning tardiness, consistent concern with getting home promptly at the end of a day, malodorousness, improper clothing for the weather, regressive behavior with peers, scrupulous avoidance of arguments and conflict, friendlessness and isolation, poor attendance, fatigue and listlessness, hyperactivity, inability to concentrate, sudden temper and other emotional outbursts, exaggerated concern with achievement and satisfying authority on the part of well-achieving children, and extreme fear about situations involving contact with parents. A sure sign of physical abuse is the "flinch" reaction by small children. In this reaction, the child automatically places his or her arms over the head as if to ward off a blow when there is nothing but a hand movement near the head. A child who has been sexually abused may either act very withdrawn and shy or be sexually precocious and engage in inappropriately seductive behavior. Since the dynamics of violence and alcoholism so closely parallel each other, these behaviors could be applied to children living in emotionally abusive or neglectful situations. When these behaviors are observed over a period of time, an interview with the child is necessary to determine the status of the home situation. If abuse is confirmed by the child, then reporting must proceed according to the law of the state in which the family resides.

For women who are the victims of an alcoholic or nonalcoholic abusive man, interruption of the cycle can begin with a call to the police. Depending on the area, the couple will either be separated or a complaint will need to be signed by the victim. In many areas, the batterer is given a suspended sentence and is thus free to resume the cycle of battering. In some areas, the court can and will mandate treatment for the batterer or the family. Berk and Newton (1985) showed that arrests substantially reduce the number of new incidents of wife battery. Whether the victim chooses to call the police or not, there are other options open. Depending on how long the cycle of battering has been allowed to continue, there may be friends or family to whom the victim can turn. For those who have lived in an abusive situation for an extended time and have become isolated from support groups, there are battered women shelters in most areas of the United States that will take in a woman and her children for varying periods of time. These shelters allow the women to determine some plan of action for themselves and to begin to create a new living situation. Some of these shelters provide counseling for the problem of the abuse as well as for financial and legal matters.

Intervention by business and industry takes place when an employee's productivity has dropped and instances of tardiness, absence, and nonreturn from lunch have been documented. The confrontation is done by the employee's manager along with the company's employee assistance counselor or a manager from personnel. The employee is told that his or her behavior has placed his or her job in jeopardy but that he or she will be given a choice of going into a treatment program. Many times, the intervention done by an employer is the beginning of the solution to many family problems as the employee is required to continue in treatment for a set period of time.

Breaking the alcohol cycle in a family is sometimes accomplished by a family member who instigates an intervention for the alcoholic. In this case, trained intervention teams assemble all the relatives and friends of the alcoholic and spend time (about 2 months of meeting weekly) preparing the concerned relatives for the confrontation. The participants of the intervention are required to write down the ways in which the alcoholic's drinking has caused them problems. Alternatives are developed for the alcoholic, much the same as an employer does. In cases where a spouse is the precipitator of the intervention, the alternative may be divorce. On the day of the confrontation, the alcoholic is taken to neutral ground and each person says his or her piece, sometimes more than once. Of the interventions about which the author knows, 75% of them have had lasting results in getting the alcoholic into treatment. There is a possibility, given the similar dynamics of a violent family, that similar interventions could get violent families into treatment.

The role of the family physician in intervention, to a large extent, has been overlooked. For many families, the family physician is the person who is contacted to heal the injuries when physical abuse occurs. The physician can then confront the alcoholic or abuser with the medical facts of the presenting problem and recommend treatment.

Interruption of the abuse cycle can be done anonymously in many places by neighbors or concerned friends. There are child abuse hot lines for reporting, and the identity of the reporting party is usually kept confidential, if he or she requests it. The cycle of abuse, whether or not it is connected with alcohol abuse, must be interrupted so that the family may obtain treatment and so that the next generation may have a different option for the future from the one learned in a dysfunctional family.

TREATMENT

There are many areas of concern in the treatment of the very diverse population of people affected by substance abuse and the other types of abuse. Treatment for the abuser is necessary if the abuse is to stop. Treating only the alcoholism will not stop the abuse. Treatment of the victims of all the various forms of abuse varies by the kind of abuse and the life situation of the victim. Treating children and spouses of an intact family is quite different from treating the adults who grew up with abuse. However, there are common issues that need to be addressed for all the people involved in abuse and alcoholism.

Issues in Treatment

Probably the two most salient issues in beginning to deal with the alcoholic and abusive family are denial and the inability to trust. Even when treatment has begun, denial persists. Many times, both the alcoholic and the abuser will insist that "it really wasn't *that* bad." Even the victim will persist in minimizing or rationalizing the damage done. The skepticism and mistrust that have become a natural state for the members of alcoholic and violent families have an impact on most therapies, stretching out the initial phase longer than that which occurs with other kinds of psychotherapy clients. In many cases there is a period of time when the people involved in alcoholism and abuse need to learn a vocabulary that can help them express their feelings and thoughts.

Treatment issues for the abuser consist of breaking down the denial. The abuser, who is often under sentence from the court and in mandated therapy, needs to admit and accept his or her responsibility for the abuse. The histories of most abusers show that they, too, were abused as children. Many of them have hideous emotional life histories. In abusers, we find issues of low self-esteem, lack of confidence in functioning as an adult, inappropriate relationships with younger people, a life stance with a paranoid quality (everybody's out to get me), lower-level functioning than their abilities would warrant, and a low frustration level. All of these issues need to be addressed in a treatment program, whether it is individual, group, marital, or family therapy.

For the children who are abused before they are born, appropriate measures must be taken to remedy the damage. These measures may consist of surgical intervention where necessary to correct the physical anomalies caused by the mother's excessive ingestion of drugs and alcohol; other treatment may consist of special training and education for children who are born with mental retardation.

Children living in an intact family where alcoholism and/or abuse has occurred need to learn that all families are *not* like the ones in which they are growing up. Since the symptoms of alcohol abuse and violence usually increase with time, there are various levels of mistrust and isolation from peer groups and other members of the family that are active within these children. The mistrust and isolation generally become more severe as children grow older. Loyalty to the family often contributes to the isolation of such children from the community at large. In some cases, older children turn to alcohol and drugs as a way of coping with and/or rebelling against the abuse occurring within the family. Growing up in a life style of alcoholism and abuse leads to another generation of abusers being formed unless there is intervention and treatment.

Parentification of the children (children taking the parental role with their parents or siblings) creates children who become overly serious and have difficulty acting in accordance with their age levels. Many times their spontaneity is lost within the seriousness of surviving and coping in an alcoholic/violent family. Many adolescents have great difficulty with self-confidence and self-esteem, but for those teenagers living in an alcoholic family, it is only with great difficulty that they can negotiate the transition of adolescence successfully.

Some children in the family appear to be self-sufficient and seem to be functioning to a high degree in spite of the alcoholism and violence. These children who are achieving well in school, athletics, and social events look as though they have transcended the alcoholism and abuse in their families. Often with these children there are adults, usually in the extended family, who have become a special source of affirmation and guidance for them. However, for others of these children, the high degree of functioning has a driven quality to it and serves as a way of physically and emotionally distancing themselves from the chaos of the family. Overachieving then becomes a form of denial.

The author is acquainted with a woman in her forties who has obtained a Ph.D. and three M.A. degrees, has raised four boys successfully, and has helped her husband establish himself in his profession. This woman was the product of an alcoholic family where all forms of abuse existed: physical, emotional, and sexual. About 6 months after the death of her father, who on his deathbed said he was sorry he had hurt his children so much, she began to manifest symptoms of night terrors, panic attacks, and thought intrusions. She was then diagnosed as having post-traumatic stress disorder as a result of facing her abusive childhood. Prior to that time, she had denied that any abuse had occurred.

Adults who were untreated children of alcoholics/abusers very often continue the cycle by marrying alcoholics and abusers or by becoming alcoholics and abusers. For those who have turned to substance abuse in order to cope with their fears and anxieties, there are more levels of denial than just those existing with the substance abuse. Recovering addicts and alcoholics may maintain that they came from an untroubled family. It can be years before they begin to acknowledge the dysfunction in their families of origin. Those adult children who have not become abusers or alcoholics also have issues of control and trust that need to be addressed. Nielsen (1984) stated that recovery issues for children of alcoholics, whether adult or still children, include the restructuring of personal boundaries and the working through of guilt and shame feelings.

Spouses who have been battered will need medical attention, if the injuries are serious enough, and, if warranted, physical rehabilitation. For the spouses in lower socioeconomic circumstances (mostly women with children), counseling is needed to assist them in exploring other options than the return to an untreated batterer. This spouse may need vocational training, information on the welfare system and other social services, financial counseling, and a place to go to explore these options. Contrary to what may be expected, women who seek help because of violent, abusing husbands do not always suffer from low self-esteem. Stacey and Shupe (1983) found that these women benefit from supportive counseling and information about the options available to them whether they decide to leave or return to the batterer.

For people who have suffered sexual abuse in alcoholic/violent families, trust is probably the most difficult issue they need to deal with. Along with trust, the sexualization of relationships when they were young indicates a need to reframe relationships to allow true intimacy to develop. Rage and anger at their betrayal by those who were supposed to nurture and protect them are other areas of treatment that need to be explored. The victims of all these forms of abuse usually believe that they were somehow responsible for the abuse that happened to them—especially victims of sexual abuse. The treatment of those victims who developed post-traumatic stress disorder as a result of sexual abuse must emphasize exploration, catharsis, and reintegration of the traumatic experience (Kovach, 1986). Treatment can be lengthy, sometimes lasting for years, but it is hoped that through treatment, the intergenerational cycles of alcoholism and abuse can be stopped.

Most of the treatment methods in existence today are the result of years of development and research in the field of alcoholism. However, the Potter-Effrons (1985) maintained that the problems of chemical dependency and family violence overlap both numerically and conceptually. Some of the similarities are: both are intergenerational, passed on by modeling and genetics or both; personality dynamics of low self-esteem, dependency, and impulsivity affect all members of the family; both kinds of family are characterized by loss of control resulting in the use of alcohol or violence as an attempt to cope; and the use of alcohol and/or violence increases family tension and increases the likelihood of more problems. The Potter-Effrons (1985) stated that these similarities provide the ground to treat both problems together, using the alcoholic crisis to intervene in child/spousal relationships.

Kinds of Treatment

Treatment of alcoholism comes in many modalities. The initial contact with sobriety for many alcoholics consists of inpatient and outpatient programs at hospitals and other units set up specifically for alcohol and drug rehabilitation. Through the United States, there are thousands of residential programs for the recovering drug addict and alcoholic. Couples therapy and family therapy are also available for treating the family. In addition, there are mental health workers in private practice who specialize in alcoholism issues and AA and other support groups. There are community and private centers that specifically serve the recovering alcoholic and drug abuser.

However, for the abuser of people, there is far less in the way of programs for treatment. The intergenerational aspects of abuse have been recognized only recently. Within the past few years treatment has been developed in addition to any sentence issues for those who had been convicted of battering and abuse. There are now 12-step programs modeled on AA that address any dysfunction thatremotely resembles addictive behavior. These include sexual addiction, abuse of food (overeating, anorexia, and bulimia), gambling, compulsive shopping, and a host of other maladaptive behaviors.

Inpatient and outpatient programs in hospitals are primarily geared to treat the alcoholic. The majority of these programs are focused on getting the alcoholic to admit and accept his or her alcoholism, with little attention paid to other issues, such as abuse. Many of these programs do involve the family in treatment, with a little family therapy or couples therapy being done. However, too little time and attention are given in these programs to the family; therefore abusive situations can go unnoticed. In many cases, because of the severity of the dysfunction, the family will sabotage treatment. Scott (1985) found that high family involvement with treatment and family referrals via intervention have reduced the against medical advice discharges at the Rimrock Foundation from 12.7% to 5.6%. Hospital programs usually run for about 1 month, with some having longer periods of treatment. Assessment for violence of any form could very well be done during the period of the alcoholic's stay.

Longer term residential treatment centers, called "halfway" or "three-quarter-way houses," also vary in their length of treatment. Usually, the substance abuser will stay anywhere from 3 months to 1 year. These residences also vary in the amount of treatment offered, from AA meetings only to some rather intense individual and group therapy. In the houses offering therapy, the issues of violence and abuse usually surface in those people who had been victims of abuse, especially sexual abuse. Referrals can then be made to those people who specialize in dealing with incest victims. Generally, the therapy occurring in those houses offering it will address the issue of risk taking, self-esteem, and interpersonal relationships, the lack of which are the outgrowths of neglect and emotional abuse. The therapists in these residences are as much required by law to report child abuse on the part of the perpetrator as are any other health care professionals, especially if there are still minor children in the family to which the abuser will return.

AA is one of the more successful treatment modalities for the treatment of alcoholism. Started in 1935 by two alcoholics who wanted to stay sober, it is an organization of recovering alcoholics who follow 12 steps in order to learn how to live a productive, sober life. Groups of alcoholics meet and share their stories of alcoholism and recovery and form a fellowship. The 12 steps are based on spiritual principles (see Appendix A). AA has proven to be the road to recovery for millions of alcoholics. The 12 steps stabilize the alcoholic in early sobriety, allow the alcoholic to take a look at those issues that trigger drinking, assist in repairing ruptured relationships, and aid the alcoholic to continue in sobriety and to help other alcoholics. AA can provide socialization for those who were isolated and alienated from peers. It can also provide grounds for forming healthy intimate relationships with others who have the same feelings and problems as the alcoholic. It has aided many in overcoming alcoholism. However, some people take objection to the spiritual focus of AA, and others balk at the sharing of experiences by members. AA meetings vary in format and content from one part of the country to another, and they vary within an area. Some meetings are more formal, some are more intimate, some are therapeutic, and some are social. While AA is not for everyone—in fact some people exchange one obsession (alcohol) for another (AA)—a large number of alcoholics have been helped by this organization. However, AA's focus is strictly on alcohol, and it discourages discussion of other issues such as abuse, drug addiction, overeating, and gambling. So while AA can be of use in a treatment plan for alcoholism, it should be supplemented with other kinds of treatment for other issues.

Because of AA's success with alcoholics, other self-help groups have sprung up to deal with other kinds of addictions. The first 12-step group of this kind was Al-Anon for the spouses and other concerned people who were connected with an alcoholic. The purpose of this group is to teach people how to live with alcoholism without getting caught up in the destruction that alcoholism can wreak. Other groups of this sort are Narcotics Anonymous for drug addicts, Cocaine Anonymous for cocaine addicts, and Nar-Anon for families of drug abusers (similar to Al-Anon). There are also Overeaters Anonymous for people with eating disorders and food addictions, Gamblers Anonymous for compulsive gamblers, Sexual Addictions Anonymous for people with sexual addictions, Parents Anonymous for abusive parents, and on and on. The author has heard various estimates of 12-step programs ranging from 95 to 148 different programs. They are an excellent source of support for people who have developed various problems as a result of familial alcoholism and violence; however they only work with each specific problem and discourage discussion of other problems.

There are numerous other groups that are not based on AA's 12 steps that offer support for a variety of problems. One group formed in reaction to AA's earlier orientation to the white male population, the primary population until 15 years ago, is Women for Sobriety. This group does not adhere to the 12 steps but has developed its own version of them. Other groups of this type are Abusing Men Entering New Directions (AMEND), a support group for men who have abused their families; Parents United, a support group for the parents of victims and abusers; Sons and Daughters United, a support group for the siblings of abusers and victims; and Victims of Incest and Child Abuse (VOICES), for those who have suffered any kind of abuse. There are many more groups of this sort; some are national, others are local. They can be found listed with community referral services and provide an excellent adjunct to other therapy.

Other forms of therapy are geared more toward individual issues rather than the general focus of support groups. These forms of therapy are individual therapy, couples therapy, group therapy, and family therapy. Each of these modes of therapy has its advantages and disadvantages.

Individual therapy has the advantage of providing a "safe" place for an alienated, isolated, and mistrustful client to experience a nonjudgmental, noncritical, one-on-one relationship. It is a setting where the victim or the abuser can begin to lower some of his or her defenses and get to some of the pain and hurt locked up inside. Of course, if the abuser is not under court-ordered treatment, and there are minor children living with him or her, when the issue of abusing comes up in therapy, the therapist will be bound by law to report it. The disadvantages of individual therapy are that it can be expensive and take many years of visits for improvement to occur. The client can also maintain a sense of difference from other people, adding to the sense of isolation, unless he or she is in an appropriate support group. Some therapists are not equipped, either emotionally or by training, to work with the victims of familial abuse, particularly incest.

Group therapy consists of one or more therapists and a group of clients who are focused on a common issue such as alcoholism or a form of abuse, such as incest. Some advantages of group therapy are the feedback given by the other members of the group, the feeling of not being alone with whatever the problem is, and the inspiration of watching others change. Therapists who specialize in abuse have told this author that group therapy is the most powerful mode of treating all forms of familial abuse. A disadvantage of group therapy is that all of the clients cannot explore their own particular issues in depth in each session. Therefore the client could feel lost in the crowd or overlooked. Because there are more participants in the therapy, it is less expensive for each client than individual therapy, and improvement usually comes about more rapidly than with individual therapy.

Couples therapy is a group form of marital therapy. In just about all families where abuse has occurred, the relationship between the parents is usually extremely dysfunctional. In this kind of therapy, the issues that deal with the parental relationship are treated under the assumption that when the parental unit is functioning in a healthy manner, the family as a whole will function better, and the abuse will cease. Treating one couple has the same advantages and disadvantages of individual therapy. Treating more than one couple is analogous to treating a group, with its attendant advantages and disadvantages.

Family therapy is a most powerful method of treatment. Since all members of the family are affected by the abuse, each to a greater or lesser degree than another, treatment is necessary for all. Each family member has a chance to hear the other without interference. Changes in the growth of each member can be observed by all other members of the family, and new understandings can be developed. The advantage of having the family treated is that all are getting the treatment instead of just one victim or just the alcoholic or abuser. Each person can see how he or she contributes to the problem. The disadvantages to family therapy are the cost and the logistics of assembling all members of the family in one place at the same time.

The trend in treatment has been to view alcoholism and other kinds of abuse as 2 separate issues. Therefore an abuser who is an alcoholic would receive treatment for the alcoholism, but, because of the assumption that treating the alcohol abuse would cause the other abuse to stop, none of the other problems is addressed as a primary treatment issue. Vega and Vega (1986) maintained that physically abusive behavior should not be condoned on the basis of drunkenness and, further, that treatment professionals need to be aware of the misconception that men under treatment for alcoholism will stop abusing their families. Since the two phenomena of alcoholism and family violence coexist, the variety of treatment programs designed with specific services for specific problems should be broadened to serve the entire family unit more effectively and efficiently under one treatment program (Hassett, 1985; Spieker, 1983). A multimodal treatment approach would be the ideal, with perhaps family, group, and individual therapy being supplemented by a support group.

PREVENTION

Prevention of alcoholism and familial abuse begins to occur when a crisis occurs in a family where alcoholism and abuse occur. It is by breaking the cycle through treatment of this generation's abusers and alcoholics that one can begin to prevent alcoholism and abuse in the next generation. Organizations such as Mothers Against Drunk Drivers (MADD) and Students Against Drunk Driving (SADDJ), as well as the National Council on Alcoholism, are raising public consciousness on the cost of alcoholism in lives lost and wasted. The media as well as various school systems are beginning to recognize their roles in the prevention of both alcoholism and abuse. Cohn (1982) stated that media can encourage openness and the reporting of abuse problems, can give the facts on the problem, and can increase the public's awareness. Spieker (1983) believed that an awareness of problems leads to treatment, and, therefore, that both prevention and treatment can be implemented through public education.

There are a number of ways in which school systems are contributing to the prevention of alcohol abuse. Drug and alcohol awareness programs and classes on what drugs and alcohol can do to a life are being offered. Many schools have become more strict with students who use drugs and alcohol. Parenting classes beginning in elementary schools are being started in order to teach children how to be healthy parents.

Social services provided by the community at large include drop-in centers for adolescent and other substance abusers and day programs for mothers where they can socialize with other mothers and their children. Carter (1982) listed play groups for children and family day care centers where children and parents meet under the supervision of workers as methods of preventing further abuse within the family. Prevention is the responsibility of all in the community—the media, the schools, and the public at large. Regan (1982) stated that the first step in breaking the twin cycles of alcoholism and abuse is to raise public consciousness of the pervasiveness of alcoholism and family violence in our society today.

SUMMARY

The twin family secrets of alcoholism and violence have a long history. Cultural attitudes have allowed these problems to continue within the family for thousands of years. It is only with the advent of the social movements of the late 1960s and early 1970s that both alcoholism and abuse have begun to be studied and treated. The connection between alcohol abuse and violence has been known for a long time but has been formally studied only within the past 10 years. Although estimates of the involvement of alcohol with violence vary widely, all studies indicate a significant relationship between them. The forms of abuse are neglect, prenatal abuse, physical abuse, emotional abuse, and sexual abuse. Both alcoholic and violent families exhibit the same dynamics of severe dysfunction.

The transmission of alcoholism and abusing is intergenerational, caused by parental role modeling and the experience of living in an alcoholic and/ or violent family. The consequences of living in a family where alcoholism and abuse occur range from medical interventions, mental retardation, various forms of addiction, and low self-esteem to abuse and alcoholism in the following generation. A powerful way of breaking the intergenerational cycling of these problems is an intervention that can be done by the courts, by employers, or by families. Treatment issues include denial, trust, and self-esteem, along with the alcoholism and the abuse. Hospital and residential treatments available are mainly for the alcoholic, although the psychosocial treatment issues are the same for both problems. While hospital programs focus mainly on the alcoholism, residential programs and half-way and three-quarter-way houses may begin to address the issues of abuse for their clients. Other forms of therapy include self-help groups and individual, group, marital, couples, and family therapy, each of which contributes its own strengths in the treatment of abuse and alcoholism. Prevention is a community responsibility. The media are cooperating with messages and programs about the effects of drugs and alcohol. School systems have programs relating to drugs and alcohol, as well as classes in parenting for their students. Communities are providing centers where professional help is available for families and individuals with both of these problems. With public awareness of the twin problems of alcoholism and violence in the family, there is hope for the next generation as more resources are allocated to their treatment and prevention.

REFERENCES

Abel, E. (1984). Fetal alcohol syndrome: A case of prenatal child abuse? In *Fetal alcohol syndrome and fetal alcohol effects* (pp. 213–219). New York: Plenum.

*Adult Children of Alcoholics, Chicagoland Area. (1985). *Traits list*. Chicago: Author.

Berk, R.A., & Newton P.J. (1985). Does arrest really defer wife battery? An effort to replicate the findings of the Minneapolis spouse abuse experiment. *American Sociological Review, 50*, 253–262.

Black, C. (1981). *It will never happen to me*. Denver, CO: M.A.C.

Black, C. (1984). Children of alcoholics: The clinical profile. In *Changing legacies: Growing up in an alcoholic home. (pp. 73–76)*. Hollywood, FL: Health Communications.

Black, C., Bucky, S.F., & Widder-Padilla, S. (1986). Interpersonal and emotional consequences of being an adult child of an alcoholic. *International Journal of Addictions, 21*, 213–231.

Block, M.R., & Sinnott, J.D. (1979). *Battered elder syndrome: An exploratory study*. (Contract No. G-90-A-1674 01). Washington, DC: Administration on Aging.

Borrill, J. (1986). Facing up to booze. *British Journal of Medical Psychology, 60*, 71–77.

Bottom, W., & Lancaster, J. (1981). Ecological orientation toward human abuse. *Family and Community Mental Health, 4*(2), 1–10.

Califano, J. (1986, September 23). National attack on addiction is long overdue. *New York Times,* p. 2.

Campbell, J. (1986). Nursing assessment for risk of homicide with battered women. *Advances in Nursing Science, 8*(4), 36–51.

Carducci, B.J., & McNeely, J.A. (1981). *Attribution of blame for wife abuse by alcoholics and nonalcoholics.* Paper presented at the Annual Convention of the American Psychological Association, Los Angeles.

Carnes, P. (1983). *Out of the shadows: Understanding sexual addiction.* Minneapolis: CompCare.

Carter, J. (1982). Family day care centers and child abuse. In K. Oates (Ed.), *Child abuse: A community concern.* (pp. 204–214). Secaucus, NJ: Citadel.

Cohn, A. (1982). The role of media campaigns in preventing child abuse. In R. Oates (Ed.), *Child abuse: A community concern.* (pp. 215–230). Secaucus, NJ: Citadel.

Condon, J. (1986). Spectrum of fetal abuse in pregnant women. *Journal of Nervous and Mental Disease, 174,* 509–516.

Covington, S. (1986). Facing the clinical challenges of women alcoholics: Physical, emotional, and sexual abuse. *Focus on Family and Chemical Dependency, 9*(3), 10–11, 37, 42–44.

Deutsch, C. (1982). *Broken bottles, broken dreams: Understanding and helping the children of alcoholics.* New York: Teacher's College Press.

Edwards, D., & Gil, E. (1986). *Breaking the cycle: Assessment and treatment of child abuse and neglect.* Los Angeles: Association for Advanced Training in the Behavioral Sciences.

Famularo, R., Stone, K., Barnum, R., & Wharton, J. (1986). Alcoholism and severe child maltreatment. *American Journal of Orthopsychiatry, 56,* 481–485.

Flanzer, J. (1984). Alcohol abuse and family violence: The domestic chemical connection. *Focus on Family and Chemical Dependency, 7*(4), 5–6.

Goodrick, J.H. (1983, February). *Clues for early identification of sexual abuse of children in alcohol abusing families.* Paper presented at the conference: Working with Adolescent Alcohol/Drug Problems: Assessment, Intervention and Treatment, Madison, WI.

*Hassett, D. (1985). Family alcoholism and child abuse: Where do you start? *Focus on Family and Chemical Dependency, 8*(4), 14–15.

Julius, E.K., & Papp, P. (1979). Family choreography: A multigenerational view of an alcoholic family system. In E. Kaufman & P. Kaufman (Eds.), *Family therapy of drug and alcohol abuse* (pp. 201–214). New York: Gardne.

Kantor, G., & Strauss, M. (1986, April). *Drunken bum theory of wife beating.* Paper presented at the National Council on Alcoholism Forum, San Francisco.

Kaufman, E. (1985a). Critical issues in family research: drug abuse. *Journal of Drug Issues, 4,* 463–475.

Kovach, J.A. (1986). Relationship between treatment failures of alcoholic women and incestuous histories with possible implications for post traumatic stress disorder. *Dissertation Abstracts International, 44,* 710A.

Krupp, S., & Lehmann, N. (1984). Incidence of alcohol-related domestic violence: An assessment. *Alcohol Health and Research World, 8*(2), 23–27.

Lawson, G., Peterson, J.S., & Lawson, A. (1983). *Alcoholism and the family.* Rockville, MD: Aspen.

Lipson, A. (1984). Contamination of the fetal environment: A form of prenatal abuse. In R.K. Oates (Ed.), *Child abuse: A major concern of our times* (pp. 42–48). New South Wales, Australia: Butterworths.

Lundy, C. (1986). Social role enactment and the onset, maintenance and cessation of alcohol dependence in women. *Dissertation Abstracts International, 46*(10), 3158-A.

Marsden, D. (1978). Sociological perspectives on family violence. In J. Martin (Ed.), *Violence and the family* (pp. 118–123). New York: Wiley.

May, M. (1978). Violence in the family: A historical perspective. In J. Martin (Ed.), *Violence and the family* (pp. 136–165). New York: Wiley.

Meagher, M. (1987). *Beginning of a miracle: How to intervene with the addicted or alcoholic person.* Pompano Beach, FL: Health Communications.

Middleton, J.L. (1984). Double stigma: Sexual abuse within the alcoholic family. *Focus on Family and Chemical Dependency, 7*(5), 6, 10–11.

Miller, A. (1983). *For your own good: Hidden cruelty in child rearing and the roots of violence.* New York: Farrar, Strauss, Giroux.

Miller, A. (1986). *Thou shalt not be aware: Society's betrayal of the child.* New York: Farrar, Strauss, Giroux.

Morgan, P. (1982). *Alcohol and family violence: A review of the literature.* (Alcohol and Health Monograph No. l). Berkeley, CA: University of California, Social Research Group.

Morris, G. (1985). *The kids next door: Sons and daughters who kill their parents.* New York: William Morrow.

National Council on Alcoholism. (1987). *Acts on alcohol related birth defects.* New York: Author.

Neidig, P., Freidman, D., & Collins, B. (1985). Domestic conflict containment: A spouse abuse treatment program. *Journal of Contemporary Social Work, 66*(4), 195–204.

Nielsen, L.A. (1984). Sexual abuse and chemical dependency: Assessing the risk for women alcoholics and adult children. *Focus on Family and Chemical Dependency. 7*(6), 6, 10–11, 37.

Oates, R. (1982). Failure to thrive: Part of the spectrum. In R. Oates (Ed.), *Child abuse: A community concern* (pp. 119–129). Secaucus, NJ: Citadel.

Parkin, W. (1982). Domestic violence against women: The role of health professionals. *Australian Nurses Journal, 12*(4), 41–44.

Pelton, C. (1982). Intervention in family violence: A role for the physician and for society. *Postgraduate Medicine, 72*(5), 163–165.

Potter-Effron, R., & Potter-Effron, R. (1985). Family violence as a treatment issue with chemically dependent adolescents. *Alcoholism Treatment Quarterly, 2*(2), 1–15.

Priest, K. (1985). Adolescent's responses to parent's alcoholism. *Social Casework, 66*(9), 533–539.

Regan, R. (1982). Alcohol problems and family violence: A message to the helpers. In J.P. Flanzer (Ed.), *The many faces of violence* (pp. 106–120). Springfield, IL: Charles C Thomas.

Russell, L. (1985). Child abuse and alcoholism: A suggested model for future research and treatment. Rutherford, NJ: Thomas W. Perrin.

Sandburg, D. (1986). Child abuse/delinquency connection: Evolution of a therapeutic community. *Journal of Psychoactive Drugs, 18,* 215–220.

Schaefer, S., Evans, S., & Sterne, M. (1985). Incest among women in recovery from alcoholism and drug dependency: Correlation and implication for treatment. Alcohol, drugs, and tobacco: An international perspective: Past, present and future. *Congress on Alcoholism and Drug Dependence, 2,* 268a–269.

Schatzman, M. (1973). *Soul murder: Persecution in the family.* New York: Random House.

Scott, L. (1985). *AMA discharges: Variables and solutions.* Unpublished report, Rimrock Foundation, Billings, MT.

Sedge, S. (1979). Violence in American society. In M.R. Block & J.D. Sinott (Eds.), *The battered elder* (Contract No. G-90-A-1674). Washington, DC: Administration on Aging.

Sienkiewicz, J. (1983). Evaluation of court intervention with maltreatment of family members by alcoholics. *Problemy Alkoholizmu, 30*(7–8), 119–21.

Spieker, G. (1983). What is the linkage between alcohol abuse and violence? In Gotteheil E., Druley, K., Skolada, T., & Waxman, W. (Eds.), *Alcohol, drug abuse and aggression* (pp. 125–136). Springfield, IL: Charles C Thomas.

Stacey, W., & Shupe, A. (1983). *The family secret: Domestic violence in America.* Boston: Beacon.

Stark, R., & McEvoy, R., III. (1970). Middle class violence. *Psychology Today, 4,* 52–55.

Swanson, R. (1984). Battered wife syndrome. *Canadian Medical Association Journal, 130,* 709–712.

Vega, C., & Vega, D. (1986, April). *Addiction connection: Chemical dependency, domestic violence, and sexual abuse.* Paper presented at the National Council on Alcoholism Forum, San Francisco.

Viken, R. (1982). Family violence: Aids to Recognition. *Postgraduate Medicine, 71*(5): 115–117, 120–122.

Weil, A., Rosen, W., Slater, P., Macdonald, D., & Holden, C. (1985). What are the causes of drug abuse? In C.D. Debner (Ed.), *Chemical dependency: Opposing viewpoints series* (pp. 15–47). St. Paul, MN: Greenhaven.

Woititz, J. (1983). *Adult children of alcoholics.* Hollywood, FL: Health Communications.

Zimmern, A. (1986, April). *Parent/family interactions in the recovery of substance abusing youth.* Paper presented at the National Council on Alcoholism Forum, San Francisco.

Chapter 14

Indigent Alcoholics on
Skid Row

Thomas J. Young

INTRODUCTION

The term *skid row* is derived from "skid road," the name used for a logging center in Seattle, Washington, more than a century ago. Saloons, gambling houses, and dilapidated hotels were built along the thoroughfare where logs were skidded to sawmills, and eventually the area became referred to as "skid row" by the lumberjacks who lived and worked there. Over the years the term grew to include other urban regions inhabited by "marginal" men (Levinson, 1970; McSheehy, 1979).

It is extremely difficult to provide an accurate estimate of the skid row population, but its size has varied with time. In 1911, for example, somewhere between 40,000 and 60,000 men lived on the skid rows of Chicago (Solenberger, 1911) and this number increased after World War I and during the depression of the 1930s. The government work programs of the 1940s reduced the skid row population considerably, and with the prosperous years following World War II, the number of inhabitants declined further. By 1957 the skid row population in Chicago totaled approximately 12,000, and in the 1960s some scholars speculated that many of the skid row areas were disappearing as a result of urban renewal (Bahr, 1967; Bogue, 1963; Rubington, 1971; Wallace, 1965). This optimism was brought to a halt as the 1970s witnessed three factors that contributed to the emergence of a "grate society": an economic recession, the return of Vietnam veterans, and the deinstitutionalization of mental patients and the mentally retarded. In a survey of mission directors in 23 cities, Levinson (1979) reported a population increase among 15, a decrease among 4, and no change among 4. Overall, the United States is faced with a homeless mass that is estimated to number 250,000 to 2 million people (French, 1986).

The U.S. government has noted that it has not had a street count of this magnitude since the Great Depression, but the official stance has been that the vast majority of the contemporary skid row population is suffering from mental illness, mental deficiency, or both. This perspective does not

305

place any blame on the economic system but rather on the community mental health centers (CMHC) and the mental health network mandated to care for the deinstitutionalized (French, 1986). While the deinstitutionalized are rather heavily represented among those on the street, the literature seems to suggest that they do not account for more than 30% of this population (Mowbray, 1985). Actually, the skid row population is a relatively heterogeneous population composed of at least seven groups: the deinstitutionalized, occupational itinerants, resident workers, impoverished pensioners, unemployed young black men, drug addicts, and alcoholics. It should also be noted that there is some intergroup mobility on skid row with the most typical pattern being the movement of occupational itinerants, resident workers, and pensioners to the alcoholic subculture (Levinson, 1979).

Another commonly held misconception is that drunkenness is the norm on skid row. As Rubington (1971) noted: "the surveys in Chicago, Minneapolis, and Philadelphia all report that about one-third of the skid row residents are abstainers, one-third are moderate drinkers (by skid row standards) and only a third are alcoholics" (p. 127). Such findings tend to support the position held by Bogue (1963) and by Blumberg, Shipley, and Shandler (1973) that alcoholism has probably been overemphasized in discussions of skid row inhabitants and their problems. Yet within the skid row community is a subculture in which alcohol is central to everyday life. This chapter explores the drinking practices of skid row alcoholics and examines other issues such as alcohol related health problems, treatment, and prevention.

DRINKING PRACTICES

Contrary to popular folklore, skid row alcoholics do not represent a monolithic mass. Unfortunately, their diversity is often ignored and intervention programs are commonly implemented without an adequate understanding of the homogeneous nature of this population. At least four types of alcoholics can be found on skid row, each marked by considerable diversity in terms of drinking practices, values, and status. Included in this typology are isolated alcoholics, lushes, winos, and drunks (Gammage, Jorgensen, & Jorgensen, 1972).

In comparison with other skid row alcoholics, the isolated type is more likely to be suffering from an affective or schizophrenic disorder. They tend to be chronically depressed, withdrawn, and characterized by extremely low self-esteem and self-punishing behavior. Retreatism has been adopted as an autoplastic adaptation to life, and they represent what Merton (1957) called "double-losers" in that they have been rejected by the larger society and shunned by other skid row alcoholics because of their inability to conform to group drinking patterns and norms (Docter, 1967; Fox, 1967; Gammage et al., 1972; Jackson & Connor, 1953).

Lushes are the most prestigious alcoholics on skid row (Jackson & Connor, 1953), mainly because they can afford to drink in bars and are employed as casual day laborers (Rooney, 1961). Their acquaintances are usually the bar crowds on skid row, and they tend to shun the wino and the drunk as much as possible to avoid social stigma and the attention of law enforcement officials.

Lushes are part of the skid row subculture for a variety of sociological, psychological, and economic factors. Sociologically, some are voluntary participants (Sagarin, 1979) in the skid row subculture because they are simply alienated from the norms and values of "the harried suburbanite— the whole organization, briefcased, gold-and-bridge, scotch-and-soda set" (Bendiner, 1962, p. 409). These lushes, as Bendiner (1962) has noted, have rejected the protestant work ethic and are among "those who no longer aspire, who do not wish to rise on anybody's shoulders, who do not wish to sell more, make more, show more, even give more than others" (p. 409). Psychologically, some lushes meet the diagnostic criteria for mental, personality, and developmental disorders. In such cases impairment in social and occupational functioning results in a drift to the skid row subculture and acculturation into the norms and general life style of the lush group. Economically, forces within the political economy push some workers out of the dominant culture and into the surplus labor population of daily wage earners, and some of these individuals find that becoming a lush tempers their harsh social reality.

The primary difference between a wino and a drunk is that the former needs a drink every day while the latter will go on drinking sprees with periods of abstinence between binges (Gammage et al., 1972). Thus, winos are characterized by Delta alcoholism and drunks are marked by Epsilon alcoholism (Jellinek, 1960). Both will resort to nonbeverage alcohol consumption on occasion, but only a small subpopulation of winos referred to as "rubby-dubs" do so habitually (Gammage et al., 1972; Jackson & Connor, 1953; Peterson & Maxwell, 1958). Many winos and drunks have mental and personality disorders, but extrapsychic factors are often relevant, too. For example, skid row binge drinking is more prevalent among Native American urban migrants than other ethnic groups because their preparation for successful, unstressful urban living is far poorer (Graves, 1971; Young, in press).

Group drinking in a "bottle gang" is perhaps the most dominant drinking pattern for most indigent alcoholics on skid row. The bottle gang is composed of two to six men who collectively pool their limited economic resources to buy an inexpensive bottle of alcohol, which is shared in a public place such as an alley, door step, or street corner (Archard, 1979). According to Rubington (1968), there are six stages in the bottle gang cycle: salutation, negotiation, procurement, consumption, affirmation, and dispersal. Each stage is marked by explicit norms and sanctions for breaches of the rules.

During the salutation stage, potential bottle gang members meet and share information about "the boys." The rules of this stage include: never snub a "drinking man," greet friends and acquaintances alike, and always be ready to pass the time of day with an equal. Obviously the primary function is to cement past ties, to become acquainted with new members, and to signify in-group solidarity. Exclusion is the ideal penalty for salutation breaches, but it is rarely applied.

Negotiation is entered into when an initiator asks if others wish to "go in on a bottle." At this stage the only requirement is that each member has a few cents. If the members do not have enough money for a bottle, a brief excursion in panhandling is undertaken until the price is collected. Negotiation rules include: show your money and be willing to share it, buy or work your way into a bottle gang, and never "chisel" in. Negotiation breaches usually entail attempts at illicit entry into a bottle gang. Among these rule violators are "lap dogs" (i.e., those who stand at the periphery of the drinking group hoping for a free invitation), "actors" (i.e., those who feign withdrawal symptóms), and "hold-out artists" (i.e., those who contribute less than can be afforded).

At the procurement stage, a "runner" is sent after a bottle while the rest of the members await his return. The runner must not be shabbily dressed or acutely intoxicated, and he must be dependable. Using a runner for procurement serves to reduce the visibility of the bottle gang's activities, and it also creates a drinking-centered drama as members await the runner's return. Procurement breaches include failure to return with the bottle, returning too slow, or returning with a bottle from which the runner has already drunk or has offered a few "pulls" to people to whom he owes a drink. Failure to return is not always by design. Sometimes it is due to accident, loss of memory, or arrest. Because of the difficulty of knowing what has really happened, the gang generally labels such a runner as "Dick Smith," a name used to describe a man who "went south with the bottle."

Consumption begins with the leader making a big show of breaking the seal and taking the first drink. The bottle then passes to the leader's left with each man taking two short gulps. Drinking is surreptitious, and each member is expected to watch for police officers or other outsiders who might jeopardize the activity of the bottle gang. After the bottle has been passed full circle, it is placed in the leader's pocket until someone calls for another drink. Drinking too fast, too much, or too obviously can result in exclusion from subsequent bottle gangs, but there is a reluctance to apply sanctions unless the breach is blatant.

During affirmation, the leader sets the style, tone, and topics of talk. The function of the affirmation is to promote solidarity among gang members in the immediate situation by signifying that each is a "good man" and a good drinking partner. Members compliment the leader on how well or fast he "promoted" bottle money, praise the runner for his speed, and favorably compare the sociability of the present gang with others they have been in. Outsiders are criticized, especially men who are currently in skid row missions as well as mission directors, preachers, and staff. The theme is that members and staff alike are "a bunch of phonies" and that the former are "not real drunks." Affirmation violations include incorrect talk or actions. It is taboo to discuss troubles or the past or to ask personal questions of any kind. Exclusion is most likely, however, in cases of "acting up," either by fighting in the gang or by engaging in antics. These men are called "jail bait" and are avoided whenever possible.

Once the bottle is emptied, the gang is ready to disband. The primary rule at this stage is "duck the empty" and "say goodbye while the going's good." Dispersal violations include calling attention to oneself or the activities of the gang, begging money from gang members, and trying to rob, steal, or beat up members thought to have money. Those who breach the rules of dispersal through violence are quickly stigmatized and are excluded from future bottle gangs.

HEALTH PROBLEMS

The harsh environment of skid row takes a heavy toll on the health of its residents, particularly skid row alcoholics. For example, no other segment of American society approaches the unfortunate prevalence rate of tuberculosis that one finds for indigent alcoholics on skid row (Hudson & Rhodes, 1971). In a study by Blumberg et al. (1973), the prevalence rate for active tuberculosis was 5 times greater for skid row alcoholic patients than for nonalcoholic skid row patients. Specifically, active tuberculosis was diagnosed in 21% of the skid row alcoholics compared with 4% of the nonalcoholics. Furthermore, the prevalence rate for inactive tuberculosis was twice that found for nonalcoholic skid row patients (10% vs. 5%). The development or redevelopment of tuberculosis among skid row alcoholics commonly arises through an alcoholism–to malnutrition–to tuberculosis cycle; or through an alcoholism–to peptic ulcer–to gastrostomy–

to nutritional deficiency–to tuberculosis cycle. In any case, the relationship between alcoholism and tuberculosis on skid row is evident.

Pulmonary disease other than tuberculosis is also a health problem for skid row alcoholics with a prevalence rate 2.5 times greater than the rate for nonalcoholics on skid row. In the Blumberg et al. (1973) sample, 32% of the skid row alcoholics were diagnosed with pulmonary disease other than tuberculosis, compared with 12% of the nonalcoholics. These pulmonary diseases included emphysema, chronic bronchitis, bronchial asthma, bronchiectasis, various forms of pleural disease, neoplasm, and other respiratory conditions.

Rib fractures are another clinical mark of skid row alcoholics. Due to the high incidence of trauma, either accidental (e.g., falling) or produced by others (e.g., being "rolled"), Blumberg et al. (1973) found that 25% of the alcoholics had evidence of rib fractures, whereas the nonalcoholic sample had a prevalence rate of 4%. Thus, the prevalence rate for rib fractures was more than 6 times greater among skid row alcoholics than among nonalcoholics.

The Blumberg et al. (1973) study also revealed that about 24% of the alcoholic and 17% of the nonalcoholic patients were anemic. Undoubtedly malnutrition is a contributor, but an additional factor is that more than half of the alcoholics sold blood too often. There is a common misconception held by skid row alcoholics that the drinking of port wine will build up any hemoglobin loss suffered as a result of selling blood. Actually, selling blood too frequently along with drinking too much and malnutrition can cause the hemoglobin count to drop precipitously in less than 2 months with a net result of lowered resistance to disease processes.

Cirrhosis of the liver was 3.5 times more prevalent among the alcoholics than the nonalcoholics in the Blumberg et al. (1973) study. While this finding is not unexpected, it is worth noting that the prevalence rate for the alcoholic population was only 7%. The prevalence of enlarged liver, fatty liver, or acute alcoholic hepatitis was much higher, but for the most part this represented reversible liver damage that could be corrected through nutrition, vitamins, and abstinence from alcohol.

Varicose veins occurred more than 5 times as often among skid row alcoholics than among nonalcoholics on skid row. The prevalence rate for varicose veins for the alcoholics in the Blumberg et al. (1973) sample was 11% compared with 2% for the nonalcoholics. This finding can be partly explained by the fact that the life style of the skid row alcoholic is marked by prolonged periods of standing or sitting without movement, which places a heavy strain on the veins.

Disorders such as central nervous system diseases, cardiovascular disease, inguinal hernia, and hemorrhoids were 2 to 3 times more frequent among skid row alcoholics than among nonalcoholics on skid row (Blumberg et al., 1973). The prevalence rate for diseases of the central nervous system was 17% for alcoholics and 5% for nonalcoholics. For cardiovascular disease the prevalence rate for alcoholics was 10%, compared with 3% for nonalcoholics. Inguinal hernia and hemorrhoids were diagnosed in 8% and 10%, respectively, of the alcoholics compared with 4% and 5%, respectively, of the nonalcoholics. Rates for hypertension and musculoskeletal disorders for alcoholics were 14% and 18%, respectively, compared with 10% and 14%, respectively, for nonalcoholics. Prostatism was slightly higher among nonalcoholics than alcoholics, with prevalence rates of 9% for the former and 7% for the latter. It has been speculated that liver impairment leading to elevated estrogen levels may protect the prostate, but this theory is not conclusive.

Clearly, many skid row alcoholics are ill and in need of medical care. Unfortunately, they often do not receive treatment unless they come to the attention of the police or some other agency. In the limited cases where contact is made with a clinic or hospital, the chances of carrying the treatment through to a successful conclusion are poor. Skid row alcoholics are easily discouraged and frustrated by the typical obstacles to health care in the United States: having to wait to see a physician, filling out forms, making appointments for return visits, and the aloofness of Western medicine. These structural problems must be overcome if successful health programs are to be implemented for this population.

PREVENTION AND TREATMENT

Intoxification has been pursued throughout history and it is quite unlikely that this autoplastic/alloplastic response to life will ever cease to exist (Malcolm, 1973). In fact, one can argue from a Durkheimian (1979) perspective that a society without some degree of substance abuse would be pathological. Such an argument, however, should not be used to reify the existing social order. Efforts toward the primary prevention of alcoholism on skid row can and should be made through a multimodal approach. The starting point for such an approach is an understanding that skid row alcoholics represent a diverse population. Some are on skid row because of mental or developmental disorders, others drift into this subculture because they are alienated from the dominant society, and many are pushed by forces within the political economy. Thus, primary prevention must entail efforts along the lines of community mental health, social change to reduce alienation, and economic justice.

Treatment must be based on a professional evaluation of the patient's psychological, sociological, and medical profile (Lawson, Peterson, & Lawson, 1983; Young and Lawson, 1984). A complete multiaxial evaluation in the American Psychiatric Association's (1980) *Diagnostic and Statistical Manual of Mental Disorders* (DSM III) includes the following axes:

1. *Axis I*

   • clinical syndromes
   • conditions not attributable to a mental disorder that are a focus of attention of treatment (V. codes)
   • additional codes

2. *Axis II*

   • personality disorders
   • specific developmental disorders

3. *Axis III:* physical disorders and conditions
4. *Axis IV:* severity of psychosocial stressors
5. *Axis V:* highest level of adaptive functioning past year.

The use of multiaxial classification "ensures that attention is given to certain types of disorders, aspects of the environment, and the areas of functioning that might be overlooked if the focus were on assessing a single presenting problem" (American Psychiatric Association, 1980, p. 23).

Following hospitalization, aftercare must be provided to guard against relapse. This may include a referral to Alcoholics Anonymous, group therapy, individual therapy, social skill training, or other supportive measures depending on the client's profile. At any rate, the gradual transition from the skid row alcoholic subculture to mainstream society requires considerable social and emotional support.

REFERENCES

American Psychiatric Association. (1980). *Diagnostic and statistical manual of mental disorders* (3rd ed.). Washington, DC: American Psychiatric Association.

Archard, P. (1979). Drinking schools. In D. Robinson (Ed.), *Alcohol problems* (pp. 31–38). New York: MacMillan.

Bahr, H.M. (1967). The gradual disappearance of skid row. *Social Problems, 15,* 41–45.

Bendiner, E. (1962). Bowery man on the couch. In E. Josephson & M. Josephson (Eds.), *Man alone: Alienation and modern society* (pp. 401–410). New York: Dell.

Blumberg, L., Shipley, T.E., Jr., & Shandler, I.W. (1973). *Skid row and its alternatives: Research and recommendations from Philadelphia.* Philadelphia: Temple University Press.

Bogue, D.J. (1963). *Skid row in American cities.* Chicago: Community and Family Center of the University of Chicago.

Docter, R.F. (1967). Drinking practices of skid row alcoholics. *Quarterly Journal of Studies on Alcohol, 28,* 700–708.

Durkheim, E. (1979). The normal and the pathological. In D.H. Kelly (Ed.), *Deviant behavior* (pp 51–55). New York: St. Martin.

Fox, R. (1967). A multidisciplinary approach to the treatment of alcoholism. *American Journal of Psychiatry, 123,* 769–778.

French, L. (1986). Treatment considerations for the mentally retarded inmate. *Corrective and Social Psychiatry, 32,* 124–129.

Gammage, A.Z., Jorgensen, D.L., & Jorsensen, E.M. (1972). *Alcoholism, skid row and the police.* Springfield, IL: Charles C Thomas.

Graves, T.D. (1971). Drinking and drunkenness among urban Indians. In J. Waddell & O. Watson (Eds.), *The American Indian in urban society* (pp. 274–311). Boston: Little, Brown.

Hudson, R.M., & Rhodes, R.J. (1971). A follow-up study of tuberculous skid row alcoholics. *Quarterly Journal of Studies on Alcohol, 32,* 116–122.

Jackson, J.K., & Connor, R. (1953). The skid row alcoholic. *Quarterly Journal of Studies on Alcohol, 14,* 468–486.

Jellinek, E.M. (1960). *The disease concept of alcoholism.* New Haven, CT: United Printing.

Lawson, G., Peterson, J.S., & Lawson, A. (1983). *Alcoholism and the family.* Rockville, MD: Aspen.

Levinson, D. (1979). Changes in skid row life. In D. Robinson (Ed.), *Alcohol problems* (pp. 37–46). New York: MacMillan.

Malcolm, A.I. (1973). *The pursuit of intoxification.* New York: Pocket.

McSheehy, W. (1979). *Skid row.* Cambridge, MA: Schenkman.

Merton, R.K. (1957). *Social theory and social structure.* New York: Free.

Mowbray, C.T. (1985). Homelessness in America: Myths and realities. *American Journal of Orthopsychiatry, 55,* 4–8.

Peterson, J.W., & Maxwell, M.A. (1958). The skid row "wino." *Social Problems, 5,* 308–316.

Rooney, J.F. (1961). Group processes among skid row winos. *Quarterly Journal of Studies on Alcohol, 22,* 444–460.

Rubington, E. (1968). The bottle gang. *Quarterly Journal of Studies on Alcohol, 29,* 943–955.

Rubington, E. (1971). The changing skid row scene. *Quarterly Journal of Studies on Alcohol, 32,* 123–135.

Sagarin, E. (1979). Voluntary associations among social deviants. In D.H. Kelly (Ed.), *Deviant behavior* (pp. 448–463). New York: St. Martin.

Solenberger, A.W. (1911). *One thousand homeless men.* New York: Russell Sage Foundation.

Wallace, S.E. (1965). *Skid row as a way of life.* Totowa, NJ: Bedminster.

Young, T.J. (In press). Substance use and abuse among Native Americans. *Clinical Psychology Review.*

Young, T.J., & Lawson, G. (1984). AA referrals for alcohol related crimes: The advantages and limitations. *International Journal of Offender Therapy and Comparative Criminology, 28,* 131, 140.

Chapter 15

Chemical Dependency and Treatment of the Professional Athlete

Herbert Martin and Delia Thrasher

INTRODUCTION

This chapter provides an overview of one of the most pervasive problems affecting the modern day professional (pro) athlete: drug usage. While hard and reliable data regarding the amount and frequency of drug use among athletes have not been published, there is considerable controversy surrounding the causes, the consequences, and the approaches used to combat this problem.

This chapter examines the profile of the athlete, the drugs used, the reasons for use, and the physiological effects these drugs produce. The etiology of drug abuse in professional sports is explored from a sociological and psychological perspective, and various existing treatment and prevention models are discussed. Suggestions for future directions and approaches are outlined.

THE ATHLETE

This section examines the typical profile of the male pro athlete with particular emphasis on the pro football, basketball, and baseball player, as these athletes have been frequently associated with drug abuse and dominate the interest of the American public. Although this chapter focuses on male pro athletes, many of the issues raised are pertinent to female and amateur athletes as well. Women in sports unquestionably have specific concerns that may be related to substance abuse. Similarly, athletes at the high school, collegiate, national, and Olympic levels of competition experience circumstances that may lead to different trends in substance abuse than those for pro athletes. Clearly, these topics deserve attention in terms of treatment and prevention. As a large and influential group, male pro athletes were chosen for this discussion in the hope that a broad variety of concerns would be illuminated concerning the treatment and prevention of substance abuse problems for athletes in general.

Pro male athletes typically enter professional sports via college and have generally spent most of their earlier life involved in organized athletics. The average age of the athlete entering sports is 21, with the exception of the baseball player who may enter out of the minors a few years earlier. The career span for the pro athlete is 3 to 4 years, with baseball being the exception at 4 to 5 years. The median income reported for pro athletes is approximately $400,000 a year, with some players demanding as much as $2 million a year. The typical player is single and may reside in any part of the country (*Sport*, 1987).

In perhaps no other profession is the individual required to compete and function as competently and consistently, despite pain, physical injury, and pressure, than in pro sports. It is believed that every player who has participated in pro sports has faced these realities. Unfortunately, the tremendous pressures to perform at consistently optimal levels have frequently resulted in the use of drugs to maintain or improve performance. The "performance enhancement" drugs are used because many athletes believe they will give them the "competitive edge" over their opponents by increasing their endurance, level of energy, and strength. Some individuals also believe that these drugs will help reduce pain and will speed recovery from injury. Many athletes use these drugs to counter the numerous stressful areas in sports. Finally, many athletes use drugs for reasons other than performance enhancement, and it becomes difficult at times to distinguish between "recreational" use and use to improve performance.

The athlete reveals no specific genetic or biological predisposition to substance abuse. However, research has supported the contention that individuals raised in homes and families in which there is substance abuse or alcoholism will be at higher risk for developing alcohol or substance abuse problems themselves. In order to put these issues into perspective, it is important to examine some of the drugs used by athletes and their effects.

DRUGS AND SUBSTANCES USED BY ATHLETES

Psychomotor Stimulant Drugs

Amphetamines

Amphetamines are central nervous system (CNS) and cardiovascular stimulants and are classified as a pressor or sympathetic amine. They are chemically related to epinephrine or ephedrine but are greater CNS stimulants. Amphetamines stimulate activity of the post ganglionic and synaptic nerves and possibly stimulate andfacilitate synaptic transmission in the spinal cord (Kallant, 1958; Thompson & Shuster, 1968). As a CNS stimulant, amphetamines increase alertness, respiration rate, blood pressure, muscle tension, heart rate, and blood sugar and often induce an overall sense of physical well-being. These drugs also increase the production and release of dopamine and noradrenaline in parts of the brain known as "the limbic system." Amphetamines can increase the level of arousal and elevate one's mood by acting on the brain. They also increase the release of neurotransmitters in the part of the brain that initiates movement, thereby increasing motor activity.

Symptoms of large doses of amphetamines may include restlessness, agitation, nausea, rapid pulse, dilation of the pupils, cardiac arrythmia, anxiety, and amphetamine induced euphoria, alternating with periods of apathy and depression. In addition, large doses of amphetamines have been reported to produce symptoms similar to those seen in patients identified as paranoid schizophrenics. Some of the toxic symptoms, which are not necessarily related to overdosage, include dizziness, headaches, confusion, and possibly hormonal reactions resulting in the loss of libido and impotence. Amphetamines are highly addictive, and users are apt to develop a rapid tolerance to them. Unfortunately, this leads to withdrawal and may contribute to periods of severe depression.

There have been numerous studies to determine the effects of amphetamines on performance. One of the most widely known was conducted by Beecher and Smith in 1959. They suggested that administration of small doses of amphetamines to athletes (swimmers, runners, and weight throwers) would delay fatigue and improve performance. They found that this occurred when brief and explosive responses were needed. They concluded that although these improvements were minimal, athletes reported feeling better. In another study, Clark (1970) found that amphetamines may improve performance but only under special circumstances and at some risk to the athlete. More specifically, he found that use of amphetamines would sustain attention and that in order to improve performance reliably using amphetamines, three elements are necessary: (a) an exciting sustained attention to the task, (b) habituation to the task, and (c) habituation to the drug. Thus, the findings revealed that the athlete must not only guess the timing and dosage necessary for the desired performance effects but must also paradoxically risk deteriorated performance due to habituation to the drug.

In contrast to these findings, several studies revealed that the use of amphetamines provided little if any improvement in athletic performance. Golding's extensive study in 1963 on the use of amphetamines and athletic performance found no significant differences between athletes' mean and placebo times on all-out treadmill runs. His tests were given to fatigued as well as rested athletes to test the alleged endurance provided through the use of dextroamphetamine (a common form of the drug). During recovery following rested athletes' runs, d-amphetamine significantly retarded recovery for blood pressure but had no significant effect on heart rate. During the recovery period following the fatigued athletes' runs, d-amphetamine significantly retarded heart rate recovery and blood pressure recovery. Thus, administration had no significant effect on the all-out treadmill runs of either the conditioned or unconditioned athlete. Wyndham (1971), however, found that an athlete could exercise for an extended period of time by using as little as 10 mg of methamphetamine (Desoxyn). He found, however, that the amphetamines did not increase the athletes' capacity for aerobic exercise. He proposed that the drug's action enabled the athlete to tolerate acute discomfort, possibly becoming aware of the pain at a later time. Similarly, in a more recent study (Chandler & Blair, 1980) it was found that after administering small doses of Dexedrine to athletes, there was improvement in terms of endurance, knee strength, and acceleration. Although endurance was increased, no difference in sprinting speed was observed.

The studies on amphetamine use and athletic performance provide inconsistent findings, with the exception of the masking of fatigue. However, the fact remains that if an athlete believes the use of drugs will improve his performance, he may use the drug despite the consequences.

This point was well illustrated in the controversial book *The Nightmare Season* by Mandell (1976).

As a team psychiatrist for the San Diego Chargers, Mandell (1976) shocked the public and the pro sports world when he provided a personal account of the widespread use of amphetamines in pro football. Mandell was responsible for prescribing drugs to players for pain and injury and was banned by the National Football League (NFL) for allegedly overprescribing drugs to players (3 years after the NFL had banned the use of amphetamines). In a later paper, "The Sunday Syndrome," Mandell stated that amphetamines were used in three ways by the players: (a) only on game days for the induction of analgesia and rage (30 to 150 mg or more); (b) only on game days to increase speed and combat pain (5 to 30 mg), and (c) per day to aid speed (15 mg). He revealed that the drugs were typically used more by older players and those in defensive positions. He reported that players were more apt to use the drug because opponents may have done so. Although Mandell admitted writing large prescriptions, he claimed he was treating athletes with long-term addictions. He argued that this had occurred primarily because team trainers had routinely handed out amphetamines before games. He felt that by writing prescriptions he could protect athletes from turning to black market sources and thus could win their cooperation in a program of self-reform (Donahue & Johnsen, 1986). However, players continued to use the black market to obtain amphetamines and other drugs in order to maintain the competitive edge.

Cocaine

If amphetamine use in pro sports was the shock of the 1970s, then cocaine is the scourge of the 1980s. Countless articles on widespread drug use in pro sports have appeared, and the highly publicized deaths of collegiate star Len Bias and pro football player Don Rogers have rocked the nation. Considerable attention is now focused on understanding the nature of cocaine, its effects on the body, and the reasons for the widespread use by pro athletes.

Cocaine is an alkaloid derived from a deciduous shrub found in the Peruvian Andes, Bolivia, and Columbia. Each (3 to 5 ft plant/shrub tall) is steeped in kerosene, sulfuric acid, and alkali to produce a coca paste. The paste is 20% to 85% cocaine sulfate. With the addition of hydrochloric acid, cocaine sulfate becomes powdery flakes or rocks of nearly pure cocaine hydrochloride. At that point cocaine is a colorless or white crystalline powder, which is odorless.

Pharmacologically, cocaine acts as an anesthetic that blocks nerve conduction at the cellular membrane. It is a very powerful stimulant that is short-acting with a low margin of safety. The actions of this drug are related to the administration route (snorting, 1 to 3 min; eating, 30 min; shooting, 14 sec; and free-basing, 6 sec) as well as to the set and setting (Dourtey, 1984). Cocaine can be absorbed through any mucous membrane and is carried by the blood to the heart, the lungs, and the rest of the body. Cocaine is metabolized quickly by the blood and the lungs. Its chemical action on the sympathetic nervous system minimizes the body's fight or flight response to fear or challenge. CNS effects include dilation of pupils; elevation of pulse, blood pressure, temperature, and blood sugar; digestive slowing; hypothalamic stimulation (thirst, hunger, sexual arousal); and creation of symptoms of euphoria, agitation, restlessness, pacing, teeth grinding, sweating and vomiting, and disturbance of the heart regulatory center, causing fever and seizures (NIDA, 1984).

Cocaine effects are very similar to those of amphetamines and are characterized by the intense sequence of euphoria followed by depression and irritability. However, the euphoric effects of cocaine quickly taper off, resulting in physiological and psychological depression.

Effects of chronic cocaine use (as little as 3 g weekly via nasal inhalation) can induce blackouts, damage to the liver, and acute high blood pressure, which can cause blood vessels in the brain to rupture and cause a stroke. Heavy use can also cause angina and irregular heartbeats. It can worsen preexisting heart disease and bring on a heart attack. The individual is also plagued by an inability to concentrate, insomnia, fatigue, lack of sexual interest, or impotence when trying to perform. Some individuals experience panic attacks and become aggressive. Weight loss is common, as is the neglect of personal needs and activities such as bathing and eating. In addition, because many chronic users lose weight, users are prone to malnutrition. This can lower immune defenses and make the user susceptible to fungal disease, tuberculosis, and infections. These problems are often compounded by lack of sleep and neglect of personal hygiene. Unfortunately, the more cocaine is used, the more pronounced the symptoms will be.

In addition, the more cocaine is consumed the more likely it is that a pattern of uncontrolled use will occur. Animal research in monkeys showed that monkeys given a choice between food and cocaine preferred cocaine and may have died without investigator intervention. Such research suggests that a physiological basis for cocaine dependence may be rooted in its strength as a reinforcer. This may explain why some people, especially those with constant access to the drug, may become compulsive users despite adverse consequences.

Compulsive users of cocaine are almost certain to develop a psychological dependency. Direct methods of use, such as smoking (free-basing) and intravenous injection, are strongly linked with the obsessive behavior associated with psychological addiction. Habitual users are also certain to develop a physical tolerance for the drug. Thus the user will often increase the dose or frequency in order to obtain an intense high. It has been reported that the individual can never obtain a high like the first one. While users may develop a tolerance for the cocaine high, they do not develop a tolerance for the cardiovascular actions of the drug. This overstimulation of the cardiovascular system can cause sudden death from cardiac standstill. CNS overstimulation may also lead to violent and fatal seizures.

The effects of cocaine on performance are very similar to those of amphetamines and include euphoria, hastened reflexes (particularly during exhaustive events), an increased endurance capacity, and an alteration in perceived reality (IOC, 1984). Probably the most striking characteristic of cocaine use is related to the extreme increase in confidence and the resulting belief that performance can undoubtedly be improved by using this drug. However, in contrast to amphetamines, the addictive qualities of cocaine may result in such a total absorption in obtaining the drug that athletes may lose interest in the sport. Thus, the athlete becomes less competitive and motivated. As mentioned before, there can often be a tendency to neglect physical health. The athlete may become increasingly out of shape, often resulting in as much as a 25% to 30% drop in physical fitness (Collings, 1986). The physical demands of a long and enduring season figure prominently in amphetamine and cocaine use as pro athletes try to maintain consistent levels of performance throughout the season.

While widespread cocaine and amphetamine use in pro sports has been well documented, the use of anabolic steroids among athletes has recently emerged as another means of gaining the competitive edge.

Anabolic Steroids

Anabolic steroids are derivatives of testosterone that were developed in an attempt to disassociate adrogenic (growth/maintenance of primary characteristics) and anabolic (tissue building) effects so that only the anabolic effects were maintained and the androgenic effects were minimized (Goodman & Gillman, 1975). Anabolic steroids have been acceptably used in medicine to treat certain types of anemia, and they have been useful in stimulating sexual development in hypogonadal men (Goodman & Gillman, 1975).

Anabolic steroids were reportedly used during World War II when they were given to German troops to increase aggressiveness (Wade, 1972). Their first use in athletics was in 1954, and in the late 1950s, studies were conducted on American athletes (Wade, 1972). Initially these studies were focused on weight lifters or disc throwers; however, usage spread to football players and other track and field participants.

Today an estimated 1 million athletes use steroids, apparently to maintain or improve performance (Taylor, 1985). In order to comprehend this phenomenon fully, one must understand that athletes use steroids because they believe their use will result in increased muscle size and strength. While it has been established that anabolic steroids result in an increase in both total and lean body mass in animals, there has been controversy surrounding gains in strength. Haupt and Rover (1984) reported in a review of the literature that the use of anabolic steroids will result in increased strength when athletes engage in intensive weight training prior to a steroid regimen and then continue to use weights while taking steroids.

Anabolic steroids have been reported to produce potentially harmful side effects including liver damage and liver cancer, endocrine abnormalities (such as decreased plasma testosterone, decreased luteinizing hormone, and atrophy of the testes), decreased libido, acne, salt retention, and stunting of bone growth in children. Anabolic steroids in large doses and with prolonged use produce puffiness in the face and trunk and, possibly, cardiovascular disease. In addition, the androgenic effects of steroids can contribute to aggressive behavior by the individual.

The use of steroids to provide gains in strength and muscle is desirable in a sport such a pro football, and increased aggression is viewed as beneficial as well. For this reason it is not surprising that many pro football players have used steroids during competition. In fact, a report in *Sports Illustrated* (1985) suggested that 95% of pro football players have tried anabolic steroids at some time and that 75% are regular users. While these estimates appear high, the fact remains that players believe steroids will enhance performance. This frightening reality, despite the constant reports of the hazards associated with use, typify what the athlete will do to maintain the competitive edge.

While some athletes may turn to drugs to enhance performance, there are probably some who use drugs to help them deal with the stress, pain, and injury that are inherent in pro sports.

Alcohol

The physiological and psychological demands placed on the athlete are enormous. The constant pressure to complete and achieve despite adversity often results inextreme anxiety for the athlete. To overcome these obstacles, the athlete must learn to relax. For many, however, this means resorting to drugs. The most accessible and commonly used drug is alcohol. Alcohol is a CNS depressant, which may be also used to counteract the effects of other drugs. Some of the physiological effects of excessive alcohol intake include nausea, dehydration, headaches, amnesia, impotence, and depression. Alcohol is highly addictive and as tolerance develops, the user may become both physically and psychologically addicted (Donahue & Johnson, 1986). However, alcohol in moderation can be used to diminish fatigue or worry and generally has a sedating effect. The effects of alcohol on performance reveal that use can impair motor coordination and reaction time. Excessive intake can have a deleterious effect on the athlete who participates in sports that require precise and quick body movements (football, basketball, and baseball). Yet despite the well-documented problems associated with drinking, alcohol remains interwoven with sports.

It appears, then, that alcohol can have many effects on athletic performance. For example, moderate amounts can minimize or alleviate worry. However, alcohol can also impair skills that are dependent on fine motor judgment, motor coordination, and reaction time. Thus, in sports like baseball, basketball, and football, heavy use can be extremely counterproductive. Despite these effects on performance, the use of alcohol in pro sports continues and appears to be a complicated issue. Perhaps this is true because players have not learned adaptive ways to deal with stress and anxiety, or perhaps alcohol is used because a player believes it will aid his performance, or it could be used because "all great athletes" have been associated with drinking (as evidenced by all the advertising campaigns promoting the use of alcohol). Obviously, there is no one answer to this complex problem.

Pain Killers

In many ways the phrase "no pain, no gain" symbolizes the experiences and expectations of the pro athlete. This is particularly true today when the stakes are higher. The players are more competitive and the training is more demanding. In fact, it is not uncommon to hear that a player is competing despite being in severe pain. So what can a player do when the pain becomes so severe that he is unable to continue? Simply ask the trainer or team physician for a pain killer or analgesic to alleviate the discomfort? Unfortunately, this may often be the case, and it becomes even more serious when the athlete takes things into his own hands. To understand this clearly, it is important to examine some of the common pain killers used and their specific effects (see Exhibit 15-1).

For example, local anesthetics such as Novocain, Xylocaine, and Marcaine are often used prior to game times. These drugs are generally ingested and have prolonged effects. However, they have also been reported to cause cardiac disorders and should not be used during games (IOC, 1984). In fact, large doses of these drugs have been reported to cause overstimulation of the CNS, convulsions, and even death (Gardiner, 1983).

Another group of substances known as anti-inflammatory drugs act to reduce the aches, pain, and inflammation that are associated with tissue damage. These drugs include Indorin, naproxen, Tandearil, Butazolidin ("bute"), and the most commonly used anti-inflammatory agent: aspirin. "Bute" (Butazolidin) is the most commonly abused drug by athletes in this category. The unfortunate side effects of the prolonged use of these drugs (with the exception of aspirin) are gastrointestinal problems including ulceration of the intestine and stomach, diarrhea, headaches, dizziness, and disorientation.

Drugs that act by suppressing the inflammatory response to tissue injury are corticosteroids. These drugs are typically delivered precisely to the

Exhibit 15-1 Prohibited Drugs

The International Olympic Committee has developed a list of drugs and substances that athletes are prohibited from using. Although these well-established guidelines have not been fully adopted by pro teams, they have been reported to be used as models.

Psychomotor Stimulant Drugs
Amphetamine
Benzphetamine
Chlorpheniramine
Cocaine
Diethylpropion
Dimethylamphetamine
Ethylamphetamine
Fencamfamin
Meclofenoxate
Methamphetamine
Methylphenidate
Norpseudoephedrine
Pemoline
Phendimetrazine
Phenmetrazine
Phentermine
Pipradrol
Prolintane
And related compounds
Sympathomimetic Amines
Chlorprenaline
Ephedrine
Estafedreine
Isoetharine
Isoprenaline
Methoxyphenamine
Methylephedrine
And related compunds
Miscellaneous Central Nervous System Stimulants
Amiphenazole
Bemegride
Caffeine[1]
Crolethamide[2]
Cropropamide[2]
Doxapram
Ethamivan
Leptazol
Nikethamide
Picrotoxin
Strychnine
And related compounds

Narcotic Analgesics
Anileridine
Codeine
Dextroaoriamide
Dihydrocodeine
Dipipanone
Ethylmorphine
Heroin
Hydrocodone
Hydromorphone
Levorphanol
Methadone
Morphine
Oxycodone
Oxymorphone
Pentazocine
Pethidine
Phenazocine
Piminodine
Thebacon
Trimeperidine
And related compounds
Anabolic Steroids
Clostebol
Dehydrochlormethyltestosterone
Fluoxymesterone
Mesterolone
Methenolone
Methandienone
Methyltestosterone
Nandrolone
Norethandrolone
Oxymesterone
Oxymetholone
Stanozolol
Testosterone[1]
And related compounds

Exhibit 15-1 continued

> [1]The definition of positive depends on the following: for caffeine, if the concentration in urine exceeds 15 μg/ml; for testosterone, if the ratio of the total concentration of testosterone to that of epitestosterone in the urine exceeds 6.
> [2]Components of Micoren.

injured area by injection into a joint with a local anesthetic. Corticosteroids (cortisone) are reported to be used frequently by pro basketball and football players and can produce feelings of well-being and euphoria in addition to relief of pain. However, prolonged use of these drugs can result in serious side effects including cardiovascular problems, infections, and even psychotic reactions.

In addition to the anti-inflammatory drugs, narcotic analgesics are used in the treatment of pain. The term *narcotic analgesic* refers to a group of substances that includes various alkaloids as well as a number of synthetic drugs. The prototypic drug for this group, morphine, produces a narcotic action characterized by analgesia, sedation, mood changes, and decreased mental activity. Individuals given morphine for analgesia experience either a disappearance or lessening of pain. Drowsiness is a common effect of morphine, but because much safer drugs are used for sedatives, morphine is not used for its sedative effects. Other effects of morphine may include poor motor coordination, depressed respiration, lethargy, and loss of appetite. Morphine may also produce agitation in the individual, particularly when given to an individual not experiencing pain. Occasional nausea and vomiting may occur. Some individuals using morphine may experience euphoria, an effect that is more commonly associated with a related compound: heroin. Heroin is a much more powerful drug than morphine, and while it was originally developed to treat severe pain, it is no longer used medically. Chronic use of these drugs can result in permanent injury or death, as the player will not experience the pain signals to warn him to slow down.

It appears, then, that the pro athlete uses drugs in sports for a variety of reasons, and it is obvious that there are many problems that can result. To compound these problems, players often have difficulty determining the boundaries between performance enhancement and recreation. For example, a player may start off by using amphetamines to help him fight fatigue before or during a game. Next, he may increase his use or dose to "get up" for the following game. Suddenly, the player cannot function at home or on the field without the use of the drug. Problems like these become increasingly more serious with drugs like cocaine because of its extremely addictive properties. In addition to these issues there are many sociological and psychological factors that also contribute to (and result from) the athlete's use of drugs.

SOCIOLOGICAL FACTORS CONTRIBUTING TO DRUG ABUSE IN PRO SPORTS

This section focuses on the sociological factors that may be associated with a high risk for drug abuse by athletes. In order to begin this examination, it is important to understand the interdependency of sports and society.

Pro sports in America in many ways embody the idealized conceptions of the traditions, virtues, values, and practices of the larger society. Competitiveness, achievement, authority, and social competence are but a few of the ideals that link sports and society. However, sports also mirror the tensions, anxieties, and problems of society. Poor interpersonal relationships, violence and aggression, failure and dismay, exploitation, racism, cheating, and the unethical behaviors often observed in pro sports reflect the disorganization patterns of society.

Social Disorganization in Sports

Elliot and Merrill defined social disorganization as social structures or processes that are engaged in by many over considerable lengths of time and that are dysfunctional with regard to meeting the goals of the individual members. Social disorganization results from one or more of four preconditions (Merton & Nisbet, 1966). First, disorganization may be the effect of faulty communication, e.g., flaws in the communication channels or networks in a social system. A second source of disorganization occurs when various status groups and social strata have values and interests that are both different and incompatible. The third source of disorganization is insufficient or defective socialization: inadequacies in the structures or processes through which one learns values, skills, attitudes, and behaviors associated with social roles. The fourth source of disorganization arises from the inevitability that people will occupy multiple status to the extent that they experience status inconsistency. Within this framework, Rosenberg's (1980) preliminary examination of disorganization in sports suggests that this phenomenon will inevitably take place during the career and post career of the pro athlete.

The old saying that "great athletes are born and not made" paradoxically describes a phenomenon that occurs long before the individual can participate in sports. This is particularly true in American society where fathers will often purchase bats and ball for their little boys long before they reach the first grade. However, in reality, it generally takes considerable time, training, and preparation to become an athlete. This usually begins in elementary school, where little boys compete for the first time in organized athletics. These early experiences are designed to encourage a competitive spirit, teamwork, and unity among one's fellow man. However, during this process children often learn that aggression and violence are accepted and that there are really no alternatives to winning. More important, the fragile self-concept of these children often become intricately interwoven with their success and failure in sport. Thus, the rewards and guidance of the parent and coach have a tremendous impact on the child during his introduction to organized athletics.

Those children who excel early in sports typically pursue high school athletics. During this period, the athlete is not only applauded by his parents but by his peers also. This becomes a very important part of the adolescent's identity: the need to belong and be accepted and a feeling of being in control in a world that he generally feels out of control in. Quite often, the rewards of athletic participation begin to take precedence over the demands of school, as the adolescent may begin to feel that those rewards outweigh academic responsibility and even school rules. In addition, if an athlete reveals considerable promise, he may receive local media attention and perhaps become the focus of college coaches. For many, this may represent their only avenue into college. This is certainly true today as the cost of college tuition may prohibit the average student's attendance at a major university. It is apparent that many of these student athletes are often ill prepared to meet the rigors of college.

When one examines the disorganizational elements, it is important to keep in mind that the disorganization is from the perspective of the athlete. There are several of these elements that are of particular importance to the child/adolescent athlete. First, when a child enters sports, he generally does so because he wants to have fun and wants to be with his friends. There is no particular emphasis on winning or losing. This abruptly changes when the child participates in organized athletics. Unfortunately, it is rare that parents put winning into the proper perspective (faulty communication), and thus the child may equate his failure in sports with a sense of self. This occurs in part because many parents vicariously try to meet their own needs of competency (various status groups may have interests that are incompatible) through their children. Second, adolescence is often characterized by the intense search for one's identity. Sports participation can certainly facilitate this process and enhance the self-esteem of the individual. This can prove to be problematic, however, for the "gifted athlete" who may have difficulty understanding the boundaries between his real and imagined power (defective socialization). This is often evidenced by an individual defying certain rules and regulations in school and at home (multiple status) and his being absolved from wrong doing because of his athletic status. Finally, given the demands of practice and training, the athlete may lag behind his peers socially and academically (defective socialization and values and interests that are incompatible). Many of the latter issues continue on into college, as the student athlete may begin to ponder a "career" in sports.

The standard high school athlete is typically a highly recruited individual who must choose a college to meet his athletic and academic needs. For many individuals, however, this may never take place. Thus, there has been considerable controversy and concern regarding the eligibility of student athletes who are unable to meet the demands of college. This is particularly true of the black athlete who may reveal considerable athletic promise but is disproportionately deficient in academic skills. This disparity is often a result of a lack of creditable academic expectations and standards and the disportionate emphasis placed on the development of athletic talents since early childhood (Edwards, 1984).

Edwards (1984) found that an estimated 25% to 35% of black high school athletes qualifying for scholarships on athletic grounds could not accept those scholarships because of accumulated high school deficiencies. Yet, many of these black athletes are accepted into college solely on the basis of their athletic ability despite their marginal academic skills. The tragedy of this situation is evidenced by the studies that indicate that as many as 65% to 75% of those black athletes awarded college athletic scholarships never graduate from college.

In addition to academic demands, many student-athletes experience difficulty adjusting to the social demands of college. This may include developing and maintaining relationships with other students, teammates, and coaches. For many college athletes this proves to be quite stressful, as many of these students may have had quite different backgrounds (e.g., culturally and ethnically). Thus, many of these individuals may not have had an opportunity to interact with such a diverse group of people. Quite often this results in a further emphasis on athletic training, and the richness of college may often be missed. Despite this "goal directed" behavior, only 8% of the draft-eligible in basketball, football, and baseball are actually drafted by pro teams each year.

The major disorganizational elements in sports revolve around the issues of students trying to balance the demands of college and of athletics (status conflict and conflict of values and interest) and social adjustment within a large cultural and ethnic milieu (conflicts of values and interests and defective socialization). The institutional goals associated with running a smooth and efficient business operation may conflict with the interests of the athlete (conflicts of interest).

The draft of "judgment day" represents that moment in time that will often reshape the direction of a young athlete's life. For those drafted, this generally results in a number of adjustments that can have a tremendous impact on the individual. These include: immediate and substantial wealth, greater visibility, increased expectations, relationship issues, and transition and career termination issues. Pro athletes are among the highest paid individuals in America. A recent survey (*Sport,* 1987) revealed that the average player salary for the NFL, National Basketball Association (NBA), and the National League was $400,000, $450,000, and $450,000, respectively. For most players entering the league this represents an enormous change in life style. New places to go, new friends, and the ability to buy just about anything one wants at any time are among some of the issues that face the young athlete. This new "status" is not without its problems, however, as players often have difficulty managing or deciding what to do with their money. This is particularly true for the athlete who has had to defer immediate gratification all of his life.

In addition, those athletes from disadvantaged socioeconomic backgrounds often have a heightened sense of responsibility toward their families. Hence, finding a balance between meeting one's own needs and meeting the needs of others can create additional pressure for the athlete. The pro athlete is also one of the most highly visible individuals in our society. His actions on and off the field are magnified and are often under constant scrutiny. Therefore, being in the public eye subjects the athlete to biased evaluation and perhaps unrealistic expectations of idealized standards. These standards are further imposed because athletes are expected to be role models for our society. Sanctions on the behavior of the athlete often result in his retreat into a world isolated from the larger society. Therefore, it is not uncommon to observe athletes frequently engaged together as reciprocal sources of support, further alienating themselves from the unscrupulous demands of the public.

The pro athlete, much like his college counterpart, must form a new series of relationships, e.g., team players, coaches, and management. However, there are some distinct differences that deserve discussion.

First, when players' social contact with each other is examined, changes and patterns in these relationships resulting from the transient nature of pro sports are revealed. For example, it is not uncommon that a pro player is traded during his brief tenure in sports (3 to 4 years). This undoubtedly makes forming and maintaining relationships difficult. There may also be a greater degree of competitiveness, resentment, and distrust among team players because of the high stakes involved. Therefore, group cohesion for the pro athlete and college athlete may be functionally the same, but systematically different.

While college institutions are rarely defined as businesses, the pro franchise can be clearly identified as one of the more successful and profitable organizations/businesses in the country. This reality is often a source of confusion, resentment, and misunderstanding among pro athletes. The apparent conflicts that occur in this relationship may involve contract disputes, salary negotiations, and even trade issues. Thus, in a relationship that must exist by design, there are problems that can have a tremendous effect on the life of a player and possibly his subsequent performance.

Yet, for some players, conflict may not occur until the day of retirement. Imposed or self-imposed career termination probably represents one of the most traumatic experiences for the pro athlete. The decline in status, social contact, and income can all have a deleterious effect on the individual. These problems are generally compounded by the residual effects of inadequate educational training, and for the average pro athlete, this means starting all over with little or no viable working skills.

The issue of racism in sports has been a long-debated topic and has recently reached the forefront of national concern. This has occurred primaily as a result of the growing numbers of minorities, specifically blacks, who dominate pro sports such as football and basketball. Yet, despite the preponderance of numbers, there are very few minorities or blacks represented in governing or managerial positions in their respective sports. It is for perhaps this reason that the commissioner of the NFL, Pete Rozelle, stated that he would like to see a black coach directing a team by 1990. Interestingly, at the time of this statement, and despite the fact that approximately 57% of pro players are black, there was only one starting black quarterback among the entire roster of 28 teams of the NFL.

There are many reasons these situations exist, and perhaps one of the fundamental issues revolves around the belief that blacks are naturally endowed ("gifted") with superior athletic skills that enable them to function more effectively than their white counterparts in sports that require speed, quickness, and agility. Unfortunately, this line of thinking has reinforced the notion of black athletic superiority and intellectual inferiority. Thus, for many black players, feelings of inferiority and inadequacy are recapitulated and reinforced as the result of racism in sports. Paradoxically, this occurs when many players entering the world of pro sports are seeking refuge from the realities of the outside world. However, their subsequent denial of these issues often contributes to their use of drugs.

Each of the sources of social disorganization affect the pro athlete. First, for the rookie and the seasoned veteran who are always vulnerable to trade, there are constant personal adjustments to new players, coaches, and management that may create stress (defective socialization and conflicts of interest). Second, pro athletes receive large salaries, which often propel them into social situations and experiences that can be very anxiety-provoking (inadequate socialization and multiple status). Those players who receive large sums of money may have increased feelings of responsibility, thus creating a situation in which players must decide what they should give to family members (conflict of interest). Each player is also under constant pressure to conform to the expectations of society, regardless of his personal life (multiple status and conflict of interests), which can result in a retreat into one's own world to minimize the external pressures of the public (defective socialization). Career termination is a period in which an athlete must reevaluate his marketable skills in order to become a viable working individual within the society (defective socialization). Finally, racism in sports may serve to perpetuate existing disorganizational patterns within the society and contribute to the maladjustment of the athlete.

PSYCHOLOGICAL FACTORS THAT CONTRIBUTE TO SUBSTANCE ABUSE IN SPORTS

The pro athlete is basically reared and functions in a world faced with the same psychological issues and concerns as the rest of humanity. However, there are social disorganizational elements that may place a particular burden on the athlete. Thus, the athlete's view of the world and his reaction to that world are mediated by psychological factors that are specific to the athlete and the athletic experience and therefore should be considered in the treatment of the individual. The authors have identified four factors that are believed to have a major influence on the behavior of the player and his potential for substance abuse: identity and self-image issues, fear of winning and losing, aggression, and relationship issues.

For many pro athletes, sports is a way of life. From the first time the child athlete participates in organized sports until long after he hangs up his jersey, he is an athlete. This unique life experience may be markedly different from the experience of his peers and generally has a tremendous impact on the social and psychological development of the individual. Therefore, it is not uncommon for the athlete to be rewarded and valued by others on the sole basis of his athletic ability. Unfortunately, the athlete may view this as the only thing he has to offer. Thus, the success and failure of the athlete take on great importance to the individual. If he fails, the rewards (social and monetary) may cease to exist, and if he succeeds, he is expected to do so always. This undoubtedly causes conflict for the injured or aging athlete who must slow down. Therefore, it is not uncommon to observe players resorting to just about anything to maintain a high level of perceived or real competency. The former issues are also of particular importance to the retiring athlete who will no longer receive the rewards and recognition associated with his previous athletic status. Thus, this individual must often redefine his life emotionally, economically, and socially. The interrelationship of these issues can also be examined from the perspective of the fears that pervade the life experience of the athlete.

Fear and anxiety are experiences that are not only common but are necessary for human existence. The athlete is particularly vulnerable to these experiences as his behavior is constantly being scrutinized in terms of his performance. In order to understand this phenomenon more clearly, it is important to examine some of the common fears of the athlete relating to diminished self-esteem. These include fears associated with winning and losing, the adequacy of performance, fear about the physiological condition of one's body, and the consequences of aggressive behavior. In a society that places so much value on the idea of winning, it is not unexpected that players fear losing. Losing may reflect a player's feeling of inadequacy, and in a practical sense, losing may have a direct bearing on whether an athlete will play or be traded during the following season, which serves to heighten feelings of inadequacy. However, some athletes may be afraid of winning, and this can certainly create a complex situation for the individual as well as his coach. This situation may result when the player feels that a team or coach requires more and more from him and may also occur when opposing teams and players become increasingly more challenging because of his previous successes. Perhaps this is one of the reasons teams are rarely back-to-back champions.

Other fears related to impaired self-esteem are associated with physical functioning. Most athletes are concerned about their bodies: its functioning and durability. It becomes obvious that these are necessary ingredients of athletic performance. However, in most athletic endeavors there is always a risk of injury. These injuries can often result in a temporary departure from competition, or they can often end the career of a player. Thus there may be considerable preoccupation in self-protection from injury and pain. Unfortunately, a false sense of invulnerability may occur when a player takes drugs to diminish the real pain that results from injury.

Some athletes may also experience fear associated with aggression. This may involve their aggression directed toward another player or aggression directed toward a team. Although strong sanctions against aggression and violence exist, violence is often encouraged in sports. Individual beliefs differ widely regarding the nature and extent of acceptable aggression in sports. Consequences of aggressive behavior are also continually in question.

The pro athlete is often in a unique position to meet many people throughout his career. Some of these contacts can be made through sports networks or even socially, as athletes rarely escape the public eye. However, for the typical athlete, establishing and maintaining these contacts and relationships may prove to be difficult. There are several reasons for this, including the realities of scheduling. For example, for the NBA player who plays 88 games per season, it is not uncommon that he could be in one city one night and in another part of the country the next. Thus, the nature of pro sports necessitates that players be on the road for perhaps weeks at a time, making it extremely difficult for the athlete to maintain constant contact with his family and loved ones. Therefore, it appears that the athlete would be particularly susceptible to tensions resulting from these separations from family and important others. In addition, pro athletes are often subjected to all kinds of advances from fans, and this too can create tension in their relationships. Finally, the pro athlete may have difficulty differentiating between those interested in him as a person and those interested in him only as an athlete. This undoubtedly can make it difficult for the athlete who is trying to develop real and meaningful relationships.

The relationship between management and the pro athlete is a very intriguing one. In this relationship, as in any business relationship, players are expected to perform tasks on the basis of contractual agreements. However, when this relationship between pro players and management is examined closely, it can be likened to the structure of the family, with many of the same dynamics, issues, and conflicts. For example, during player contract negotiations there is typically a fight for control, e.g., how much am I going to give vs. how much I think I deserve (parent-child). Another example may reflect the issue of when players fail to meet management's expectations and the resulting consequences (punishment-limits). Perhaps one of the more potentially frightening aspects of the control issue results from the individual (child) using control to gain control. For example, the player's use of drugs could be interpreted as a vehicle to control management (adolescent rebellion). Thus, some of these issues recapitulate dysfunctional family systems that induce and maintain substance abuse. Denial of conflict and the severity of the drug/alcohol problem between parents and children can be compared with the previous denial and/or minimization of substance issues by coaches and management.

TREATMENT APPROACHES FOR ATHLETES

Drug abuse among athletes is clearly a serious and complicated matter. Involvement in pro sports creates specific physical, social, and psychological concerns that must be addressed when considering the etiology of drug abuse in athletes. Increased understanding of these issues is crucial, especially in the development of effective treatment approaches for pro athletes.

It may be argued that some of the same factors that contribute to or exacerbate drug abuse in athletes also provide formidable obstacles to prevention and treatment. While such physical demands of pro sports as long hours of rigorous training, extensive traveling, and pressure to perform consistently can contribute to drug use, they can also make standard treatment efforts difficult if not impossible. Traditional treatment methods such as inpatient hospitalization, psychotherapy, and self-help groups are simply not compatible with the monumental demands of pro sports without posing a major career disruption. Similarly, the high public profile of pro athletes often deters them from seeking treatment. Issues of privacy and confidentiality become magnified, and players seeking rehabilitation face strong public reaction. For example, a star basketball player requiring inpatient hospitalization must deal not only with the media attention but also with responses from fellow patients. The idealization of athletes and the resulting elevation of self-esteem can also contribute to a strong reluctance to seek help. The perception of competitive athletes as strong and powerful contradicts the need to seek external help for drug problems.

Athletes often receive insidious encouragement for drug abuse in the sports environment itself. Pressure by peers to use drugs to improve performance or for recreational purposes also makes it difficult to confront the negative aspects of drug use. Drug use prescribed by team physicians for the purpose of maintaining performance despite pain and injury unconsciously sanctions drug abuse in the interest of competition. Until relatively recently, pro management maintained a rather hands-off approach to drug use among athletes; i.e., unless a player was unable to perform, drug abuse was not a management concern. In addition, attempts to regulate and treat drug use are plagued by inconsistencies. Different sports and the organizations within them have a wide variety of policies and procedures designed to combat drug abuse. Consequences for drug use vary from mild to severe, depending on the team or program in question and perhaps even on the value of the individual player. Great controversy has recently been focused on drug testing and the ethical and economic implications involved. (Readers interested in further information on drug testing are referred to Rovere, Haupt, and Yates, 1986.)

Drug abuse treatment is often conceptualized at the levels of primary, secondary, and tertiary prevention. Understanding each of these and its application to athletes can be extremely useful in the development and assessment of treatment effectiveness. Primary prevention is aimed at preventing drug use that is harmful to the individual and/or society. Generally, primary prevention models focus on information about the dangers of substance use and may take an educative or moralistic stance. Primary models are implemented prior to abuse and include policy measures, customs, values, and mores. Alternative activities to drug use may be explored and resources developed. Individuals at high risk and contributing risk factors are identified and modified wherever possible (Lawson, 1983). Identified factors include the physiological, sociological, and psychological concerns discussed earlier. Adequate prevention components for athletes must involve all these aspects. Generalized drug education does not address the perceived benefits and negative consequences of drugs on sport performance, which is the core of the matter for athletes. A myriad of factors can predispose athletes to drug abuse, and these factors must be attended to as prevention issues.

Secondary prevention is generally considered to involve early identification of use and the provision of intervention to halt more serious long-term problems. As a result of controversy regarding what constitutes use vs. abuse (especially regarding alcohol), there is considerable blurring between primary and secondary prevention. Tertiary prevention is more clear-cut, however, and involves the treatment of more serious cases and hospitalization and/or detoxification.

Successful efforts at combating drug use in the world of pro sports must include provisions for all three levels of prevention. Existing programs at the pro level approach prevention and treatment in a variety of ways. A brief examination of three programs highlights the crucial issues discussed in this section.

NBA Program

In September, 1983, the NBA and the National Basketball Player's Association set forth an antidrug program. It contains policies for drug seminars and treatment and penalties for drug policy violators. The prevention component consists of requiring all players to attend two specific drug seminars throughout the year. Rookies must attend an additional preseason seminar dealing with the potential problems facing the pro athlete. The rationale for this is that involved problems (e.g., travel, losing games) might lead to drug abuse. Aspects of treatment are also set forth in the NBA program. The first time a player voluntarily requests help, he is referred to treatment at team expense, no penalty is imposed, and he continues to receive his paycheck. Treatment consists of referral and involvement in a California-based hospital program with specified aftercare conditions. The second time a player voluntarily seeks help, the provisions are the same, but pay is suspended. Any subsequent illegal drug use, even if voluntarily disclosed, will result in immediate dismissal from the NBA. Players may appeal for reinstatement after 2 years. The program also contains provisions for drug testing under certain conditions and outlines predetermined penalties for drug use (NBA, 1983).

The NBA program model has certain advantages, including a written league-wide policy agreement between the association and players. However, primary prevention appears cursory, and treatment is separated from the team milieu in which it occurred. Active work on underlying ethnic, social, and psychological considerations is minimal, and there is little mention of the family involvement of players. Programs such as those developed by the Hazelden Foundation and the Cleveland Clinic Foundation appear more comprehensive in scope.

NFL Program

The NFL's drug abuse program is overseen by the Hazelden Foundation in Minnesota. The multifaceted program began in 1982 and is well respected for its emphasis on confidentiality regarding the media and legal authorities. The primary prevention components include drug education for coaches and players and seminars on attitudes concerning drug use. Program referral includes an initial assessment of medical, psychological, personal, and familial aspects of use and a 28-day inpatient program. Although the program initially focused on players as individuals rather than as athletes, in 1985, Hazelden demonstrated increased consciousness of sport influences. A $7 million sports education training center was developed that involves in-depth educational programming and on site athletic training facilities (Moore, 1983; "Operation Cork," 1984). Although it is far more extensive than the NBA program, the Hazelden program also treats athletes with drug problems separately from the team environment.

Cleveland Clinic Program

The Cleveland Clinic Foundation has developed a comprehensive drug abuse program for a professional football team through a cooperative effort by the team's management and a psychiatrist/substance abuse specialist. This program, as described in 1984 by Collins, Pippinger, and Janesz, considers a number of factors to be related to drug abuse. These include developmental immaturity, an unhealthy environment, idle time, isolation, a high income, overreliance on athletic talent, and minimal accountability.

The involvement of all team components is aimed at mobilizing resources and commitment to deal with the complexity of drug-abusing athletes. These "links in the chain" include the owner, coaches, the team physician, a drug specialist, prevention education, a rehabilitation center, group therapy (known as "The Inner Circle," a specialized self-help group for drug-using players), employee assistance counseling, administrative assistants, therapeutic urine monitoring, a spiritual guidance program, security personnel, and a family program. Clearly, the crucial aspects of this team-oriented program are the awareness of the tremendous scope of drug problems and the willingness to address all available resources for support and change. Reportedly, the Cleveland Clinic program has led to significant improvement in 75% of cases over an 18-month period and improvement in playing ability for all participants. This model thoroughly develops the primary, secondary, and tertiary elements of treatment (Collins et al., 1984).

All three of the models discussed attempted to integrate primary prevention strategies with treatment. Indisputably, prevention is a complex area, yet it can and should be the first thrust of defense against drug abuse. Enhanced prevention efforts can be accomplished through improved agreement and interaction. A recommendation to facilitate this might be widespread efforts by pro leagues in all sports to hire athletes (as part of the regular playing contract) to educate student athletes at all levels about the realities of life in pro sports. For example, in such an agreement a player's contract for 5 years at $100,000 per year would be extended for several years at a lower rate of pay. This might mean a 9-year contract at $75,000 per year. The benefits of this to the player would include deferred tax and income as well as extended employment (under contact despite injuries that might otherwise shorten his athletic career).

The rationale of such an approach is threefold. First it would provide first-hand information to student athletes, a preventative measure, and heightened awareness for all athletes. Second, it could increase player utility and provide increased job security. Stress related to career termination and overemphasis on athletic performance could also be diminished in this manner. Third, this type of effort would foster joint responsibility for fighting drug abuse because it would involve the entire organization. It could also strengthen the relationship between players and management and thereby benefit overall performance. This type of approach could be implemented in conjunction with existing treatment and rehabilitation efforts.

SUMMARY

Drug abuse among athletes is a pervasive and difficult problem involving a wide variety of elements. These include physiological, sociological, and psychological aspects, as well as demands and pressures inherent in pro competition. A clear and thorough understanding of these factors is necessary for the development of successful programs aimed at prevention and treatment of substance abuse in pro athletes.

REFERENCES

Adams, E. & Durrell, J. (1984). *Cocaine: Pharmacology, effects, and treatment of drug abuse.* National Institute on Drug Abuse, Research Monograph Series, *50.*

Beecher, H., and Smith, G. (1959). Amphetamine sulfate and athletic performance. *Journal of the American Medical Association, 170,* 542–547.

Chandler, J., & Blair, S. (1980). *Medical Sciences in Sports, 12,* 65.

Clark, K. (1970). Drugs, sports and doping. *Journal of the Maine Medical Association, G1*(3), 55–58.

Collings, G. (1986). Drugs and sports. *Sport and Fitness.*

Collins, G.B., Pippenger, C.E., & Jenesz, J.W. (1984). Links in the chain: An approach to the treatment of drug abuse on a professional football team. *Cleveland Clinic Quarterly, 51,* 485–491.

Donohoe, T., & Johnson, N. (1986). *Foul play: Drug abuse in sports.* New York: Blackwell.

Dorety, R. (1984). *Pharmacology of cocaine abuse/misuse.*

Edwards, H. (1984). The black dumb jock: An American tragedy. *College Review Bulletin.*

Elliot, M.A., & Merrill, F.E. (1961). *Social disorganization,* 4th ed. New York: Harper.

Golding, L. (1963). The effects of *l*-amphetamine sulfate on physical performance. *Journal of Sports Medicine, 3,* 221–224.

Goodman, L.S., & Gilman, A. (1975). *The pharmacologic basis of therapeutics.* New York: Macmillan.

Goth, A. (1978). *Medical pharmacology* (9th ed).

Haupt, H., & Rovere, G. (1984). Anabolic steroids: A review of the literature. *American Orthopedic Society for Sports Medicine,* 479–483.

Johnson, W. (1985). Steroid explosion. *Sports Illustrated,* May 13, pp. 38–51.

Kallant, O.T. (1968). The amphetamines: Toxicity and addiction. *Behavioral pharmacology.* Englewood Cliffs, NJ: Prentice-Hall.

Kopvick, P.V. (1959). The effect of amphetamine sulfate on athletic performance. *Journal of the American Medical Association, 170,* 558–561.

Lawson, G., Peterson, J. & Lawson, A. (1983). *Alcoholism and the family: A guide to treatment and prevention.* Rockville, MD: Aspen Publishers.

Mandell, A.J. (1976). *The nightmare season.* New York: Random House.

Mandell, A. (1978). The Sunday syndrome: A unique pattern of amphetamine abuse indigenous to professional football. *Pharmacological Newsletter, 7,* 8–11.

NBA Pamphlet (1983). The anti-drug program of the National Basketball Association and the National Basketball Players Association.

Operation Cork, Hazelden: Cork program to address sports related alcohol and drug abuse (1984). *Operation Cork Communicator,* Summer.

Pesman, C. (1987). Sports 100 salary report. *Sport Magazine,* June. 23–38.

Rosenburg, E. (1980). Sport as work: Characteristics and career related patterns. *Sociological Symposium, 30,* 39–61.

Rovere, G.D., Haupt, H.A., & Yates, C.S. (1986). Drug testing in a university athletic program: Protocol and implementation. *The Physician and Sportsmedicine, 14*(4), 69–76.

Taylor, W.N. (1985). *Hormonal manipulation: A new era of monstrous athletes.* Jefferson, NC: McFarland.

U.S. Olympic Committee Sports Medicine Program (1983). *Coping control: Questions and answers.*

Wade, N. (1972). Anabolic steroids: Doctors denounce them but athletes aren't listening. *Science, 176,* 1399–1403.

Wyndham, H. (1971). Physiological effects of the amphetamines during exercise. *South African Medical Journal, 45,* 247–252.

Chapter 16

Treatment and Prevention of Alcoholism and Substance Abuse in the Military

Daniel Ray Benson

INTRODUCTION

Alcoholic beverages and military servicemen have gone hand in hand for generations, as military customs and traditions have condoned, if not dictated, alcohol abuse. Recently, however, the trend has begun to shift. Today's military is concerned with identifying and treating the problem of substance abuse within its ranks. Changes have been made in policies and programs, reaping significant results in all branches of the service. Programs of education, prevention, detection, intervention, and treatment have been instrumental in bringing about these changes. This chapter discusses major findings of the 1985 Worldwide Survey of Alcohol and Non-Medical Drug Use among Military Personnel (Bray et al., 1986) as well as various approaches to prevention and treatment of active duty military personnel and veterans.

1985 WORLDWIDE SURVEY

The 1985 Worldwide Survey was conducted by the Research Triangle Institute (RTI) of Research Triangle Park, North Carolina. The purpose of the survey was to evaluate and determine the prevalence of substance abuse in the military. This survey also provided information that is helpful in evaluating the nature, causes, and consequences of substance use and how it affects the military and provides a useful tool in the assessment of programs and policies. Worldwide surveys are conducted periodically among military personnel in order to monitor fluctuations and for comparative purposes.

The views, opinions, and findings contained in the 1985 Worldwide Survey of Alcohol and Non-Medical Drug Use among Military Personnel are those of the authors and should not be construed as an official Department of Defense position, policy, or decision, unless so designated by other official documentation.

In analyzing changes in substance abuse rates over a period of time, caution must be taken in determining reasons for such fluctuations. Changes may be due to effective substance abuse policies and programs; however, differences in attitudes,values, and characteristics of those being surveyed must also be taken into consideration.

As stated in the 1985 Worldwide Survey (Bray et al., 1986, p. 1):

> Six specific objectives guided the conduct of the study:
> 1. Assess the prevalance of alcohol use, nonmedical drug use, and tobacco use.
> 2. Identify the physical, social, and work consequences of use.
> 3. Identify demographic/behavioral characteristics of users.
> 4. Determine trends in military drug and alcohol use over time.
> 5. Compare military drug and alcohol use to civilian use.
> 6. Assess health attitudes and behavior of military personnel.

The distribution of survey respondents covered all ranges of paygrades, male and female, with the heaviest representation in the E-4 to E-9 categories. Overall, the largest number of respondents were frm the Army, followed by the Air Force, Navy, and Marine Corps, for a total of approximately 17,000 usable questionnaires.

Approximately 87% of military personnel consume some alcohol. Significant changes over a period of time have occurred in all areas of drug use and in heavy alcohol consumption. Marijuana use dropped 10% and the overall use of any drug dropped 10.1% betwen 1982 and 1985. Figure 16-1 shows alcohol use by military rank.

Patterns of heavy alcohol use were more prevalent in the E-1 to E-3 paygrades than in the E-4 to E-6 paygrades. These were also seen more in men, those with less education, the unmarried, and younger service personnel. Fewer significant differences were observed among the categories of time on active duty, race/ethnicity, region, and service.

The 1985 Worldwide Survey revealed that the most-used alcoholic beverage is beer, followed by hard liquor, and finally, wine. Daily consumption, however, has been decreasing since 1980. The pattern of drinking with the highest frequency proved to be drinking less than once a week (1 to 3 drinks per occasion). Very few drink more than 7 drinks per occasion. Overall, 87% of service personnel drink on occasion; more than 65% are moderate to heavy drinkers, and those in the heavy drinker category total 12%. The average alcohol consumption per day is 1.22 ounces of ethanol.

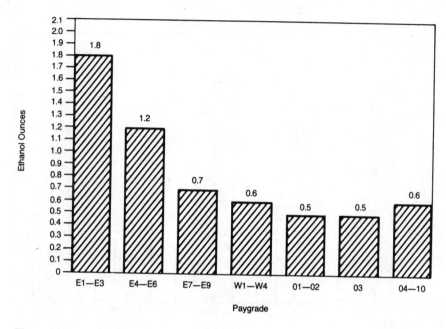

Figure 16-1 Average Daily Ounces of Ethanol by Pay Grade, 1985. *Source:* From *1985 Worldwide Survey of Alcohol and Nonmedical Drug Use among Military Personnel* by R.M. Bray et al., 1986, Research Triangle Park, N.C.: Research Triangle Institute. Copyright 1986 by Research Triangle Institute. Reprinted by permission.

Concerning service differences and alcohol consumption, the differences in levels were not significant.

When comparing drug use among the four service branches, there were significant differences found between the 1982 report (Bray et al., 1983) and the 1985 report. The Army, Marine Corps, and Air Force reported significantly more abstainers, while the Navy had significantly more moderate drinkers. All four branches had significantly less marijuana use (both in the past 30 days and in the past 12 months). Similar usages were significantly less for any drug use in all four branches in 1985. Even cigarette smoking was reduced significantly in the Navy, Marine Corps, and Air Force. Figure 16-2 illustrates these dramatic drops in drug use in the last 30 days.

The 1985 Worldwide Survey showed:

- Approximately 9% of military personnel reported having used drugs in the past 30 days, and 13% in the past 12 months.
- The highest usage of any drug came from the ranks of E-1 to E-3, followed by E-4 to E-6.

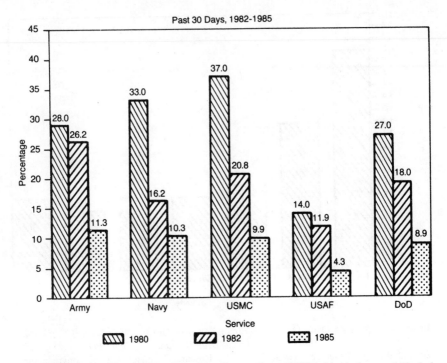

Figure 16-2 Service Trends in Any Drug Use. *Source:* From *1985 Worldwide Survey of Alcohol and Nonmedical Drug Use among Military Personnel* by R.M. Bray et al., 1986, Research Triangle Park, N.C.: Research Triangle Institute. Copyright 1986 by Research Triangle Institute. Reprinted by permission.

- The use of marijuana compared to other specific drugs was, by far, the most frequent.
- There has been a progressive decline in drug usage in the military since 1980. These statistics are in regard to all services. The same findings are true of productivity loss due to drug use.
- Similar to alcohol consumption, drug use is greater among the young, less educated, unmarried, and low-ranking personnel. Race/ethnicity, location of duty station, and sex did not have a significant impact on usage.
- Differences between the services were partially attributed to socio-demographics within the military.

Even though the majority of personnel surveyed did not show negative side effects, a significant number did experience problems as a result of alcohol use. Approximately 27% experienced productivity loss, while in other areas i.e., work impairment, physical damage, social disturbances, and other consequences, or dependence, less than 10% reported a loss.

There were, however, significant changes from 1982 to 1985 in the categories of work impairment, social disturbances, and productivity loss. Physical damage, other consequences, and dependence showed little change.

As of 1985, the military had few service members using nonmedical drugs, but of the personnel who did use drugs, relatively few experienced negative effects.

Between 1982 and 1985, the most significant drop in negative effects showed up in productivity loss, followed by work impairment, social disturbances, physical damage, and other negative effects.

These negative effects were measured by the following criteria:

1. *work impairment:* includes any Uniform Code of Military Justice (UCMJ) punishment, lowered performance evaluation level, or loss of 3 or more working days
2. *physical damage:* occurrence of injury by accident to self, property, or others, or illness that causes disability from duty, 1 week or longer
3. *social disruption:* occurrence of driving while intoxicated (DWI), arrest, marital threats of separation, actual separation, or fights
4. *other consequences:* due to alcohol and/or drug abuse, failure to be promoted, spouse and/or child abuse, being detoxified
5. *productivity loss:* lowered performance, skipped work, intoxicated while on the job, late arrival to work, leaving work early
6. *dependence (alcohol):* blackouts, tremors, loss of control over drinking, or morning alcohol consumption (Bray et al., 1986).

The results of this survey revealed an overall decrease in substance use in all branches of the military from 1980 to 1985. Also evident was the seriousness of alcohol use and its effects, which still remain high. The negative effects of alcohol consumption are far more widespread than that of drug use because the problem still involves so many, the E-1 to E-3 personnel especially. Most of the negative effects fell into categories of productivity, social relationships, and health. Even though a decline is evident, these problems still requrie serious attention.

Programs and policies should be strengthened in the areas of greatest need, which included: males, those with less rank, the younger, and the unmarried. Also highly affected were the alcohol/drug dependent personnel and the heavy drinkers. The further reduction of alcohol use appears to be the primary need.

Nonmedical drug use declined significantly since 1980, primarily due to drug deterrent programs such as urinalysis testing. It is still an area of concern, however, because nonmedical drug use still exists and its negative effects continue within the military.

Substantial progress has been made in all areas of substance use, nonmedical drug use in particular. Efforts toward further reduction of use should continue, and prevention and treatment programs should be especially directed toward the high-risk groups.

TREATMENT

The military recognizes that problems with alcohol and drug abuse can be effectively addressed through education, counseling, and inpatient treatment programs. These programs have proved to be a cost-effective means of retaining personnel with potential for continued military service.

Levels of Treatment

The Navy has developed three levels of treatment that are available to all personnel, appropriate to their degree of abuse or dependency:

• *Level I:* The local command program is managed by the command drug and alcohol program advisor (DAPA), who has been trained in the field of drug and alcohol abuse. The primary goal of the DAPA is to provide assistance to the commanding officer concerning all drug and alcohol matters of the command. It is also his duty to manage prevention efforts by ensuring personnel awareness of the consequences of drug/ alcohol abuse and to monitor urinalysis testing, drug detection dog teams, and inspections. The DAPA also monitors interventions through discipline, administrative screening, and referral of personnel to level II treatment. Any person believed to have, or is at high risk of, drug or alcohol related problems could be placed on a command program to deter further abuse.

Education is also provided through a course given by the University of Arizona called the "Navy Alcohol and Drug Safety Action Program" (NADSAP). NADSAP is an experiential model that encourages students to be active participants in the learning process. The course teaches stress management, values clarification, decision-making skills, communication skills, and information on drugs and alcohol.

• *Level II:* Counseling and Assistance Center (CAAC) programs are located at major afloat commands and shore installations throughout the world. These centers are normally manned by a paraprofessional staff of officers and enlisted personnel who have graduated from the Naval Drug and Alcohol Counselor School (NDACS). These trained counselors provide screening, evaluation, and supportive counseling, usually on a 14-day outpatient basis. Programs may vary in length based on the commanding officer's and the counseling staff's recommendations. This level of counseling is designed for personnel who are not drug and/or alcohol dependent yet require attention beyond the capacity of level I programs.

 • *Level III:* If it is determined by the CAAC that a person is drug and/ or alcohol dependent (physiologically and/or psychologically) or chronically obese, and is judged to be beyond the scope of CAAC treatment, or is recommended by a medical officer, the person will be sent to a residential rehabilitation program. This level III treatment is conducted on a full-time, live-in basis for approximately 6 weeks.

Naval Alcohol Rehabilitation Center

The largest of the military's inpatient treatment facilities is the Naval Alcohol Rehabilitation Center (NARC) located at the Naval Air Station–Miramar in San Diego, California. The overall mission of NARC is to restore to full duty personnel who have been formally evaluated and diagnosed as alcohol and/or drug dependent, or chronically obese, and who, in the opinion of their commanding officer, have demonstrated potential for continued military service. NARC, being a naval command, bases its operations on Navy policies and regulations, coupled with appropriate military behavior. The military structure promotes a spirit of camaraderie among patients, as well as enhancing unit pride and cooperation.

NARC offers a structured, 6-week inpatient program that treats active duty military personnel from the Navy, Marine Corps, Air Force, Army, and Coast Guard and, on a case-by-case basis, their dependents. The treatment center is housed in two three-story converted barricks buildings. The bottom floor of each building houses support services such as administration, medical, training and video. The upper two floors of each buildings serve both as living spaces for the four treatment units and as therapy facilities. Male patients share open bay berthing areas, and female patients share six-person rooms. Lounge, laundry, TV, and game areas are also in the building. Base dining facilities are within walking distance. At present, the maximum inpatient capacity is 200, which enables approximately 1,700 active duty military personnel to be treated annually.

NARC's treatment modality states that alcohol and/or drug dependence and compulsive overeating are diseases that affect both the individual and the family physically, socially, psychologically, and spiritually. NARC believes these diseases are treatable by a multidisciplinary model involving the ongoing recovery process to include the individual and his or her family.

This model is implemented through education, with emphasis on the disease and total abstinence through 12-step recovery programs, group therapy, physical training, and workshops. The Twelve Step Recovery Programs include Alcoholics Anonymous (AA), Narcotics Anonymous (NA), and Overeaters Anonymous (OA) (only a partial listing) as well as Al-Anon, O-Anon, Nar-Anon, Al-Ateen, and Al-Atot for the families. These are support programs where individuals meet regularly for mutual support and guidance in applying the 12 steps to maintain a lifetime of sobriety and abstinence. The 12 steps of AA are set forth in Appendix A.

Rehabilitation is an intense process. A patient's work day begins at 0500 (5:00 AM) and ends at 2100 (9:00 PM). A daily schedule is shown in Exhibit 16-1.

The staff is composed of naval officers; Navy, Marine Corps, and Coast Guard enlisted personnel; and civil service employees. Thearpy groups at NARC are faciliated by civilian and enlisted paraprofessional counselors trained at the command's Naval Drug and Alcohol Counselor School (located at the Naval Station–San Diego site). All patient groups are supervised by military and civilian psychologists to ensure quality of treatment.

Group therapy is the foundation of the rehabilitation process along with the various 12-step programs. Each group is composed of 8 to 12 individuals, including counselors. At the present time all groups are open-ended,

---

Exhibit 16-1 NARC Daily Schedule

0500	Reveille
0530	March to breakfast
0545-0615	Breakfast
0615	March to NARC
0630-0700	Field day
0700-0800	Physical training
0830	Muster
0845-1000	Group
1015	March to lunch
1015-1115	Lunch
1115	March to NARC
1130-1245	Workshop or group
1300-1500	Workshop or group
1515	March to dinner
1515-1615	Dinner
1615	March to NARC
1615-1700	Personal time
1700-2000	Evening program (workshop/NA/AA/OA meetings)
2000	Uniform preparation
2100	Taps

with new patients being added to the group as other patients are leaving. During group therapy, personnel explore personal issues affecting each member's sobriety or abstinence and learn to take responsibility for their actions. Video taping of selecting group sessions is used as a training device for staff as well as an outstanding way for patients to receive feedback on their verbal and nonverbal communication skills. A women's group is offered twice weekly to afford woman an exclusively female setting in which to explore personal issues. A post-traumatic stress group is also offered for those who have experienced trauma through war or natural disaster.

Daily therapeutic workshops are designed within a 12-step model to emphasize recovery from addiction. The workshops are arranged in a sequential order to optimize growth.

Summary of Treatment Program Workshops

• *Week 0:* Workshops offer a series of indoctrination/orientation workshops to introduce patients to treatment, group therapy, the family program, physical training, military issues, and medical aspects of alcoholism/addiction and compulsive overeating.

• *Week 1:* Workshops begin to educate and offer hope to patients about their respective diseases.

• *Week 2:* Workshops extend the educational process by exploring how the disease of chemical dependency is also a family disease requiring treatment and ongoing recovery.

• *Week 3:* Workshops focus on self-healing; a time to understand and heal the wounds caused by shame, guilt, resentment, and anger.

• *Week 4:* Workshops emphasize extending the healing process by reaching out and reestablishing relationships, building support systems, and improving communication skills.

• *Week 5:* Workshops present practical tools to incorporate and develop spiritiuality, thus aiding in a life after recovery.

• *Week 6:* Workshops focus on transition from treatment to the mainstream of society. Aftercare plans are developed, and patients are given the opportunity to say goodby to those who have become significant.

Workshops are also a vital part of the evening programs in addition to 12-step inhouse meetings and community meetings.

Summary of Evening Program Workshops

• *Week 1* offers a growth workshop to explore attitudes and projections, thus allowing patients to assume appropriate responsibility for their behaviors.

- *Week 2* introduces patients to the 12-step recovery programs.
- *Week 3* focuses on the first three steps of AA, allowing patients the opportunity to focus on themes such as powerlessness, unmanageability, and the realization of a power greater than themselves that can restore them to sanity.
- *Week 4* integrates steps 1, 2, and 3 of the 12 steps of AA into daily decisions. Patients also begin preliminary work necessary for working the fourth and fifth steps of AA, NA, and OA.
- *Week 5* is a time for patients to begin step 4. The fourth step reveals an understanding of oneself through an undertaking of a "searching and fearless" moral inventory. As patients work through step 4, they discover how many of their addictive behaviors have affected the many people in their lives. Patients are introduced to the fifth step of AA at the conclusion of the fifth week.
- *Week 6* focuses on the warning signs of relapse and provides a time to strengthen sobriety and recovery.

Familial Support in Treatment

Perhaps the most important factor in improving productivity, retention, and morale in the Armed Services has been the increasing support and recognition of the military family. NARC uses "systemic" thinking by including families of addicts, alcoholics, and overeaters.

When the active duty member enters treatment, he or she is screened by the united family counselor to determine marital and family status or whether he or she is involved in a significant relationship. If appropriate, weekly family counseling commences early in the patient's treatment program.

In addition to family counseling, spouses have the opportunity to attend weekly spouse and couples workshops. Families are educated from a systems approach. The family discovers how they as a whole and as individuals have been affected by the service member's addiction.

The spouse workshops educate the co-dependents toward understanding addiction and recovery and how they are involved in the process. Co-dependency is defined, characterized, and discussed in these workshops. Assertiveness training and its importance in recovery is explored, as well as the relapse process and prevention. It is in these workshops that spouses develop their personal recovery programs as co-dependents, involving Al-Anon, speakers meetings, counseling, education, and reading literature. The use of films, group interactions, speakers, and homework assignments are also incorporated into this program.

The couples workshop is another weekly program that is a powerful tool at NARC. The progression of alcoholism, addiction, and compulsive overeating for the substance abuser and the spouse/partner is examined, as are the behaviors, stages, symptoms, and recovery of the disease. Typical survival roles in families are identified, stressing the importance of family treatment and communication. Also included are exercises and education in the area of sexuality, including sexual abuse, spousal rape, and sex and recovery. Anger and resentment are usually major issues surrounding substance abuse and the family. Exercises are implemented to assist couples in sharing their anger and resentments in a clear, nonthreatening manner, conducive to enhancing communication. In addition, family violence, including physical and emotional abuse, is defined and discussed. Families with violent tendencies are referred to family advocacy for specialized treatment. Families with eating disorders exhibit as much violence as alcoholic/addict families. NARC attempts to return active duty personnel back to duty with the foundation necessary to continue building and maintaining healthy family relationships.

Physical Fitness

In keeping with the concept of treating the whole person, heavy emphasis is also placed upon developing physical fitness and health. Each week patients engage in physical exercises, calisthenics, aerobics, and running (walking for compulsive overeaters). Patients start out running/walking 1½ miles daily and work up to 3 miles by the completion of treatment.

Aftercare

Once the patient's clinical course of treatment has been completed and fully documented by the group counselor and the unit psychologist, a final prognosis is forwarded to the commanding officer for final approval. This prognosis, with supporting documentation, is forwarded to the patient's ultimate duty station. Patients receive a recommended 1-year aftercare plan to assist with their sobriety and abstinence. It is the duty of the individual, with command monitoring, to ensure that the aftercare plan is followed. Aftercare recommendations may include attendance of two to four 12-step recovery program meetings per week, Antabuse, random urinalysis testing, family counseling, a food plan for overeaters, meetings with the DAPA, professional counseling, and other related referrals.

It is important to note that the treatment provided by the Navy has a high success rate. The success of treatment can be closely monitored and is tied to the job performance of the treatment participants. The impressive changes in drug and alcohol use in the military can be attributed to policies and programs that came from the top and are institution-wide.

PREVENTION

A multimethod approach is used by the military to prevent, monitor, regulate, and lessen drug and alcohol abuse. This multiapproach focuses on the host, agent, and environment:

- *Host:* The host or individual becomes the military person in this context. Also, his or her knowledge about alcohol, the attitudes that influence drinking patterns, and drinking behavior itself become the focus when viewing the host. The military has developed a "zero-tolerance" attitude concerning drug and alcohol use since 1981. Responsibility for the abuse and use of drugs and alcohol has shifted to the individual. If abused, the individual faces the consequences of the zero tolerance position. Efforts continue to discourage excessive alcohol consumption. This has been done by eliminating traditional practices that encouraged servicemen to drink unresponsibly and ordering all levels of the chain of command to establish a command environment that discourages the use of drugs and/or alcohol. Efforts are being made to strengthen the image of service personnel by glamorizing health and fitness and deglamorizing drug and alcohol abuse.

- *Agent:* Preventative measures used on the agent, the alcohol, focus on its content, distribution, and availability. Educational programs are presented to all personnel to give reliable facts on the effects of drugs and alcohol on health, welfare, and personal safety. Classes are given during boot camp, change of duty station, and following all drug and alcohol related incidents. The military is now regulating the hours of distribution of alcohol on board military facilities and prices for sale of alcohol, as well as enforcing DWI violations.

- *Environment:* The environment includes the setting in which drinking and drug use occur. The military's zero tolerance has lowered the sociological risks by creating a social climate that no longer accepts drug and alcohol abuse.

Discharges are at an all-time high for personnel testing positive for drugs on urinalysis testing. "In 1985 more than 16,500 were discharged and another 55,900 were provided with rehabilitation and counseling." Entire units can be screened for drugs with a very short notice, and random tests are also conducted.

It is believed by the majority of military personnel that the urinalysis testing program has reduced drug use in the military by 64% since 1981. However, many do not feel the tests are reliable. This doubt is greatest among users, which may be due to not being detected while using drugs.

Preventative measures used by the military are also found in the Navy's three levels of treatment. These levels of treatment can also be viewed as primary, secondary, and tertiary levels of prevention.

DRUG USE AMONG MILITARY VETERANS

Drug use among military personnel was relatively unknown in World War I, World War II, and the Korean War. However, drug abuse among personnel involved in the Vietnam War was very common, especially after the Tet Offensive of 1968. According to a survey conducted in 1970, 63% of the 173D Airborne Brigade admitted to smoking marijuana. Later studies of soldiers leaving Vietnam show even higher rates of substance abuse (Baker, 1986).

The high rates of drug and alcohol abuse in Vietnam are believed by Baker (1986) to lower the neuropsychiatric casualty rate of the Vietnam soldier (World War II, 101 per 1,000; Korea, 37 per 1,000; Vietnam, 12 per 1,000). Baker (1986) found that self-medication of the Vietnam soldier was done by abusing alcohol and drugs, along with antipsychotic drugs by the Medical Corps. All helped reduce anxiety, insomnia, and frightening dreams (Baker, 1986). However, debate continues to explore the impact Vietnam has had on our society. Many of the survivors of Vietnam have experienced and continue to experience psychological symptoms such as nightmares and flashbacks and feeling jumpy and irritable. These symptoms are labeled *post traumatic stress disorder* (PTSD).

During the entire course of the Vietnam War, O'Donnell (1976) studied the drug use patterns of men from 11 birth cohorts. They found evidence of a historical effect. The United States experienced a major epidemic of drug use from 1965 to the early 1970s. Men born between 1950 and 1954 were the major users of illicit drugs during that time. This age group of men was also the majority of men serving in Vietnam in 1970 or later. Therefore, what appeared to be substantial drug increase problems in Vietnam actually coincided with the epidemic of drug use in the United States, hitting essentially the same birth cohorts. It would not be surprising if a large percentage of Vietnam veterans receiving treatment for PTSD and drug and/or alcohol abuse were in Vietnam from 1970 or later.

REFERENCES

Baker, G.R. (1986). *PTSD differences between treated and non-treated veterans of the Vietnam era: Service, race, and symptom applications.* Unpublished doctoral dissertation. San Diego: United States International University.

Bray, R.M., Guess, L.L., Mason, R.E., Hubbard, R.L., Smith, D.G., Marsden, M.E., & Rachal, J.V. (1983). *1982 worldwide survey of alcohol and nonmedical drug use among military personnel.* (RTI/2317/01-01F). Research Triangle Park, NC: Research Triangle Institute.

Bray, R.M., Marsden, M.E., Guess, L.L., Wheeless, S.C., Pate, D.K., Dunteman, G.H., & Iannacchione, V.G. (1986). *1985 worldwide survey of alcohol and nonmedical drug use* among military personnel. (RTI/3306/06-02FR). Research Triangle Park, NC: Research Triangle Institute.

Burt, M.R., Biegel, M.M., Carnes, Y., & Farley, E.C. (1980). Worldwide survey of non-medical drug use and alcohol use among military personnel: 1980. Bethesda, MD: Burt Associates.

Chromy, J.R. (1979). Sequential samples selection methods. In Proceedings of the American Statistical Association, 1978. Washington, DC: American Statistical Association.

O'Connor, C., & Miller, M. (1986). The military says no: A tough program cleans up drugs in the service. Newsweek, Nov. 10, 26.

O'Donnell, J.A. (1976). Young men and drugs: A nationwide survey. Washington, DC: Government Printing Office.

Polich, J.M., & Orvis, B.R. (1979). Alcohol problems: Patterns and prevalence in the U.S. Air Force. Santa Monica, CA: Rand Corporation.

U.S. Department of Defense. (1980, August 15). Directive No. 1010.4: Alcohol and drug abuse by DoD personnel. Washington, DC: Author.

U.S. Department of Defense. (1986, March 11). Directive N. 1010.10: Health promotion. Washington, DC: Author.

The Twelve Steps of AA

1. We admitted we were powerless over alcohol—that our lives had become unmanageable.
2. Came to believe that a power greater than ourselves could restore us to sanity.
3. Made a decision to turn our will and our lives over to the care of God as we understood Him.
4. Made a searching and fearless moral inventory of ourselves.
5. Admitted to God, to ourselves and to another human being the exact nature of our wrongs.
6. Were entirely ready to have God remove all these defects of character.
7. Humbly asked Him to remove our shortcomings.
8. Made a list of all persons we had harmed, and became willing to make amends to them all.
9. Made direct amends to such people wherever possible, except when to do so would injure them or others.
10. Continued to take personal inventory and when we were wrong, promptly admitted it.
11. Sought through prayer and meditation to improve our conscious contact with God as we understood Him, praying only for knowledge of His will for us and the power to carry that out.
12. Having had a spiritual awakening as the result of these steps, we tried to carry this message to alcoholics, and to practice these principles in all of our affairs.

Source: Reprinted with permission of A.A. World Services, Inc.

Index

About the Editors

Gary W. Lawson, Ph.D., is a professor of psychology and director of graduate studies in chemical dependency at United States International University. He is a licensed clinical psychologist in California and Nebraska. He has worked in the field of alcoholism and substance abuse for 18 years during which time he directed both inpatient and outpatient addiction treatment programs. He serves as a consultant for schools, agencies, and companies, including San Diego Services for the Blind and Sherman Indian High School in Riverside, California. His specialty area is the treatment of high-risk and reluctant-to-recover individuals. He has lectured nationally and internationally. Dr. Lawson's other books include *Alcoholism and the Family: A Guide to Treatment and Prevention, The Essentials of Chemical Dependency Counseling,* and *Clinical Psychopharmacology: A Practical Reference for Nonmedical Psychotherapists.*

Ann Lawson, Ph.D., MFCC, is the Director of the Addiction Counselor Training Program at United States International University. She is a licensed marriage, family and child counselor in California. She has worked in the mental health field for 11 years; the last 7 of these have been in the field of chemical dependency. Before coming to USIU, she was the creator and director of the Children of Alcoholic Families Program at the Lincoln Child Guidance Center, Lincoln, Nebraska. Her publications include *Alcoholism and the Family: A Guide to Treatment and Prevention* and "Geriatric Populations and Drugs," in Gary Lawson (Ed.), *Clinical Psychopharmacology: A Practical Reference for Nonmedical Psychotherapists.* She is a consultant to drug and alcohol prevention programs and has presented at many national and regional conventions and workshops.

About the Contributors

Robert J. Aguilar, Sr., R.N., M.A., is a licensed marriage, family and child counselor with offices in Chula Vista and La Jolla, California. He is a doctoral candidate in psychology at the California School of Professional Psychology, San Diego, and has more than 10 years' experience in the field of chemical dependency.

David Archambault, M.A., is a probation counselor with adolescents in the Los Angeles area. He is also a doctoral student in psychology at United States International University in San Diego.

Daniel Ray Benson, M.A., is a family counselor at the Naval Alcohol Rehabilitation Center at NAS Miramar in San Diego. He is a marriage, family, and child counselor intern and was named counselor of the year at NAS Miramar in 1988.

Freida Brown, Ph.D., is an assistant professor of psychology at United States International University, San Diego, California. She holds a doctorate in developmental psychology from Northwestern University with a minor in clinical psychology. Her specialty areas include child development and minority issues.

Stanley L. Eden, Psy.D., is a private practitioner specializing in substance abuse issues. He is a candidate for the doctoral degree in psychology from United States International University in San Diego, California, with an area of specialization in chemical dependency. He also holds substance abuse counseling credentials for the state of Michigan.

Peter G. Fellios, M.A., is a teacher at Fallbrook (California) High School. He has a masters degree in education and is a credentialled school counselor. Presently, he is enrolled in the doctoral program in psychology at the United States International University in San Diego, California. Mr. Fellios has a special interest in the problems of dysfunctional families.

Benita Anne Glow, M.A., is a teacher of the learning handicapped with a masters degree in Education and credentials in Reading and Special Education of the Handicapped. She is a doctoral student at the United States International University in chemical dependency. In addition, she works with Daughters United and Tradition #1 as a therapist.

Audrey Hill is a Mohawk Indian from the Six Nations Indian Reserve in Ontario, Canada. She worked as a native social worker in her home communities before coming to San Diego for graduate studies in chemical dependency at the United States International University. She is currently doing prevention work with Indian children for the Southern Indian Health Council. She has also presented material on alcoholism in native families in the San Diego area.

Susann M. Jordan, M.A., is a doctoral candidate in clinical psychology at the United States International University in San Diego. She is the coordinator of the AIDS Counseling Program at the Center for Social Services in San Diego. She also works as a registered psychological assistant in private practice and focuses on treatment pertaining to death and dying, women's issues, and alternative life styles.

Yvonne Kress, M.A., is a native of West Germany and a licensed marriage, family and child counselor in California. She specializes in chemical dependency treatment as a consultant and in private practice. Ms. Kress has worked for several years as a substance abuse counselor in outpatient treatment facilities. She has conducted numerous seminars and workshops in the area of psychopathology and chemical dependency and frequently lectures on these topics at local universities. She is currently completing her doctorate in psychology at the United States International University in San Diego, California.

Gary R. Lewis, Ph.D., R.N., is in private practice as a clinical nurse specialist and psychological assistant. He has 6 years of experience in the field of chemical dependency in a variety of inpatient and outpatient settings. Dr. Lewis received his doctorate in clinical psychology from United States International University in San Diego, California.

Herbert Martin, M.A., is a doctoral student at United States International University. He has worked as a consultant in sports psychology.

Nancy P. Moore, M.A., has a masters degree in psychology from United States International University. She is currently a doctoral candidate in clinical psychology at the same institution. She is a drug and alcohol abuse counselor at her doctoral intern site.

Christine M. O'Sullivan, M.A., is a doctoral student in chemical dependency at United States International University in San Diego, California. She holds an M.A. from Northeastern Illinois University in Chicago where she began her studies of alcoholism and the alcoholic family. She has experience working with recovering alcoholics and alcoholic family problems.

P. Clayton Rivers, Ph. D., is professor and director of the alcohol training program in the psychology department of the University of Nebraska-Lincoln. He is co-author with Lawson and Ellis of *Essentials of Chemical Dependency Counseling* and recently edited the *34th Volume of the Nebraska Symposium on Motivation* (1987) entitled: *Alcohol and Addictive Behavior*.

Delia Thrasher, M.A., is a doctoral candidate at United States International University and a doctoral intern at St. Lawrence Hospital, Mental Health Services, in Lansing, Michigan. Her primary interests are working in sports psychology and with children. Her other publications include a chapter on lithium in *Clinical Psychopharmacology: A Practical Reference For Nonmedical Psychotherapists*.

Joan Tooley, M.A., is a psychological assistant at the Psychological Center in Inglewood, California. She is also a doctoral student in psychology at United States International University in San Diego, California.

Thomas J. Young, Ph.D., is an assistant professor of criminal justice at Kearney State College in Nebraska. He received his Ph.D. in psychological and cultural studies from the University of Nebraska-Lincoln and has completed 2 years of postdoctoral study in developmental psychology at the University of Kansas. He has published articles on psychopharmacology and substance abuse among special populations.